To Provide
for the General Welfare

To Provide for the General Welfare

A History of the Federal Spending Power

Theodore Sky

Newark: University of Delaware Press
London: Associated University Presses

© 2003 by Rosemont Publishing & Printing Corp.

All rights reserved. Authorization to photocopy items for internal or personal use, or the internal or personal use of specific clients, is granted by the copyright owner, provided that a base fee of $10.00, plus eight cents per page, per copy is paid directly to the Copyright Clearance Center, 222 Rosewood Drive, Danvers, Massachusetts 01923. [0-87413-793-4/03 $10.00 + 8¢ pp, pc.]

Other than as indicated in the foregoing, this book may not be reproduced, in whole or in part, in any form (except as permitted by Sections 107 and 108 of the U.S. Copyright Law, and except for brief quotes appearing in reviews in the public press).

Associated University Presses
2010 Eastpark Boulevard
Cranbury, NJ 08512

The paper used in this publication meets the requirements of the American National Standard for Permanence of Paper for Printed Library Materials Z39.48-1984.

Library of Congress Cataloging-in-Publication Data

Sky, Theodore, 1933–
    To provide for the general welfare : a history of the federal spending power / Theodore Sky.
       p. cm.
    Includes bibliographical references and index.
    ISBN 0-87413-793-4 (alk. paper)
      1. Government spending policy—United States. 2. United States—Politics and government. I. Title.
HJ7537 .S55   2003
343.73′034—dc21   2003001364

Second paperback printing 2010/ISBN 978-0-87413-061-4(paperback)

PRINTED IN THE UNITED STATES OF AMERICA

To Vera, Catherine, and Victoria
With abiding love

Contents

Preface	9
Acknowledgments	13
Introduction	19

Part I. Framing and Ratification

1.	The Framing of the General Welfare Clause	33
2.	Ratification and the General Welfare Clause	55

Part II. The Framing of the First Precedents

3.	The Washington Administration	79
4.	Hamilton's Interpretation—Washington's Legacy	93

Part III. The Virginia Presidents and the General Welfare Clause: The Quest for a Constitutional Amendment

5.	Jefferson's Dilemma	111
6.	Madison's Precept	130
7.	Monroe's Turn	144

Part IV. John Quincy Adams and the Jacksonians: A Clash of Visions

8.	John Quincy Adams's "Spirit of Improvement"	167
9.	Internal Improvements in the Age of Jackson	198
10.	Madison's Testament, Story's Commentary, and the Postulates of the Antebellum Presidents	212

Part V. Lincoln's Role

11.	Lincoln's General Welfare Clause	243
12.	Lincoln's General Welfare Legacy	262

Part VI. Reconstruction, Realignment, Revolution, Resolution

13.	Reconstruction, T. R., and Wilson's Realignment	283
14.	The New Deal and Judicial Resolution	304

Part VII. Modern Exercise

15. Truman to Ford—Toward Consensus — 327
16. Carter to Clinton—Accommodating Budget and National Investment Imperatives — 342

Part VIII. Constitutionalism and National Progress: The General Welfare Clause Contribution

17. The Spending Power, the Constitutional Amendment, and the Evolving American Presidency — 357
18. "Perseverance" — 371

Appendix: The Constitution, Article I, Section 8 — 381
Notes — 383
Bibliography — 422
Index — 430

Preface

MOST AMERICANS HAVE COME TO ACCEPT THE FEDERAL SPENDING power or its manifestations as part of the fabric of life in today's United States. Social Security, Medicare, Medicaid, student financial aid, federal aid to elementary and secondary education, food stamps, welfare benefits, supplemental security income are, if not household words, familiar government programs that affect the daily lives of millions who inhabit the United States. Americans have a general sense that, in the aggregate, these programs cost billions. In fact, federal domestic spending for assistance programs to states, individuals and other recipients accounts for the bulk of the annual federal budget, now approximately $2.1 trillion, after deducting outlays for defense and interest.

Most Americans do not ask where in the United States Constitution these programs are mentioned. Are Social Security, Medicare, Medicaid, food stamps, and welfare specified in that revered document as activities about which Congress may legislate? Is federal aid to education mentioned among the so-called enumerated powers? What of aid to the arts, community development, highway construction, and federally-assisted housing?

In fact, none of these programs or areas are specifically identified in the Constitution as matters of federal or congressional concern. If this is so, how does the federal government and, more specifically, Congress enter them? On what basis does Congress annually provide billions of dollars to assist individual Americans or the states in which they reside in the many mission areas that constitute the federal budget?

The answer lies in Article I, section 8, clause 1 of the Constitution: "The Congress shall have Power To lay and collect Taxes, Duties, Imposts and Excises to pay the Debts and provide for the common Defence and general Welfare of the United States...." This provision of the Constitution authorizes Congress to tax and, implicitly, to spend, for the purposes specified. The provision has come to be known as the Spending Clause or, as used here in its domestic context, the General Welfare Clause. It encompasses the federal spending power. On the basis of that spending power Congress has come to authorize or appropriate funds for the activities mentioned above and many others.

Article I, section 8, clause 1 was included in the Constitution when it was drafted in Philadelphia in 1787 and later ratified by the requisite number of states. That clause has never been amended. However, in the early history of the country, it was not universally thought to grant the broad spending power that it is now generally understood to confer. During that time a profound controversy raged around the true meaning of these words. Each of the framers and founding fathers adopted his own position, Hamilton, Jefferson, Madison, and Monroe among them. Succeeding generations took up the fight. The issue of the scope of the spending power, whether it warranted the application of federal resources for internal improvements (canals, roads, and the like), was a major concern from one administration to another largely during the Federal period. Presidents and presidential aspirants took differing positions on the issue. It separated Federalist from Jeffersonian Republican, Whig from Democrat.

Ultimately, the "contest," to use Benjamin Cardozo's term, surrounding the scope of the spending power was settled by the Supreme Court in the course of adjudicating the constitutional propriety of key pieces of Franklin Roosevelt's New Deal architecture. The Court did so in a few spare paragraphs. However, long before that happened, the "contest" was settled as a practical matter by the political process, through the adoption of legislative precedents—the enactment of laws regarding roads, canals, river and harbor upgrades, railroads, institutions of higher education, and other internal improvements.

The spending power evolved over time so that, when the Court came at last to formally ponder its meaning, it had acquired an interpretative gloss through long usage. The massive authority that the clause today affords was derived through application and interpretation during that early period in our history. That history establishes a foundation for the modern benefit state that we know today. The contest, while judicially resolved, and the American experience of which it was a part are still pervasive.

It is the purpose of this work to trace that evolution. In describing the history of the General Welfare Clause from 1787 to the end of the Lincoln Administration—the early formative years of the nation—this work seeks to give readers a better sense of the origins of the spending power and thus the basis upon which the modern federal government seeks to provide assistance in a multitude of areas critical to our national life and progress, while remaining true to the framework of the Constitution. In further tracing that history from the Lincoln period to the present, the work seeks to give the reader a better sense of the contemporary interpretation of the clause and its modern application in light of its origins. It is hoped that these insights will better enable the reader to gauge the force of that power and its role in the growth of government, as well as its potential contribution to internal improvement writ large in the new millennium. It is hoped as well that these insights will enable the reader better to evaluate the changes in the constitutional concept of "providing for the general welfare" that might be posed in this new century.

Acknowledgments

I WISH TO EXPRESS DEEP APPRECIATION TO MY FORMER COLLEAGUES in the United States Department of Education who have given support and encouragement to me in the course of this project, without in any way suggesting that they had knowledge of, or bear responsibility for, its content. To Secretary Richard W. Riley, I owe a deep debt of gratitude for his encouragement and support, a reflection of his strong leadership coupled with caring consideration for all staff members throughout his eight year tenure at the Department. From my good friend, Marshall (Mike) Smith, the Under Secretary of the Department and a driving force during a very productive period, I also received welcome and much valued insight.

Colleagues in the senior staff of the Department's Office of the General Counsel, a hallmark of committed government professionalism, with which I served for many years, were a source of good counsel and support. In particular, I thank, Judith Winston, the universally admired general counsel during those years, for her invariably wise and welcome counsel, and my long-term and well-respected senior staff colleagues, Jack Kristy, Phil Rosenfelt, and Steve Winnick, for inspiration and encouragement. Kamina Pinder, with whom I had the everlasting good fortune to work during my final year in the Department, gave her much welcome support. From my longtime co-workers, Kay Rigling and Miriam Whitney, I gained much insight.

I have been blessed with valued colleagues and friends in the program components of the Department and at the Institute of Museum and Library Services who have become lasting friends. Sue Kenworthy and Nancy Weiss have been particularly supportive. The writing and publishing experience was fortified by my colleague and co-worker, Millicent Bentley-Memon. I thank her for her gentle cheerleading and valuable insights graciously dispensed at many stages of the writing process. She reinforced for me the merits of perseverance, a sustaining value in confronting the myriad of tasks involved in such a project.

One's academic environment is at once a spur and a haven for serious scholarship. At the Columbus School of Law of the Catholic University of America, where I have taught for over a decade, the administration and faculty have been generous in support of research by colleagues. In particular, I am grateful to Professor William A. Kaplin for his invaluable guidance on matters constitutional, as well as his continuing confidence and good wishes. At the excellent law school library, I owe much to Dawn Sobol, who arranged for many interlibrary loans, and Yvette Brown, the very helpful reference librarian. Most importantly, I have been motivated by the talented and dedicated students that I have taught at the Columbus School of Law, many of whom have found satisfying careers in legal pursuits grounded on the federal spending power and have demonstrated an appreciation for its historical origins.

In the process of review and copyediting, the University of Delaware Press has been of immense help in transforming a manuscript into a book. Reader suggestions regarding scope and content were invaluable. Karen Druliner, managing editor of the Press, devoted many painstaking months to the copyediting process, providing a forthright, thorough, and professional review. Her sound advice and suggestions greatly improved the final product. It was a privilege as well to work with Dr. Donald Mell, the Chair of the Press, ever gracious and forthcoming with good suggestions on substance and publishing practice alike. To the staff of the Associated University Presses, particularly Lawra Rogers and Mary Ann Hostettler, who have contributed to the production of this work, I owe a deep debt of gratitude.

I thank as well Dave Felton for his fine assistance on computer technology at important junctures, my friend and colleague, Lawrence Hollman, for his valuable advice on various legal aspects of the publishing process, and Sandy Rinck, secretary to Secretary Riley at NAFSA, for her invaluable assistance at crucial stages.

No work of this sort is possible without collaboration, sacrifice and patience from one's family. Such work gains in satisfaction if it is a family affair. In this regard, I have been greatly blessed. My wife, Vera, has been a steady and wonderfully supportive influence throughout. She shared my progress at every stage and wisely spurred me to find a good home for the end product. My beloved daughters, Catherine and Victoria, have been a source of constant inspiration in the writing of this book, enriching it with their affection, their good words, and their artistic talents.

The memory of our good friends, the late Joan and David Greenstone, who in their lives and writings communicated a deep sense of social justice, was a guiding light.

I have been motivated and inspired as well by my extended family, who blend into their daily activities a fine sensitivity to the needs of others less fortunate, a sensitivity that is at the core of the general welfare concept. My sisters, Davida Sky and Marcia Bregman, were generous with advice growing from their own experience as authors as well as with boosts at critical times. My cousin, Lisa Port White, gave graciously of her valuable store of knowledge about indexing. My brother Asher Sky and brother and sister-in-law, Phil and Rosalind Sky, their daughter, Tobi Rispoli, and my cousins, Steve and Phyllis Port, have been kind and generous with ideas for promotion and outreach.

While I have benefited greatly from all the help described above, I take full responsibility for all errors, omissions, and lapses unintended as they may be.

I also express appreciation to:

(1) The Ohio University Press for permission to quote excerpts from *Notes of Debates in the Federal Convention of 1797 reported by James Madison*. Ohio University Press, 1966, rev. 1985. In this work I have used the Norton Bicentennial Edition.

(2) The State Historical Society of Wisconsin for permission to quote excerpts from *The Documentary History of the Ratification of the Constitution*, edited by John P. Kaminski and Gaspare J. Saladino (Reprinted with permission of the Wisconsin Historical Society press and the The Documentary History of the Ratification of the Constitution). This material is found in *The Debate on the Constitution, Federalist and Antifederalist Speeches, Articles and Letters During the Struggle Over Ratification*, 2 vols. (New York: The Library of America, 1993).

(3) The Abraham Lincoln Association for permission to quote selections from the *Collected Works of Abraham Lincoln*. (Springfield, Ill.: The Abraham Lincoln Association, 1953).

(4) The Yale University Press for permission to quote selections from *The Records of the Federal Convention of 1787*, ed. Max Farrand, 3 vols. (New Haven: Yale University Press, 1966).

To Provide
for the General Welfare

Introduction

THE GENERAL WELFARE CLAUSE OF THE UNITED STATES CONSTITUTION confers upon Congress a formidable but useful power: the power to tax in order to provide for the general welfare of the United States. It enables Congress to appropriate federal funds to provide assistance in many areas of American life, including the environment, education, science and technology, the arts, social security, health research, and health care, as well as in easing the burden of poverty, to name but a few. The General Welfare Clause is found in Article I, section 8, clause 1 of the Constitution: "The Congress shall have Power To lay and collect Taxes, Duties, Imposts and Excises, to pay the Debts and Provide for the common Defence and general Welfare of the United States." We refer here to that aspect of the clause that confers authority upon Congress to appropriate funds generally as the spending power and to the words: "The Congress shall have Power To lay and collect Taxes . . . to . . . Provide for . . . the general Welfare of the United States" as the General Welfare Clause. It also is called the Spending Clause.

The availability of the General Welfare Clause to support the authority of Congress to appropriate federal funds for broad economic or social purposes was not always uniformly recognized. Jefferson and Madison, on the one hand, and Hamilton, on the other, espoused different readings of the clause as it appeared in Article I of the Constitution drafted in the Philadelphia Convention of 1787. Madison urged that the spending power be confined to federal spending that would implement the enumerated powers of Congress found in the clauses of Article I, section 8 that follow the General Welfare Clause. These powers relate to such matters as regulating commerce, coining money, establishing post offices, and constituting federal courts. Hamilton saw the General Welfare Clause as an independent grant of spending authority not confined to the purposes encompassed within the enumerated powers.[1]

For 150 years the dispute remained unresolved by the courts, although the General Welfare Clause was used to justify federal expenditures for a variety of purposes, such as transportation and other internal improvements, objectives that the framers supported irrespective of their views about the scope of the clause. The key Supreme Court decision in *United States v. Butler* confronted the issue posed by the dispute between Hamilton and Madison and adopted Hamilton's view. The decisions that followed used Hamilton's theory to give judicial approval to the New Deal initiatives in social security, unemployment compensation, and other areas. These decisions provided the constitutional underpinnings for Lyndon Johnson's Great Society with its emphasis on education, health, and welfare, and for the important legislation in these areas enacted during succeeding presidencies.[2]

The purpose of this book is to trace the evolution of the General Welfare Clause as the constitutional underpinning of today's federal spending power. That account may give us a more informed sense of the roots of that important power and, hopefully, greater insight as to the opportunity it affords the nation to address the profound problems it confronts.

The General Welfare Clause has played a critical role in the massive growth of the federal government in the United States. This has been accomplished without constitutional amendment, although, in our early history, many of our presidents proposed such an amendment. An historical retrospective on this subject affords us the occasion to step back and contemplate for a moment whether there are alternative constitutional frameworks that may allow us more effectively to "provide for the general welfare of the United States."

What brought the framers of the federal Constitution together was an uneasy sense that the inadequacies of the Articles of Confederation might succeed in doing what Britain had been unable to do—they might destroy the new nation. It was not the narrow reach of the spending power that troubled them so much. Rather, it was the inability of Congress to obtain resources from reluctant states to pay for past spending on the Revolutionary War or future spending to support new initiatives that would help the nation grow. Congress had the power to request that a state provide resources. It could issue countless requisitions to the member states, but lacked the power to enforce any of them.

As James Madison described it, a primary source of discontent was the fiscal weakness of Congress under the Articles. He wrote: "[T]he radical infirmity of the 'arts of Confederation' was the dependence of [Congress] on the voluntary and simultaneous compliance with its Requisitions, by so many independent Communities, each consulting more or less with its particular interests & convenience and distrusting the compliance of the others."[3]

In May of 1787, the Convention convened in Philadelphia. Decades later, in his preface to his notes of the momentous gathering of the best minds of the nation, Madison recalled the defects which prompted it. "It was seen that the public debt rendered so sacred by the cause in which it had been incurred remained without any provision for its payment." Further: "[t]he reiterated and elaborate efforts of Cong. to procure from the States a more adequate power to raise the means of payment had failed." The need for a means to repay the debt and provide for the expenses of the new nation was the driving issue. Thus, on the eve of the Convention, a central question for resolution was the framing of an adequate taxing power that would permit the central government to meet this need. The framing of that power—and the spending power that accompanied it—became a primary goal of the delegates.[4]

The constitutional convention did not turn to the actual language of the General Welfare Clause until deep into the process of constitution-making. It took up the subject during the debate that began on August 6, 1787, on the first draft to emerge from the Convention's Committee of Detail. However, the issue of federal taxation and spending was only slightly beneath the surface of the delegates' deliberations from the very start. The critical but elusive concept of the "general welfare of the United States" played the role of a touchstone, marking the divide between the functions of the states and those of the new national government.

On May 29, in introducing the Virginia resolutions—the opening salvo of the Convention encompassing Virginia's bold vision of what the new constitution should look like—Governor Edmund Randolph of Virginia invoked the "various blessings" it would confer. These blessings had a spending power thrust to them: the "establishment of great national works—the improvement of inland navigation—," as well as agricultural and manufacturing advances. Moreover, the general welfare, along with national defense and the security of liberty, were named as the principal purposes of the establishment of a new form of government to replace the ailing Articles of Confederation.[5]

In explicating the resolutions, Gouverneur Morris explained

that they would create a national government that would not depend on compliance with requisitions made to the states for its fiscal survival; instead, the national government would have a "compleat and *compulsive* operation." As George Mason of Virginia put it, such a government would "directly operate on individuals." A citizen of a state would also be a citizen of the United States. The fundamental implications of such an arrangement seemed clear; such a national or central government would have ultimate responsibility for the "general welfare" of its citizens.[6]

After the committee of the whole initially adopted the Virginia resolution calling for a three-branch national government consisting of a legislative, executive, and judicial branch, James Madison tentatively proposed that the powers of the legislative branch be expressed in a set of enumerated powers.[7] The delegates at first adopted a broader formulation, conferring on the new legislature the same legislative rights as were vested in the Confederation Congress. However, Madison's idea of enumerated powers would take hold when the Convention turned to drafting the actual language of the document. The process of enumeration ensured that the power to tax would be explicit, for the delegates realized that a priority for the new Congress under the Constitution was an adequate taxing power.[8]

Alarmed at the breadth of the Virginia resolutions, the small states counter-attacked. With William Paterson of New Jersey as their spokesman, they put forth a set of propositions known as the New Jersey resolutions. Delegates from Connecticut, Delaware, and New York, as well as New Jersey, joined in the effort. The New Jersey resolutions, less iconoclastic than Randolph's proposals, would have preserved the existing one-house national legislature with its equal representation for all the states. However, the New Jersey resolutions squarely recognized the need for an explicit central taxing power. The second New Jersey resolution would have authorized the Congress "to pass acts for raising a revenue" and apply the proceeds of such revenue "to such federal purposes as [it] shall deem proper [and] expedient."[9] While the proposed taxing power was limited to import duties, the expression of an explicit, stronger taxing and spending power indicated a consensus among small and large states' delegates on the need for specificity on the point.[10]

When he finally took the floor on June 18, Alexander Hamilton argued from the opposite end of the spectrum for a much stronger national government than that proposed by the Virginians. His proposal involved not only an adequate revenue-raising authority—broader than that reflected in the New Jersey plan—but also, significantly, an adequate and "indefinite" authority to determine how the revenues would be spent. The states should not be left with power to negative national spending decisions.[11]

On June 19, following a long analytical speech by Madison in support of the Virginia plan, the delegates, in committee of the whole, rejected both the New Jersey plan and Hamilton's approach and opted for the Virginia resolutions.[12] The full Convention then began its debate, with George Washington quietly presiding. Much of the monthlong debate was the issue of representation in the legislative branch. How much voting power would each state have? Would it be proportional to the population of each state or would each state have an equal voice in the legislature? The Virginia resolutions called for proportional representation in both houses of Congress, and leading delegates, including Madison and James Wilson of Pennsylvania, regarded that principle as central to the adoption of an adequate structure.[13]

While the debate was about representation, the delegates recognized that the taxing power lay at the heart of it. Roger Sherman put the matter squarely in the opening debate: "The national debt & the want of power somewhere to draw forth the National resources, are the great matters that press."[14] On June 29, the delegates approved the principle of proportional representation in the first branch of the legislature—the present House of Representatives. The debate shifted to the structure of the second branch—the Senate-to-be. On July 2, the Convention deadlocked on the proposition that the Senate be structured on a proportional representation basis. The deadlock made clear that the large state delegations would not prevail on this issue, as they had before on the Virginia resolutions. The deadlock paved the way for the emergence of a compromise pushed by the Connecticut delegation, and joined by delegates from other smaller states, the so-called Connecticut Compromise: proportional representation in the first branch, the House, and an equal voice for each state in the Senate.[15]

Again, money lay at the heart of the matter. The sage but aging Benjamin Franklin injected the power of the purse into the controversy by proposing that, on matters relating to supplying the national treasury, proportional representation would apply in the second branch of the legislature; on other matters, the equal voice per state principal would obtain.[16] The Gerry Committee, to whom the matter had been referred after the July 2 vote, picked up the flavor of Franklin's approach by proposing that, while the Senate would involve an equal voice for each state, all bills for raising and appropriating revenue would originate in the House. As a corollary to this, the committee proposed that the Constitution require that money be drawn from the treasury only through appropriations made by law, thus ensuring that appropriations be made through the legislative process—under the control of the legislature.[17]

When Madison and Wilson objected to this aspect of the compromise as a mirage, Franklin defended it, observing: "[A]s it had been asked what would be the use of restraining the 2nd branch from medling with money bills, he could not but remark that it was always of importance that the people should know who had disposed of their money & how it had been disposed of." This could be accomplished by confining money bills to the "immediate representatives of the people." These concepts were worked into the compromise package that the Convention finally adopted on July 16 in the context of the Connecticut Compromise.[18]

The large state delegations winced but did not bolt; they swallowed hard and proceeded with the other delegates to debate the sixth Randolph resolution which dealt with the express powers of the national legislature. This in effect constituted the first debate on the spending power because the sixth resolution conferred on the new legislature all the powers of the Congress under the Articles of Confederation. As that Congress had enjoyed a spending power, the sixth resolution *implicitly* granted such a power to the legislature to be established under the constitution-in-formation. On July 16, the delegates did not debate the merits of conferring that power; on that issue, they adopted the sixth resolution without debate.[19]

The debate that did take place on the sixth resolution that day focused on the language of the resolution that would have conferred on the new Congress the power to legislate in all cases in which the "States are separately incompetent or which the harmony of the United States may be interrupted by the exercise of individual legislation." In the end, the Convention adopted language that would be converted into what is now the Supremacy Clause.[20] Before this took place, however, the Convention considered a formulation proposed by Roger Sherman that encapsulated the ideas that he would ultimately propose in the form of the General Welfare Clause. On July 17, regarding the sixth resolution, Sherman proposed that the national legislature be empowered to "make laws binding on the people of the United States in all cases which may concern the common interests of the Union; but not to interfere with the Government of the individual States in any matters of internal police which respect the [Government] of such States only, *and wherein the general welfare of the U. States is not concerned.*" James Wilson, the consummate nationalist, seconded Sherman's motion. It was not adopted at that stage, but it anticipated the framing of the General Welfare Clause later in the proceedings. On July 26, the Convention adjourned for a period, leaving the next steps to a drafting committee.[21]

THESIS

At this stage, it is appropriate to state a thesis regarding the evolution of the spending power that began with the Convention's efforts in August 1787 and has continued to this day. While language that would support an explicit federal spending power was ultimately included in the Constitution that took form that August and was signed on September 17, no clear consensus emerged from the delegates as to its scope. The language of Article I, section 8, clause 1 recommended by the cognizant committee, the so-called Committee on Unfinished Parts, was adopted by the Convention without debate. The way was thus paved for the expression of alternative and divergent interpretations to which the language was susceptible. Even before the signatures were affixed, one view was informally expressed by Gouverneur Morris to the effect that the clause could be invoked to support federal financial assistance for federal improvements to the port of Baltimore earnestly sought by delegate James McHenry. On the other hand, the first formal interpretation expressed by James Madison in "Federalist No. 41" was sharply to the contrary: spending must be confined to purposes that fell within the enumerated powers.

Madison's interpretation was not universally embraced by other contributors to the *Federalist* or by those who contributed to both sides of the debate on ratification. Moreover, it was flatly contradicted by Alexander Hamilton in his *Report on Manufactures* provided by him to Congress in his capacity as Washington's secretary of the treasury. Hamilton urged that the General Welfare Clause would support federal spending for any national purpose that Congress conceived to be for "the general welfare of the United States," including support for manufacturing, agriculture, and education. This reading was hotly contested by both Madison and Thomas Jefferson who regarded it as rank heresy and a subversion of republican principles. The solution offered by Jefferson and Madison, when they took the reins of the Executive Branch and determined federal support for internal improvements to be a sound and necessary policy, was to propose an amendment to the Constitution that would specifically authorize a federal role regarding such improvements as part of a national program. Congress declined to adopt this suggestion and never proposed such an amendment to the states. Sufficient numbers of legislators believed that Congress already possessed the power so as to deny the proposers the necessary two-thirds majorities. Faced with this impasse, President Monroe reached for a compromise doctrine. He maintained that Congress could appropriate money to the states for the construction or repair of internal improvements but could not directly establish a national program and take jurisdiction over such improvements. The compromise enabled his successor, John Quincy Adams, who fervently wished to give effect to an even broader "spirit of internal improvement," to propose an ambitious program of nationally funded public works. Adams's policies were decried by Andrew Jackson, who tried to limit application of the spending power while conceding that the constitutional interpretation that permitted its exercise could not be rolled back. Jackson's Democratic successors, Polk, Pierce, and Buchanan, tried even more forcefully to stem the spending power tide. The commentaries of nineteenth-century jurist and constitutional scholar Joseph Story, however, provided legitimacy to a reading of the General Welfare Clause that did not embrace the limitation that both Jefferson and Madison had earlier urged.

By the time the nation came to focus on the extension of slavery, the internal improvement issue had receded in importance as a focal point of national controversy. The election of 1860 brought to the White House a president prepared to use the spending power broadly, without constitutional amendment, to achieve internal improvement and other national goals, a president prepared to sign progressive legislation that his conservative Democratic predecessors had vetoed on constitutional grounds. Lincoln's administration marks the effective end of Executive Branch opposition to the Hamiltonian reading of the spending power. Moreover, Lincoln's Republican successors invoked the power to propose legislation that would have provided federal financial assistance to primary and secondary education in order to raise the literacy level of citizens newly enfranchised by the Fifteenth Amendment. Grant, Hayes, and Harrison in particular embraced this cause.

Theodore Roosevelt, while focused on government control of business, increasingly became an advocate of strong government and extended the spending power to resource conservation, public power, and land conservation. Roosevelt, along with his successor, William Howard Taft, gave the spending power a great boost by their support of the income-tax-authorizing Sixteenth Amendment. Woodrow Wilson's New Freedom, with a progressive agenda aimed at achieving higher levels of social justice, realigned the Democratic Party in support of the broad use of governmental power, including the spending power, without the amendment earlier called for by Jefferson and Madison. Indeed, both Roosevelt and Wilson laid the philosophical groundwork for the programmatic initiatives of the New Deal that in turn gave rise to the Constitutional Revolution of 1937.

In 1936, in *United States v. Butler*, the Supreme Court squarely addressed the ancient dispute between Hamilton and Madison over the scope of the General Welfare Clause and affirmed the Hamiltonian reading. The authority of Congress to spend "for public purposes," it said, "is not limited by the direct grants of legislative power found in the Constitution." Nevertheless, the Court struck down the Agricultural Adjustment Act on Tenth Amendment grounds. In response to this and other decisions invalidating New Deal programs, Franklin Roosevelt gave some thought to a corrective constitutional amendment but ultimately opted for his ill-fated court-packing scheme. In 1937, the Supreme Court sustained the New Deal unemployment compensation and retirement insurance programs under the Social Security Act, on the basis of the General Welfare Clause, as interpreted in *Butler*. The application of the clause, read Hamilton's way, to affirm the constitutionality of two key New Deal programs settled the ancient contest without the need for a constitutional amendment and paved the way for expansion of the federal role through the vigorous exercise of the spending power during the Great Society. None of the presidents who followed Roosevelt sought such an amendment. All proposed the initiation or reauthorization of programs that required a broad reading of the clause. All did so without calling for the constitutional amendment that Madison, Jefferson, and certain of their successors had urged. The matter was settled by practice, application, and interpretation that spanned the decades following the framing.

The history recounted in this book provides no basis for a clear conclusion as to a uniform original intent on the part of all of the framers. The various framers and presidents of the framing generation, or that which immediately followed, differed as to the meaning of the General Welfare Clause. While the Father of the Constitution, James Madison, advocated a strict reading of the clause that would have precluded expenditures for other than purposes within the enumerated powers, a contrary view was expressed or implied by other framers, notably Hamilton, James Wilson and Morris, and by presidents Monroe and John Quincy Adams. The amendment of the Constitution, if it was that, took place, not through the formal Article V process, but through a long evolution in which the people spoke through their elected representatives or national leaders, manifesting their desire for national growth through federal appropriations to serve the "general welfare," a process ultimately affirmed by the Supreme Court in the Social Security Act cases.

Whether this evolution has been a positive development or whether the nation would have been better served by a formal change is subject to debate. That the scope of federal activity has been vastly expanded by the exercise of the spending power is not to be doubted. That this expansion has been accomplished under an interpretation of the instrument's original language has shielded it from numerous amendments that would have been necessary had an amendment been made a precondition each time Congress undertook a new mission. Arguably, this restraint has enhanced the durability of the charter as a stable, flexible Constitution, responsive to the changing needs of society and the great growth of the United States in role, size, and population. Certainly, during our earlier period, the representatives of the people were invited to consider such an amendment and chose not to propose it to the states.

On the other hand, the absence of an amendment has had consequences. It has limited the potential role of the federal government in such areas as education, health, and welfare to what can be accomplished through federal spending and related grant conditions. It has precluded the central government from occupying the field in those areas, assuming that to be a desirable end. What progress has been made is dependent upon a high level of state-federal cooperation under programs in which the federal government implements policy through grants to states and upon the adequacy of limited budgetary resources to achieve desired ends.

If there is room for amendment in our future, it is not through a mere confirmation of the Hamiltonian reading of the General Welfare Clause. That has been accomplished through usage and judicial interpretation. An attempt to confirm it, at this late stage, through constitutional amendment is unnecessary and potentially disadvantageous, as John Quincy Adams concluded in 1825. Much has been and can be accomplished through the framework of the spending power so interpreted in such areas as transportation, the environment, natural resources, community development, education, health, income maintenance, and social insurance, as well as civil rights, the arts, science and technology, veterans' benefits, the administration of justice, and a host of other areas. Much more can be accomplished through more effective program formulation and administration, as well as creative cooperative federalism.

If the perception is that the federal government must play a greater role in one or more of these areas, one that takes it beyond the confines of the General Welfare Clause read as a spending power, then the limits of that constitutional power may be reached. Should the people see such an enlargement of the federal role to be desirable, then the question would arise: should Congress be specifically empowered to regulate, in that area, in order to provide for the general welfare of the United States, without regard to federal appropriation? Such an enlargement would require a constitutional amendment to accomplish the end. Such a transformation would require an overwhelming level of public and state legislative support and an overwhelming certainty that legislation enacted under it would be substantially more effective than that available under the current spending power. It would constitute a step at odds with the intent of the preponderance of the framers and those who later advocated Hamilton's position. Such a step would require a large dose of what Bruce Ackerman calls "higher lawmaking." While such a step now seems unlikely, it should be kept in mind that the Constitution does afford a process for taking it, a consideration that Madison was fond of repeating in his quest for the type of constitutional change that he recommended.

At this stage, in the area of domestic federal programs, it seems much more practical to address appropriate problems through the prudent and effective exercise of the spending power and other constitutional authorities, carried out with imagination and good faith, and through meaningful state-federal partnerships created within the framework of such exercise. The possibilities of such an amendment, and the concerns to which it gives rise, should provide a renewed incentive to so administer the spending power as currently understood, in light of an appreciation of the history recounted here.

I
Framing and Ratification

1
The Framing of the General Welfare Clause

IN AUGUST OF 1787, BUILDING ON THE WORK OF THE PRECEDING DEbates, the Convention's Committee of Detail produced a draft Constitution that the delegates would debate through the balance of that month and into September. The draft contained an explicit taxing power but was silent on the purposes for which tax proceeds could be spent. The Convention debated the issue of what might and might not be taxed but it did not dwell at length on the scope of the spending power. One delegate, Roger Sherman, proposed that the taxing power should be qualified. Under his formulation, Congress could lay taxes "for the payment of the debts and for defraying the expences that shall be incurred for the common defence and general welfare." While it initially rejected Sherman's proposal, the Convention ultimately adopted it on the recommendation of its cognizant committee with the stipulation that the "general welfare" in question be that "of the United States." Adoption, however, was unaccompanied by debate as to the true scope of the embryonic spending power. Individual members took away from the meeting a variety of perceptions as to the scope of the new General Welfare Clause. A definitive determination of its meaning was left to later generations.

ENUMERATED POWERS AND THE COMMITTEE DRAFT

On August 6 the Convention reconvened to hear the report from the Committee of Detail, delivered by John Rutledge of South Carolina. It consisted of a draft constitution in printed form. Articles III–VI vested the legislative power of the national government of the United States of America in a Congress, consisting of a House of Representatives and a Senate. The members of the House would be chosen every second year by the people. The first House was to consist of 65 members, with the number of members for each state specified in the document. Thereafter, the number of representatives would be apportioned at the rate of one for every 40,000 inhabitants.

All bills for raising or appropriating money would originate in the House and would not be subject to alteration or amendment by the Senate. "No money," the draft provided, "shall be drawn from the public Treasury but in pursuance of appropriations that shall originate in the House of Representatives."

The Senate was to be chosen by the state legislatures. Each legislature would select two members to represent the state. Each member would serve six years and have one vote. This was the draft's version of the Connecticut Compromise, so acrimoniously reached in the preceding debates.

Every bill that passed the House and Senate, before it became law, would be required to be presented to the president of the United States. If the president signed it, it would become law. If the bill appeared to the president "improper for being passed," it would be returned to the originating house and would not become law unless both houses again approved the measure by a two-thirds vote.

Provision was made in Articles X–XI for executive and judicial branches. The executive power was vested in a president of the United States to be elected by the legislature for a single seven year term. He was to take care that the laws of the United States "be duly and faithfully executed." The judicial power was to be vested in a Supreme Court and such inferior courts as the Congress would constitute. The jurisdiction of the Supreme Court would extend to all cases arising under laws passed by the Congress, as well as other matters specified in the document.

Article XIII would prohibit the states from laying imposts or duties on imports. Later articles provided for the admission of new states, for amendments to the Constitution, and for ratification of the document.[1]

This was the framework within which Article VII of the August 6 draft was cast. Article VII reflected the work of the Committee of Detail on the sixth Randolph resolution that had been debated by the Convention on July 16 and 17. What the committee had done was to convert the sixth resolution, with its general terms, into a set of enumerated powers, stated in section 1 of Article VII.

The first clause of this section contained the taxing power. As crafted by the committee, it would have provided that "The Legislature of the United States shall have power to lay and collect taxes, duties, imposts and excises." Significantly, the language did not confine the taxing power to duties, imposts and excises. By including the word "taxes," the provision constituted a broad, comprehensive taxing authority.

There followed a lengthy list of specific enumerated powers. These included, the power to regulate commerce with foreign nations and among the several states, establish a uniform rule of naturalization, coin money, regulate the value of foreign coin and fix the standard of weights and measures, establish post-offices, borrow money and emit bills on the credit of the United States, establish tribunals inferior to the Supreme Court of the United States, make war, raise armies, and build and equip fleets, and call forth the militia.

Then came a "necessary and proper" clause, giving the Congress the right to make "all laws that shall be necessary and proper for carrying into execution the foregoing powers...." Section 3 of the article provided for apportioning direct taxes by a formula based on population, the numbers after six years to be established by a census. Under the fourth section, no tax or duty could be laid by Congress on articles exported from a state. The fifth section would have precluded any capitation tax except in proportion to the census.

Article VIII embodied a supremacy clause significantly modified from the form in which delegate Luther Martin had proposed it on July 17.[2]

In essence the versions of Article VII and VIII encompassed the enumerated powers approach that James Madison had proposed during the early debate on Randolph's sixth resolution on May 31, together with certain restrictions on the taxing power, as well as a necessary and proper and a supremacy clause.[3]

On August 16, the Convention deferred action on a controversial issue: whether Congress would have power to lay taxes on exports, a move that the Southern delegates feared. With that issue deferred, the Convention adopted the language of Article VII as it then stood. Congress would have power to lay and collect taxes, duties, imposts, and excises.[4] For what purposes could it do so? On that, the article was silent. Subsequent debates would address the gap. The first took place on August 18 in a colloquy between James Madison of Virginia and Charles Pinckney of South Carolina.

August 18: The Madison, Pinckney and Morris Proposals

It did not take long for the gap in Article VII to be recognized. Having provided the power to tax, how would the revenues be used? The Convention began to consider that question on August 18. However, it did not do so in the context of a broad spending power formulation. Instead, it considered a set of proposals by James Madison of Virginia and Charles Pinckney of South Carolina that would have specified additional enumerated powers for the new Congress—powers that included the authority to spend funds for narrowly defined, specific purposes.

Madison began the discussion. He suggested adding to the draft that had come from the Committee of Detail a list of additional powers that he believed were needed to render the government effective. He began with a list of regulatory activities. Congress should have power to regulate affairs with the Indians. It should exercise exclusive legislative authority over the seat of government. It should be able to grant charters of incorporation. It should be empowered to secure copyrights for authors for a limited period.

Madison then turned to another set of specific proposals that would call for the expenditure of federal funds. He would give Congress power:

- to "establish an University,"
- to "encourage by premiums & provisions, the advancement of useful knowledge and discoveries," and
- to "authorize the Executive to procure and hold [land] for the erection of forts, magazines and other necessary buildings."[5]

In much the same vein, Charles Pinckney proposed his own list, in some respects with powers similar to those proposed by Madison and in other respects with powers broader than those that Madison had put forward. Pinckney went further than Madison on education. He would give to the new Congress power "to establish seminaries for the promotion of literature and the arts & sciences." He would also give it power to "establish public institutions, rewards and immunities for the promotion of agriculture, commerce, trades and manufactures."[6]

Both of these proposals were promptly dispatched, without discussion, to the Rutledge Committee that had prepared the August 6 draft (also known as the Committee of Five). However, the absence of discussion should not shroud their significance.

1: THE FRAMING OF THE GENERAL WELFARE CLAUSE 37

These proposals were put forward at the time the Convention was debating the central tax and spend power. Their tenor suggests that, at that time, at least some delegates contemplated authorizing Congress to exercise power to spend federal funds for activities that would promote the economic, educational, and cultural future of the new nation, including expenditures for seminaries (institutions of higher education) and subsidies to promote or encourage agriculture, trades, and manufactures, or the advancement of useful knowledge.

Moreover, the specific references to "rewards" for the promotion of economic activities and the "establishment" of institutions indicate that Madison and Pinckney had in mind federal *financial* assistance. The essence of federal financial assistance is the granting of federal funds, generally upon conditions, to institutions or other recipients to support activities that the government believes will foster the public interest. The Madison and Pinckney proposals suggest that this is what their authors had in mind.

The question, at least for these delegates, it appears, was not whether empowering Congress to provide federal aid to support specific enterprises or missions—education and the like—was wise but how that power should be set forth in the Constitution. Should it be made explicit through specific enumerated powers or could it be granted through a broad, general formulation—a generally phrased spending power? It seems obvious that Madison was of the former view. He might believe in an activist federal government—to a point—but the activities must be clearly stated in a set of *enumerated* powers and not left to broad speculation based upon an amorphous generalization. Policy-wise, he apparently had no objection to the new Congress establishing "an university" or providing incentive money for the "advancement of useful knowledge." However, if Congress was going to exercise those powers, the new Constitution should so say. Hence, he carefully made the proposals on August 18 in the form of microadditions to the enumerated powers. This principle of amendment by amendment accretion to the powers of Congress he was to maintain in his public life and in his private correspondence until his death in 1836.[7]

Madison and Pinckney were not alone in proposing a framework for affirmative investment activities by the new government-in-the-making. Not surprisingly, given his views on a strong national government, Gouverneur Morris joined them on August 20, but in a different context. Along with Pinckney, he proposed sweeping language that would have established a cabinet for the Executive in the Constitution. Morris's August 20 Cabinet proposal included, as one would have expected, a secretary of foreign affairs, a secretary of war and of the "marine," and a secretary to the council of state. It also included a post he called the secretary of domestic affairs. The position would have involved the following duties: "to attend to matters of general police, the State of Agriculture and manufactures, the opening of roads and navigations, and the facilitating [of] communications thro' the U.States." The secretary of domestic affairs would also be directed, as Morris saw it, "to recommend such measures and establishments as may tend to promote those objects." The position was apparently to be a secretary of the interior, agriculture, commerce and transportation rolled into one. Charles Pinckney seconded the proposals and they were also dispatched to the already overburdened Committee of Five.[8]

It seems clear that, at this stage of the debate a group of delegates, including Madison, Morris, and Pinckney, was setting forth a vision of the central government under the Constitution as empowered not merely to attend to the defense of the nation and the regulation of its interstate and foreign commerce but also to engage in certain promotional activities, through federal financial assistance or otherwise, that fell into the category of national investments. How the Convention ultimately responded to those proposals was the business of late August through early September.

August 21–23: About Debts

Before the Convention could return to the Madison, Morris, and Pinckney proposals, it was obliged to turn to another vexing issue that accompanied the fashioning of the General Welfare Clause. This was the question of the assumption of the debt—largely the war debt that would be inherited from the Congress under the Articles of Confederation.

The debate in the Convention on August 21 began with the delivery by the Committee of Eleven, chaired by Governor Livingston of New Jersey, of a report concerning the disposition of the debt. The committee's report proposed to give Congress "power to fulfill the engagements which have been entered into by Congress, and to discharge as well the debts of the U.S. and the debts incurred by the several States during the late war, for the com-

1: THE FRAMING OF THE GENERAL WELFARE CLAUSE   39

mon defence and general welfare." Here again the general welfare formulation appears as a shorthand phrase for domestic program needs. However, on August 21, the Convention was in no mood for a debate on the debt issue. It promptly tabled the proposals and turned instead to a lengthy and acrimonious debate on the issues of taxes on exports and direct taxation. The Convention ultimately approved the language of Article VII, sec. 4 prohibiting the federal government from taxing exports. The exporting states, particularly in the South, were protected.[9]

A decision had been made: duties and imposts could be adopted by the new Congress but not taxes on exports. The Congress would have to depend upon import taxes as a major source of revenue. It was time to turn again to the question of how to use the revenues.[10]

When the convention returned to the question of the substantive powers of Congress and received the report of the Rutledge Committee (the Committee of Detail) to which the Madison and Pinckney proposals had been referred on August 18, the committee recommended that the matters it had been considering be handled by additional language added to Article VII, the enumerated powers provision. First, the committee proposed adding to the first clause of Article VII, section 1, the clause which then authorized the laying and collection of taxes, duties, and imposts, language which would describe the purpose of these tax measures as, "for payment of the debts and necessary expenses of the United States." To this was appended a proviso that would have limited appropriations for a term of years.[11] This appears to be the first formulation of *an explicit spending power* to reach the floor.

The committee further proposed that language be added to Article VII in the form of an additional enumerated power that would have authorized Congress to exercise broad regulatory and promotional powers with respect to the "general interests and welfare of the United States." The language would have authorized the new Congress "to provide, as may become necessary, from time to time, for the well managing and securing the common property and general interests and welfare of the United States in such manner as shall not interfere with the governments of individual states, in matters which respect only their internal police, or for which their individual authorities may be competent."[12]

What the Rutledge Committee had evidently done with the Madison and Pinckney proposals was not to adopt them verbatim as specific additions to the already specific enumerated powers in the August 6 draft, but rather to merge them into a general grant of authority to Congress to provide and regulate for the "general interests and general welfare." The familiar "general welfare" formula would do nicely to encapsulate the ideas about promoting education and aid to the economic interests that Madison and Pinckney had put forward on August 18. Apparently the committee's solution was neither to engraft them nor to reject them but to generalize from them.

Nor had the committee forgotten Morris's far-reaching cabinet proposals. With respect to these, the committee would have added to Article X (relating to the Executive Branch) a new section that would provide for a presidential privy council consisting of, among other members, the principal officers of the departments of foreign affairs, war, marine, and finance. As Morris had proposed, a department of domestic affairs also would be represented in the cabinet. Interestingly enough, the cabinet, as envisioned by the Rutledge Committee, would have included the president of the Senate, the Speaker of the House, and the chief justice.

While the committee's notion of separation of powers may not have been acute, as reflected in this proposal, it seems clear that, in general, the committee had accepted the broad thrusts of the Madison-Morris-Pinckney proposals for an activist federal role in the investment areas upon which those delegates had focused. It had also recognized a distinct role in domestic affairs for the central government.

In short, the Executive Branch would include a department of domestic affairs that would consider public investments or promotional proposals to increase the nation's economy and perhaps also attend to educational interests, at least at the university level. There would be a Congress with an enumerated power able to respond to these proposals insofar as they related to an opaque term—"the general welfare"—and did not interfere with the local police powers of the states. Moreover, the enumerated power was not confined to the expenditure of funds. Tax revenues could be used to pay the expenses of the United States, presumably including those incurred in carrying out the general welfare power proposed by the committee.

There was much in these proposals to digest, so it was not surprising that the Convention needed more time to digest them. Thus it deferred considering them in order that "each member might furnish himself a copy."[13]

With progress made on the question of *what* to tax and a hiatus in considering a report that proposed a broad interpretation of *how* the revenues might be used, the Convention was able to return to a third vexing question about the enumerated powers: to what extent should the new revenues be used to address the national debt that remained from the Revolutionary War?

Accordingly, the Convention took up the report of a so-called Committee of Eleven and its suggestion that Congress have power "to fulfill the engagements which have been entered into by Congress." Madison thought the power necessary to avoid conveying the impression that the war had dissolved the debts of the old government. Gouverneur Morris proposed even stronger language. He would *direct* Congress to "discharge the debts & fulfill the engagements of the U.States." His proposal was adopted as the Convention adjourned on August 22.[14]

On August 23, after a long debate on the powers of Congress with respect to the militia, the Convention again returned to the debt. It agreed to language in Article VII that would join the debt-related power (in the language that Morris had convinced the Convention to adopt the prior day) and the tax power that had been previously adopted on August 16. The language as agreed to on the 23rd would have constituted Article VII, section 1 and would have read: "The Legislature shall fulfill the engagements and discharge the debts of the U.S. & shall have the power to lay & collect taxes duties imposts and excises." On the same day, the Convention approved revised language for the supremacy clause in then Article VIII.[15] The spending power was slowly coming together by connecting the taxing and debt-paying powers.

But it was not without controversy. Pierce Butler of South Carolina vigorously contested the language relating to the debt. He complained that it would compel payment to the "blood-suckers" who had speculated on the distress of others. He promised that he would move for reconsideration. On August 24, as promised, Butler moved for reconsideration. Edmund Randolph joined with him, wishing to have the Convention focus on the issue of state debts. Debate was scheduled for the following day, Saturday August 25.[16]

AUGUST 25: ROGER SHERMAN PROPOSES THE GENERAL WELFARE CLAUSE

On August 25, intense debate resumed on Article VII, section 1. The focus was the plight of the war veterans and others who had sold their debt instruments for less than fair value. George Mason of Virginia thought it unwise to compel the central government under the new Constitution to pay the debts under these circumstances. He moved to change the previously adopted language to focus on debts incurred by or under the authority of the Congress under the Articles of Confederation as valid against the new central government. Mason objected to the "shall" in the language that had previously been adopted because it obliged the new government to discharge the debts without establishing necessary distinctions.

Morris on the other hand defended the mandatory language as necessary to establish the full faith and credit of the United States. The Convention compromised with language proposed by Edmund Randolph: "All debts contracted & engagements entered into, by or under the authority of Congress, shall be as valid [against] the [United] States under this constitution as under the Confederation." The vote was 10–1. The "shall" was gone but the Constitution would make clear that the debt was not dissolved by adopting a new basic charter, but remained valid under the government to be formed pursuant to the Constitution.[17]

All this set the stage for Roger Sherman to propose an amendment to Article VII, section 1 that, would, as he put it, "connect with the clause for laying taxes duties &c an express provision for the object of the old debts &c." He moved to add to the first clause of Article VII, section 1 (relating to the taxing power) the following language: "for the payment of said debts and for the defraying the expences that shall be incurred for the common defence and general welfare." An explicit spending power was again before the Convention.[18]

The man who proposed it, Roger Sherman, was a canny New England legislator with a practical cast of mind and a penchant for crafting compromise measures that spanned the views of opposing factions and permitted a deliberative body to move its agenda forward. History may have failed to pay him his due. Catherine Drinker Bowen has described him as he was in his Convention days. "At sixty-six he was tall, lean, sharp nosed. His dark hair, streaked with gray and cut straight across the forehead hung to his collar; he was plainly dressed. His hands and feet were big; his gestures, someone noted, 'rigid as buckram.' Yet in the craggy face was dignity, the wide spaced brown eyes had depth behind them."

While not a proponent of a strong central government or, for that matter, major changes in the confederation government,

1: THE FRAMING OF THE GENERAL WELFARE CLAUSE 43

Sherman, as has been noted, had properly recognized the critical importance of providing the new central government with an adequate revenue base that would permit it to pay its debts and meet its needs. Originally inclined to confine the Federal Government to the impost as its sole source of revenue, Sherman had been willing to concede Madison's point that the impost might not be adequate. After the Convention adopted the Connecticut Compromise, which he had first suggested on June 11, on July 16, Sherman apparently felt comfortable with the taxing power in the August 6 draft from the Committee of Detail, including the power to lay direct taxes. On August 25, therefore, Sherman, as he told the Convention, was casting about for a formulation that would connect the tax and debt issues that the Convention had been debating into a single neat phrase that would authorize both functions. One may speculate that he particularly wanted language that would limit the taxing power by differentiating federal from state functions. Reference to payment of the debts and provision for common defense were obvious touchstones and would do nicely.

The addition of the key phrase that qualifies the General Welfare Clause, "to provide for . . . the General Welfare," was perhaps more problematic but would perhaps also do. The term had been used in the Articles of Confederation. It had earlier cropped up in the debates before the Convention as a convenient shorthand reference for what the central government might "do" for the people of the United States, as distinguished from what the individual states might do. Sherman himself had used the term in the July 17 debate on the taxing and spending power implicit in the Randolph resolutions. Just three days earlier, the Rutledge Committee had employed the words in suggesting the broad promotional and regulatory power to be added to Article VII. Congress would have power to "provide . . . for securing the . . . general interests and welfare of the United States." Accordingly, it should not be surprising to see Sherman picking up the phrase and attaching it to the taxing power, as a phrase of *limitation*, rather than a broad grant of affirmative power as suggested by the Rutledge Committee.

On the other hand, there is no record that, on August 25, Sherman sought explicitly to limit or circumscribe the phrase "General Welfare" through definition or cross-reference to the other enumerated powers in Article VII. Madison's notes do not record such an effort. Madison became deeply invested in the issue almost from the close of the Convention to the end of his life. Had

Sherman made such an attempt on August 25, Madison surely would have recorded it. Madison was to argue with consummate skill, consistency, and passion throughout his life that the term, as used in Sherman's proposal, was no more than a cross-reference to the enumerated powers and that spending for the general welfare was confined to spending for carrying out functions described in the enumerated powers. If this was also Sherman's idea on August 25, he did not say. Sherman was cautious about giving vast power to the government and cautious about taxation. It is possible that his thought was consistent with Madison's even though he did not so express it on August 25. However, Sherman was also careful and cautious about language. If he had intended his general welfare clause to mean nothing more than a license to the new Congress to levy taxes in order to fund the activities in the enumerated powers sections of then Article VII (e.g., the costs of regulating foreign or interstate commerce or establishing rules of naturalization), his suggestion would have been a mere tautology—a needless or repetitive statement. The August 6 draft of the Constitution contained a Necessary and Proper clause. Fairly read in conjunction with the taxing power, that clause would have authorized the incurring of any necessary expenditures for carrying out the enumerated powers. Long after the Constitution had been signed and ratified, commenters, ranging from James Monroe to Joseph Story to Justice Roberts in the *Butler* case, would observe that the General Welfare Clause would be a mere tautology if so confined. There is thus considerable question that a man of Sherman's talent and sagacity would have invested his energy in such a gesture without making clear that it was his intent to so confine the spending power if that had been his true design. For what it is worth, Madison himself did not support the Sherman formulation on August 25.

Yet another possible explanation of Sherman's proposal arises from the change in the impost practices that delegates could anticipate from the exercise of the tax power then contained in then Article VII, section 2. Previously, import taxes had been collected by the states where the imports arrived. Massachusetts, New York, and Pennsylvania, with their large ports, were principal beneficiaries. Under the new constitution, imposts would be collected by the United States, presumably for the benefit of the people of all the states, including those that had not fully shared in the their proceeds. The small states, in part as a consequence of the compromise that Sherman had suggested, would now have a voice in determining how these proceeds would be used, through their equal voice in the Senate. As a leading advocate of the small states, it would have been reasonable for Sherman to wish to ensure that the tax revenues could be spent for the "common interests" of all the states—for the "general welfare" of their people.

One more speculative aspect of Sherman's August 25 introduction of the General Welfare Clause may be worth noting. It has been suggested that, during August 1787, there was in operation a Connecticut–South Carolina coalition in which John Rutledge of the latter state and Roger Sherman were principal players. The coalition was apparently designed to advance Connecticut's interest in avoiding taxes on exports and South Carolina's interest in avoiding limitations on the importation of slaves. Sherman may have focused on the Rutledge Committee's language from August 22, recognizing that, phrased as a general regulatory power, it went too far, but concluding that, if connected to the taxing power as a modifier, it might serve better by performing two functions: (1) limiting the taxing power to the stated purposes so as to reassure those concerned about that power and (2) providing some basis for the appropriation of federal funds for "general welfare" purposes, as well as national defense and debt repayment, purposes that the small states could monitor through their equal representation in the Senate. Literally read, whether it was Sherman's intent or not, the language would also help another South Carolinian. As has been seen, only a few days before Sherman made his proposal, Charles Pinckney had offered a string of additions to the enumerated powers that would have involved the federal government, through the spending power, in encouraging education, commerce, and agriculture. The Pinckney proposals, and those of Madison, had not been adopted by August 25. Sherman's general welfare clause would, if read literally, have embraced them. In our own age, this is indeed what has happened. All this is, of course, mere speculation. There remains for discussion the record that was made about the clause on and after August 25 until the close of the Convention and, more importantly, the record that was made thereafter.[19]

Sherman's motion had a rude beginning. It was promptly rejected on August 25 as "unnecessary." Only Connecticut supported it. Presumably, the Convention on August 25 believed that the concept, while not unwise, was already inherent in the taxing power as contained in the draft constitution as amended up to that point in the debate. Sherman characteristically bided his time while the Convention turned to other matters.[20]

Over the next days, the Convention moved on to other articles, resolving some issues, leaving some unresolved. Finally, on August 31, again on the motion of Roger Sherman, the Convention agreed to refer "such parts of the Constitution as have been postponed, and such parts of Reports as have not been acted upon" to a committee composed of one member from each state. The committee has come to be known as the Committee on Unfinished Parts. It consisted of Nicholas Gilman of New Hampshire, Rufus King of Massachusetts, Roger Sherman of Connecticut, David Brearley of New Jersey, Gouverneur Morris of Pennsylvania, John Dickinson of Delaware, Daniel Carroll of Maryland, James Madison of Virginia, Hugh Williamson of North Carolina, Pierce Butler of South Carolina, and Abraham Baldwin of Georgia. (Hamilton was not included in the list, although, at the time, he was the sole delegate attending for New York, and on September 8 was appointed to the Committee of Style. It appears that Hamilton had absented himself from the Convention during the month following the submission of the report of the Committee of Detail and did not return to Philadelphia until September 6.) It was the Committee on Unfinished Parts that reported favorably the General Welfare Clause.

The membership of the committee reflected such diversity as the times could muster. Daniel Carroll of Maryland, one of the two Catholics among the delegates, was a formidable man of property, and a business partner of Washington. Dickinson of Delaware was a distinguished patriot, had composed the first draft of the Articles of Confederation, and was to author the *Letters of Fabius* in support of the Constitution. Sherman had proposed the original language, and several of the committee members were to play a significant role in the later interpretation of the General Welfare Clause, most notably, Madison and, to a much lesser degree, Morris, each of whom apparently took away different understandings of its reach. Some, such as Baldwin, were to be heard from, but only incidentally on related subjects in the ensuing years.[21]

September 4: The Report of the Committee on Unfinished Parts—The Convention Adopts the General Welfare Clause

When the Convention convened on Tuesday, September 4, Brearley of New Jersey again made a "further partial Report."[22]

The first item in the report dealt with the taxing and spending power then in Article VII, section 1 of the draft. The committee recommended that it read as follows: "The Legislature shall have power to lay and collect taxes, duties, imposts, and excises, to pay the debts and provide for the common defence and general welfare of the United States."[23]

Roger Sherman was a member of the committee. William Pierce of Georgia observed that Sherman "seldom fails." His observation applied to the General Welfare Clause. Sherman had evidently finally prevailed on his proposal of August 25. His general welfare proposal had been included in the committee's report, with the highly significant addition of the words "of the United States" as modifying the words "general welfare." The taxing authority had been connected to the authority to pay debts and to spend appropriated funds for the common defense and "general welfare of the United States." The issues about assumption of debts had been partially resolved by connecting an authority to pay the nation's debts to the taxing power.[24]

What had been done with the Madison and Pinckney proposals? The committee made no explicit mention of them. Possibly, they had been part of the jurisdiction of the committee as sections of reports which had not been acted upon after their referral to committee on August 21. It is at least plausible that they were disposed of by providing to Congress the authority to tax "to" (in order to) "provide for . . . the general welfare," although Madison in his later writings clearly did not see it that way.[25]

The committee's version of Article VII, section 1—now containing the spending power or General Welfare Clause—was adopted on the same day that the committee reported it favorably. The Journal for September 4 records, on the question of agreeing to the first clause in the report, "it passed in the affirmative." Madison records that it was agreed to "nem. con." No ayes and noes were recorded in the Journal. Thus, there was no recorded debate on the General Welfare Clause and the committee's report that would provide posterity with a source of legislative history on the day of its adoption.

Roger H. Brown tells us that the Convention's adoption of the taxing power without debate is evidence of a consensus that affected a number of issues to come before that body. Brown further observes that "the Framers' experience with the inability of the state governments to collect taxes had educated them to the system's inadequacy and predisposed them to radical reconstitution." At the same time that consensus, insofar as it was reflected in the adoption of the taxing power in Article I, section 8, clause 1, disinclined them to thoroughly debate the purposes for which funds could be used. The existence of the General Welfare Clause effectively precluded that discussion.[26]

MCHENRY'S CONVERSATIONS

Some contemporaneous informal discussion among delegates would support the theory that the General Welfare Clause was perceived by some of them as providing the authority to carry out certain of the types of investment activities that had been proposed in the early days of the debate and in the August proposals of Morris, Pinckney, and Madison. Two days after the action of September 4, on September 6, Maryland delegate James McHenry spoke to several members regarding the inclusion of a power to enable the national legislature to erect piers to protect shipping in winter and preserve the navigation of harbors. He probably had in mind using the federal spending power to aid in improving the port of Baltimore. McHenry, who had lost little time in contemplating how the new taxing authority might benefit his constituents, had been thinking about the issue since September 4, the day the General Welfare Clause was adopted. His own notes record his musings on that day. "Upon looking over the constitution, it does not appear that the national legislature can *erect light houses* or *clean out or preserve the navigation of harbours*—This expence ought to be borne by commerce—of course by the general treasury into which all the revenue of commerce must come—." He further noted that a motion on lighthouses would be made on September 5.[27]

September 5 brought no motion. On September 6, McHenry consulted Gouverneur Morris and other delegates. According to McHenry, Morris was in favor of the policy, but, "thinks it may be done under the words of the I clause I sect 7 art. amended—'and provide for the common defence and general welfare.'"[28] Max Farrand, in his classic account of the framing cites these conversations as "an indication of what Morris would have liked to have this clause mean." Farrand attributes to Morris, as well as Sherman, the phrasing of the clause and its recommendation by the Brearley Committee.[29] All this would suggest that at least some among the draftsmen of the clause (Morris was on the Brearley Committee) regarded it as broad enough to confer authority to spend on matters that went beyond the enumerated powers, even in the absence of specific language in the Constitution. This would accord with the theory that the clause was intended or understood by some to confer authority to spend funds on the types of purposes envisaged in the Madison and Pinckney proposals.

Madison, however, was not among them. He had proposed his policy ideas as specific additions to the enumerated powers and spent portions of his career advancing the proposition that the General Welfare Clause was of limited effect and conferred no power to spend on purposes outside the enumerated powers. However, on September 4 and the days following, there is no record of his views or those of any other delegate regarding the potentially enormous reach of the spending power that the framers had adopted on September 4.

Sherman's Catch: The Significance of a Semicolon

Between September 4 and September 10, the Convention debated various provisions of the report from the Brearley Committee as well as recommendations from other committees. But no further action was taken with respect to the language of the General Welfare Clause. Nor was there any further debate with respect to the meaning of that clause.

On September 8, the Convention approved a motion to appoint a committee of five to revise the style and arrange the articles as they had been revised and amended during the debates on the report of the Committee of Detail's draft of August 6. The committee of five included Samuel Johnson of Connecticut, Alexander Hamilton of New York, once more a participant in the Convention, Gouverneur Morris of Pennsylvania, James Madison of Virginia, and Rufus King of Massachusetts. The version of Article VII, section 1 referred to this committee retained the same language that had been recommended by the Brearley Committee and approved on September 4, namely: "The Legislature shall have power to lay and collect taxes, duties, imposts and excises, to pay the debts and provide for the common defence and general welfare of the United States."[30] Significantly, both Madison and Hamilton, who were to take widely divergent views regarding the meaning of the General Welfare Clause, served on the committee.

On September 12, the Committee of Style made its report. The legislative powers in the draft recommended by that committee were now arranged in Article I. Section 8 of Article I contained the enumerated powers. The second clause of that section gave to Congress the power "To lay and collect taxes, duties, imposts and excises; to pay the debts and provide for the common defence and general welfare of the United States." The language was in the form that the Convention had adopted on September 4, with one exception. In place of the comma after the word "excises" the committee had substituted a semicolon.[31]

Much meaning is attributed to this change and its reversal. When the Constitution was finally engrossed on September 17, Article I, section 8, clause 1 read as follows: "The Congress shall have Power To lay and collect Taxes, Duties, Imposts and Excises, to pay the Debts and Provide for the common Defence and general Welfare of the United States; but all Duties, Imposts and Excises shall be uniform throughout the United States." The semicolon had been deleted after "excises" and replaced by a comma.[32]

The uniformity clause was added during the debates that followed September 12. There is no record of any debate on the committee's insertion of the semicolon. However, Max Farrand notes that the semicolon might have supported a construction of the clause that gave it significance independent of the taxing power. Thus, Congress would have authority to provide for the common defense and general welfare quite apart from spending legislation. Its general welfare power would extend to regulatory measures independent of appropriations and the exercise of the power of the purse. It is for these reasons that the semicolon was removed. Farrand attributes this change to Roger Sherman. He suggests that Sherman was instrumental in causing the change to be made, presumably as a technical drafting matter, to ensure that the general welfare language would not provide legislative authority to Congress independent of the taxing power, as the Rutledge Committee had proposed, but would be regarded as a limitation on the taxing and spending power.

History further records that the semicolon episode reflected an effort by Morris to enlarge the powers of the Congress in this respect. Morris served on the Committee of Style and was a principal draftsperson of the document at this stage.[33] The semicolon episode, if true, suggests that Morris read the clause broadly and not, as Madison later urged, constituting a mere cross-reference to the enumerated powers. Otherwise, there would have been no point in manipulating the semicolon.

There is no record of a vote on this change nor of a debate about it. But there is in the record the variation in the versions of Article I, section 8, clause 1 delivered by the Committee of Style on September 12 and the engrossed version on September 17.

What seems clear at the inception was that the General Welfare Clause did not confer a separate power independent of the spending power. The reversal of the semicolon had clarified this. The event was recalled during a session of the Fifth Congress on June 19, 1798 when Albert Gallatin, then a representative from Pennsylvania, is recorded as having discussed the issue in debate before the House. Gallatin said that he was aware that the words (presumably the General Welfare Clause) had been originally inserted into the Constitution "as a limitation to the power of laying taxes." In his words, "After the limitation had been agreed to, and the Constitution was completed, a [Pennsylvania] member of the Convention . . . being one of a committee of revisal and arrangement, attempted to throw these words into a distinct paragraph, so as to create not a limitation, but a distinct power." Gallatin continued, "The trick, however, was discovered by a member from Connecticut, now deceased, and the words restored as they now stand."[34] The references are apparently to Gouverneur Morris and Roger Sherman. Having proposed the language, Sherman had made the catch that would preserve its original meaning as a limitation on the taxing power.

The final version of the General Welfare Clause, with the comma restored, was sufficiently elliptical to give rise to differing constructions from the very founders who were present at the creation. Evidently, the framers had intended to limit the taxing and spending power, rather than create an express new power to provide for the general welfare of the United States, but they had not expressly confined that limitation to spending solely in order to implement the enumerated powers. This left Article I, section, 8, clause 1 *susceptible* to the construction that Congress could tax, and then appropriate tax funds, in order to provide for the general welfare of the United States, to carry out purposes encompassed by the enumerated powers as well as purposes that extended beyond them.

Morris might have been foiled in his effort to legislate by punctuation. However, his overall approach of favoring indefinite language that might embrace specific proposals without specifying them was ultimately to prove more successful. One example of that approach occurred in the reported colloquy between Morris and McHenry following the September 4 vote. Yet another was to take place following the report of the Committee of Style on September 12.

That quality of creative ambiguity, whether intended or not, enabled three different members of the Committee of Style, Hamilton, Madison, and Morris, to defend, espouse, or intimate different perspectives on the General Welfare Clause before and after the Convention adjourned. That same quality also gave to the Constitution sufficient flexibility to enable it to serve the Nation superbly through the decades that followed its formulation and to continue to so serve during the coming millennium.

The Final Debates: The Franklin and Madison Proposals and the Engrossment

On September 14, the Convention debated the version of Article I, section 8, clause 1, the spending power, contained in the report of the Committee of Style submitted on September 12. That version still contained the semicolon that history has attributed to Gouverneur Morris, but no mention was made of the semicolon. Instead, the Convention annexed to the clause language providing that all duties, imposts, and excises must be "uniform" within the United States. Apparently satisfied with the text, they made no other changes. The work on the language of the spending power was complete but for the later removal of the semicolon.[35] The spending power and the General Welfare Clause that conveyed it, in the form of a limitation on the taxing power, had been adopted essentially *without* debate.

The disposition of some motions on related issues demonstrate the differing approaches of key delegates. Madison's preference was for specific enumeration; Gouverneur Morris preferred generalized statements of encompassing authority. Both, along with Wilson, were groping for ways to authorize the new Congress to engage in limited investment in support of internal improvement and education. Benjamin Franklin thus moved to add to Article I, section 8 a specific power to provide for "cutting canals where deemed necessary." His motion was seconded by James Wilson but ultimately failed to pass.[36]

Madison and Pinckney, with Wilson's support, unsuccessfully renewed their proposal on universities. They moved to insert into section 8 language that would give Congress the power "to establish an University in which no preferences or distinctions should be allowed on account of Religion." Gouverneur Morris observed that the power was already implicitly contained in the Constitution through resort to the power of Congress over the seat of government contained in Article I, section 8, reflecting in this context the advice regarding the General Welfare Clause that he had previously given to McHenry.[37]

Language was added regarding periodic reports of expenditures. As a result, Article I, section 9, clause 7 of the Constitution now reads: "No money shall be drawn from the Treasury but in consequence of Appropriations made by Law; and a regular Statement and Account of the Receipts and Expenditures of all public money shall be published from time to time." The phrase "from time to time" was adopted in lieu of "annually" following a motion made by Madison and seconded by Wilson. Whatever their differences as to the scope of the spending power, the framers knew that the making of appropriations would be an important function of the new Congress and they wanted the operation of that function to be known to the people.[38]

On September 15, the Convention clarified the limitation on state imposts or duties on imports or exports without the consent of Congress. Article I, section 10, clause 2 now reads: "No State shall, without the consent of the Congress, lay any Imposts or Duties on Imports or Exports, except what may be absolutely necessary for executing its Inspection Laws; and the net Produce of all Duties and Imposts laid by any State on Imports or Exports, shall be for the Use of the Treasury of the United States." Clarifying language was also added that would restrain the states from laying duties of tonnage without the consent of Congress, now Article I, section 10, clause 3. This was done following a motion by delegates McHenry and Carroll from Maryland, still seeking to ensure funds for clearing harbors and erecting lighthouses.[39]

In these debates, the Convention was polishing the limits on state access to resources through taxes on the same sources to which Congress would look for revenues. Those limits would eventually affect the scope of the spending power. With their power to tax imports or exports limited, the states' ability to support the general welfare within their borders was constrained. Accordingly, states could in the future argue, like McHenry, that they should gain the benefits of the federal taxing power through federal aid for projects that enhanced the general welfare of their citizens.

The Signing of the Constitution and the Convention's Adjournment

When the Convention reconvened on the following Monday, September 17, it was to hear the reading of the engrossed Constitution and to ponder sage observations by Benjamin Franklin that have been handed down to posterity. Franklin expressed surprise that the document had turned out as "near to perfect" as it had: "Thus, I consent, Sir, to this Constitution," he told the Convention, "because I expect no better, and because I am not sure, that it is not the best." He urged the delegates to support the Constitution despite their objections to individual provisions and followed his plea with a motion that the Constitution be signed by the members with the formula: "Done in Convention by the unanimous consent of *the States* present."[40]

Thirty-nine delegates followed Franklin's recommendation and signed the Constitution. Among those who declined was Elbridge Gerry who complained, among other things, about the power of the national legislature to "raise armies and money without limit."[41] Edmund Randolph, "animadverting on the indefinite . . . power given by the Constitution to Congress," also declined to sign the document, although it embraced large portions of the Virginia plan that he had originally proposed.[42]

Ultimately on the 17th of September, Franklin's motion carried. The members who had determined to sign the Constitution did so. As Madison noted, "The members then proceeded to sign the instrument." As they attended to this task, Franklin made his famous observation about the sun painted on the back of Washington's chair. "[N]ow at length I have the happiness to know that it is a rising and not a setting Sun."[43] The Convention then dissolved by adjournment sine die.[44]

A General Welfare Clause, carved out of Roger Sherman's express attempt to limit the taxing power, would now be part of the Nation's basic charter. At least it would be so if the requisite number of states ratified the document as Franklin had fervently urged the delegates that September Monday in Philadelphia.

2
Ratification and the General Welfare Clause

THE DEBATE OVER THE RATIFICATION OF THE CONSTITUTION PITTED the proponents of the document against its opponents—Federalists against Anti-Federalists. The latter launched a bitter attack against the taxing power in the charter produced by the Philadelphia convention. They charged that limiting the taxing power to the laying of those taxes that would provide for the general welfare of the United States was essentially meaningless. In their view, Congress would have the laboring oar in determining the scope of the General Welfare Clause. The taxing power was thus overly broad and would leave the states with only crumbs to meet their own needs. In response, Madison, in "Federalist No. 41," put forth an alternative interpretation that sought to narrow the scope of the clause. For him, the language operated merely to introduce the more specific limitations in the enumerated powers rather than to constitute a separate grant of power. Implicit in Madison's argument was the thesis that Federal spending could encompass only that spending designed to carry out the enumerated powers. Madison's partner in this enterprise, Alexander Hamilton, did not embrace Madison's theory but rather defended the need for a broad taxing power on grounds of expediency, without explicitly laying out his own vision as to its scope. Other delegates, notably James Wilson, adopted a similar approach. The Bill of Rights, the product of the ratification debates, did not specifically deal with the issue of the scope of the spending power. In sum, that issue, while a subject of conversation, was never definitively resolved in the ratification debate. Rather, it was left for alternative interpretation by those who became responsible for staffing the new government established under the Constitution—primarily, but not exclusively, presidents and their close advisors.

Anti-Federalist Rhetoric

The breadth of the General Welfare Clause, as the Anti-Federalists perceived it, contributed to the profound antagonism with which they viewed the product of the Philadelphia Convention. It prompted them to oppose ratification vigorously. In their campaign against it, they used what they saw as the unlimited power of Congress to raise money for any purpose that body saw fit as a convenient weapon with which to arouse popular feeling against the proposed Constitution.

Repeatedly, they pointed to the vagueness of the General Welfare Clause as a means of dramatizing their opposition to direct taxation. Both the power and the objects of direct taxation were broad. Congress could lay taxes on countless objects and back up collection with force. In this the Anti-Federalists focused on that part of the tax power that granted Congress authority to lay taxes, as distinguished from imposts and excises. They might be able to live with import taxes, but they feared the power to engage in direct taxation.

Moreover they saw in the General Welfare Clause no meaningful limit on the taxing power. The clause had been added to the taxing power in Article I, section 8, as a means of modifying or limiting that power. Congress could not tax for just any purpose: it could tax only to provide for the common defense or the general welfare of the United States. However, the Anti-Federalists remained unconvinced that this language constituted an effective limitation. Their concern was that the term "general welfare" could be interpreted to mean whatever Congress wanted it to mean. The Anti-Federalists proclaimed that the concept was so broad that Congress could formulate initiatives in many areas of national life and then support requests for taxation on the basis of need for revenues to finance those initiatives.

Indeed, the Anti-Federalists did not bother to answer the argument that Madison put forward in response, namely, that the "general welfare" was a shorthand for the specific enumerated powers in Article I, section 8. Congress, Madison urged, could spend money to carry out those enumerated powers but not for other purposes. Disregarding this argument, the Anti-Federalists continued to press the charge that the breadth of the spending power and its weak brake upon the taxing power was a powerful reason for rejecting the new Constitution. From this point, they launched their broader attack—that the federal power of the purse would be used by aristocrats, under an aristocratic constitution, to serve aristocratic ends. So they warned the people.[1]

Nowhere was this theme expressed more explicitly than in the Brutus VI essay attributed to Robert Yates. Yates, a member of the New York delegation to the Philadelphia Convention, had sat largely silent during the debates, although he took notes that were later published.

Yates left the Convention early and declined to sign the Philadelphia document. Back in New York, he helped lead the fight against ratification. "Brutus VI," published in December 1787, is one of a set of essays that appeared in the press and was attributed to Yates. Its main purpose was to object to the threat of excessive taxation, particularly direct taxation. Interwoven in the argument against that broad power was the author's response to the General Welfare Clause.

The author of "Brutus VI" responded to the argument made by the Federalists that the power to lay and collect taxes was limited to the purposes for which money could be appropriated: to pay the debts and to provide for the common defense and the general welfare. Yates asked "those, who reason thus, to define what ideas are included under the terms, to provide for the common defence and general welfare? Are these terms definite, and will they be understood in the same manner, and to apply to the same cases by every one?" Brutus quickly answered his own rhetorical flourish, "It will . . . be a matter of opinion, what tends to the general welfare; and the Congress will be the only judges in the matter." He continued: "To provide for the the general welfare, is an abstract proposition, which mankind differ in the explanation of, as much as they do on any political or moral proposition that can be proposed. . . ." To the author of Brutus VI, it was absurd to suggest that the power of Congress was meaningfully limited by these general expressions. Hence, the power of taxation constituted a real threat to states' rights.[2]

The same theme was reflected in the first article of the Brutus series, Brutus I, which appeared in the *New York Journal* in October of 1787. It carried the dramatic heading: "If you adopt it . . . posterity will execrate your memory," hardly an accurate prediction. Here, the core of the Anti-Federalist position was set forth. The new government would possess "absolute and uncontroulable power . . . with respect to every object to which it extends." The Necessary and Proper Clause and the Supremacy Clause, along with the General Welfare Clause, were cited as evidence of this broad power.[3]

Moreover, Congress could regulate the people without the buffer that would be created if the central government were forced to operate through the states. Turning to the taxing power, Brutus complained: "[T]here is no limitation to this power, unless it be said that the clause which directs the use to which those taxes, and duties shall be applied, may be said to be a limitation. . . ." But this limitation, he argued, constituted no meaningful effective brake on the power to lay taxes.

"By this clause [the spending power]," the Brutus I analysis proceeded, "[the tax revenues] are to be applied to pay the debts and provide for the common defence and general welfare of the United States; but the legislature have the authority to contract debts at their discretion; they are the sole judges of what is necessary to provide for the common defence, and they only are to determine what is for the general welfare; this power therefore is neither more nor less, than a power to lay and collect taxes, imposts, and excises, at their pleasure. . . ." Thus, in the business of laying taxes and collecting taxes—"the most important of any power that can be granted"—the idea of "confederation" was "totally lost" and that of "one entire republic" was embraced.[4]

It was this central concern about an unlimited taxing power that so bothered the Anti-Federalists and led them to so vigorously oppose ratification. The theme was picked up as the fall of 1787 wore on. In October of that year Samuel Bryan's article, published under the heading of "Centinel," appeared in the *Independent Gazeteer* in Philadelphia. "Centinel I" flatly rejected the argument that a system of checks and balances as reflected in the Constitution would preclude a despotic aristocracy. A far better scheme of government was that represented by the unicameral Philadelphia legislature, whose members were elected annually and who could thus be held more responsible to the people. This clearly responsible government was best, Bryan argued.

Like his fellow Anti-Federalists in New York, Bryan pointed to the breadth of the taxing power contained in the proposed constitution to establish his hyperbolic proposition that the new government was "a most daring attempt to establish a despotic aristocracy among freemen, that the world has ever witnessed." High among the concerns that Bryan cataloged was vesting Congress with the power to engage in "every species of *internal* taxation." Bryan complained, "[W]hatever taxes, duties, and excises that they may deem requisite for the *general welfare*, may be imposed on the citizens of these states. . . ." The breadth of the power was made manifest by the language of the General Welfare Clause itself. "The Congress may construe every purpose for which the state legislatures now lay taxes, to be for the *general welfare*, and thereby seize upon every object of revenue."[5]

Several aspects of this attack on the General Welfare Clause are worthy of note here. First, the objection to the clause clearly implied that the Anti-Federalists understood it to confer what the Supreme Court held it to confer 150 years later: a power to spend independent of the enumerated powers. Second, the attacks on the clause focused on its failure to limit the taxing power rather than on the proposition that Congress could spend money for initiatives that came within the scope of the term "general welfare." The Anti-Federalists, understandably, were more concerned about the pocketbooks of their readers than with the kinds of projects that might be financed under the General Welfare Clause. Finally, a broadly phrased taxing and spending power ran counter to the core beliefs of the Anti-Federalists.

As Herbert Storing has observed, they believed in the efficacy of the "small republic." In their view, the most efficient and effective government was that closest to the people. That the general or central government would possess power to do things that states could already do, such as providing for the common good or general welfare, was antithetical to their political thought. It was also antithetical in the sense that a broad general welfare clause would make it difficult to distinguish between those functions that were assigned to the central government and those that were assigned to the states.[6] In fact, the growth of federal functions under the spending power has been in part attributable to the recognition that the "small republics" or states were unable effectively to address their general welfare problems, e.g., internal improvements, transportation, education of the disadvantaged, without federal assistance.

In the ratification debate before the Virginia convention, both Patrick Henry and Richard Henry Lee expressed the fear that an unlimited taxing power would subvert the authority of the states. In June 1788 Henry made invidious comparisons between the guarantees against taxation in a bill of rights and the unlimited power of taxation contained in the Constitution. On June 7 of that year, in the course of the debate before the Virginia Convention, Henry rose to respond to Governor Edmund Randolph's defense of the Constitution—a constitution that Randolph himself had not signed. Henry pointed to the perceived dangers in the Constitution and, at the end of his address, returned to the issue of taxation and his disagreements with Randolph and Madison who had preceded him.

Henry contended that the exercise of the federal taxing power would not save money or reduce public burdens. The costs of the new government would offset any savings. Double collection of taxes—at both federal and state levels—would increase the expenses of government. In addressing the argument that the taxing power was vital to the new government, Henry responded that it was also vital for the states. States would be shortchanged because the central government was also collecting taxes on the same sources.[7] The potential loss of sources of revenues to state governments was a theme that Henry and others would continue to sound during the debates and beyond. Later, the same theme would provide a basis for broader use of the federal spending power. The concern over loss of state resources would eventually be reflected in the argument that assistance to states under the General Welfare Clause was a means of returning resources to the states that had given them up in acceding to the federal taxing power.

Henry also sounded another theme: the breadth of the power granted—including the taxing power—warranted a bill of rights. Henry objected to reserving power to the states by implication: "They say that every thing that is not given is retained. The reverse of the proposition is true by implication. They do not carry their implication so far when they speak of the general welfare. No implication when the sweeping clause comes. Implication is only necessary when the existence of privileges is in dispute...." In short, as Henry saw it, the spending power inherent in the General Welfare Clause constituted a sweeping power that had not been implied, but that had been expressly written into the Constitution.

What was sauce for the goose was sauce for the gander. The notion that powers unexpressed in the Constitution were reserved to the states could not be left to implication. An explicit bill of rights *was* necessary. The "sweeping" language of the General Welfare Clause helped to undergird that argument.[8]

In sum, the Anti-Federalists, in their press attacks and their ratification convention speeches, pointed to the breadth of the General Welfare Clause as a prime reason to fear the Constitution. That fear was focused on what they perceived as an unlimited power in Congress to lay taxes, particularly direct taxes. The General Welfare Clause was so broad that it provided no meaningful limitation on that power. In arguing from the breadth of the General Welfare Clause, the Anti-Federalists implicitly recognized that the clause could be read as authorizing Congress to spend for those purposes that Congress, in its discretion, deemed within the scope of the "general welfare of the United States." In making this argument so expressly, the Anti-Federalists provide convincing evidence that those who ratified the Constitution did so with a keen awareness that the General Welfare Clause—and the Constitution of which it was a part—were *susceptible* to that construction, the construction that the courts ultimately placed upon that clause. Whether they agreed with the construction or not, those who ratified the Constitution knew that it could be read to include a spending power of indefinite scope. The Anti-Federalists did not let them adopt this bold new charter without that awareness.

To be sure, the Anti-Federalists did not object that the General Welfare Clause conferred a power to "provide for" the "general welfare" independent of the taxing and spending power. They did not read the General Welfare Clause as it would have read had Morris's substitution of a semicolon for a comma succeeded in separating the words "to . . . provide for . . . the general welfare" from the authority to lay taxes that preceded them. The Anti-Federalists recognized the General Welfare Clause for what it was—an effort to limit the taxing power. A limitation on a power, however, can be seen as a grant of power. By empowering Congress to enact only tax (and necessarily appropriation) measures the purpose of which was "to provide for . . . the general welfare," the Constitution makers had precluded Congress from enacting measures that exceeded that limitation. By the same token, however, Congress was empowered to enact tax and appropriation measures that did provide for the general welfare of the United States and thus fell within the bounds of the limitation. The argument of the Anti-Federalists was that the limitation was so broad and left Congress with such complete discretion to define "the general welfare" that it provided no effective brake on the taxing power. The Anti-Federalists thus clearly posed the issue that had not been debated fully in the Convention of 1787.

The Anti-Federalists also laid the groundwork for the movement that led to the 1791 adoption of the Bill of Rights that reserved specific rights to the states and to the people. This was the second great compromise of the constitutional period. The first led to adopting the Constitution that established a central, federal government with broad taxing power; the second involved appending to it an express bill of rights that included the

Tenth Amendment: "The powers not delegated to the United States by the Constitution, nor prohibited by it to the States, are reserved to the States respectively, or to the people."[9]

THE FEDERALISTS RESPOND: MADISON'S CONSTRUCTION

Those who supported ratification—commonly referred to as Federalists—responded vigorously to attacks by the Anti-Federalists on the proposed constitution that emerged from the Philadelphia Convention. That response took the form of a set of articles by Hamilton, Jay, and Madison that have come down to us as the *Federalist Papers* or *The Federalist*, familiar to all students of constitutional history. The Federalist response also included a body of other articles in the popular press and speeches in the ratifying conventions that are an important part of the fabric of the debates on the adoption of the federal constitution— and essential to understanding it. This Federalist response addressed the totality of the Anti-Federalist critique. It also focused on specific aspects, including those attacks that identified the supposed breadth of the spending power in the eighth section of the first article of the Constitution.

The defense of the General Welfare Clause took several forms. One approach was that offered by Madison in "Federalist No. 41." The gravamen of Madison's argument in No. 41 was that the Anti-Federalists flatly misread Article I, section 8, clause 1 for their own forensic purposes. Contrary to the their argument about breadth, Congress was not vested by the General Welfare Clause with broad power to legislate for the general welfare, beyond the scope of the enumerated powers in Article I, section 8. The "general welfare" language, Madison urged, was merely an introductory or shorthand for the set of enumerated powers that followed it. This laid the foundation for the argument that Madison later spelled out with greater specificity: Congress could, under the General Welfare Clause, spend money to carry out, for example, the interstate commerce power because that was specified in Article l, section 8. However, it could not spend money for purposes not specified in that section and that were outside the scope of the enumerated powers. The power to tax and spend was thus a mere funding mechanism for the enumerated powers. The spending power was strictly confined by the terms of the section in which it was contained. The General Welfare Clause therefore constituted an appropriate limitation on the taxing power.

"Federalist No. 41" was but one of a series of many essays that Madison contributed to the project that Hamilton had conceived as a means of generating support for the proposed Constitution in New York. After completing the project, Madison tersely described his role in it in a letter to Thomas Jefferson. Madison observed that the project had been undertaken by him, together with Jay and Hamilton, at the behest of the latter two and that, with the illness of Jay, he and Hamilton assumed the major burden. He then added the following significant disclaimer: "Though carried on in concert, the writers are not mutually answerable for all the ideas of each other, there being seldom time for even a perusal of the pieces by any but the writer before they were wanted at the press, and sometimes hardly by the writer himself." This disclaimer seems particularly pertinent to the views that both Hamilton and Madison expressed regarding the General Welfare Clause.

"Federalist No. 41" is significant enough to warrant further discussion. It appeared in the *Independent Journal* in New York during January 1788. Because it followed Yates's Brutus I and VI essays, it appears to have been designed as a response to both. The subject of No. 41 was the new national government's power with respect to the issues of defense and taxation, and it addressed two, overarching questions: "[w]hether any part of the powers transferred to the general Government be unnecessary or improper?" and "[w]hether the entire mass of them be dangerous to the portion of the jurisdiction left to the several States?" To Madison the first question boiled down to a central issue: was the power conferred on the central government by the Constitution "necessary to the public good"?

To answer this question, Madison classified the powers conferred into a number of categories in terms of their purpose, including "security against foreign danger," regulation of commerce with foreign nations, "maintenance of harmony" among the states, restraint of the states from "certain injurious acts," and provision for giving "due efficacy" to all of these powers. He then devoted a large portion of No. 41 to explaining and justifying the national security powers in the Constitution, particularly to those relating to the national defense—raising armies and equipping fleets.[10]

A major purpose of No. 41 was to reassure its readers that a peacetime defense establishment was necessary and not a threat to individual liberty. Madison began by arguing that a standing force was a "necessary provision" for the defense of the nation. That the new nation was unified under the Constitution would itself provide a barrier against hostile action and internal dissension and thus would destroy "every pretext for a military establishment which could be dangerous."[11]

He then pointed to the spending power in the Constitution, arguing that, aside from the union, the best precaution against danger from standing armies was limiting the term for which revenues could be appropriated for their support. Here, Madison invoked the limitation in Article I, section 8 that authorizes the Congress to "raise and support Armies, but no Appropriation of Money to that Use shall be for a longer Term than two Years." Madison may also have had in mind the constitutional provision for reconstituting the House of Representatives every two years. These provisions established a safeguard: appropriations for defense would be made only on a biennial or more frequent basis. This argument was followed by a stout defense of the need for both a standing army and navy.[12]

In No. 41, having established a solid foundation for the defense power, Madison then used it to defend the taxing power which had been attacked ferociously by the Anti-Federalists. "The power of levying and borrowing money" was "the sinew of that which is to be exerted in the national defence." It was therefore properly classified in the same class of powers with the defense power. The taxing power and the defense power were thus clearly intertwined.

Having related the taxing power to the defense power, Madison felt bold enough to respond to the argument made by the Anti-Federalists that the power of taxation under the Constitution should be limited to external taxation—the laying of taxes on imports. To this Madison made the response that had been voiced in the Convention: the United States could not depend solely on import taxes to meet its needs. As soon as domestic manufacturing increased, the importation of manufactured products would decrease. At the same time, the population would increase as would the need for services, presumably from the government. The new government must be sufficiently flexible to respond to these changes and have at its disposal alternative sources of revenue. Madison wrote: "A system of Government, meant for duration, ought to contemplate these revolutions, and be able to accommodate itself to them."[13]

Finally, in further defense of the taxing power, Madison felt compelled to turn to the arguments of the Anti-Federalists based on the breadth of the General Welfare Clause. Because of its importance, it is appropriate to quote the following passage from "Federalist No. 41" for it is in this passage that Madison established the foundation for his lifelong interpretation of the clause in response to the Anti-Federalists. Madison first characterized the arguments of the Anti-Federalists: "Some who have not denied the necessity of the power of taxation, have grounded a very fierce attack against the Constitution on the language in which it is defined. It has been urged and echoed, that the power 'to lay and collect taxes, duties, imposts and excises, to pay the debts: and provide for the common defence and general welfare of the United States,' amounts to an unlimited commission to exercise every power which may be alledged to be necessary for the common defence or general welfare." Madison hurled contempt at this interpretation: "No stronger proof could be given of the distress under which these writers labour for objections, than their stooping to such a misconstruction."

In responding to the "misconstruction," Madison may have restated the Anti-Federalist argument in ways that expanded its scope. "Had no other enumeration or definition of the powers of the Congress been found in the Constitution, than the general expressions just cited, the authors of the objection might have had some colour for it," Madison conceded, however awkward the formulation, "A power to destroy the freedom of the press, the trial by jury or even to regulate the course of descents, or the forms of conveyances, must be very singularly expressed by the terms 'to raise money for the general welfare.'"

He then turned to his central rebuttal—the tie between the General Welfare Clause and the enumerated powers and the proposition that the former was merely an introduction, or encapsulation, for the latter: A broad reading of the General Welfare Clause would deny effect to the enumerated powers that followed it. He asked rhetorically, "But what colour can the objection have, when a specification of the objects alluded to by these general terms, immediately follows; and is not even separated by a longer pause than a semi-colon. If the different parts of the same instrument ought to be so expounded as to give meaning to every part which will bear it; shall one part of the same sentence be excluded altogether from a share in the meaning; and shall the more doubtful and indefinite terms be retained in their full extent and the clear and precise expressions, be denied any signification whatsoever?" For Madison, the presence of the enumerated powers precluded interpreting the words, "to provide for the general welfare," as conveying a general, indefinite power to regulate.

> For what purpose could the enumeration of particular powers be inserted, if these and all others were meant to be included in the preceding general power? Nothing is more natural or common than first to use a general phrase, and then to explain and qualify it by a recital of particulars. But the idea of an enumeration of particulars, which neither explain nor qualify the general meaning, and can have no other effect than to confound and mislead, is an absurdity which as we are reduced to the dilemma of charging either on the authors of the objection, or on the authors of the Constitution, we must take the liberty of supposing, had not its origin with the latter.

In short, the enumerated powers in Article I, section 8, clauses 2 and on, qualified the General Welfare Clause in Article I, section 8, clause 1. So read, the General Welfare Clause did not confer a broad and undefined general power as Madison alleged the Anti-Federalists claimed.

Madison went on to support his argument by referring to the Articles of Confederation. Here, he maintained that the General Welfare Clause imported into the Constitution the limitation that bound the Congress under those articles. Again, his contention is worth quoting in full, given its significance in his theory and the attention which critics of his theory, notably Joseph Story, would give it.

> The objection here is the more extraordinary, as it appears, that the language used by the Convention is a copy from the articles of confederation. The objects of the Union among the States is described in article 3rd, are, "their common defence, security of their liberties, and mutual and general welfare." The terms of article 8th. are still more identical. "All charges of war, and all other expences, that shall be incurred for the common defence or general welfare, and allowed by the United States in Congress, shall be defrayed out of a common treasury &c" A similar language again occurs in art. 9. Construe either of these articles by the rules which would justify, the construction put on the new Constitution, and they vest in the existing Congress a power to legislate in all cases whatsoever. But what would have been thought of that assembly, if attaching themselves to these general expressions, and disregarding the specifications, which ascertain and limit their import, they had exercised an unlimited power of providing "for the common defence and general welfare"? I appeal to the objectors themselves, whether they would in

that case have employed the same reasoning in justification of Congress, as they now make against the Convention. How difficult is it for error to escape its own condemnation!¹⁴

It is to be noted that, in the quoted paragraphs, Madison did not specifically dwell on spending, as distinguished from general regulatory activities. To the extent that Madison's argument in "Federalist No. 41" maintained that the General Welfare Clause did not confer upon Congress power to regulate in all areas pertaining to the "general welfare of the United States," independent of the taxing and spending power, it was consistent with the action of the Convention and with the weight of the interpretations that followed ratification during Madison's lifetime, including Story's commentaries. It was generally understood, as Madison argued, that the General Welfare Clause did not confer power to regulate agriculture beyond what would be possible under the interstate and foreign commerce power as a means of "providing for the general welfare." Nor, as Madison urged, was the clause thought to confer power to regulate the course or descents or the forms of conveyances, let alone power to "destroy" freedom of the press or trial by jury. The question that Madison's analysis in No. 41 raised, however, was whether the General Welfare Clause was qualified by the enumerated powers so as to limit *spending* for purposes encompassed within the enumerated powers and thus to preclude federal *spending* for such matters as education, internal improvements, economic subsidies and social services, without a constitutional amendment. It was this question, so ably posed by Madison as a means of defending the Constitution against the Anti-Federalist onslaught, that would confound statesmen during Madison's life and after his death until the Supreme Court quietly put the issue to rest in 1936 in addressing legislation to confront the Great Depression. Madison later claimed that spending was so limited; Hamilton denied that it was.

Madison's observations in No. 41 constituted the only specific interpretation of the General Welfare Clause to appear in the *Federalist Papers*. However, other key players in the Convention, notably, James Wilson and Alexander Hamilton offered defenses of the taxing power that did not invoke or rely upon Madison's narrow reading. Roger Sherman, the author of the original proposal that led to the inclusion of the clause did not opine on the matter in his fairly limited and subdued contributions to the debate. In his speech to the Pennsylvania ratifying convention in December of 1787, Wilson counseled the assemblage that it would be "unwise" to deny ratification because the Constitution "grants congress power to lay and collect taxes, for the purpose of providing for the common defence and general welfare of the United States."[15]

Perspectives on the Taxing Power: Wilson, Hamilton, and Others

In his summation, Wilson did not attempt to interpret the General Welfare Clause. Certainly, he did not adopt the interpretation that Madison was to give the clause in "Federalist No. 41" which appeared in the month following Wilson's speech. On the contrary, Wilson's summation appeared to comprehend the clause as part of a set of broad powers necessary to turn the separate states into a nation. This said, Wilson turned to domestic powers: He asked: "Can we expect to make internal improvement, or accomplish any of those great national objects which I formerly alluded to, when we cannot find money to remove a single rock out of a river?"

Wilson thus saw the Constitution as carrying a promise of national progress that went beyond mere public safety in time of war. It embraced "internal improvement" and provision for the general welfare of individual citizens. This aspect of nation building commended the constitution to the ratifying convention: "This system, sir, will at least make us a nation, and put it in the power of the union to act as such."[16]

To make good on that vision, Wilson did not find it necessary to narrow the scope of the General Welfare Clause. Rather, he alluded to its promise. The power of internal taxation was useful not only in time of war but also in providing the sinews of nation building. The Pennsylvania convention ratified the Constitution on December 12, 1787, one day after Wilson's summation and rebuttal.[17] This significant event took place before the publication of Madison's "Federalist No. 41" with its narrowed interpretation of the General Welfare Clause. Thus it can be argued that, at least in some state conventions, ratification took place on the basis of an understanding—put forth both by the opponents and the proponents of the Constitution—that the General Welfare Clause could be given a broad construction that would provide support for "internal improvements" and other initiatives that would promote the "general welfare," although not confined to missions embraced within the enumerated powers.

When Wilson's speech in the Philadelphia ratifying convention is compared to Madison's "Federalist" No. 41, a picture emerges of alternative approaches to the defense of the taxing power and the breadth of the General Welfare Clause. Both documents defend the power of internal taxation, as distinguished from external taxation, on the ground that the nation should not be dependent for its fiscal existence on the latter, particularly during time of war. Madison seems to respond to the Anti-Federalist argument regarding the breadth of the General Welfare Clause by treating that clause as a shorthand for the enumerated powers in Article I, section 8. Wilson, perhaps somewhat less explicitly, defends the same provisions on the basis of a vision of a new nation pursuing national objectives in the domestic as well as the international arena and as a nation turning its back on the fundamental weaknesses of the experience under the Articles of Confederation. This dual vision may be considered part of the fabric of the adoption of the Constitution, its approval by the states, and its construction during the early years of the nation's history.

Like Madison and Wilson, Hamilton recognized the taxing power as a central concern in the ratification debate. In a series of articles that constituted numbers 30 and 36 of *The Federalist*, and in a crucial speech before the New York ratifying convention, he described his vision of that power and its role in the governmental system. Like Wilson, he argued fervently that an adequate taxing power was essential to the effective functioning of the national government and that the power, to be adequate, must include authority to levy internal as well as external taxes. To Hamilton, the power of direct taxation was indispensable not only to meet the wartime emergencies that Wilson had dramatically depicted for the Pennsylvania ratifying convention, but also as a continuing authority to serve domestic as well as national defense needs.

In "Federalist No. 30," published in September of 1787, Hamilton began his realistic analysis of the taxing power as contained in the yet-to-be-ratified Constitution. He started by describing the contribution of money to a well-functioning government. "Money," he explained, "is with propriety considered as the vital principle of the body politic; as that which sustains its life and motion, and enables it to perform its most essential functions." Examples of the principle were hardly difficult to find. Support of the civil list, payment of the national debt, and adequate provision for "all those matters which call for disbursements out of the national treasury" were among the functions calling for the application of money that Hamilton cited. Influenced perhaps by the need for caution in the debate with the Anti-Federalists, Hamilton did not offer any details as to what matters might call for "disbursements" from the Treasury.[18]

His reticence was no accident. Throughout his career, Hamilton urged the need for creative ambiguity that would give the government sufficient flexibility to meet needs no one could foresee. Rather than tying Congress to a limited number of specified powers that might be inadequate for the future, Hamilton preferred to leave an elliptical clause or a broad, vaguely phrased grant of power that could be invoked when unexpected crises or opportunities called for it. This notion lay at the heart of his constitutional thinking. It particularly characterized his thinking about the taxing power and the general welfare authority that accompanied it.

To rely upon requisitions to meet these needs, once the revenues from the imposts had been exhausted, would recreate the very problems that had required the calling of the Philadelphia Convention in the first place. "How," he asked, "is it possible that a government half supplied and always necessitous, can fulfill the purposes of its institution—can provide for the security of—advance the prosperity—or support the reputation of the commonwealth?" Here he elaborated: "How can it undertake or execute any liberal or enlarged plans of public good?"[19]

In these references to "plans of public good" or advancement of "prosperity," Hamilton comes closest in "Federalist No. 30" to expounding a broad vision of the spending power directed to advancing a program of public investment to enhance national growth or improvement. He declined to talk about specific objects such as internal improvements or educational projects. At the same time, he clearly refrained from adopting the interpretation, later identified with Madison, that the spending power was limited to the scope of the enumerated powers. For Hamilton, the need justified the means. No concession regarding the scope of the power was necessary to his analysis.[20]

For Hamilton as well as Wilson, without adequate resources gathered through the proceeds of taxation, the exercise of the spending power could not be expected to achieve very much, whatever its scope. Conversely, the taxing power would not accomplish the positive objectives which both framers intimated unless it was accompanied by a spending power with coextensive scope. An adequate taxing power must be accompanied by an equally adequate spending power, sufficiently flexible to enable the legislature to respond readily to changing national circumstances. Hamilton's discussion of the taxing powers in the "Federalist" Nos. 30 and 36, discussed above, as well as Wilson's analyses in 1787, can be regarded as arguments for a broad spending power, couched in the framework of a defense of an adequate power of internal taxation in the Congress.[21]

Taken together, the Hamilton-Wilson propositions—set forth in articles, speeches, and addresses before various ratifying conventions—constitute a rationale for both a broad taxing and spending power. An *adequate* taxing power, both internal and external, is essential to an effective central government and a vigorous union. Exercising these powers will not sap the vitality of the states; using these powers will enhance the prosperity of the nation. That the General Welfare Clause does not substantially limit the taxing power is not, under this analysis, a fatal flaw. A limited interpretation of the General Welfare Clause to sustain the taxing power is not essential to that analysis. On the contrary, it is inconsistent with the vision of an energetic union not "half necessitous" in satisfying its money needs. On the basis of this rationale, rather than on Madison's limiting interpretation in "Federalist No. 41," the ratifying conventions in Pennsylvania and New York can be regarded as having taken their decisions in 1787 and 1788. These sentiments were consistent with those expressed by other advocates of the Constitution in other state ratifying conventions where the taxing power was debated or questioned.[22]

Sherman's Role

Roger Sherman of Connecticut had played a key role in formulating the spending power in the federal Constitution. He had first proposed the language of the General Welfare clause during the Philadelphia Convention and served on the Committee on Unfinished Parts which included the language in its report of September 4, 1787. Sherman had also promoted, at an early stage in the Convention, the critical Connecticut Compromise that enabled the delegates to bridge the gap between large and small states. A frequent speaker in the deliberations of the Convention, Sherman had contributed substantially to the framing of the Constitution and, along with his fellow delegate, Oliver Ellsworth, signed it on behalf of Connecticut, just as he had signed the Declaration of Independence and the Articles of Confederation.

Surprisingly, Sherman did not play as a prominent a role in the debates on ratification as other key players in the Philadelphia Convention, notably Hamilton, Madison, and Wilson. He did not contribute to the *Federalist Papers*, and the most comprehensive contemporary anthology of the debates on ratification devotes only a few pages to Sherman's role. Thus, there is little evidence of how he responded to Anti-Federalist attacks on the breadth of the General Welfare Clause that he had helped to frame.

Shortly after the close of the Philadelphia Convention, Sherman and his fellow delegate Ellsworth reported succinctly to the Governor of Connecticut on the results of the proceedings of 1787. Commenting on the "particular parts of the constitution," they led off with the Connecticut Compromise that they had helped to engineer. "The equal representation of the states in the senate, and the voice of that branch in the appointment to offices, will secure the rights of the lesser, as well as of the greater states." The "additional powers . . . vested in Congress . . . extend only to matters respecting the common interests of the union, and are specially defined, so that the particular states retain their sovereignty in all other matters." Then they briefly paraphrased Article I, section 8, clause 1, and the spending power that it conferred in the following terms: "The objects, for which congress may apply monies, are the same mentioned in the eighth article of the confederation, viz. for the common defence and general welfare, and for the payment of the debts incurred for those purposes."[23] Sherman's later contributions to the ratification debate in the New Haven press do not amplify this terse encapsulation, which on the surface runs counter to Madison's limiting interpretation.

On the other hand, Sherman's colleague, Oliver Ellsworth, strongly defended the taxing power before the Connecticut ratifying convention in January of 1788. Ellsworth, in an important speech before that body, responded to a three-pronged attack against Article I, section 8, clause 1, which he correctly characterized as "a most important clause in the constitution." To the objection that the clause extends to all objects of taxation, Ellsworth countered that, except in the case of the impost, all the sources of taxation available to Congress were also available to the states. Moreover, he observed, much in the same vein as Hamilton and Wilson, that the taxing power would enable Congress to assume the state debts incurred as a result of the imperfections in confederation government. "The State debt," he said, "which now lies heavy upon us arose, from want of powers in the federal system. Give the necessary powers to the national government, and the State will not be again necessitated to involve itself in debt for its defence in war. It will lie upon the national government to defend all the States, to defend all its members, from hostile attacks." Ellsworth firmly believed that the most powerful economic incentive for ratifying the Constitution was Congress's ability to relieve the states of the burden of debt.

Then Ellsworth advanced the classic argument that had been made by other defenders of the Constitution to sustain a broad taxing power—the inability of the framers to anticipate all the problems that might arise in the future. While making the point in the context of potential war, Ellsworth phrased it comprehensively: "It is necessary, that the power of the general Legislature should extend to all the objects of taxation, that Government should be able to command all the resources of the country; because no man can tell what our exigencies may be." This was in essence the argument that Hamilton was to make in favor of a broad reading of the General Welfare Clause and the spending power during his tenure as secretary of the treasury in the Washington administration. Ellsworth did not embark on a defense of the specific language of the clause in his speech to the Connecticut Convention, but the thrust of his remarks was in the same direction. Sherman, history records, like Ellsworth, voted for ratification in his capacity as a delegate to the Connecticut ratifying convention. He also gave to his fellow citizens the advice he had earlier given the governor: "The objects of expenditure will be the same under the new constitution, as under the old."[24]

OTHER WITNESSES

A number of other speakers at the state ratifying conventions, who also had participated in the Philadelphia Convention, expressed their views on the General Welfare Clause in a manner that suggests they viewed the clause as reflecting a broad power. One of these was Governor Randolph of Virginia, who had contributed greatly in the Convention by introducing the Virginia resolutions. Speaking in response to Patrick Henry, Randolph observed:

But the rhetoric of the gentleman [Henry] has highly colored the dangers of giving the general government an indefinite power of providing for the general welfare. I contend that no such power is given. They have power "to lay and collect taxes, duties, imposts, and excises to pay the debts and provide for the common common defence and general welfare of the United States." Is this an independent, separate, substantive power, to provide for the general welfare of the United States? No, sir. They can lay and collect taxes, &c. For what? To pay the debts and provide for the general welfare. Were not this the case, the following part of the clause would be absurd. . . . Take it altogether, and let me ask if the plain interpretation be not this—a power to lay and collect taxes, &c., in order to provide for the general welfare and pay debts.

This observation suggests that Randolph, at the time, did not believe that the General Welfare Clause was limited by the enumerated powers, as did his fellow, Virginian, Madison. Evidently, a number of understandings were in play at the time of the ratification debates. Long after ratification some framers, or members of the framer generation, expressed views of the Constitution consistent with a broad view of the authority of the Congress to support internal improvement. Thus, in a colloquy involving Madison in 1796, Rep. Baldwin (evidently Abraham Baldwin of Georgia who had represented that state in the Philadelphia Convention) observed that it was "properly the business of the general government to undertake the improvement of the roads."[25]

RATIFICATION AND PROPOSED AMENDMENTS

After the interplay of arguments and counter arguments, the Constitution was ratified, and the new government was launched. It has been observed that this was foreordained. The new nation faced great difficulties under confederation government. The constitution that emerged from the Philadelphia Convention was the only viable alternative before the people that offered a reasonable promise of relief. The Anti-Federalists could oppose. However, they had no serious, coherent alternative to propose. The prevailing view was perhaps best expressed by Washington in a letter to Bushrod Washington written in November of 1787. The presiding officer of the recent Convention candidly recognized the document's imperfections: "The warmest friends and the best supporters the Constitution has, do not contend that it is free from imperfections; but they found them unavoidable and are sensible, if evil is likely to arise therefrom, the remedy must come hereafter; for in the present moment, it is not to be obtained...."[26]

The comprehensive defense of the taxing power made by Hamilton and Wilson, as well as Ellsworth, was not dependent upon a narrow reading of the General Welfare Clause but assumed uses of tax revenues that would aid the general prosperity. Thus there was no clear, unified vision of the scope of the General Welfare Clause that could be said to have accompanied ratification. The ratifiers could expect a variety of readings that ultimately would be resolved by future generations.

In ratifying the Constitution, some states recommended an amendment to the document that proposed amendments that would reinvigorate the old requisition process. Under these proposals, Congress would have the authority to issue requisitions to the states for additional revenues in situations where the imposts provided insufficient resources. Internal taxation by Congress would be authorized only in the event that a state refused to honor the requisition.[27]

It was just this sort of proposal that Hamilton had warmly opposed in his speech to the New York ratifying convention. Probably, for the reasons he put forward, Congress never adopted the proposal when it came to write amendments to the Constitution now known as the Bill of Rights. But the concern about infringement of state power through the taxing power may have contributed to the adoption in the Bill of Rights of the Tenth Amendment : "The powers not delegated to the United States by the Constitution, nor prohibited by it to the States, are reserved to the States respectively, or to the people." A bill of rights containing such a formulation was recommended by a number of the ratifying conventions; it was these recommendations that moved Madison and others to propose such a bill in the initial Congress in 1789. The contribution of the Anti-Federalists to the framing of the Constitution can be seen in their insistence on a bill or rights, growing in part from their perceptions about the breadth of the General Welfare Clause as a broad grant of spending power.[28]

Significantly, none of the state ratifying conventions in 1787 and 1788 proposed amendments to the Constitution that would have altered the language of the General Welfare Clause. No proposal was made that would have codified Madison's interpretation in "Federalist No. 41" that spending for the general welfare was confined to spending to carry out the enumerated powers in Article I, section 8, clause 2 and the empowering clauses that followed. And, of course, no amendment changing the language of the General Welfare Clause has ever been adopted, despite the controversy that has swirled around it and around the legislation enacted under the umbrella of its authority. The concern of the Anti-Federalists was with the reach of the taxing power. Their quarrel with the General Welfare Clause was not that spending initiatives would be carried out that affected internal improvements or other matters not specified in the Constitution. Their concern was that the General Welfare Clause was so broadly crafted that it would constitute no effective brake upon the taxing power. If, by amendment, they could cut back on the congressional power of internal taxation or direct taxation by substituting a modified requisition scheme, as the Massachusetts resolution proposed, they would be satisfied to leave the "provide for the common defence and general welfare" formulation alone. Or, so it appears from the voluminous records of the ratification debates.[29]

Delaware was the first state to ratify the Constitution. It did so on December 7, 1787. Four other states, Pennsylvania, New Jersey, Georgia, and Connecticut, ratified before January 19, 1788, when Madison's "Federalist No. 41" appeared in the press. Thus, it is difficult to conclude that all States that ratified did so against a background of a uniform interpretation of the General Welfare Clause.[30] And, after ratification, Anti-Federalists continued to press their complaint that the Constitution vested in the Congress a power of the purse that was "complete and unlimited."[31] It would take almost 150 years before the Supreme Court confirmed that conclusion.

II
The Framing of the First Precedents

3
The Washington Administration

A POLARITY OF VISIONS REGARDING THE REACH AND PROMISE OF THE General Welfare Clause and the congressional spending power that it encompassed arose early in George Washington's first term as president. It took the form of a profound rift between two of the ablest members of his cabinet, Alexander Hamilton, the brilliant and energetic secretary of the treasury, and Thomas Jefferson, the extraordinarily talented secretary of state. Hamilton saw the General Welfare Clause as a powerful and broadly phrased charter for the vigorous national government that he championed and for at least some of the fiscal and economic measures that he proposed to Congress as essential to set the new nation on the path toward independence and prosperity. Jefferson and Madison, then a leading member of the House of Representatives, viewed Hamilton's expansive construction of the clause as antithetical to their vision of a federal government that was effective but also held in check by a discrete and limited body of enumerated powers. At root was a profound clash of national aspirations—economic independence and viability to be secured through a bold program of debt refinancing and government support for manufacturing versus a predominantly agrarian society of sovereign states unified under a central government of distinct and limited powers. At stake was the preservation of the "sacred fire of liberty" which Washington invoked in his first inaugural address.[1]

EARLY INTIMATIONS OF A FEDERAL INVESTMENT ROLE: WASHINGTON'S FIRST ANNUAL MESSAGE

George Washington's simple and moving inaugural address, delivered on April 30, 1789, was not the occasion for proposing explicit legislative measures to Congress. The president contented himself with citing to that body the provisions of Article II of the Constitution that called upon the holder of that office "'to recommend to your consideration such measures as he shall judge necessary and expedient.'" He then deferred to the Constitution. "The circumstances under which I now meet you will acquit me from entering into that subject further than to refer to the great constitutional charter under which you are assembled, and which, in defining your powers, designates the objects to which your attention is to be given."[2]

However, in his first annual message to Congress, delivered in person in January 1790, Washington did not decline to impart a brief summary of the measures that he deemed necessary and expedient. After congratulating the first Congress on the measures that it had adopted in its first session, Washington began by directing members' attention to the common defense: "To be prepared for war is one of the most effectual means of preserving peace." He called for arrangements for the "proper establishment of the troops" and for the "comfortable support" of officers and soldiers. In this early invocation of national defense as a rationale for domestic initiatives, he also urged that the people's "safety and interest require that they should promote such manufactories as tend to render them independent of others for essential, particularly military, supplies."[3]

Washington returned to the theme of economic self-sufficiency in the domestic portion of his address. "The advancement of agriculture, commerce, and manufactures by all proper means," he said, "will not, I trust, need recommendation." He also commended to his listeners "the expediency of giving effectual encouragement as well to the introduction of new and useful inventions from abroad as to the exertions and skill and genius in producing them at home."[4] Always a proponent of more efficient means of transportation, Washington recommended, when he turned to the subject of postal and related issues, "facilitating the intercourse between the distant parts of our country by a due attention to the post-office and post-roads."[5]

It was to the subject of education rather than infrastructure, however, that Washington devoted the bulk of the domestic portion of his first annual address. He began by addressing the essential role of education in the political system that had just been established. "Nor am I less persuaded," he began, "that you will agree with me in opinion that there is nothing which can better deserve your patronage than the promotion of science and literature." He continued in this vein, noting that "Knowledge is in every country the surest basis of public happiness. In one in which the measures of government receive their impressions so immediately from the sense of community as in ours it is proportionately essential."

He ended with an eloquent discourse on the relationship between knowledge and civic virtue that warrants quotation in full in the context of a discussion of the constitutional authority to provide for the general welfare: "To the security of a free constitution [knowledge] contributes in various ways—by convincing those who are intrusted with the public administration that every valuable end of government is best answered by the enlightened confidence of the people, and by teaching the people themselves to know and to value their own rights; to discern and provide against invasions of them; to distinguish between oppression and the necessary exercise of lawful authority; between burthens proceeding from a disregard to their convenience and those resulting from the inevitable exigencies of society. . . ."[6]

Having thus eloquently described the contribution of knowledge to an enlightened government under the Constitution, Washington was circumspect in suggesting educational measures that Congress might consider: "Whether this desirable object will be best promoted by affording aids to seminaries of learning already established, by the institution of a national university, or by any other expedients will be worthy of a place in the deliberations of the Legislature."[7]

Douglas Southhall Freeman's great biography of Washington characterizes this message as "unexciting."[8] It was, especially when compared to the bold fiscal and economic program that followed it in the form of Hamilton's proposals for financing the debt and establishing a national bank. Many of the measures that Washington proposed in his annual message were not new. Madison and Pinckney had proposed federal support for a national university or for seminaries of learning during the Constitutional Convention. Franklin had urged support for better transportation through the cutting of canals.

What is remarkable, however, is that we find the first president giving priority in his first annual message to matters in which Congress could function only through the power of the purse and suggesting an affirmative role for the federal government in providing for the common defense and/or general welfare in such diverse areas as agriculture, manufacturing, arts and sciences, and education. While these proposals may have been couched in modest terms consistent with the tenor of the times, their appearance in the message suggests a shrewd appreciation of the role that the central government might play under the new Constitution. A number of the measures that Washington suggested clearly implied using the spending power for both domestic purposes and the national defense. Moreover, from the perspective of an era in which there has been profound controversy over the federal government's proper role in education, it is interesting to note that Washington devoted a major portion of his first state of the union address to education—"knowledge"—at a time when education was largely a nongovernmental responsibility.

While Washington read this address to the first Congress, he did not actively lobby for the proposals that it contained. He believed strongly that, having made recommendations in pursuance of the constitutional role that he had alluded to in his inaugural address, his duty did not extend to importuning Congress to enact those measures. He left to Congress the responsibility for making legislative judgments, subject to his exercise of the veto power if he believed a bill to be unconstitutional.[9] Washington saw his major role with respect to legislation as guardian of the Constitution. He was to have ample occasion to consider that role when Congress came to address the proposals that his secretary of the treasury put forward later in 1790 and in the years that followed.

HAMILTON'S PROGRAM: OF DEBT AND THE BANK

More immediately far-reaching and controversial proposals followed Washington's message in the form of recommendations that flowed from the creative and energetic mind of Alexander Hamilton. Hamilton had at least three goals: (1) to establish the credit of the new nation through measures to finance its existing war debt and assume the debts of the states; (2) to establish a national bank that would provide the financial services that the nation needed; and (3) to inaugurate a system for supporting domestic manufacturing through protective tariffs and federal subsidies. These proposals raised profound legal as well as policy concerns and sparked a fundamental controversy over the proper role of the federal government in providing for the general welfare under the new constitutional framework.

The federal government's assumption of the state debt was an essential part of Hamilton's plan. He supported it by advancing a number of distinct policy considerations related to the taxing power. He argued, for example, that, if public creditors could look to one source for payment, they would have a common interest and would tend to support the "fiscal arrangements of the Government," such as revenue laws. Moreover, assumption would provide for a uniform means of managing the state debt rather than relying on the varying payment capacities of the individual states.[10]

Assumption was intimately tied up with the adoption of the taxing and spending power in the Constitution. Article I, section 8, clause 1 and section 10, clause 2, taken together, gave Congress exclusive power to lay imposts (taxes on imports). Their revenue capacity thus diminished, it was regarded, at least in some quarters, as equitable that the states' obligation to service the debt would be assumed by the federal government—the very type of trade-off that had been intimated during the ratification debates on the taxing power. Hamilton's own financing report observed that state creditors would be better off looking to the federal government, in part because the new constitution precluded a state from taxing imports without the consent of Congress.[11]

Madison's opposition to assumption has been attributed to a belief that assumption was manifestly unfair to his state, as well as to a determination to delay adoption of assumption in order to gain advantages for Virginia and the South in terms of the legislation for the permanent location of the seat of the new government. Whether these motives or those that Madison described were paramount, the assumption proposal ultimately was adopted by Congress at the same time that legislation moved the temporary seat of the central government to Philadelphia and the permanent seat to the Potomac, a move that the Virginia delegation obviously favored and promoted. Provision was also made to compensate Virginia for inequities that Madison urged were inherent in the formula for implementing assumption. These arrangements overcame the opposition to assumption and apparently gave Madison and others the adjustments they needed to abandon their equity arguments and support assumption.[12]

In his further reports to Congress on the public credit issue after funding, assumption, and sinking fund measures had been enacted into law, Hamilton turned to three initiatives that he regarded as essential to implement his program fully: the adoption of new internal excise taxes to provide revenues to support, among other things, debt service under the new funding program; the creation of a national mint; and the establishment of a national bank. The bank that Hamilton proposed in his report on the subject would be chartered by Congress with a capitalization of not more than $10 million. In order to give an early extension to the bank's operations, $2 million of this amount would be subscribed for by the federal government, to be be paid out of moneys borrowed by the government under recently enacted authorizing legislation. The balance would be taken up by the public through subscriptions. Subscribers could pay for three-fourths of their stock in federal government securities representing public debt and bearing an interest rate of 6 percent. The interest on these securities would, as Hamilton put it, "enlarge" the bank's income and increase the attractiveness of its stock. Public credit would be enhanced as the government securities gained in value.[13]

While these plans made eminent economic and fiscal sense, they pointed inevitably to an enlarged federal role. For those alarmed by such an enlargement, the Constitution, strictly interpreted, provided a counterweight. At first the bill to charter the bank was noncontroversial. It passed the Senate in January 1791, largely in the form that Hamilton had proposed. However, during the later stages of the measure's consideration by the House, Madison attacked the bank bill's constitutionality. He argued that Congress lacked the constitutional authority to charter a bank. The enumerated powers afforded no specific authority. Neither did Article I, section 8, clause 1, including the General Welfare Clause. The Necessary and Proper Clause could not be interpreted to grant the power because the relationship between the bank and express powers was too tenuous. Madison's advocacy of a doctrine of strict construction of the Constitution was met in the House with the opposition of those who favored a broader construction. Ultimately, the bank bill was passed over Madison's objection. It was engrossed and sent to the president.[14]

Washington requested opinions from Attorney General Randolph and Secretary of State Jefferson. Both opined that the bill was unconstitutional, largely for the reasons that Madison had raised in the House. Jefferson, however, leavened his opinion with pragmatic advice. If in doubt, Washington could sign the measure as expedient. Washington also requested Hamilton's response to the legal opinions he received from other members of the cabinet. In the meantime, in an exercise in inter-branch technical assistance, Washington sought Madison's help in preparing a veto message in case Washington could not be persuaded to sign.

Hamilton's response constituted a comprehensive defense of the bill in the context of a broad construction of the Constitution. In essence, Hamilton defended the bank as a proper exercise of the sovereign power of the government and of the Necessary and Proper Clause. The bank was an appropriate means of carrying out certain express powers relating to taxation and the borrowing of funds, presumably those included in Article I, section 8, clause 1. The thrust of Hamilton's contention was that the government could not function under the strict construction of the Necessary and Proper Clause that proponents of a veto put forward. As Hamilton saw it, if a measure was reasonably related, although not absolutely necessary, to the exercise of an enumerated power, it passed constitutional muster. The absolutely necessary standard, he contended, was so erroneous that it had to be "exploded." He said, "The only question must be, in this, as in every other case, whether the mean to be employed, or in this instance, the corporation to be erected, has a natural relation to any of the acknowledged objects or lawful ends of the government." The Constitution therefore sanctioned the establishment of the bank. Washington sided with Hamilton and signed the bank bill into law. On the same day, amendatory legislation was enacted that assured moving the capital to the Potomac on a schedule earlier than that established in the 1790 legislation.[15]

The battle over the constitutionality of the bank signaled the beginning of a fundamental philosophical rift between Hamilton, on the one hand, and Jefferson and Madison on the other. Apart from the influence of sectional interests on such issues of immediate interest as the location of the capital, that rift took the form of differing perceptions of the scope of constitutional power and the approach to constitutional construction. The perceptions were in part, of course, driven by policy considerations. Hamilton proposed and believed strongly in his financial programs and the individual initiatives that were part of that program. To support them, he was obliged to reach for broad constructions of the Constitution. His forceful and compelling opinion in support of the bank bill was perhaps the first major opportunity to propose such a construction after *The Federalist*. But that opinion is consistent with a reasonable extension of his expositions in *The Federalist*, Nos. 30 and 36. Madison and Jefferson reached for narrower constructions as a means of preserving their concept of an effective government of limited, enumerated powers. The controversy was inevitable and had its origins in the philosophical differences that surfaced in the Convention: Hamilton's yearning for a Congress with "indefinite" authority; Madison's insistence on airtight enumerated powers. Whatever the immediate private, political, or constituent interests that impelled the making of these arguments, and putting to one side that they may not have been consistently espoused or applied, these considerations came to characterize the bedrock positions of the combatants as the battle shifted to the scope of the spending power.[16]

The theories that Hamilton expounded in his opinion are of considerable significance to a study of the General Welfare Clause and of the development of concept of "providing for the general welfare" in the American polity. At issue was the proposition, in Hamilton's view, that the Constitution must be interpreted flexibly and creatively to justify strong measures to secure the economic future and stability of the nation. Hence, the sovereign powers and necessary and proper doctrines that he expounded in 1791 are not mere arguments to overcome an internecine political battle but the components of a coherent philosophy of government.

The same may be said of the propositions put forward by Jefferson, Madison, and Randolph. In the case of Hamilton, however, the philosophy and propositions advanced to support the constitutionality of the bank bill can also be advanced to support strong government action or intervention in the sphere of domestic legislation to confer benefits on particular activities, economic or otherwise, and ultimately on individuals, where the interests of the overall polity, the central government, or the "general welfare" so warrant. This prospect no doubt alarmed Madison and Jefferson, despite their earlier avowals of admiration for Hamilton and despite their sympathy for support for education and other internal improvements that would benefit from federal backing. This prospect became even clearer in Hamilton's *Report on Manufactures* and Jefferson's and Madison's response to it.[17]

HAMILTON'S GENERAL WELFARE AGENDA: THE *REPORT ON MANUFACTURES*

Hamilton's *Report on Manufactures* was a comprehensive and lengthy discourse on "the expediency of encouraging manufactures in the United States." It was issued on December 5, 1791, in response to a request by the House of Representatives in January 1790 when Hamilton was secretary of the treasury. Hamilton was almost two years late, so he began his report with a graceful apology. He did not, however, apologize for his lengthy and vigorous brief in support of positioning the United States as an industrial nation. To convey its pivotal impact on thinking under the General Welfare Clause and modern spending power doctrine, and to provide a sense of the context in which the now governing interpretation of the General Welfare Clause was first enunciated, it is necessary to discuss the content of that report in some detail.

As Jacob Cooke puts it, "[t]he major thrust of Hamilton's argument was the essentiality of flourishing manufactures not only to the nation's security and defense but also to the growth and prosperity of its economy." Hamilton began his discourse by responding to the argument that it would be unwise for the United States to encourage manufacturing. He characterized those who took this position as strongly urging the superiority of agriculture as "the most beneficial and productive object of human industry." This applied with particular force to the United States with its "immense tracts" of uninhabited and unimproved territory. The United States, so it was argued, should give priority to taming this wilderness rather than embarking on a program of encouraging manufacturing. The market should be left to its own devices. Moreover, labor shortages, the greater mobility of agricultural pursuits, and the shortage of capital made the prospect of competition with Europe in manufacturing pursuits little short of desperate. Even if tariff protections or bounties could stimulate manufacturing, they would simply raise the prices of the manufactured goods.[18]

To this Hamilton responded at length. He rejected the argument that agricultural production was superior to manufacturing. He argued that the labor of the "artificer" was as productive as that of the agricultural worker and would augment the value of the goods in the market, independent of agricultural production. To Hamilton, there was no distinction between earning a profit on land and earning a profit on capital invested in a manufacturing enterprise.

In making these arguments, Hamilton assured his readers that he was not taking the view that manufacturing was more productive than agriculture. He was merely trying to advance the argument that the supposed "superior productiveness of tillage" should not be an obstacle to "inducements" to encourage manufacturing. Hamilton was fully aware that many of his fellow citizens thought that the proper destiny of the United States was to be an agrarian nation populated with yeoman farmers who would hold liberty dear and oppose expanding the powers of national government. He "readily conceded" that the "cultivation of the earth" included "a state most favorable to the freedom and independence of the human mind" and that it intrinsically had "a strong claim to preeminence over every other kind of industry." This concession presumably would mollify Jefferson and Madison, as well as Washington, with their agrarian backgrounds and constituencies.[19]

However, Hamilton refused to abandon his claim that manufacturing would not divert labor from profitable employment and would augment revenue and productivity. If the farmer alone had to work to make the goods (clothing and other articles) that could otherwise be procured from the artificer, the farm would be less productive. If there were both a farmer and an artificer, the farmer could devote exclusive attention to the farm. The artificer could supply the farmer and respond to his own needs as well. Thus there would be "two quantities or values in existence . . . [and] the revenue and consumption would be double." The labor of the artificer and the farmer would be equally productive for this purpose. The labor of both would occasion a "positive augmentation of the total produce and revenue of the society."[20]

It was this argument that lay at the core Hamilton's thesis. If society's revenues could be increased by the policies he was proposing, additional resources would be available to pay the debt service on the loans that the new nation would incur to establish its credit under his earlier funding and assumption programs. The increased revenues would support the manufacturing subsidies he was proposing. Sound credit, sound currency, and stronger economic growth through manufacturing as well as agricultural pursuits were all interrelated in Hamilton's program.[21]

After explaining the general advantages of manufacturing, Hamilton turned to discussing the factors that would contribute not only to augmenting the produce and revenue of the society but also to making them greater than they would be without manufacturing establishments. Thus he argued that the division of labor between manufacturing and agricultural pursuits would, as a result of specialization, enhance efficiency.[22]

Finally, Hamilton reserved his most comprehensive discussion for what he regarded as a major policy consideration—the creation of "a more certain and steady demand for the surplus produce of the soil." Here Hamilton held out the strongest inducements for the agricultural interests whom he was obliged to convince if his program were to be adopted. Farmers, he continued, were susceptible to the fluctuations of the market. Creating a stable domestic market in place of an uncertain foreign market for agricultural products was highly desirable.[23]

Benefits for the New Nation

The general considerations that he initially enumerated, Hamilton concluded, were sufficient to establish "that it is the interest of nations to diversify the industrial pursuits of the individuals who compose them" and that the introduction of manufactures would not only increase the "general stock" of productive labor but also advance the "interests" of those engaged in agriculture. He then explained how these considerations related to the "particular situation of the United States" and to the objections that had been raised to encouraging manufacturing in the new nation. His central vision was a "diversified economy" for the new nation.[24]

First, Hamilton addressed the argument that, whatever might be true generally, the United States could rely upon foreign sources for its manufactured goods and should instead concentrate on cultivating and populating its immense tracts of unsettled land. In short, why not leave each nation free to engage in those economic pursuits that it was best able to conduct? The United States could not trade on equal terms with Europe, Hamilton observed. If the new nation refrained from manufacturing, it would be cast into a position of constant dependency on Europe for manufactured goods with only "a partial and occasional demand" for its agricultural commodities. This in turn would relegate the nation to a "state of impoverishment" despite its political and natural advantages. Avoiding this fate was a central concern of Hamilton's report. While complaining about the practices of other nations was pointless, the United States must "consider by what means, they can render themselves least dependent on the combinations, right or wrong, of foreign policy."[25]

Here, Hamilton took pains to point out that the obstructions to foreign trade had prompted the United States to "accelerate" its "internal improvements." The promotion of internal improvements, it is important to note, was intimately related to the successful establishment of manufactures which, as we have seen, was in turn tied up, not merely with economic prosperity, but with the survival of the nation. "To diversify and extend these improvements," he warned, "is the surest and safest method of indemnifying ourselves for any inconveniences which these or similar [foreign anti-trade] measures have a tendency to beget. If Europe will not take from us the products of our soil upon terms consistent with our interest, the natural remedy is to contract, as fast as possible, our wants of her." Here, economic independence was to follow political independence. For these reasons, Hamilton urged that a policy of encouraging manufactures should be pursued even if it resulted in reducing the amount of land that otherwise would be under tillage.[26]

Finally, he observed, "the greatest obstacle of all to the successful prosecution of a new branch of industry in a country in which it was before unknown consists, as far as the instances apply, in the bounties, premiums and others aids which are granted in a variety of cases by the nations in which the establishments to be imitated are previously introduced." The answer to the free trade proponents was that there was no free trade and that, to survive, the United States had to be in a position to resort to the same practices as its competitors. Thus, Hamilton made his principal case for federal aid for manufactures: "The existence or assurance of aid from the government of the country in which the business is to be introduced may be essential to fortify adventurers against the dread of such combinations, to defeat their effects, if formed, and to prevent their being formed, by demonstrating that they must in the end prove fruitless." In essence, a policy of protectionism was essential if the United States were to defend itself in the economic arena of the late eighteenth century. In sum the prodigious report was, as Richard Brookhiser puts it, "another window on [Hamilton's] vision for America."[27]

A Case for Federal Aid for Manufactures

At the next stage of his report, Hamilton turned to the strategies which the central government of the United States might employ to give life to that vision and elaborated on four: (1) protective duties; (2) prohibitions of rival articles; (3) prohibitions of the exportation of the materials of manufactures; and (4) "pecuniary bounties." This part of the report renders it, in the words of Cooke, "the most memorable plan for national economic planning that our early history affords."

While the late nineteenth-century revival of interest in Hamilton's report focused particularly on its support of protective tariffs, Hamilton himself devoted the bulk of his attention to the subject of *pecuniary bounties* in an effort to analyze alternative strategies for aiding domestic manufactures. For this study of the evolution of the General Welfare Clause doctrine, that portion of Hamilton's report assumes the highest significance, for it was in connection with his advocacy of the pecuniary bounty that Hamilton advocated a species of federal financial assistance. The pecuniary bounty, among the strategies that Hamilton discussed, bears the closest resemblance to modern federal aid, involving a grant of money to entities outside the federal government in order to *support* an activity that the federal government wishes to promote but cannot, or wishes not to, compel. Moreover, it was in the defense of the bounty strategy, from a legal perspective, that Hamilton propounded his interpretation of the meaning and scope of the General Welfare Clause and the congressional spending power that it confers.

Hamilton began his analysis by pronouncing the pecuniary bounty, or manufacturing subsidy, as one of "the most efficacious means of encouraging manufactures, and in . . . some views the best." Several reasons persuaded him of this. First, it was the most "positive and direct" form of encouragement. The manufacturing enterprise would be directly subsidized by the government, increasing the likelihood of profit and diminishing risk. Second, the bounty did not have the tendency to raise prices in the first instance as much as, say, a protective duty. Even where the revenues for funding the bounty were derived from a duty on the same article, the manufacture of which was to be encouraged, the effect on prices was small because the bounty would be designed to stimulate a domestic industry and thus encourage competition.[28]

In light of these circumstances, Hamilton regarded the bounty as "indispensable to the introduction of a new branch" of an industry. "There is no purpose," he said, "to which public money can be more beneficially applied than to the acquisition of a new and useful branch of industry, no consideration more valuable than a permanent addition to the general stock of productive labor." Thus, the use of the bounty—direct government aid for an enterprise—lay at the core of Hamilton's economic thinking. Encouragement of manufacturing was essential to make the nation economically independent, to enhance its resources, and to supply the revenues needed to fund its debt. Of all the strategies to achieve that encouragement, the bounty, a species of federal assistance, was one of the most efficacious.[29]

However, in order to promote and advocate a program of government aid, whether carried out through bounties or otherwise, Hamilton was obliged first to confront a *constitutional* issue. In doing so, he announced what was to become the most significant—and the most controversial—doctrine in his lengthy report, his interpretation of the General Welfare Clause.

4
Hamilton's Interpretation—Washington's Legacy

TO COMPLETE A CONVINCING ANALYSIS IN THE *REPORT ON MANUFACtures,* Hamilton was compelled to respond to a basic legal question. The federal bounty might be very effective in speeding the nation's journey to economic self sufficiency and strength. However, was its enactment into law constitutional? To answer this question, Hamilton invoked the General Welfare Clause. That clause, Hamilton unequivocally maintained, authorized Congress to spend federal funds to aid manufactures, as well as agriculture, commerce, and learning. In "Federalist No. 41," Madison had urged that the General Welfare Clause was no more than a reference to the enumerated powers in Article I, section 8 and did not authorize Congress to legislate for the "general welfare." Federal support for manufactures was not an enumerated power. Madison's theory, if adopted, would have presented a serious problem for Hamilton's proposed program. When Hamilton's constitutional thesis appeared in the *Report on Manufactures*, Madison unsurprisingly responded that the General Welfare Clause confined Congress to spend only for purposes within the enumerated powers. For both Madison and Jefferson, Hamilton's proposal was constitutional heresy that dangerously expanded the federal role, contrary to the understanding of the framers. Hamilton's effort opened up a profound rift over the scope of the General Welfare Clause that would exacerbate the tensions within the Washington Administration and reverberate for decades beyond—a controversy that was not definitively resolved by the judicial branch until 1937, 150 years after the framing. While the constitutional issues were never settled by Washington, his administration quietly continued to promote a federal role in the areas that Hamilton's report had cited as proper for congressional appropriation under the General Welfare Clause.[1]

THE GENERAL WELFARE CLAUSE INTERPRETED

Hamilton began by acknowledging the issue. "A question has been made concerning the constitutional right of the Government of the United States to apply this species of encouragement. . . ." However, he quickly brushed the question aside. "[T]here is certainly no good foundation for such a question." He turned to the General Welfare Clause for his argument: "The National Legislature has express authority to 'lay and collect taxes, duties, imposts, and excises, to pay the debts, and provide for the common defense and general welfare,' with no other qualification than that 'all duties, imposts, and excises shall be uniform throughout the United States; that no capitation or other direct tax shall be laid, unless in proportion to numbers, ascertained by a census or enumeration, taken on the principles prescribed in the Constitution,' and that 'no tax or duty shall be laid on articles exported from any State.' "[2]

In short, the Constitution on its face provided a broad spending power subject only to the qualifications stated in the Constitution. Hamilton then explained how he interpreted that power. His theory, as set forth below, relied upon the broad language of the General Welfare Clause and upon the conviction that it must have been intended to convey flexibility to address, through the appropriation power, national problems that could not be adequately anticipated in the text of the Constitution.

> These three qualifications excepted, the power to raise money is plenary and indefinite, and the objects to which it may be appropriated are no less comprehensive than the payment of the public debts and the providing for the common defense and general welfare. The terms "general welfare" were doubtless intended to signify more than was expressed or imported in those which preceded; otherwise, numerous exigencies incident to the affairs of a nation would have been left without a provision. The phrase is as comprehensive as any that could have been used; because it was not fit that the constitutional authority of the Union to appropriate its revenues should have been restricted within narrower limits than the "general welfare"; and because this necessarily embraces a vast variety of particulars which are susceptible neither of specification nor definition.[3]

This is the core of Hamilton's constitutional theory of the spending power and the concept of "general welfare" as used in Article I, section 8. The concept is as broad and all-encompassing as possible in order to provide for those "exigencies" that the framers could not have anticipated. This argument regarding the need for flexibility had been advanced by Hamilton previously in the debates on ratification of the Constitution. He invoked it here in this "general welfare" analysis as a central point: the framers had no choice but to preserve an avenue of flexibility to address important national issues that could not be the subject of specific provision in the Constitution. The "general welfare" language was that avenue. It provided the "indefinite" grant of authority to the federal legislature for which Hamilton had been desperately groping since his June 18, 1787 speech before the Philadelphia Convention.[4]

At the same time it should be noted that, in the quoted passage, Hamilton treated the General Welfare Clause as a *limitation* on the taxing power and not as an independent grant of "regulatory" authority as Gouverneur Morris might have contended, at least if his use of the semicolon had prevailed. Hamilton discussed the clause as describing the "objects" to which "money" raised under the taxing power "may be appropriated." The General Welfare Clause, as discussed in the *Report on Manufactures*, circumscribes, however broadly, the power to appropriate and spend.

Having described the breadth of the General Welfare Clause, Hamilton then stated his conclusion about its reach with regard to specific areas of national concern: "It is, therefore, of necessity, left to the discretion of the National Legislature to pronounce upon the objects which concern the general welfare, and for which, under that description, an appropriation of money is requisite and proper. *And there seems to be no room for doubt that whatever concerns the general interests of learning, of agriculture, of manufactures, and of commerce is within the sphere of the national councils, as far as regards an application of money.*"[5]

The General Welfare Clause was thus a constitutional basis not only to support the manufacturing subsidy proposals that Hamilton suggested in the report; it would also support initiatives in education and agriculture—areas that would be of interest to southern lawmakers. After all, Madison had proposed aid to universities in the constitutional convention and Washington had done so in his first inaugural address. The conclusion probably was designed to gain support for the interpretation from those who might object to it, as well as to support administration goals.

Hamilton, perhaps recognizing the broad grant of power that

he was proposing ran counter to Madison's central thesis as to the meaning of the clause, despite the report's effort to include an "education sweetener," added one qualification: the objects of the appropriation should be *general* rather than *local*. Hamilton said: "The only qualification of the generality of the phrase in question which seems to be admissible is this: That the object to which an appropriation of money is to be made be general and not local; its operation extending, in fact or by possibility, throughout the Union and not being confined to a particular spot."[6]

Hamilton declined the opportunity to address directly the arguments that Madison had made in "Federalist No. 41," that the "general welfare" formulation was a mere shorthand or introductory for the enumerated powers that followed. Nor did he attempt fully to refute the central point that would be made in opposition: by broadly construing the "general welfare" language in the federal constitution, that document would give Congress authority to enter a vast array of areas that the framers had not mentioned in the enumerated powers. This, of course, he must have anticipated, would be Madison's concern. Hamilton recognized the problem and tried to deal with it in two somewhat elliptical sentences: "No objection ought to arise to this construction from a supposition that it would imply a power to do whatever else should appear to Congress conducive to the general welfare. A power to appropriate money with this latitude, which is granted, too, in express terms, would not carry a power to do any other thing not authorized in the Constitution, either expressly or by fair implication."[7]

As Hamilton apparently perceived it, the power to appropriate did not extend to the power to regulate directly. Congress could spend to encourage activities thought to be of benefit to the public in a particular area, such as education. That did not mean, in the absence of specific constitutional authority, that Congress had plenary power directly to regulate in that area. The Constitution gave Congress spending authority through the express language of Article I, section 8, clause 1. Otherwise, it confined the legislative power of Congress to regulate through the enumerated powers. This was the closest Hamilton came to directly confronting the implications of Madison's general welfare theory expressed in "Federalist. No. 41." The new central government was, indeed, one of express enumerated powers. However, one of these express powers, the spending power, was as comprehensive as Congress wished in order to provide flexibility to deal with unanticipated problems. The equation thus becomes: broad power to spend; limited power to engage in direct regulation through the enumerated powers that appear in the Constitution after the General Welfare Clause. Evidently, Hamilton thought this response sufficient without mentioning "Federalist No. 41" or its author; clearly, it would not do to take on Madison by name, particularly since Hamilton was a coauthor of the set of essays in which Madison's interpretation of the General Welfare Clause had appeared.

Hamilton's theory in the *Report on Manufactures*, of course, did not convince Madison or those who shared his views. It is instructive to note that Hamilton implicitly recognized Madison's position and attempted to deal with it by contending that the power of the purse is different than regulatory power, at least on the surface. However, Hamilton did not try to elaborate on the point or to develop distinctions between the two powers that might have strengthened his central interpretation. He did not, for example, urge that the spending power could be expressed by grants or other instruments which the recipient would be free to reject or that it would generally be exercised through appropriations, measures limited in time in a way that permanent regulatory legislation is not. This is not surprising since the *Report on Manufactures* was not intended to serve as a constitutional treatise. It was a proposal for urgent legislative action which included a legal argument on the basis of which legislators could support the action constitutionally if they decided to take it.

The significance of Hamilton's "general welfare" interpretation in the *Report on Manufactures* is threefold. In the first place, it represents the views of one of the framers of the Constitution, who, while not always present at the deliberations and absent when the General Welfare Clause was proposed, debated, and reported favorably by the Committee on Unfinished Parts, was present when the clause was finally included in the draft of the Committee of Style on which he served. Second, Hamilton was one of the major defenders of the Constitution and authored a majority of the essays that constituted *The Federalist,* a factor which gives some weight to his views on the meaning of the basic charter. Third, the *Report* provides a framework for evaluating the significance of the interpretation in light of the development of government policy in a major area early in the first term of the first president.

The interpretation was not merely an insignificant, speculative legal sidebar in a long, unfocused tract on economic policy. Hamilton had laboriously made the case, in a report to Congress, that the United States needed to adopt a policy of encouraging manufactures in order to stimulate economic growth and increase revenues. To do this it needed to consider such initiatives as federal subsidies (bounties) to manufactures. A broad reading of the Constitution was *essential* in order to implement that policy. That reading could be achieved only through a flexible construction of the General Welfare Clause. Hamilton viewed the clause as a pivotal force in supporting the new nation's efforts to achieve economic independence, to enhance its political independence, and to establish its status as a nation to be respected. Moreover, while not expressly stated, the implication is that a broad reading of the General Welfare Clause is needed to preserve the Constitution itself. Only if it can be read to respond to the type of unanticipated "exigencies" of the sort Hamilton invoked could it adequately serve future generations. Hamilton had from the first regarded some repository of "indefinite" legislative power as critical to the effective working of the Constitution whose ratification he had labored so hard to achieve. That repository was the General Welfare Clause. This understanding was at the heart of his analysis. That he reflected deeply over the matter is evinced in a letter he wrote to Washington some months before the report's release expressing concern as to the scope of the government's power regarding the funding of manufacturing subsidies.

In the generations that followed, Hamilton's analysis was to be used to support not only programs of benefit to business but programs of social welfare of particular benefit to the vulnerable citizens in the society. In the words of Samuel Konefsky: "That contemporary America should be more in tune with Hamilton's conception of the constitutional possibilities for promoting the public welfare through federal action may be too obvious a phenomenon to require further proof. What does need to be said, perhaps, is that this inversion of the logic of ideology is probably as good a testimonial to the resourcefulness of the American Constitution as the history of the document has furnished."[8]

In fact, the constitutional analysis in the report was subject to bitter attack from the time of its issuance. It contributed to the growing rift in the Washington administration. Perhaps, the animosity was due in part to the fact that the analysis was put forward to serve a policy position and did not purport to be the product of an objective study of the Constitution. The report itself was never adopted or implemented by the Congress that received it. The significance of the document came to focus on the constitutional theory that it contained. The controversy over the reach of the General Welfare Clause, as maintained in the report, extended long after Hamilton's death and after Madison's decades later. It was finally resolved in 1936 by the Supreme Court in the *Butler* case dealing with a federal program to help farmers rather than manufacturers.

Samuel Konefsky has aptly summarized the constitutional significance of the *Report on Manufactures*: "Judged by the importance of the role which the federal government has come to play in the promotion of social welfare, none of Hamilton's prophetic ideas is more strikingly significant than his conception of the 'general welfare' clause...." For Konfesky, "Hamilton was doing more than expounding constitutional theory." He was furnishing posterity with "a rationale which would free Congress to adopt measures he deemed essential to the nation's growth and power."[9]

Hamilton himself recognized that there were some limits in the Constitution that might preclude certain aspects of his program. He strongly supported aid for internal improvements, including the cutting of canals, but conceded that constitutional authority might be lacking, perhaps reflecting the abortive efforts to include language on the subject during the September 14 debate in the Constitutional Convention. With respect to improvements in inland navigation, he said: "There can certainly be no object more worthy of the cares of the local administrations; and it were to be wished that there was no doubt of the power of the National Government to lend its direct aid on a comprehensive basis." He also recognized that the language in the Constitution might not be sufficient to support subsidies for introducers of new inventions, but it is not clear why he hesitated to invoke the General Welfare Clause in these areas. These reservations aside, the *Report on Manufactures* proposed a comprehensive program of federal investment for economic growth through encouraging manufacturing and expanding the means of transportation. Wherever possible, federal investments in these areas would be posited on the one clear basis of constitutional authority—the General Welfare Clause. That was the vision embodied in Hamilton's report.[10]

Madison's Reaction

James Madison did not lose time in reacting to the *Report on Manufactures* and the legal analysis that it contained. He wrote to Edmund Pendleton, a longtime family friend and colleague in Virginia politics dating back to 1776 when the young Madison had served in the Virginia convention of that year. On January 21, 1792, Madison wrote to Pendleton, as was his habit, on issues pending before the House. At the end of his letter he told Pendleton: "I have reserved for you a copy of the Report of the Secretary of the Treasury on Manufactures." Madison had wanted to send the copy by private conveyance because it was "rather bulky" for the mail but had not yet had an opportunity to do so. Instead, he enclosed a newspaper account. He then described his deepest concern with the the report that he regarded as antithetical to the established understanding of the Constitution and as eroding the principles embodied in the concept of enumerated powers that he had personally championed:

> [The Report] broaches a new Constitutional doctrine of vast consequence and demanding the serious attention of the public. I consider it myself as subverting the fundamental and characteristic principle of the Government; as contrary to the true and fair, as well as the received construction, and as bidding defiance to the sense in which the Constitution is known to have been proposed, advocated, and adopted. If Congress can do whatever in their *discretion* can be *done by money*, and will promote the *General Welfare*, the Government is no longer a limited one, possessing enumerated powers, but an indefinite one, subject to particular exceptions. It is to be remarked that the phrase out of which this doctrine is elaborated is copied from the old Articles of Confederation, where it was always understood as nothing more than a general caption to the specified powers, and it is a fact that it was preferred in the new instrument for that very reason, as less liable than any other to misconstruction.[11]

These observations are consistent with the constitutional views that Madison had expressed in the "Federalist No. 41," and they no doubt constituted his deeply held convictions regarding Hamilton's interpretation of the General Welfare Clause at the time of the issuance of the *Report on Manufactures*. The question was not academic for Madison. It went to the heart of his philosophy of government. By taking the position that he had, Hamilton was "subverting the fundamental and characteristic principle of the Government." It is understandable that Madison would take this view. As he saw it, by so expanding the reach of the General Welfare Clause, Hamilton had converted the Constitution from a document granting limited, enumerated powers to the national legislature into a document granting unlimited powers, as long as the exercise of the power was expressed through an appropriation. This was strong medicine for Madison who had, throughout the Constitutional Convention, as consistently and strongly as any delegate, urged that the powers of Congress be specifically enumerated. If greater power in an area was needed, it should be given by constitutional amendment through the amendatory process. Indeed, Madison himself had urged amendments on such matters as the establishment of a university at the time of the Convention.

Quite apart from sectional or political interests, or personal animosities, the gap between Madison and Hamilton must have been widened considerably by their different perspectives on the meaning of the General Welfare Clause. The argument was not necessarily over the specific initiatives proposed or alluded to in the report as areas appropriate for federal assistance. Hamilton saw the General Welfare Clause as a basis for federal financial support for learning. Madison had proposed the addition of language into the Constitution to authorize federal financial support for a university or "seminaries of learning." Later, when he was president, Madison urged federal assistance for internal improvements, a national need that Hamilton also clearly perceived and expressed in the *Report*. In short, on a number of discrete policy issues, Madison supported, or would come to support, initiatives similar to those favored by Hamilton. The argument was, to some extent, over constitutional means. As each step along the way toward greater federal participation was taken, should the people's blessing be asked through a formal amendment to the Constitution? Madison said, yes. Hamilton said that the Constitution, unamended, must be interpreted as sufficiently elastic to enable the national legislature to respond immediately to such unanticipated "exigencies."

The *Report on Manufactures* did, however, bring to a head profound broad differences between Madison and Hamilton over the fundamental direction that the nation should take. As Lance Banning has observed: "[A]s a capstone of a systematic program to remold the infant government into a shape that would subvert the Revolution, the Report on Manufactures was, to Madison, the trigger and the context for a great campaign to rouse the people to defend the revolutionary order they and the Convention had intended to complete."[12]

Jefferson's Complaint

In May and September of 1792, the year in which the report was transmitted to Congress, Thomas Jefferson cataloged his complaints in two lengthy and heated communications to President Washington. In the first of these, Jefferson recounted his difficulties with the funding of the debt and with the rise of the "paper men," the holders of and speculators in government securities, many of whom held seats in Congress. Hamilton's program, in Jefferson's opinion, was leading the country toward monarchism rather than the republicanism which Jefferson saw as the true course of the new nation. Moreover, the direction taken in Hamilton's program was at the expense of the South and to the benefit of northern commercial interests.[13]

Hamilton's legal interpretation of the spending power played a key role in this exchange. Jefferson alluded to it in the first letter in the course of castigating the "corrupt squadron" that had "manifested their dispositions to get rid of the limitations imposed by the Constitution on the general legislature. . . ." This was clearly an ill-disguised reference to Hamilton's broad construction of the General Welfare Clause. However, the major burden of Jefferson's May letter was to urge Washington to remain in office for a second term rather than retire. Jefferson argued that only Washington could help the new nation survive the domestic divisions that it faced and overcome the threat of monarchism posed by Hamilton's program. The alternative to the direction that Jefferson portrayed in this May letter would be a split in the Union reflecting the disappointments of the South.

Distressed, Washington asked Hamilton to respond to this and other allegations. In his reply, Hamilton brushed aside Jefferson's accusation with a breezy observation that captures the essence of the contest over the meaning of the General Welfare Clause that was to ensue, although he did not specifically mention that provision: "There are some things which the general government has clearly a right to do. There are others, which it has clearly no right to meddle with; and there is a good deal of middle ground, about which honest and well-disposed men may differ."[14]

At the end of the following summer, Jefferson repeated his litany of complaints to Washington. Here he was more specific in his negative references to Hamilton and in his concern regarding the debate over the General Welfare Clause. Jefferson was responding to an August letter from Washington in which the latter had expressed concern regarding the "internal dissensions which have taken place without our government, and their disagreeable effect on its movements." Jefferson readily conceded that "dissensions" had indeed taken place among those who were "nearest" to Washington in the administration. Rather than confessing the error of his ways, however, Jefferson used the occasion once more to attack Hamilton and his policies. If Jefferson had regrets, it was for supporting them in the earlier conflict over assumption.[15]

Jefferson acknowledged that, privately, he had "utterly disapproved" of Hamilton's "system" as "flow[ing] from principles adverse to liberty . . . and calculated to undermine and demolish the Republic, by creating an influence of his [Hamilton's] department over the members of the Legislature." Jefferson's concern was that the funding and assumption programs had been adopted by the votes of members who had personal interests in the programs because they would benefit from an increase in the value of the debt securities that they held. Those who had so voted were "deserters from the rights and interests of the people." Hamilton's interpretation of the General Welfare Clause had only compounded the felony. Jefferson dramatized this for the president in the following biting and accusatory passage:

> If, what was actually doing, begat uneasiness in those who wished for virtuous government, what was further proposed was not less threatening to the friends of the Constitution. For, in a report on the subject of manufactures, (still to be acted on,) it was expressly assumed that the General Government has a right to exercise all powers which may be for the *general welfare,* that is to say, all the legitimate powers of government since no government has a legitimate right to do what is not for the welfare of the governed. There was, indeed, a sham limitation of the universality of this power *to cases where money is to be employed.* But about what is it that money cannot be employed?[16]

Jefferson saw Hamilton's interpretation of the spending power as a central ingredient of a two-part Federalist plot, the steps of which he luridly described to Washington. First Hamilton's object was to "draw all the powers of government into the hands of the general Legislature." This, presumably would be done through broadly interpretating the General Welfare Clause. A corps of the Legislature "corrupted" by the funding program, under Hamilton's command, would then subvert "step by step, the principles of the Constitution. . . ."[17]

The rift between the two secretaries would probably have arisen, even without the *Report on Manufactures* and the interpretation it contained. They differed on foreign policy, as well as domestic, constitutional concerns. However, the interpretation of the General Welfare Clause in the *Report on Manufactures* strongly reinforced Jefferson's central suspicion that Hamilton would control a portion of the legislature because it benefited financially from Hamilton's program to restore credit and increase the value of government securities. Under Hamilton's control the legislature would be more powerful than the Constitution intended because, according to the treasury secretary's theory, it could pass whatever legislation it wished under the guise of spending measures to provide for the "general welfare of the United States." It could therefore intervene in areas uncontemplated by the Constitution, strictly read in light of the enumerated powers.

Because the drift of Hamilton's program was disadvantageous to the South (high tariffs, excises on whiskey, funding and assumption of debt at the expense of original holders who had sold their certificates at depreciated prices, emphasis on manufacturing rather than agriculture, benefits to the creditor class), the alleged conspiracy was particularly noxious. The solution was for Washington to remain in power until Jefferson, and presumably Madison, could muster forces, reverse the program, and restore balance and the original notion of republicanism in the form of a more limited central government with pared-down legislative powers under a General Welfare Clause strictly confined to spending to implement the enumerated powers. This was the core strategy set forth in Jefferson's correspondence with Washington that followed the issuance of the *Report on Manufactures* and reflected Jefferson's complaint.

Forrest McDonald urges that Jefferson's accusations were exaggerated and that they were rejected by Washington. Flexner describes Washington's profound distress at the rift and his inability to quell it. In a letter to Jefferson in August 1792, Washington complained of "internal dissensions" that were "harrowing and tearing our vitals." Flexner observes that Washington did not openly support the *Report on Manufactures* because he thought the nation was unprepared for it. How he came down on the specific issue of Hamilton's broad interpretation of the General Welfare Clause versus Jefferson's and Madison's more narrow reading is not clearly documented. Unlike the situation regarding the bank bill, Washington was never obliged to opine on the issue because no legislative action was ever taken on the famous and controversial *Report on Manufactures*. Flexner suggests that Washington declined to openly repudiate Hamilton's theory of the General Welfare Clause. When Jefferson, in conversation, afforded him an opportunity to do so, Washington "remained silent." Washington did, on the other hand, accede to the political advice of Jefferson, Madison and, for that matter, Hamilton, all of whom urged him to run again. At first, he vacillated, requesting of Madison a draft letter announcing his retirement. Ultimately he reluctantly allowed himself to be reelected.[18] But his reelection did not end the rift between his fellow Virginians and Hamilton and did not resolve the controversy over the scope of the General Welfare Clause that contributed to the schism.[19]

The Whiskey Rebellion, the Last Annual Message, and the Farewell Address: Washington's General Welfare Clause Legacy

While he never specifically addressed the legal schism over the scope of the General Welfare Clause that sharply divided his closest advisors, Washington's actions in his second term suggest his inclination in favor of an energetic taxing and spending power. In 1794, he led what he termed "the army of the Constitution" to quell the Whiskey Rebellion, an uprising in the western counties of Pennsylvania opposed to the excise tax enacted to supply revenues for Hamilton's program. Washington saw the experience as proof that his fellow citizens understood "the true principles of government and liberty" and were "ready to maintain the authority of the laws against licentious invasions." It represents as well a determination to enforce the taxing power when challenged and thus to ensure that the new government would have the revenues to carry out its programs.[20]

To the nature of such programs, Washington turned again in his final state of the union message, delivered in person on December 7, 1796. In it, Washington continued to promote a national agenda that included assistance to domestic activities, including "the encouragement of manufactures" by means unspecified. As to agriculture, he recommended "[i]nstitutions for promoting [agriculture]" "supported by the public purse." As a means to this end, he suggested establishing boards to diffuse information, "enabled by premiums and small pecuniary aids to encourage and assist a spirit of discovery and improvement."[21] At the same time, he reinstituted his earlier proposal for a national university that would provide for "the education of our youth in the science of *government*." He asked Congress: "In a republic what species of knowledge can be equally important and what duty more pressing on its legislature than to patronize a plan for communicating it to those who are to be the future guardians of the liberties of the country?" Washington's correspondence indicates that his advocacy for educational and agricultural establishments was the result of his own personal reflection and commitment, rather than acquiescence to ideas pressed by Hamilton.[22]

While his Farewell address, delivered in the September preceding the eighth annual message, did not press his domestic recommendations, it did lay a framework for successful exercise of an energetic spending power. Washington admonished his fellow citizens to maintain fiscal integrity ("cherish public credit" and avoid the "accumulation of debt"), and he stressed the importance of a solid revenue base: "[T]oward the payment of debts, there must be revenue; . . . to have revenue there must be taxes."[23] Read together both messages implicitly reflect the thrust of Hamilton's interpretation of the scope of the General Welfare Clause.

The Washington Administration established a foundation for the broad exercise of the authority contained in the General Welfare Clause in Article I, section 8 of the Constitution. Clause 1 of that section, embracing the taxing and spending power, had clearly been put into play. The taxing power had been vigorously applied to support the major domestic initiative of the administration—the establishment of public credit on a sound footing through the Hamilton program. A central aspect was the adoption, not only of higher imposts, but also of internal excise taxes on domestic products to gain revenues to service the debt. When challenged by internal obstructions during the Whiskey Rebellion, the exercise of the taxing power had been upheld and enforced, where necessary, by force of arms assembled and led by none other than the chief executive.

In terms of the thesis proposed earlier in this work, it seems appropriate to note that the Washington administration, while exercising and enforcing the taxing power, had not ignored the spending side of the equation. In the course of laying out a vision of national prosperity through a definitive policy of support for domestic manufactures, Washington's secretary of the treasury had formulated a bold legal theory for interpreting the General Welfare Clause that gave it independent force as a discrete *spending* power. Hamilton had emphatically declined to limit its reach to the purposes encompassed within the enumerated powers in Article I, section 8. That reading had been fiercely challenged by Jefferson and Madison and the challenge had contributed to the formation of the Democratic-Republican party under their leadership and to the emergence of the "spirit of party" that Washington warned against in his Farewell Address. Notwithstanding the challenge, however, a broad reading or vision of the General Welfare Clause had been squarely announced—a reading or vision that was to be adopted by Justice Story in the nineteenth century, in his *Commentaries on the Constitution,* and ultimately by the Supreme Court in the twentieth century.[24]

It is true that Washington never articulated his own interpretation of the General Welfare Clause. Indeed, Washington took pains to avoid constitutional theorizing. However, the policies he recommended, most notably in the eighth annual message, ultimately depended for constitutional support on the broad reading of the clause that Hamilton gave it. While the first president did not specifically bless that reading, neither did he explicitly reject it. On the contrary, he continued to collaborate with its author, seeking advice, as well as drafting services. Regarding the domestic initiatives in that message, Washington, not Hamilton, was driving the agenda.

The campaign that both Madison and Jefferson had launched against Hamilton's bold interpretation of the General Welfare Clause continued unabated after Washington departed. During the administration of John Adams, it took the form of the Virginia Resolutions of 1798, drafted by Madison, and the Kentucky Resolutions of 1798 and 1799, drafted by Jefferson. While particularly addressed to the Alien and Sedition Acts, the Virginia Resolutions (prepared for adoption by the Virginia House of Delegates) took clear aim at the "spirit . . . manifested by the federal government to enlarge its powers by forced constructions" of the Constitution. The resolutions complained of "a design to expound certain general phrases . . . so as to destroy the meaning and effect of the particular enumeration which necessarily explains and limits the general phrases." The inevitable result of such a design would be a "consolidation of the states" into "one sovereignty" and the transformation of the "republican system" into a "mixed monarchy." If there were doubt as to the reference, in an accompanying report Madison named the *Report on Manufactures* as the documentary evidence of the culpable design, and he lashed out at Hamilton's interpretation of the General Welfare Clause whether it was confined to the appropriation of federal funds or not. Here, Madison made explicit and public his view of the General Welfare Clause: "Whenever . . . money has been raised by the general authority, and is to be applied to a particular measure, a question arises whether the particular measure be within the enumerated authorities vested in Congress. If it be, the money requisite for it may be applied to it. If it be not, no such application can be made." The Kentucky Resolutions, while more prolix, made the same points. Delaware, among other states, rejected the Virginia Resolutions as a "very unjustifiable interference with the general government."[25] With the passing of the Adams administration in the election of 1800, both Jefferson and Madison became vested with authority to apply their thesis of the General Welfare Clause to the administration of government.

III
The Virginia Presidents and the General Welfare Clause: The Quest for a Constitutional Amendment

5
Jefferson's Dilemma

THE JEFFERSON PRESIDENCY SUGGESTS THAT, EVEN FOR A CHIEF executive who sincerely emphasized the limited role of the federal government and a strict construction of Article I, section 8 of the Constitution, federal encouragement for internal improvements was difficult to resist despite the absence of an appropriate constitutional amendment. Maintaining strict adherence to a condition that a constitutional amendment be secured before Congress legislated to provide such encouragement through general welfare legislation was an elusive goal. Jefferson signed and administered the Cumberland Road legislation. No amendment preceded its enactment, just as no amendment accompanied Senate ratification of the Louisiana Purchase treaty. The Democratic-Republican administrations of Madison and Monroe that followed struggled with the same dilemma that confounded Jefferson, but pursued different paths to its resolution.[1]

JEFFERSON'S INAUGURAL ADDRESSES

The General Welfare Clause and its possibilities were far from Jefferson's thoughts as he took the oath of office on March 4, 1801, at high noon. He delivered his barely audible inaugural address in the Senate chamber. Joseph Ellis observes: "Simplicity and austerity, not equality or individualism, were the messages of his inaugural march." The address began with a note of awe and humility: "A rising nation, spread over a wide and fruitful land, traversing all the seas with the rich productions of their industry, engaged in commerce with nations who feel power and forget right, advancing rapidly to destinies beyond the reach of the mortal eye—when I contemplate these transcendent objects, and see the honor, the happiness, and the hopes of this beloved country committed to the issue and the auspices of this day, I shrink from the contemplation, and humble myself before the magnitude of the undertaking."[2]

The new president next alluded to the "contest of opinion through which we have passed" and assured his audience that "all will . . . arrange themselves under the will of the law, and unite in common efforts for the common good." He referred to the divided opinions about the measures of safety that had been taken in the face of the foreign threats—presumably a reference to the Alien and Sedition Acts. Then he sought to conciliate. "But every difference of opinion is not a difference of principle. We have called by different names brethren of the same principle. We are all Republicans, we are all Federalists."

His belief in freedom and his confidence in his fellow citizens warranted tolerance even for those who opposed the union. "If there be any among us who would wish to dissolve the Union or to change its republican form, let them stand undisturbed as monuments of the safety with which error of opinion may be tolerated where reason is left free to combat it." For those who feared that the government was insufficiently strong, he posed this question: "I know, indeed, that some honest men fear that a republican government can not be strong, that this Government is not strong enough; but would the honest patriot, in the full tide of successful experiment, abandon a government which has so far kept us free and firm on the theoretic and visionary fear that this Government, the world's best hope, may by possibility want energy to preserve itself?" He stated his own conviction: "I believe this, on the contrary, the strongest Government on earth. I believe it the only one where every man, at the call of the law, would fly to the standard of the law, and would meet invasions of the public order as his own personal concern."[3]

Jefferson urged his audience to pursue "with courage and confidence" their "own Federal and Republican principles," their "attachment to union and representative government." Then he turned to his own vision of the scope and functions of government and asked what was necessary to make Americans a "happy and prosperous people"? "Still one more thing," he answered: "a wise and frugal Government, which shall restrain men from injuring one another, shall leave them otherwise free to regulate their own pursuits of industry and improvement, and shall not take from the mouth of labor the bread it has earned. This is the sum of good government, and this is necessary to close the circle of our felicities."

After painting this broad picture, Jefferson had one last

task—to outline the principles that would shape his administration and to "compress them within the narrowest compass they will bear." These principles he packed into a single paragraph:

> Equal and exact justice to all men, of whatever state or persuasion, religious or political; peace, commerce, and honest friendship with all nations, entangling alliances with none; the support of the State governments in all their rights, as the most competent administrations for our domestic concerns and the surest bulwarks against antirepublican tendencies; the preservation of the General Government in its whole constitutional vigor, as the sheet anchor of our peace at home and safety abroad; a jealous care of the right of election by the people . . . ; absolute acquiescence in the decisions of the majority . . . ; a well disciplined militia . . . ; the supremacy of the civil over the military authority; economy in the public expense, that labor may be lightly burthened; the honest payment of our debts and sacred preservation of the public faith; encouragement of agriculture, and of commerce as its handmaid; the diffusion of information and arraignment of all abuses at the bar of the public reason; freedom of religion; freedom of the press, and freedom of person under the protection of the habeas corpus, and trial by juries impartially selected.[4]

In his private correspondence following the delivery of his first inaugural address, Jefferson expansively disclosed his strategy and mused about its potential success. Several days after the inaugural, he wrote to his friend John Dickinson describing the recent course of national affairs under the Federalists in nautical terms. "The storm through which we have passed, has been tremendous indeed. The tough sides of our Argosy have been thoroughly tried. Her strength has stood the waves into which she was steered, with a view to sink her. We shall put her on her republican tack, and she will now show by the beauty of her motion the skill of her builders."[5]

In the compressed statement of "sound principle" found in the first inaugural, federalism, frugality, fiscal restraint, and limited taxation are central themes. Only a limited role—involving the encouragement of some activities and the diffusion of information—is assigned to the central government. This vision guided Jefferson in his first administration. He pared the rolls of the civil service, eliminated functions, cut public expense, and sought to reduce or eliminate internal taxation.[6]

Writing again to Dickinson in December 1801, Jefferson discoursed on his fiscal policy. The abolition of internal taxes was "perfectly safe," Jefferson assured Dickinson. Government economies would reduce the need for those revenues. The impost would provide sufficient resources to support the government, pay the interest on the debt, and discharge the principal within a reasonable period. The capital set free could be employed, among other ways, "in agriculture, canals, bridges or other useful enterprises."[7] Jefferson's view, in his first term, was that his policies of paring spending and reducing internal taxes would still result in sufficient revenue to pay off the principal of the debt in a shorter period of time than required. The repaid principal would then be used by recipients of the payments for general welfare investments of the kind described in the letter. Government economy would enhance private investment.

By the time of his second inaugural address, in March 1805, Jefferson could point to a surplus. His suggestion for its use added another dimension to the compressed vision of government that he had expressed in his first inaugural. After a reference to foreign affairs, he expressed pride and took credit for the progress of his administration in the "suppression of unnecessary offices, of useless establishments and expenses" which had "enabled us to discontinue our internal taxes." The continuing impost he justified in terms of ability to pay: "The remaining revenue on the consumption of foreign articles is paid chiefly by those who can afford to add foreign luxuries to domestic comforts, being collected on our seaboard and frontiers only, and, incorporated with the transactions of our mercantile citizens, it may be the pleasure and the pride of an American to ask, What farmer, what mechanic, what laborer ever sees a taxgatherer of the United States?"[8]

Able to take credit for government economy and reduced taxation, Jefferson was now emboldened to turn affirmatively to spending. "These contributions," he told the inaugural assemblage, "enable us to support the current expenses of the Government, to fulfill contracts with foreign nations, to extinguish the native right of soil within our limits, to extend those limits, and to apply such a surplus to our public debts as places at a short day their final redemption. . . ." The question he turned to was what to do with the newly available revenue when redemption had been accomplished. He answered in this way: "[T]hat redemption once effected the revenue thereby liberated may, by a just repartition of it among the States and a corresponding amendment of the Constitution, be applied *in time of peace* to rivers, canals, roads, arts, manufactures, education, and other great objects within each State."⁹

This appears to be a change of direction from the tone of the first inaugural with its emphasis on frugality and limited government. Here was a vision of government exercising its spending power to assist states in their efforts to improve transportation, aid the arts, encourage manufactures, and enhance education. Note also that the educational initiative was not confined to the establishment of a national university, Washington's pet project, but included education within the states. However, these suggestions were accompanied by two important limitations. They would be achieved through a "just repartition" of the surplus to the states. States would have the implementing role, and they would receive the funds, presumably by way of an equitable formula. Here, then is the forerunner of the federally funded, state formula grant, a familiar form of government life in post–Great Society America.

The other limitation is the "corresponding" constitutional amendment. Jefferson, as did Madison, still adhered to the proposition that the General Welfare Clause was limited by the enumerated powers and that it was not a basis for supporting constitutional government spending in areas that fell outside the enumerated powers, the case that Jefferson sketched in his inaugural. Hence, a constitutional amendment would be needed to justify the initiatives if Congress chose to adopt them. This was important because it would mean that the people, through the amendment process, would assent to the use of federal resources in these new areas. Indeed, to Jefferson, as well as to Madison, the limitations on the General Welfare Clause and the need for amendment-by-amendment entry into new areas were articles of political faith that they adhered to during their time in office and in their private correspondence. In 1817, Jefferson was to reinforce the limited view of the General Welfare Clause as a basic tenet of the party that he had founded, separating it from the Federalists: "Whereas, our tenet ever was, and, indeed it is almost the only landmark which now divides the federalists from the republicans, that Congress had not unlimited powers to provide for the general welfare, but were restrained to those specifically enumerated," he reminded Albert Gallatin, his former secretary of the treasury. The rationale for this remained clear to Jefferson: "[A]s it was never meant that they should provide for that welfare but by the exercise of the enumerated powers, so it could not have been meant that they should raise money for purposes which the enumeration did not place under their action; consequently, that the specification of powers is a limitation of the purpose for which they may raise money."[10]

However, as a matter of *policy* for both Jefferson and Madison, it was not inconsistent with frugal, economic, and limited government—or with the foregoing constitutional tenet to assist states with river improvements, construction of canals and roads, enhancement of education and the arts, and manufacturing subsidies. It was not inconsistent to assist them with federal funds, with all that federal funds entailed, as long as the constitutional concern was satisfied through an appropriate amendment. Such an amendment would bridge the compressed principles of the first inaugural with the investment proposals of the second, would enable a strict-construction president to promote an active, investment strategy.

Jefferson did not favor his friends and colleagues with extensive discourse on the strategy that moved him in delivering the second inaugural. He contented himself with a short observation in a letter to Judge John Tyler at the end of March 1805, written from Monticello: "The first [inaugural address] was, from the nature of the case, all profession and promise. Performance, therefore, seemed to be the proper office of the second. But the occasion restricted me to mention only the most prominent heads, and the strongest justification of these in the fewest words possible."[11] There is in this no evidence that Jefferson was ambivalent about the initiatives that he had proposed or that he did not take them seriously. On the contrary, they were among the most "prominent heads." and they reappeared, as we shall see, in subsequent annual messages during his second administration.

The question arises, what—other than favorable fiscal news—caused Jefferson to favor internal improvements between March 1801 and March 1805? To be more specific, what persuaded him that public investment "in time of peace" was an appropriate means of meeting the need for internal and other improvements within each state?

The answer is the Louisiana Purchase.

During Jefferson's first term, the United States purchased the Louisiana Territory from France. The action doubled the size of the nation and made infrastructure growth and other unifying actions imperative. It also removed a source of potential friction with France which had acquired the territory from Spain. This Jefferson recognized; he vividly portrayed the dangers in correspondence with his emissaries Robert Livingston and James

Monroe, and with Pierre DuPont who played a key role as an emissary in the negotiations with Napoleon.

One potential bar stood in the way of consummating the sale and the momentous achievement it represented, the most significant of Jefferson's tenure. While delighted at the turn of events, Jefferson believed that the Constitution did not authorize the purchase or the formation of new states out of the territory that would be acquired from France. He shared his qualms with members of his party in Congress and toyed with various drafts of constitutional amendments that might supply the authority that he believed lacking. He refused to concur in broad interpretations that would cure the problem without amendment, believing them to be a departure from his strict constructionist doctrine. Thus, he told Senator Wilson Nicholas: "I had rather ask an enlargement of power from the nation where it is found necessary, than to assume it by a construction which would make our powers boundless."

In the end, however, pragmatism prevailed. The concern that France might back out of the deal or Spain might sabotage it prompted Jefferson to mute the constitutional concerns and press for early ratification without proposing a constitutional amendment that, at one point, he thought necessary to ratify an unauthorized action. Normally strict-construction Republican senators overwhelmingly supported the treaty; normally broad-construction Federalists opposed it. When then Senator John Quincy Adams offered a constitutional amendment, he received no support from the administration. The purchase was ratified. New states were admitted from the new territory. No change was made to the text of the Constitution. Long after, Adams remembered the episode when opponents attacked his broad, pro-internal improvement interpretation of the Constitution.[12]

The experience with the Louisiana Purchase underscores the limitations of the strict constructionist approach to the spending power. When necessity compelled it, both the executive and the legislative branches, according to Jefferson, were proceeding outside the bounds of the Constitution in order to effectuate a massive good by approving and implementing the Louisiana Purchase. Obtaining a constitutional amendment before negotiating or ratifying the purchase was impracticable and would have precluded successfully completing the transaction. This could not be permitted. Although he recognized the issue in his correspondence, Jefferson had counseled silence with respect to the constitutional issue in his dealings with Congress and the public. As

Joseph Ellis has observed, "The decision to bypass the constitutional issue was was unquestionably correct, for the practical reason that the debate over a constitutional amendment would have raised a constellation of nettlesome questions ... that might have put the entire purchase at risk."[13]

These conundrums may reveal why, respecting the spending power, the alternative—Hamilton's way—became so attractive and ultimately prevailed, both in Story's *Commentaries* and the Supreme Court. Quite apart from questions of textual support and the intent of the framers—after all, the framers did not consider these issues directly—calling for an amendment each time the question of internal improvement arose was not practical. Legislators could not be asked to approve spending if they were told at the same time that the measure was ultra vires under the basic charter, any more than they could be asked to approve a sensitive treaty if told that it called for action the central government could not take constitutionally.

An understandably attractive alternative was to look to the Constitution for broad interpretations rather than amend it each time a question arose. Hence the treaty-making power was construed broadly by the Senate, as Wilson Nicholas suggested to Jefferson in 1803.

The General Welfare Clause contained language that would support such an interpretation. In practice, notwithstanding Jefferson's cautions, it came to be construed broadly as embracing areas for spending not confined to the enumerated powers in Article I, section 8.[14]

The Spending Power and Jefferson's Second Term: The Strategy in the Sixth Annual Message

Despite these considerations, in his annual messages and infrequent private correspondence on the subject, Jefferson steadfastly maintained the constitutional position on the spending power that he had set forth in his second inaugural address while simultaneously recommending its beneficent exercise.[15] The sixth annual message, submitted to Congress in December 1806, reflects the most comprehensive statement of his policy. As in the case of the second inaugural address, the context was the prospect of a treasury surplus and its possible use in the public interest. Jefferson pointed to the receipts for 1806 having reached $15 million, thus enabling the government to pay claims on Louisiana, reduce the principal on the debt, and make required payments of interest. He estimated that $23 million of principal would be repaid during the course of his administration to that point. He recommended eliminating two sources of revenue. Thus, the prospect was for continued reduction of both taxes and debt. Jefferson could even forsee a surplus: "When both of these branches of revenue shall in this way be relinquished there will still ere long be an accumulation of moneys in the Treasury beyond the installments of public debt which we are permitted by contract to pay. They can not then, without a modification assented to by the public creditors, be applied to the extinguishment of this debt and the complete liberation of our revenues, the most desirable of all objects. Nor, if our peace continues, will they be wanting for any other existing purpose."[16]

Having set the stage, Jefferson posed the inevitable question, one that more recently confronted us during the second term of President Clinton when, after years of deficits, we enjoyed a balanced budget. Jefferson put it squarely: "The question therefore now comes forward, To what other objects shall these surpluses be appropriated, and the whole surplus of impost, after the entire discharge of the public debt, and during those intervals when the purposes of war shall not call for them?" He then asked rhetorically, "Shall we suppress the impost and give that advantage to foreign over domestic manufactures?" He continued, "On a few articles of more general and necessary use the suppression [of the impost] in due season will doubtless be right, but the great mass of the articles on which impost is paid are foreign luxuries, purchased by those only who are rich enough to afford themselves the use of them."[17] Then he turned to the options.

The "patriotism" of these affluent citizens, Jefferson speculated, "would certainly prefer [the] continuance [of the impost] and [its] application to the great purposes of the public education, roads, rivers, canals, and such other objects of public improvement as it may be thought proper to add to the constitutional enumeration of Federal powers." In short, the preferred policy should be to devote the surplus, hard earned by Jefferson's efforts at public frugality, to the "great purposes" he listed but only if the items on the list were added to the Constitution by amendment.[18]

Having stated this caveat, he felt free to make a strong case for these initiatives: "By these operations new channels of communication will be opened between the States, the lines of separation will disappear, their interests will be identified, and their union will be cemented by new and indissoluble ties." Jefferson's eloquent statement of the rationale for public investment in internal improvements echoed the statements of his predecessor, Washington. Ironically it even bore a resemblance to the sentiments of Hamilton that Jefferson had so warmly criticized in his correspondence with Washington.

When Jefferson turned to education, extending his statement of the rationale for federal financial assistance to that area, he made clear his commitment to the carving out of a distinct federal role: "Education is here placed among the articles of public care, not that it would be proposed to take its ordinary branches out of the hands of private enterprise, which manages so much better all the concerns to which it is equal, but a public institution can alone supply those sciences which though rarely called for are yet necessary to complete the circle, all the parts of which contribute to the improvement of the country and some of them to its preservation." Here, from Jefferson, was an early rationale for *supplementary* federal aid for education that in substance, if not in detail, reflected considerations that would be raised more than 160 years later. It should be noted that Jefferson's recommendation probably called for aid to private institutions of higher education; the role of states in carrying out programs of public education at the elementary and secondary level had not yet evolved.

Finally, Jefferson invoked the timing of his proposal and posed a precondition that reveals both his constitutional thinking and his continuing insistence on a constitutional amendment to undergird national public investment:

> The subject is now proposed for consideration of Congress, because if approved by the time the State legislatures shall have deliberated on this extension of the Federal trusts, and the laws shall be passed and other arrangements made for their execution, the necessary funds will be on hand and without employment. *I suppose an amendment to the Constitution, by consent of the States, necessary, because the objects now recommended are not among those enumerated in the Constitution, and to which it permits the public moneys to be applied.*[19]

Thus, in 1806, Jefferson concisely laid out his domestic spending strategy: use the surplus for improvements. Transportation improvements would cement the country. Supplementary educational aid would do what private educational institutions could not and would improve and, in certain cases, help preserve the country. An amendment to the Constitution was necessary. Congress should take prompt steps to propose the amendment to the states. With the ratification of such an amendment, which Jefferson apparently regarded as pro forma, all would be in place to support authorization and appropriation measures.

"CHEQUER THE WHOLE COUNTRY WITH CANALS [AND] ROADS"

Jefferson had spoken of internal improvements as an endeavor to be pursued by the nation "in time of peace." The final two years of his administration, while not a time of outright war, were absorbed with preparations for war or efforts to avoid it. During 1807, Jefferson became increasingly preoccupied with foreign and defense policy.[20] Despite these preoccupations, Jefferson found time to return, in his private correspondence, to the subject of the domestic federal assistance projects that he had raised in his sixth annual message. He had received letters from Robert Fulton, the inventor, and Joel Barlow, the noted author and poet, raising these issues. In December 1807, he responded to Barlow. "The desire of peace," he told Barlow, "is very much strengthened in me by that which I feel in favor of the great subjects of yours and Mr. Fulton's letters. I had fondly hoped to set those enterprises into motion with the last legislature I shall meet. But the chance of war is an unfortunate check. I do not however despair that the proposition of amendment may be sent down this session to the legislatures. But it is not certain." Jefferson's approach to federal assistance, even as communicated to friends and supporters of these projects, remained fully consistent with his earlier insistence that a constitutional amendment remained a necessary precondition to internal improvement or other domestic spending initiatives. The strategy he propounded would have Congress, despite its focus on national defense, propose to the state legislatures the necessary constitutional amendment: "I doubt whether precedence will be given to your part of the plan before Mr. Fulton's. People generally have more feeling for canals and roads than education. However, I hope we can advance them with equal pace. If the amendment is sent out this session, returned to the next, and no war takes place, we may offer the plan to the next session in the form of a bill, the preparation of which should be the work of the ensuing summer."[21]

Despite the "unfortunate check," as a matter of policy, Jefferson continued to favor using federal resources to assist initiatives in transportation and education, areas organized in modern budgets under the headings of functions 400 and 500. His insistence on a constitutional amendment was not a device to forestall such initiatives but a precondition based upon his deep constitutional conviction. Presumably he was prepared to support the necessary amendment and believed that the state legislatures would ratify it promptly. Certainly, there is nothing in this private letter to a respected national figure, friend, and frequent guest in the White House, suggesting that Jefferson opposed such an amendment on the grounds that he thought federal assistance in these areas was an inappropriate subject for inclusion in the enumerated powers. On the contrary, the thrust of his letter was the difficulty in moving Congress to propose such an amendment, particularly in an atmosphere of crisis. Moreover, at the end of 1807, Jefferson was contemplating an ambitious schedule that would include timely adoption of such a constitutional amendment, thus permitting his administration to draft and propose necessary legislation in a subsequent session of Congress. The letter implies that, in the presence of the necessary constitutional authority, Jefferson would not have hesitated to propose the authorizing and/or funding legislation needed to implement the ideas that Barlow and Fulton had propounded.

The legislation that Congress did enact in the session that began in October 1807 was not related to amendments to the Constitution to expand the General Welfare authority. Rather, it had to do with the continuing conflict with England, and it took the form of an embargo that Jefferson supported and which was to absorb him throughout the last year of his presidency. Both Britain and France had embarked upon a policy of interdicting United States commerce. Britain would interdict American commerce with French ports; France would do so with British ports. Jefferson concluded that it if the United States were to lose vessels, cargoes and crews, it was preferable to leave them at home; in short, he favored an embargo. Congress enacted such a measure, and it became the duty of Jefferson to administer it. So, when he again wrote to Joel Barlow in late January 1808, it is unremarkable that the subject of federal aid to education was not raised in his letter.[22]

In the spring and summer of 1808, his last full year in office, Jefferson became absorbed with questions concerning the application and enforcement of the embargo legislation, as well as with its political implications. He attributed to the Federalists an intent to use the embargo to gain political advantage. To his fellow Republicans, he expressed appreciation for their patience and patriotism in supporting the embargo. He reflected on whether the embargo would persuade the British government to repeal the hated orders of council or whether the United States would ultimately abandon the embargo in favor of war. He had to have recognized the unpopularity of the measure for he clearly noted the extent to which his fellow citizens sought to evade it, but he held to his resolve until, in the last months of the administration, Congress suddenly and unexpectedly repealed the measure on March 4, 1809.[23]

Throughout this period there was little time to return to the question of domestic improvements financed with federal revenues. When Jefferson did address the subject, it was to express regret that the absence of true peace precluded the execution of the domestic vision that he had set forth in his sixth annual message. In May 1808, he responded, with apologies for his tardiness, to Mr. Leiper, who had sent him an address of the Democratic-Republicans of Philadelphia. Jefferson speculated with Leiper as to whether the embargo would produce a repeal of the British orders of council and, accordingly a "cessation of our embargo." "To nobody," he avowed, "will a repeal be so welcome as to myself." The benefits of such a step would be manifest. "Give us peace till our revenues are liberated from debt, and then, if war be necessary, it can be carried on without a new tax or a loan, and during peace *we may chequer our whole country with canals, roads, etc.* This is the object to which all our endeavors should be directed."[24]

True peace did not come. In his eighth annual message, his last, Jefferson returned to the theme of the second inaugural and the sixth annual messages. The eighth annual message was delivered in November 1808, when the course of events with Britain remained uncertain. Jefferson saved his domestic recommendations until the end of the message. He referred to the surplus, after application of revenues to government operations and reduction of the debt. The disposition of these surpluses when the "freedom and safety of our commerce shall be restored" merited the consideration of Congress. "Shall it lie unproductive in the public vaults? Shall the revenues be reduced?" he asked rhetorically. "Or shall it not rather be appropriated to the improvement of roads, canals, rivers, education and other great foundations of prosperity and union under the powers which

Congress may already possess or such amendment of the Constitution as may be approved by the States?" There was no doubt as to his answer. The recommendation he made was for preparatory action during the embargo period. *"While uncertain of the course of things, the time may be advantageously employed in obtaining the powers necessary for a system of improvement, should that be thought best."* This was his last recommendation. He followed with expressions of gratitude and graceful apologies.[25]

In the final months before his leave-taking, Jefferson had one further opportunity to clarify his views on the use of federal assistance for a "system of improvement." Those views remained consistent with those that he had expressed throughout his administration and those that he was to express after it. A Doctor Maese had written to him seeking his support for the federal chartering of, and federal assistance to, an institution for the advancement of the arts. Jefferson explained that his Republican party had always denied that the Constitution granted the power of incorporation; this had been the basis for his opposition to the the chartering of the bank. He further explained that the establishment of the bank had been sustained "on the argument of its being incident to the power . . . for raising money." As to federal assistance, he observed: "It is still more settled that among the purposes to which the Constitution permits them [Congress] to apply money, the granting of premiums or bounties is not enumerated, and there has never been a single instance of their doing it, although there has been a multiplicity of applications. The Constitution has left these encouragements to the separate States." Then he restated his own policy and legal position: "I have in two or three messages recommended an amendment to the Constitution, which should extend their power to these objects. But nothing is yet done in it. I fear, therefore, that the institution you propose must rest on the patronage of the State in which it is to be. I wish I could have answered you more to my own mind, as well as yours; but truth is the first object." This was his last expression as president, and it clearly stated his policy and constitutional views. It also clearly mirrored the central tension that those views reflected.[26]

THE CUMBERLAND ROAD

During Jefferson's second term, two actions took place that reflected the vision of internal growth and improvement that Jefferson portrayed in his annual messages and in his letters to Joel Barlow and Mr. Leiper. Neither was accompanied by the constitutional amendment that Jefferson thought necessary to authorize congressional legislation to establish a system of roads and canals.

First, Congress took the steps necessary for establishing the Cumberland Road. In the second session of the ninth Congress, by the Act of March 29, 1806, Congress authorized laying out a road from Cumberland, Maryland, to the Ohio River. The exact route was to be determined by a presidential commission, subject to the consent of the affected states. Congress provided an initial appropriation of $30,000 for planning and laying out the road.

Second, Congress directed the secretary of the treasury to prepare a report setting forth a comprehensive plan for a system of internal improvements, including roads and canals, that would bind the entire nation. Secretary Gallatin responded with an ambitious and comprehensive report that the president transmitted in April 1808. Congress did not act on this report during Jefferson's term, but it pointed the way toward a system of national improvements that would be implemented, on a piecemeal basis, by administrations that would follow. In both cases, the steps set precedents for the emergence of a substantial federal role in establishing internal improvements that evolved over the decades into the major federal participation, reflected in function 400 in today's modern federal budgets, with magnitudes of over $50 billion in annual appropriations, all accomplished without the constitutional amendment that Jefferson so earnestly sought in his sixth annual message and other communications.

Even before delivering that message, Jefferson signed the Cumberland Road measure, thereby enacting into law the Act of March 29, 1806. It is not entirely clear how the president that day squared his approval of the Cumberland Road legislation with his oft-repeated admonition that federal assistance for internal improvement projects, including roads, must be preceded by an appropriate constitutional amendment. Since the measure merely provided for planning, it may be that he thought his emphatic recommendations for an amendment, transmitted in both his second inaugural address and his sixth annual message, would resolve the situation if the plans matured into actual construction. On the other hand, he may have felt that, in this discrete circumstance, his duty ended with the making of the recommendation and that he should not disapprove progressive and necessary preparatory legislation merely because Congress had not sent an amendment to the states before adopting planning legislation that, in any event, required the consent of the states through which the road was to pass. Later, his successors would struggle, in a variety of ways, to harmonize this precedent with their own views of how the General Welfare authority should be interpreted.[27]

Having signed the Cumberland Road bill, Jefferson administered it without reservation and without public comment as to how it fit in with the overall vision of internal improvements that he was communicating in annual messages or otherwise, whenever his preoccupations with foreign policy, embargo, national defense, and other weighty issues permitted. Accordingly, on January 31, 1807, he duly reported to Congress that he had appointed the commissioners under the law, and he submitted to the tenth Congress a partial report of the progress of the commissioners. He further communicated that he had taken steps to procure consent from the states through which the road the commissioners proposed would pass. He reported that he had received it from Maryland and Virginia in the form of state legislation; Pennsylvania was still pondering. He observed: "Until I receive full consent to a free choice of route through the whole distance I have thought it safest neither to accept nor reject finally the partial report of the commissioners."

In February 1808, Jefferson again reported to Congress on the progress of the road. He announced that all three states had given their consent to the route and that he had approved of it as described in the commissioners' report, "as far as Brownsville, with a single deviation, since located, which carries it through Uniontown."[28] His ultimate aim was a line of communication from Washington to St. Louis.

Dumas Malone, in his biography of Jefferson, provides background on the deviation. A few weeks after Jefferson's report to Congress on January 31, 1807, the Pennsylvania legislature had given its consent to the route of the Cumberland Road but included in its consenting legislation a resolution that the routing include a deviation that would allow the road to pass through Uniontown and Washington, Pennsylvania, to accommodate local interests. Albert Gallatin, the secretary of the treasury, who had previously represented the district containing Washington in the House of Representatives, counseled deference to the Pennsylvania legislature's request with respect to Uniontown.[29] Jefferson noted the issue, among many others, in a letter to Gallatin, dated April 21, 1807.[30]

The question of Uniontown was settled by April 1807 and was, as we have seen, communicated in the February 1808 report to Congress. The question of the deviation to Washington, Pennsylvania, did not, however, go quite so easily. In April 1808, Jefferson again wrote to Gallatin on the subject. Jefferson had been advised that there would be legal opposition (presumably in Pennsylvania) to the road's passing in any other direction than through Washington if a good road could be established through that route. The advice had apparently stiffened his back on the second deviation and his insistence on federal prerogatives where federal funds were involved. He told Gallatin:

"I know my determination was not to yield to the example of a State's prescribing the direction of the road, and I understood the [federal] law as leaving the route ultimately to me. If I have misconstrued the law, I shall be sorry for the money spent on a misconstruction, but that loss will be a lesser evil to the United States than a single example of *yielding to the State the direction of a road made at the national expense and for national purposes.*" Jefferson curtly requested a copy of the law so that he could determine whether "we are really at liberty to pursue the route we have proposed, or must adopt another which shall not enter the State of Pennsylvania."[31]

Jefferson, champion of states' rights and the limited federal role, was, nevertheless, evidently ready to uphold federal authority when it came to the use of federal funds. The more direct and presumably less expensive federal route must prevail over a less efficient alternative imposed by the state; if the state wanted the federal assistance, it must accede to the federal condition; otherwise the federally assisted road would be routed in another direction. In this, Jefferson was succinctly and definitively anticipating standard federal assistance law that would be laid down by the Supreme Court 160 years later in *King v. Smith,* when it held, in a footnote, that state conditions, contrary to a federal-funding statute, must yield to the federal requirements if the state participates in the program.[32]

In August 1808, Jefferson pursued the matter with the road commissioners. Now in a somewhat more accommodating mood, he advised the commissioners that the route through Washington to Wheeling would be advantageous. He put it as follows: "The principal object of this road," he reminded them in a reference to the overall purpose of the law, was "communication directly westwardly." He observed, however, that if "inconsiderable deflections" from the course would "benefit particular places, and better accommodate travelers," these considerations could be taken into account. Because he had "a regard to the funds that remain," Jefferson directed the commissioners to examine the best route through Washington to the Ohio River—the one offering the most advantageous route to Chillicothe and Cincinnati—and report back to him. In December 1808, one of his last acts as president was to submit a further report on the progress of the Cumberland Road commissioners.[33]

Thus, Jefferson, with the aid and advice of his secretary of the treasury, navigated the rapids of a sensitive state-federal relationship in the context of an internal improvement initiative, funded with federal money under a federal appropriation and requiring state-federal cooperation within the framework of an unamended Constitution to provide for an express federal role in the area. The constitutional dilemma was not resolved by putting aside action on the Cumberland Road legislation as a minor matter.[34] That legislation, and the action taken under it or under legislation enacted to proceed with the project, established a precedent for later internal improvement legislation that could not be squared completely with the proposition that Congress could take no spending action for internal improvements without a constitutional amendment. Because no constitutional amendment was proposed, let alone adopted, the precedent forced succeeding presidents, including those who immediately followed Jefferson and adhered to his strict constructionist views, to struggle for satisfactory arguments to rationalize the distinction or departure that the Cumberland Road legislation seemed to represent. It also provided a convenient precedent for succeeding presidents, like John Quincy Adams, who fervently believed in internal improvements and took a more flexible view of the Constitution.

In short, while Jefferson steadfastly and consistently affirmed and reaffirmed his belief that the Constitution did not afford authority to spend for internal improvements and his belief that the General Welfare Clause was limited by the reach of the enumerated powers, Congress took no steps to provide for such an amendment. Consequently, when legislation reached his desk calling for the federal government to assist in the planning or routing of internal improvements, Jefferson's choice was to sign and execute or to veto and wait for an appropriate amendment. He chose the former. When Congress, through a Senate resolution called for a report on internal improvements, he could have declined to respond to the resolution until an amendment had been secured. Nevertheless he authorized (or permitted) his secretary of the treasury to prepare the report and transmitted it when it was ready, while at the same time reiterating his constitutional views when the occasion arose.

Thus he balanced principle and pragmatism in way that is essential in the day-to-day process of governing. In that balance, however, he laid the groundwork for the exercise and implementation of the constitutional spending power in ways that seemed inconsistent with his constitutional philosophy and that, over time and through countless subsequent exercises, gradually led to the modern state in which general welfare-human resource expenditures predominate. The observations of Kelly, Harbison, and Belz regarding Louisiana seem relevant here: "The significance of the Louisiana controversy, therefore, lies not in some supposed cynicism about constitutional principles that political expediency inspires, or even in the cautionary reminder that practice must temper theory. Rather it lies in the insight it offers into the development of a distinctively American form of constitutional politics, based on rhetoric and principles that have power to influence public opinion because they express fundamental values."[35]

Both in his attempts to propose a broad program of internal improvements, and in his administration of the internal improvement legislation which Congress provided him, Jefferson contributed to establishing a role for the United States in the encouragement of public enterprises he thought appropriate: transportation, education, agriculture, manufactures, exploration, and the arts. This role became even more imperative as a result of the signature success of his administration, the Louisiana Purchase. If these initiatives involved a compromise with his views on the strict construction of the Constitution, it was not because he abandoned those principles but because he was prepared to temper them when he thought that the greater good of the nation clearly compelled it.

6

Madison's Precept

JAMES MADISON'S FIRST INAUGURAL ADDRESS FOCUSED NOT ON internal improvements but on external crises and in particular on the continuing difficulties with Britain that the fourth president had inherited from his predecessor and political partner. Only after the ensuing War of 1812 ended could Madison focus on domestic concerns, including his view that federal financial assistance for internal improvement was justified by considerations of national growth and unity. When Congress heeded Madison's recommendation, made in his seventh annual message, but failed to propose a constitutional amendment to authorize such assistance, Madison, to the surprise and dismay of the bill's supporters, vetoed the measure. His Bonus Bill veto dramatized Madison's insistence that strict enumeration should not be weakened by a broad construction of the General Welfare Clause but bequeathed to Monroe the resolution of the underlying constitutional and infrastructure issues.[1]

INAUGURAL ADDRESS AND EARLY ANNUAL MESSAGES

The end of the embargo had left the United States in economic distress. The belligerent powers—France and Great Britain—continued their hostile actions on the high seas. Like Jefferson, Madison outlined in his inaugural address the policies that he would observe in his administration: friendly intercourse with all nations; neutrality with respect to belligerent powers; maintenance of the Union; support of the Constitution as the "cement" of the Union "in its limitations as in its authorities."[2]

With respect to federal domestic assistance, he confined himself to a phrase that reflected in general, if subdued, terms, the framework established by Jefferson. His administration's policy would be to promote "by authorized means improvements friendly to agriculture, to manufactures, and to external as well as internal commerce." He would also "favor in like manner the advancement of science and the diffusion of information as the best aliment to true liberty." He thus laid out the dual aspects of the Democratic-Republican position: support for internal improvements in a broad sense, but only if carried out by "*authorized means*." The limitations and authorities in the Constitution thus would be maintained. Subsequent events and the clouds of war deferred his ability to give effect to these principles until near the end of his administration.[3]

At first it appeared that Britain might modify its antagonistic policies. However, when the time arrived for Madison to deliver his first annual message in November 1809, that hope was fast fading. Britain was refusing to change policy in ways called for by the United States.[4] By later in 1810, matters with France had improved, but the difficulties with Britain continued. While deploring these circumstances in his second annual message, Madison found time to focus on two domestic areas that were to occupy him even during the period of conflict with Britain: infant industries and education. He observed, "To a thriving agriculture and the improvements related to it is added a highly interesting extension of useful manufactures, the combined product of professional occupations and of household industry."[5] Domestic manufactures were substituting for goods formerly imported but whose importation had been barred by Jefferson's embargo. The development, Madison insightfully observed, was "more than a recompense for those privations and losses resulting from foreign injustice which furnished the general impulse required for its accomplishment." Madison asked Congress to consider tariff legislation and other regulations to protect the infant industries thus established.[6]

To the question of education, he devoted even more attention. He enthusiastically reaffirmed his support of the proposal for a national university. His predecessors, notably Washington and Jefferson, had recommended the initiative on a number of occasions. Madison began by making the traditional case for government encouragement of education through a nationally supported seminary of learning in a single sentence: "Whilst it is universally admitted that a well-instructed people alone can be permanently a free people, and whilst it is evident that the means of diffusing and improving useful knowledge form so small a proportion of the expenditures for national purposes, I can not presume it to be unseasonable to invite your attention to the advantages of superadding to the means of education provided by the several States a seminary of learning instituted by the National Legislature *within the limits of their exclusive jurisdiction,* the expense of which might be defrayed out of the vacant grounds which have accrued to the nation within these limits."[7]

Thus Madison was renewing a proposal for a national university that he had made to the Constitutional Convention years before. The convention had rejected the proposal, but, at least one member, Gouverneur Morris, had suggested that the power of Congress to legislate for the federal city encompassed the authority, making specific language unnecessary. Madison was evidently taking comfort from that history in strongly renewing the proposal in his capacity as president, notwithstanding the serious foreign policy issues that absorbed him. In his message, Madison took pains to follow the proposal with a carefully worded rationale which reveals the importance with which he regarded federal investment in education:

> Such an institution, though local in its legal character, would be universal in its beneficial effects. By enlightening the opinions, by expanding the patriotism, and by assimilating the principles, the sentiments and the manners of those who might resort to this temple of science, to be redistributed in due time through every part of the community, sources of jealousy and prejudice would be diminished, the features of national character would be multiplied, and greater extent given to social harmony. But, above all, a well-constituted seminary in the center of the nation is recommended by the consideration that the additional instruction emanating from it would contribute not less to strengthen the foundations than to adorn the structure of our free and happy system of government.[8]

The availability of a constitutional base for this proposal gave Madison a rare opportunity to promote a federal initiative he cherished without the concern that he was proposing a legislative measure that the Constitution did not warrant. Freed of that constraint he could wax more eloquent on the desirability of a federal role in an aspect of "internal improvement" that he had always considered of paramount importance—education.

The Seventh Annual Message:
Federal Investment in a Time of Peace

Madison's preoccupation with the conduct of the War of 1812 prevented him from focusing substantially upon domestic policy and the role of the General Welfare Clause in supporting federal assistance for internal improvements as an aspect of domestic policy.[9] The signing of the Treaty of Ghent, which formally ended the war in February 1815, left Madison free to return to these issues. He did so with energy and unfeigned enthusiasm in his seventh annual state of the union message, transmitted to Congress in December of 1815.[10]

The message was framed and delivered in a decidedly upbeat period for the administration. The War of 1812 had been brought to a successful conclusion, despite the frustrations and setbacks that had taken place during the hostilities, including the occupation of Washington and the burning of the White House. The battle of New Orleans, fought after the treaty was signed, had delivered a clear-cut, if after-the-fact, military victory to the United States. The nation had vindicated itself in war against a European power superior in numbers and arms. United States maritime and commercial interests would now be protected. Europe would not interfere with its freedom to grow economically and to occupy, domesticate, and integrate as states the vast territories acquired during the Jefferson administration.

With victory had come renewed prosperity in the summer of 1815. Faith in the government, sorely tried during the war, had been restored. With it came a new measure of admiration and affection for Madison who had played so profound and meaningful a role in creating the nation and who had served it so long and so faithfully. The president and the nation he led could look to ways to enhance its internal strength. Now it was time for Madison to address matters of domestic policy. The seventh annual message would constitute his vehicle for doing so.

During the summer of 1815, Madison started to plan his message. A period of respite at his beloved Montpelier worked to his advantage. There, in the comfort of his well-appointed home surrounded by fine gardens, he had time to consider the direction it should take and to consult with members of his cabinet on early drafts.[11] The resulting message "brimmed with optimism." Madison began with an account of events leading to the termination of the war and recommendations about national defense, including proposals for the support of war veterans, particularly those who had been wounded. The president further recommended enlarging the military academy, classifying and organizing the militia so as to improve its effectiveness, and strengthening the navy.[12]

While he generally favored low tariffs, Madison also mentioned the need for protecting infant industries whose manufacturing activities were related to agriculture. In advancing this policy, he had the national defense foremost in mind. "In selecting the branches more especially entitled to the public patronage a preference is obviously claimed by such as will relieve the United States from a dependence on foreign supplies, ever subject to casual failures, for articles necessary for the public defense or connected with the primary wants of individuals." But initiatives that would add to the "great fund of national prosperity and independence," particularly in agriculture, were also to be favored.[13]

Within this expansive framework, Madison next turned to internal improvements. His recommendations clearly indicate that he recognized them as an imperative in an expanding American economy. His vision included a role for the federal government in supporting their development. He said, "Among the means of advancing the public interest the occasion is a proper one for recalling the attention of Congress to the great importance of establishing throughout our country *the roads and canals which can best be executed under the national authority*. No objects within the circle of political economy so richly repay the expense bestowed on them; there are none the utility of which is more universally ascertained and acknowledged; none that do more honor to the governments whose wise and enlarged patriotism duly appreciates them." The United States, he believed, was now an appropriate locus for the application of these benefits. "Nor is there any country," he said, "which presents a field where nature invites more the art of man to complete her own work for his accommodation and benefit."[14]

That this policy would bestow a political, as well as an economic, benefit was clear. "These considerations are strengthened, moreover," he continued, "by the political effect of these facilities for intercommunication in bringing and binding more closely together the various parts of our extended confederacy." He had in mind, no doubt, not only the admonitions of Washington and Jefferson, but also the enlargement of the nation that the Louisiana Purchase had effected. Adequate facilities for transportation in the "extended confederacy" had become an absolute necessity for national growth.

After making the case for internal improvements, Madison thoughtfully articulated the justification of a federal role. "Whilst the States individually, with a laudable enterprise and emulation, avail themselves of their local advantages by new roads, by navigable canals, and by improving the streams susceptible of navigation, the General Government is the more urged to similar undertakings, requiring *a national jurisdiction and national means*, by the prospect of thus systematically completing so inestimable a work." Clearly, he envisaged a federal role, complementary to and concurrent with that of the states, as a matter of policy and expediency.¹⁵

He saved for last, and perhaps soft-pedaled, the traditional Democratic-Republican caveat: the need for a constitutional amendment to provide a legal underpinning for all these progressive initiatives. He put it with great delicacy so as not to undercut or negate his policy recommendation: "[I]t is a happy reflection that any defect of constitutional authority which may be encountered can be supplied in a mode which the Constitution itself has providently pointed out."¹⁶ The admonition may have been so low-key as to have been lost on its audience. When, in 1817, Congress passed a bill to provide funding for roads and canals, Madison vetoed it on the ground that it was not accompanied by the requisite constitutional amendment.

The seventh annual message also contained another recommendation for a funding initiative that Madison did not tie to the need for constitutional change. As he had done five years earlier, Madison included a plea for the funding of a national seminary of learning to be located in the nation's capital. The proposal echoed similar recommendations made by Madison himself during the constitutional convention, by Washington in both his first and last annual message, as well as by Jefferson, albeit in somewhat broader terms. For his part, Madison accompanied the proposal with a carefully worded rationale, comparable to that in his earlier message on the subject: "Such an institution claims the patronage of Congress as a monument of their solicitude for the advancement of knowledge, without which the blessings of liberty can not be fully enjoyed or long preserved; as a model instructive in the formation of other seminaries; as a nursery of enlightened preceptors, and as a central resort of youth and genius from every part of their country, diffusing on their return examples of those national feelings, those liberal sentiments, and those congenial manners which contribute cement to our Union and strength to the great political fabric of which that is the foundation."¹⁷

In so stating Madison not only closely reflected the views of his predecessors in their support for a national university; he added his own perspective. What seems significant is that in both his proposals for internal improvement and higher education, Madison saw, as a central purpose, the binding together—and thus the preservation—of the union. In the case of education, he added the rationale that federal aid to a national institution would assist in the establishment of a model for other institutions of higher education in the states, as well as a training ground for instructors who would then fan out in the country and strengthen private or state institutions—an early form of federally assisted professional development.

The two proposals differed in that Madison did not append to his recommendation regarding the national university an observation regarding the need for a constitutional amendment. Evidently, this was because the proposal was for a university (seminary of learning) to be established in the seat of government over which Congress had plenary authority. Accordingly, the use of the spending power to assist the university would be within the constitutional theory advocated by both Jefferson and Madison: spending under Article I, section 8, clause 1 could be authorized, without a constitutional amendment, because it related to a specific power of Congress. It seems reasonable to surmise that this consideration influenced Madison's thinking in renewing a proposal that he had first made in 1787 and relieved him of the necessity to discuss the constitutionality of federal assistance to education, while at the same time he was obliged to take up that issue in the case of the broader recommendation for internal improvements.

Robert Alan Rutland has noted the near universal appeal of Madison's message. "There was something in Madison's message for everybody except the old Republicans, who hated taxes, hated debt, and wanted the 'general welfare' clause of the Constitution squeezed dry." Political reaction to the message varied. Purist Jeffersonians attacked it as a reversion to Hamiltonism and as moving in a direction of enhanced federal power. That reaction failed to take into account the true significance of the message. Ralph Ketcham describes the political fall out in terms that convey the essence of Madison's public investment policy:

> To "Old Republicans" in Congress, the President's message, and the nationalistic fervor of Calhoun and others upholding it, was a complete surrender to Federalism. John Randolph of Roanoke, back in Congress after a two-year absence, declared that the President "out Hamiltons Alexander Hamilton.". . . What Randolph . . . failed to grasp, however, was that though Madison had a keen sense of the limiting character of the Constitution and a conviction that generally government, especially at the national level, ought to be "mild" and

shun self-aggrandizement, he did not make dogma of either strict construction or laissez-faire. These were respectively Southern states' rights and late nineteenth century business fixations wholly subordinated in Madison's view to the far more important question of finding the structure and use of government best suited to a prosperous, happy, and free people.

As Rutland puts it, "This president had decided that the war had exposed the shortcomings of a nickel-and-dime democracy, and he was anxious to hail reforms in national defense, banking, transportation, and education. Madison was not trying to stand time-honored Republican doctrine on its head, but he realized the country had gone beyond that struggling Republic of 1787."[18]

Thus, with war at end and the survival of the nation assured, Madison's turning inward toward domestic concerns and national growth reflected a high priority for proposals to expand facilities of internal improvement and institutions of higher learning. Both of these initiatives could be aided with federal funds, as a matter of national policy. In this Madison was not merely advancing the political thought of his immediate predecessor, Jefferson. He was adding to it his own conviction and his own keen sense of the direction in which the nation should move.

Toward the end of his presidency, Madison had come to the conclusion that federal assistance for internal improvements was consistent with the architecture that he had helped to erect thirty years earlier. Federal aid could constitute a useful component of that structure, if properly authorized. What was needed to reconcile this enhancement of authority with the basic charter was an amendment to the Constitution to confirm that the people favored this extension of national power. In this context the seventh message reflected a careful balancing of progressive policy formulation and constitutional constraint. The absence of that amendment was to prove critical when Madison was confronted with a bill that responded to his bold recommendations of 1815.

In his final annual message, transmitted after the election of Monroe in 1816, Madison contented himself with a passing reference to his earlier recommendations for internal improvement and education. As to the latter, he observed: "The importance which I have attached to the establishment of a university within this District on a scale and for objects worthy of the American nation induces me to renew my recommendation of it to the favorable consideration of Congress." He also called Congress's attention to "the expediency of exercising their existing powers, and, where necessary, of resorting to the prescribed mode of enlarging them, in order to effectuate a comprehensive system of roads and canals, such as will have the effect of drawing more closely together every part of our country by promoting intercourse and improvements and by increasing the share of every part in the common stock of national prosperity."[19]

The Bonus Bill Veto: The Last Official Testament of a Framer President

With early 1817 came preparations for the president's return to private life. In a letter written in mid-February of that year to his friend, Jefferson, he complained about "[t]he severe weather [which] unites with the winding up of my public business in retarding the preparations during the session of Congress. . . ." Almost as an aside, he mentioned to Jefferson that another bill had gone to the Senate which he had not seen. He described it as "of a very extraordinary character, if it has been rightly stated to me." He continued: "The object of it, is to compass by law only an authority over roads and Canals. It is said the Senate are not likely to concur in the project; whether from an objection to the principle or to the expediency of it, is uncertain."[20]

The bill in question was the internal improvements legislation that Madison had recommended in his seventh annual message. It pledged the proceeds of a bonus generated by the Bank of the United States in connection with the extension of the Bank's charter to be used for the construction of roads and canals. It was thus referred to as the Bonus Bill. It arrived on the president's desk four days before he was to leave office. It was delivered, however, without the constitutional amendment that Madison had indicated, however circumspectly, was necessary to support the legislation. Madison alerted John C. Calhoun and other allies in Congress that he planned to veto the measure as unconstitutional. Surprised and dismayed, Henry Clay, a supporter of the measure, urged him to leave the matter for his successor.[21]

The president declined to follow Clay's advice. He "relished the opportunity too much . . . to duck the issue." Madison accompanied his veto with a message that clearly outlined his thinking. His problem with the measure lay in its constitutionality, not its expediency. The bill provided federal funding for roads and canals and for improving the navigation of water courses. Madison began his veto message by stating that he was "constrained by the insuperable difficulty ... in reconciling the bill with the Constitution of the United States to return it with that objection to the House of Representatives, in which it originated." Madison then turned to the basis for his objection: "The legislative powers vested in Congress are specified and enumerated in the eighth section of the first article of the Constitution," he continued, "and it does not appear that the power proposed to be exercised by the bill is among the enumerated powers, or that it falls by any just interpretation within the power to make laws necessary and proper for carrying into execution those or other powers vested by the Constitution in the Government of the United States."[22]

He quickly brushed aside the argument that the bill could be sustained under the Interstate Commerce Clause. The power to regulate commerce among the States did not include a power to construct roads and canals and improve the navigation of rivers. To so construe the clause would involve "a latitude of construction departing from the ordinary import of the terms strengthened by the known inconveniences which doubtless led to the grant of this remedial power to Congress." His views were in keeping with Jefferson's concern regarding the use of the Commerce Clause to sustain public works appropriations for piers, less so with Jefferson's use of that clause to support the Lewis and Clark Expedition.

When Madison turned to the General Welfare Clause, he provided the analysis that he and Jefferson had applied since Hamilton had first proposed a broad reading of that provision in the *Report on Manufactures* twenty-five years earlier: "To refer the power in question to the clause 'to provide for the common defense and general welfare' would be contrary to the established and consistent rules of interpretation, as rendering the special and careful enumeration of powers which follow the clause nugatory and improper." Given the significance of the Bonus Bill veto to this account, the following paragraphs describe in detail the thrust of Madison's thinking about the General Welfare Clause as expressed in the accompanying veto message.

Here, Madison's concern, as it had been before, was with the effect of such an interpretation. "Such a view of the Constitution would have the effect of giving to Congress a general power of legislation instead of the defined and limited one hitherto understood to belong to them, the terms 'common defense and general welfare' embracing every object and act within the purview of a legislative trust." Its effect would be magnified by the Supremacy

Clause. "Such a view of the Constitution, finally, would have the effect of excluding the judicial authority of the United States from its participation in guarding the boundary between the legislative powers of the General and the State Governments, inasmuch as questions relating to the general welfare, being questions of policy and expediency, are unsusceptible of judicial cognizance and decision."

That the general welfare authority was confined to the appropriation of funds did not sway Madison here, as it had not in the past. "A restriction of the power to 'provide for the common defense and general welfare' to cases which are to be provided for by the expenditure of money would still leave within the legislative power of Congress all the great and most important measures of Government, money being the ordinary and necessary means of carrying them into execution." Gaining the assent of States to the projects would not cure the defect. "The only cases in which the consent and cession of particular States can extend the power of Congress are those specified and provided for in the Constitution."

Finally, Madison made it clear that his objection was based on the Constitution, not on the policy or *expediency* of using federal funds for internal improvements. This was only consistent with his messages on the subject. "I am not unaware of the great importance of roads and canals, and the improved navigation of water courses," he told Congress, "and that a power in the National Legislature to provide for them might be exercised with signal advantage to the general prosperity." But his fidelity to the constitutional principles that he was espousing precluded him from letting the policy advantages prevail. The following observation, in a sense a valedictory, summarizes the view that Madison had held during his public life and the view that he would continue to maintain during his retirement: "But seeing that such a power is not expressly given by the Constitution and believing that it can not be deduced from any part of it without an inadmissible latitude of construction and a reliance on insufficient precedents; believing also that the permanent success of the Constitution depends on a definite partition of powers between the General and the State Governments, and that no adequate landmarks would be left by the constructive extension of the powers of Congress as proposed in the bill, I have no option but to withhold my signature from it...."

He closed, however, by noting that he "cherish[ed] the hope that [the bill's] beneficial objects may be attained by a resort for the necessary powers to the same wisdom and virtue in the nation which established the Constitution in its actual form and providently marked out in the instrument itself a safe and practicable mode of improving it as experience might suggest."²³

Balancing National Growth with Constitutional Constraint

Congress may have been less convinced than Madison as to the need for such an amendment, believing that the Constitution already authorized internal improvement legislation. One factor that may have been influential was the availability of an alternative interpretation of the General Welfare Clause. Hamilton had urged that the General Welfare Clause could be read broadly *without an amendment* to support initiatives to promote the general welfare, including federal assistance to aid manufactures and agriculture. Moreover, some internal improvement legislation had been enacted and implemented prior to 1817 without a preceding constitutional amendment. This was the Cumberland Road legislation enacted in 1806 during Jefferson's second term. Congress may have therefore recognized that the internal improvement issue could be addressed without a constitutional amendment. Despite the recommendations of Jefferson and Madison and despite Madison's dramatic veto of the Bonus Bill, as matters unfolded, Congress did not hasten to propose the type of enhancement to the Constitution that Madison called for in his veto message.

In that message, Madison had publicly articulated his definitive view as to the limited reach of the General Welfare Clause. Moreover, he had backed up that view by vetoing a popular measure. His action was not the product of sudden impulse or limited reflection. Despite the surprise that Henry Clay expressed about Madison's action, the views that Madison expressed in the veto message reflected principles that he had advocated firmly during the thirty years that separated his service in the Constitutional Convention and the delivery to his desk of the Bonus Bill. His message was consistent with the position that he had taken in "Federalist No. 41." It also was consistent with the view he had taken in 1791 in opposing Hamilton's interpretation, in the *Report on Manufactures*, that the General Welfare Clause was not limited to spending to implement the enumerated powers. Finally, it was consistent with the position that his friend, political ally, and mentor, Jefferson, had taken in his sixth annual message that a constitutional amendment must precede internal improvements legislation. If members of Congress were surprised by the veto, Madison himself was astounded that any one might be unaware of his long-held position on the matter, although he later conceded that he may have expressed his reservations in 1815 in too low-key a manner. Rutland has observed, "In rejecting the bonus bill . . . Madison wanted to establish a presidential precedent of constitutional stewardship." So wrote Ralph Ketcham in his biography of Madison which summarizes the significance of the veto in the following terms: "Though to Clay and others Madison's last-minute scrupulousness was painful and unnecessary, the retiring President considered it an important 'last testament' in favor of exactly the form of limited republican government he had just praised in his annual message as responsible for the free, prosperous state of the nation. . . . Madison meant to make clear that truly republican, truly federal government had to remain in vital ways 'defined and limited.' To maintain this quality was to Madison a far more relevant kind of consistency than mere rigidity."[24]

In this light, however, the Bonus Bill veto may be thought by some to brand Madison as an enemy of federal assistance in such areas as transportation and education, to characterize him as believing that initiatives in such areas would be inherently inconsistent with the practice of federalism by the United States as he had helped to structure it, however the Constitution might read. This is not the case. As the veto message and the seventh annual message that preceeded it make clear, Madison, like Jefferson, supported the use of federal funds to assist internal improvements in the form of roads and canals, *as a matter of policy*. The construction of these forms of improvement, with the help of the central government, constituted a positive investment in nation-building. Indeed, Madison argued that, while state and local efforts were an essential foundation, the success of the internal improvements enterprise *required* a "national jurisdiction" and "national means." "Systematic completion" of that enterprise called for a federal aid and a federal presence. A coherent transportation system for the United States demanded a federal role. These themes, enunciated in the seventh annual message in 1815, were not abandoned two years later in the Bonus Bill veto in which Madison, while refusing to sign the legislation, recognized the "signal advantage to the general prosperity" of such legislation. Indeed, in putting forward these policy considerations, Madison was consistent with the positions that he had taken over a lifetime of public service.

It was therefore, for the Father of the Constitution, not a subversion of federalism to apply federal funds to internal improvements. Nor was it inherently inconsistent with the federal system to apply federal funds to educational pursuits in the form of a national university based in the nation's capital over which Congress had plenary legislative authority. But first there must be a constitutional amendment to preserve the integrity of that basic charter where clear constitutional authority was lacking, as Madison believed it was in the case of internal improvement legislation. In order that the federal government remain "defined and limited," the authority of Congress must be redefined to include a power over roads and canals. This done, federalism could coexist with federal aid in these areas because the Constitution would expressly provide for it. Moreover, the extension of federal authority into the funding of road and canal projects, desirable as it was, would not constitute a precedent for extension into other areas through interpretation rather than amendment. The principle of popular government would be served because the people would first approve extension through the process of constitutional ratification. This done, Congress could embark safely upon road and canal-building initiatives without harm to constitutional values. A role for Congress in the area would be consistent with the federative principle. The "reconciliation of public strength with individual liberty," of which Madison spoke in his last annual message, then would have been accomplished in the internal-improvement sphere.

The veto message on the Bonus Bill was signed on March 3, 1817. Despite Clay's support, the House attempt to override the veto failed by a vote of 60 yeas, to 56 nays. Madison learned of it on his return to Montpelier. On March 4, 1817, James Monroe took the oath of office.[25]

7
Monroe's Turn

THE EFFORTS OF THOMAS JEFFERSON AND JAMES MADISON TO PERsuade Congress and the country to adopt a constitutional amendment that would define the scope of the spending power to include internal improvements failed. It fell to their ally, compatriot and successor, James Monroe, to craft a compromise that would maintain their vision of a limited central government but allow that government sufficient flexibility to assist in the maintenance and expansion of internal improvements. At first Monroe sought to cajole Congress into adopting an amendment through a more direct and urgent recommendation than Madison had first tendered. When it became clear that Congress would not oblige, Monroe vetoed the internal-improvement bill it sent him and instead provided a comprehensive guide as to his constitutional thinking.

This took the form of a lengthy memorandum in which Monroe concluded that Congress had authority under the Constitution to appropriate funds which states could use for internal improvements but Congress could not establish a national system of internal improvements under federal jurisdiction. While gossamer-like, the compromise permitted Monroe to sign internal-improvement legislation that made available federal funds to be used for repair of the Cumberland Road and for a nationwide survey of internal improvement needs. Monroe's compromise in effect abandoned the position that a General Welfare Clause appropriation could be used solely to implement the enumerated powers. It made Article I, section 8, clause 1—the General Welfare Clause—the source of a broadened national spending power that could be used to support appropriations for a wide array of national purposes through federal financial assistance to states and state bodies. This compromise paved the way for a succession of legislative enactments that provided a basis for a broad interpretation of the General Welfare Clause upon which the twenty-first century spending power is ultimately grounded.

Initial Efforts to Resolve the Internal Improvement Impasse

Monroe confronted the thorny issue that Madison had bequeathed to him early and head-on. In his first annual message in December 1817, he candidly confessed his firm conviction that Congress lacked the right to establish a system of internal improvement. Like Madison, he strongly recommended a constitutional amendment to solve the problem. His proposal for such an amendment embraced not only traditional internal improvements but authority to establish "seminaries of learning" as well.[1]

Writing from retirement, James Madison blessed this strategy in a way that makes transparent his oft-maintained policy of support for both types of public investment initiatives, within the framework of his constitutional concerns:

> The *expediency of vesting in Congress* a power as to roads and canals I have never doubted, and there has never been a moment when such a proposition to the States was so likely to be approved. A *general* power to establish seminaries being less obvious, and affecting more the equilibrium of influence between the National and State Governments, is a more critical experiment. The feelings awakened by the proposed University within the Congressional District are a proof of the opposition which may be looked for. I should consider it as at least essential that the two propositions, whatever may be the modification of the latter, should be so distinct, that the rejection of the one by the States should not be inconsistent with the adoption of the other.[2]

Monroe continued to reflect on the troublesome issue in his correspondence with Madison. On December 22, shortly after the annual message, he evidently queried Madison about the possible role of the Cumberland Road as a precedent for claiming an authority to establish roads and canals. Madison responded promptly but somewhat lamely on December 27, explaining, as best he could, his recollection of the events surrounding Jefferson's approval of the measure: "The Cumberland road having been a measure taken during the administration of Mr. Jefferson, and, as far as I recollect, not then brought to my particular attention, I cannot assign the grounds assumed for it by Congress, or which produced his sanction. I suspect that the question of Constitutionality was but slightly, if at all, examined by the former, and that the Executive assent was doubtingly or hastily given." Given the energy that both Jefferson and Madison had invested in the contest over the General Welfare Clause, this explanation seems rather surprising. Also surprising is Madison's further observation that appropriations for the Cumberland Road had become habitual. "Having once become a law, and being a measure of singular utility, additional appropriations took place, of course, under the same Administration, and, with the accumulated impulse thence derived, were continued under the succeeding one, with less of critical investigation, perhaps, than was due to the case."[3]

This account suggests that Madison found the circumstances of Jefferson's approval of the Cumberland Road legislation somewhat difficult to explain and potentially inconsistent with his long-held position on the Constitution, particularly since it had first arisen in an administration in which he had played a key role, headed by a president who maintained the same view on the issue that was prominently expressed in successive annual messages. Madison was, no doubt, aware that the Cumberland Road precedent would be argued vigorously by proponents of internal-improvement legislation adopted without a constitutional amendment. Accordingly, the retired president gamely sought to distinguish the cases on principled grounds.

"Be all this as it may," he told his successor, seeking to dampen any adverse implication that might arise from the precedent, "the case is distinguished from that now before Congress by the circumstances." First, the Cumberland road was undertaken "for the accommodation of a portion of the country with respect to which Congress have a general power not applicable to other portions." Presumably, this was a reference to the congressional power over territories. Second, "the funds appropriated . . . were under a general power of Congress, not applicable to other funds," presumably a reference to the territories clause.[4]

In an effort to escalate the conflict in March of 1818, Henry Clay launched a bitter personal attack on the president for his internal-improvement policies. He criticized Monroe for expressing a view on the constitutionality of internal-improvement legislation before Congress had an opportunity to enact it. He also complained about the president's failure to provide substantive legal arguments to support his position on the lack of Constitutional authority to support internal improvements. The session of the Congress ended without action on Virginia Senator James Barbour's proposal for a constitutional amendment as Monroe had recommended. It seemed clear that Congress was not prepared to heed Monroe's advice in his inaugural address. Indeed, Congress and the president were at an impasse on the subject; despite Clay's opposition to the Bonus Bill veto, the House in 1817 had been unable to muster the necessary two-thirds vote to override the veto and pass the bill. On the other hand, at least a majority voted in opposition to the veto, suggesting that a two-thirds vote to propose an amendment to the Constitution, as Madison and Monroe advocated, would not be available. In light of this impasse, some compromise seemed necessary if internal improvement, so necessary to national growth in an expanding nation, were to advance.[5]

Perhaps prompted by these considerations or stung by Clay's critique, Monroe quietly proceeded to prepare a lengthly memorandum setting forth his legal views on the issue. The president originally intended to share this memorandum with Congress when he delivered his third annual message in late 1819. However, Secretary of State John Quincy Adams and other members of the cabinet dissuaded him from doing so, believing that Monroe's views would receive no better treatment in the Sixteenth Congress than they had from its predecessor. Adams concluded that it was a "moral certainty" that Congress would not act on an amendment. Deferring to his cabinet, Monroe filed the memorandum for possible future use.[6]

The issue arose again in his second term in a way that demanded an executive determination. In May 1822, Congress presented to Monroe for his signature a bill entitled, "An act for the preservation and repair of the Cumberland road." Monroe characterized it as legislation affording Congress "a power to establish turnpikes with gates and tolls, and to enforce the collection of tolls by penalties." He perceived it as legislation that implied Congress's ability to exercise "a power to adopt and execute a complete system of internal improvement." Monroe therefore vetoed it, describing his reasons in a brief message.[7] He began this message by first explaining that—as he understood it—the right to impose duties on persons passing over the road also involved the right to take land from the proprietor and to pass laws for the protection of the road. If that right existed for the Cumberland Road then, by extension, it existed for all roads that Congress might establish. In short, Monroe saw the measure before him as constituting "*a complete right of jurisdiction and sovereignty* for all the purposes of internal improvement." It did not constitute "*merely the right of applying money* under the power vested in Congress to make appropriations under which power, with the consent of the States through which this road passes, the work was originally commenced, and has been so far executed."[8]

After determining that the Constitution contained no specific grant of power that would justify the legislation presented to him, Monroe—like Madison before him—felt he had no choice about vetoing the bill. He apologized that his message did not include a longer, more formal recitation of his reasons. Monroe then reminded his audience that, since his first annual message where he had communicated his views on the subject and recommended a curative amendment to the Constitution, his "attention [had] often been drawn to the subject." From time to time, he had "committed [his] sentiments" on the matter "to paper." The paper to which he referred was not then in a form intended for Congress, for it had not been completed. Nevertheless he was prepared to send it and promised to do so no later than the following Monday. The document he promised and sent on May 4 was the same document that he had prepared in 1819 but filed away. As in the case of the Bonus Bill veto, the vote to override failed, 68 yeas to 72 nays.[9]

THE MONROE MEMORANDUM: FRAMING THE PROBLEM

The memorandum to which Monroe referred in his veto message and which he sent to Congress to explain the reasoning that undergirded that message was entitled, "Views of the President of the United States on the Subject of Internal Improvements." It is a lengthy, thoroughly reasoned document in the form of a legal memorandum. Monroe carefully and comprehensively set forth the legal arguments to support his position that Congress lacked the authority to establish a national system of internal improvements. It also set forth Monroe's evolving view of the General Welfare Clause in Article l, section 8, clause 1, and broke new ground in the interpretation of that clause.[10]

The Monroe Memorandum constitutes the most comprehensive legal discussion of the General Welfare Clause by a sitting president that I have been able to uncover. Moreover, it represents the views of the last president who came to prominence in the revolutionary era and who was a contemporary, friend, and political ally of Madison, as well as of Jefferson and others among the founding fathers. For these reasons, the views expressed therein by Monroe, as Justice Cardozo so nicely put it years later in *Helvering v. Davis*, are "entitled to weight."[11]

Monroe's Perspective on the Origins of the Constitution

As Monroe perceived it, the Constitution had been been adopted to remedy "all defects of the Confederation." It had "succeeded beyond any calculation that could have been formed of any human institution." Monroe explained and then proceeded to capture the essence of the Constitution's central role, as he perceived it. "[T]he great office of the Constitution, by incorporating the people of the several States to the extent of its powers into one community and enabling it to act directly on the people, was to annul the powers of the State governments to that extent, except in cases where they were concurrent, and to preclude their agency in giving effect to those of the General Government. The Government of the United States relies on its own means for the execution of its powers, as the State governments do for the execution of theirs. . . ." Thus, "were two separate and independent governments established over our Union, one for local purposes over each State by people of the State, the other for national purposes over all the States by the people of the United States."[12]

Monroe's Inventory of Federal and State Powers

As an initial step in addressing the issue of congressional power regarding internal improvements, Monroe inventoried all of the constitutional powers of the general government and of the states. The powers of the states were difficult to delineate because they were contained in the various state constitutions which Monroe did not undertake to summarize. Instead, he contented himself with several observations. In general, the territory within each state belonged to the state rather than the United States, except where cessions had been made to the United States. "The militia are the militia of the several States; lands are held under the laws of the States; descents, contracts and all the concerns of private property, the administration of justice, and the whole criminal code, except in cases of breaches of the laws of the United States made under and in conformity with the powers vested in Congress and of the laws of nations, are regulated by State laws." This enumeration, Monroe declared, demonstrated "the great extent of the powers of the State governments."

Returning to the powers of Congress, Monroe illustrated their extent and limitation by a reference to the power to declare war, perhaps the "most important power." If war were declared, Congress could lay taxes, raise armies, call forth the militia, seize and sell lands if taxes were not paid. However, once the war ended, the militia would return to the state involved; the lands sold would remain in the hands of the purchasers subject to state laws. The power in Congress was a power to perform certain acts which, while touching the states, did not disturb the great body of power reposed in the states.[13]

Monroe's Statement of the Internal Improvements Issue

After providing this framework, Monroe turned to an examination of the central question to which the memorandum was addressed, namely, "whether the power to adopt and execute a system of internal improvements by roads and canals has been vested in the United States." To consider this question adequately, Monroe felt compelled to describe in detail how such a power would be carried out if it existed. He hypothesized how the federal government might operate if it possessed such a power; for example it might build a road from Washington to Baltimore and a canal to connect the Chesapeake with the Delaware. It could appoint commissioners to establish a route and acquire the ground over which the road and canal would run. This would be done through land purchases or condemnation, if necessary.

Once laid out, the road and canal would have to be repaired and protected from damage and vandalism. Congress would have to pass laws to punish offenders and establish turnpikes with gates and tolls to defray the expense of improvement and repair. The power had to extend to all these objects in order to be credible. Moreover, legal challenges could arise at any point, when the Federal Government sought to acquire land or when it sought to punish those who transgressed against the road or canal. Judicial challenge to the power would inevitably arise in these contexts or in others if states challenged the authority. In brief, Monroe portrayed a Federal Government as exercising plenary jurisdiction over the internal improvement—the road or canal—in question.[14]

Did anything in the Constitution confer such broad jurisdiction? Monroe read the Constitution's power to establish post-roads as no more than a power to fix the routes by which mail should pass rather than a power to build and establish the roads themselves. The right to declare war, he reasoned, did not include the power to establish roads throughout the United States that might be used for military purposes; were it otherwise, the war power would give the United States plenary power over the entire territory of the nation. Monroe saw the power to regulate interstate commerce as designed to end the commercial conflicts between individual states and to preclude the imposition by states of duties on commercial intercourse between the states, not as a broad grant of power to construct internal improvements to aid commerce. Tracing the relevant measures that had been proposed under the confederation and that had led to the formation of the Constitutional convention, Monroe concluded that none of them had involved "the subject of internal improvement."[15]

THE GENERAL WELFARE CLAUSE: SPENDING NOT REGULATORY POWER

This comprehensive discussion brought Monroe to the core of his analysis: consideration of the spending power. Monroe interpreted the second part of this grant, the part which authorized Congress "to pay the debts and provide for the common defense and general welfare of the United States," as a "right to appropriate the public money and nothing more."[16]

At the outset, Monroe felt compelled to refute the old contention that the General Welfare authority constituted a power to regulate or legislate with respect to the general welfare independent of the power to appropriate. "This part of the grant," he said, "has none of the characteristics of a distinct and original power." Monroe characterized the spending power as follows: "It is manifestly incidental to the great objects of the first part of the grant, which authorizes Congress to lay and collect taxes, duties, imposts, and excises, a power of vast extent, not granted by the Confederation, the grant of which formed one of the principal inducements to the adoption of this Constitution." He then made explicit his view that the phrase "to provide for the general welfare of the United States" qualified the taxing power and did not constitute an independent regulatory power:

> If both parts of the grant are taken together (as they must be, for the one follows immediately after the other in the same sentence), it

seems to be impossible to give to the latter any other construction than that contended for. Congress shall have power to lay and collect taxes, duties, imposts and excises. For what purpose? To pay the debts and provide for the common defense and general welfare of the United States, an arrangement and phraseology which clearly shows that *the latter part of the clause was intended to enumerate the purposes to which the money thus raised might be appropriated.*[17]

If this was not the proper construction, then the General Welfare Clause either had no meaning at all or it would have an import much greater than the taxing power itself. Neither option was acceptable. The first was untenable because "no part of the Constitution can be considered useless; no sentence or clause in it without a meaning." The second option was untenable because it would be absurd to ascribe to the second part of the clause greater power than the first as a matter of drafting practice. Moreover, if the General Welfare Clause were construed as more than a power to appropriate money, it would "[convey] a power of indefinite and unlimited extent" that would have obviated the need for the other enumerated powers that followed: "An unqualified power to pay the debts and provide for the common defense and general welfare, as the second part of this clause would be if considered as a distinct and separate grant, would extend to every object in which the public could be interested. . . . a right to provide for the general welfare. . . . would, in effect, break down all the barriers between the States and the General Government and consolidate the whole under the latter."[18]

Continuing, Monroe elaborated on this point. If the General Welfare Clause were construed as more than a power to appropriate money, the enumerated powers would be eliminated. On the other hand, if construed as Monroe contended, then every part would have an important meaning and effect: "A power to lay and collect taxes, duties, imposts and excises subjects to the call of Congress every branch of the public revenue, internal and external, and the addition to pay the debts and provide for the common defense and general welfare gives the right of applying the money raised—that is, of appropriating it to the purposes specified according to a proper construction of the terms."[19]

The Nature of the Power to Appropriate

The appropriation of money was different. In and of itself, it did not withdraw power from the states, as Monroe saw it. "[T]he use or application of money after it is raised is a power altogether of a different character. It imposes no burden on the people, nor can it act on them in a sense to take power from the States in any sense in which power can be controverted, or become a question between the two Governments." He conceded that the right to appropriate might be abused. It might be disproportionately applied to the states or put to improper uses. But it was not a power like other powers that would withdraw authority from the state. The state might complain about the disproportionate allocation. But this was not the same as abuse under the other powers. Accordingly, the placement of the spending power as an incidental or secondary power to the money raising power was consistent with Monroe's views as to the allocation of power as between the central government and the states.

With this construction, Monroe was satisfied that he had done justice to the Constitution as a whole: "Under it we behold a great scheme, consistent in all its parts, a Government instituted for national purposes, vested with adequate powers for those purposes, commencing with the most important of all, that of the revenue, and proceeding in regular order to the others with which it was deemed proper to endow it, all, too, drawn with utmost circumspection and care."[20]

In concluding that the General Welfare Clause did not constitute an independent power apart from the power to appropriate, Monroe's thinking was consistent with that of his predecessors, Madison and Jefferson. The historical incident later related by Albert Gallatin in which Roger Sherman, the author of the General Welfare Clause had precluded a drafting change by Gouverneur Morris that would have converted the clause into a general power suggests that Monroe's conclusion at this point was consistent with the original intent of the provision. Monroe's opinion on the point was also in keeping with, and anticipated, the thinking of Justice Story, who, in his commentaries some eleven years later, came to the same conclusion: the General Welfare Clause was not a grant of broad authority to regulate regarding the general welfare, separate and apart from the power to appropriate. At this stage of his memorandum, Monroe had remained true to his Republican lineage and to the Jeffersonian party of which he had been a member and leading proponent.[21]

Monroe's Doctrine: The Enumerated Powers Do Not Confine a General Welfare Clause Appropriation

Monroe then sought to firm up his conclusion about the first part of his analysis and build a bridge to the next part. "I indulge a strong hope," he wrote, "that the view herein presented will not be without effect, but will tend to satisfy the unprejudiced and impartial that nothing more was granted by that part [the General Welfare language in clause 1 of section 8 of Article I] than a power to *appropriate* the public money raised under the other part [the power to tax language in that clause]."[22] Thus, Monroe was clear that a plenary power to regulate and establish systems of internal improvement or the like was not granted by the language "to provide for . . . the general welfare." He then invited his readers to join him in pursuing the next question: "To what extent that power [to appropriate] may be carried will be the next object of inquiry."[23]

At the outset Monroe conceded that he had a change of heart on this issue. He explained. "It is contended on the one side that as the National Government is a government of limited powers it has no right to expend money except in the performance of acts authorized by the other specific grants according to a strict construction of their powers; that this grant in neither of its branches gives to Congress discretionary power of any kind, but is a mere instrument in its hands to carry into effect the powers contained in the other grants." This was obviously a restatement of the Madison-Jefferson position, so frequently enunciated in the past. Monroe confessed: "To this construction I was inclined in the more early stage of our Government; but on further reflection and observation my mind has undergone a change, for reasons which I will frankly unfold."[24] Here Monroe was announcing an intellectual departure from his own early thinking, as well as from that of his venerated predecessors. Accordingly, he set forth his reasoning at considerable length.

Monroe characterized Article I, section 8, clause 1 as a "twofold power—the first to raise, the second to appropriate, the public money. . . ." The clause thus contained a taxing and a spending power. He noted that "the terms used in both instances are general and unqualified." Moreover, "[e]ach branch [of the twofold power] was obviously drawn with a view to other other, and the import of each tends to illustrate that of the other." This generalization made, he began with the taxing power, noting that it was plenary in the same sense as other enumerated powers: the grant of power to raise money gave "a power over every subject from which revenue may be drawn." Like other powers granted, the check upon was "the responsibility of the representative to [the] constituents."[25]

Monroe then applied this same framework—an unqualified

general formulation—to the spending power, using language reminiscent of that employed by Hamilton in the *Report on Manufactures*. "If we look to the second branch of this power [to raise and appropriate money], that which authorizes the appropriation of the money thus raised, we find that it is not less general and unqualified than the power to raise it. *More comprehensive terms than to 'pay the debts and provide for the common defense and general welfare' could not have been used.*" Thus, it was reasonable to interpret the two parts of the two-fold power—the taxing power and the spending power—in the same way as general and unqualified powers.

Monroe backed up this analysis with a subtle argument: A limited spending power would have demanded a limited taxing power, presumably more limited than that afforded in the Constitution: "So intimately connected with and dependent on each other are these two branches of power that had either been limited the limitation would have had the like effect on the other.... [I]f the right of appropriation had been restricted to certain purposes, it would be useless and improper to raise more than would be adequate to these purposes."[26]

This argument made, Monroe restated his central conclusion: "The power in each branch [of the taxing/spending power] is alike broad and unqualified, and each is drawn with peculiar fitness to other, the latter requiring terms of great extent and force to accommodate the former, which have been adopted, and both placed in the same clause and sentence." To reinforce this central conclusion, Monroe posed a series of rhetorical questions. "Can it be presumed that all these circumstances were so nicely adjusted by mere accident? Is it not more just to conclude that they were the result of due deliberation and design?" Then, he posed a key point related to the drafting of the instrument: "Had it been intended that Congress should be restricted in the appropriation of the public money to such expenditures as were authorized by a rigid construction of the other specific grants, how easy it would have been to have provided for it, by a declaration to that effect. The omission of such a declaration is therefore an additional proof that it was not intended that the grant should be so construed."[27]

In brief, Monroe's argument was basically a textual one. The General Welfare Clause was incidental to an unqualified taxing power and was itself unqualified. If the framers had intended to limit appropriations under the General Welfare Clause to those related to the carrying out of the enumerated powers, they could have said so. Monroe's interpretation gave full effect to the plain meaning of the constitutional language.

In departing so signally from Madison's views, Monroe did not discuss the writings or opinions that Madison had provided on the subject in the *Federalist Papers* or elsewhere. Nor did he cite the views of other founding fathers, notably those Hamilton expressed in the *Report on Manufactures*, that would clearly have supported the conclusions that Monroe was reaching. It is probable that he wanted to avoid injecting the prior political controversy into his memorandum. Clearly, he would have wanted to avoid relying on Hamilton, the mortal political enemy of his own political allies, Madison and Jefferson. The better course was to provide a memorandum that relied on textual analysis.

Related Policy Considerations

When he turned to the broad policy considerations that supported his interpretation, Monroe did not put forward Hamilton's appealing rationale that the Federal Government must have flexibility to deal with problems that could not be anticipated and that the taxing/spending power embraced within the General Welfare clause gave it that flexibility. Instead, Monroe put forward a more subtle but related policy argument to support his general conclusion. To have subjected the taxing/spending power to a restriction that would have limited its use to appropriations for the enumerated powers would have, Monroe argued, exposed the Federal Government to "very serious embarrassment." If the power had been made dependent upon the states, the federal government would have been subjected to the fate of the confederation under the Articles of Confederation. Had the Supreme Court been authorized to pass on the propriety or utility of appropriations, the "whole system [would have been] disorganized."[28]

Moreover, "[h]ad it been declared by a clause in the Constitution that the expenditures under this grant should be restricted to the construction which might be given of other grants, such restraint, though the most innocent, could not have failed to have had an injurious effect on the vital principles of the Government and often on its most important measures." Opponents of an appropriation measure would construe the underlying power narrowly; proponents would construe it broadly. In sum, had the framers explicitly confined the spending power to the appropriation of funds to carry out the enumerated powers, the construction of those enumerated powers might have been artificially constrained or expanded in legislative disputes over appropriation measures. Monroe's interpretation neatly avoided this peril.[29]

Finally, Monroe summarized the practical advantages of his construction of the General Welfare Clause as a government-wide power but not as a power to regulate independent of the appropriation of funds. In doing so, the president recognized the significance of his interpretation as conveying both a "useful" and "safe" interpretation of the clause: "[T]he words 'to provide for the common defense and general welfare' have a definite, safe, and useful meaning. The idea of their forming an original grant, with unlimited power, superseding every other grant is abandoned. They will be considered simply as conveying a right of appropriation, a right indispensable to that of raising a revenue and necessary to expenditures under every grant."[30]

Moreover, the dangers of misconstruing of the other powers would be avoided. In particular, Monroe warned against the consequences of a narrow construction of the spending power, as distinguished from the other powers. "All the other grants are limited by the nature of the offices which they have severally to perform, each conveying a power to do a certain thing, and that only, whereas this is coextensive with the great scheme of the Government itself." He continued: "It is the lever which raises and puts the whole machinery in motion and continues the movement . . . Each of the other grants is limited by the nature of the grant itself; this, by the nature of the Government only. Hence it becomes necessary that, like the power to declare war, this power should be commensurate with the great scheme of the Government and with all its purposes."[31] Hamilton could not have said it better.

The Limitations of the Spending Power: National vs. Local Purposes

After abandoning the Madison-Jefferson constraint on the General Welfare Clause, Monroe addressed the question of whether the spending power, as he construed it, was unlimited. It is this passage of his memorandum that has been most often quoted:

If, then, the right to raise and appropriate the public money is not restricted to the expenditures under the other specific grants according to a strict construction of their powers, respectively, is there no limitation to it? *Have Congress a right to raise and appropriate the money to any and to every purpose according to their will and pleasure? They certainly have not.* The Government of the United States is a limited Government, instituted for great national purposes, and for those only. Other interests are committed to the States, whose duty it is to provide for them. Each government should look to the great and essential purposes for which it was instituted and confine itself to those purposes.

State governments would not apply money to national purposes; the Federal Government would not appropriate for local purposes. Clearly, then, as Monroe saw it, while not limited by the enumerated powers, the spending power could be exercised only in favor of national purposes for the the general welfare of the United States. Congress had broad discretion in determining what was a "national" purpose. A Congress that overreached in the exercise of this broad discretion would be corrected by the people at the polls rather than the courts.[32]

From this reading of the General Welfare Clause, Monroe easily concluded that roads and canals fell into the ambit of "national purposes:" "Good roads and canals will promote many very important national purposes. . . . To the appropriation of the public money to improvements having these objects in view and carried to a certain extent I do not see any well-founded constitutional objection," so as long as the role of Congress was confined to appropriation. "All the Congress could do in the case of internal improvements," Monroe explained, "would be to appropriate the money necessary to make them." The states would do the rest. To support his conclusion, Monroe exhaustively listed and described the appropriation measures that comported strictly with the view he was taking of the spending power. In this way, bereft of case law support, he assembled a list of *legislative* precedents that supported his reading.

High on the list was the Cumberland Road, but others were included. He also carefully cited the legislative measures and their dates, making clear that these measures had been enacted during the administrations of his predecessors, Madison and Jefferson, despite their strict view of the General Welfare Clause. It seems clear from this listing that Monroe had not been persuaded by Madison's explanation that the Cumberland Road measure was of doubtful constitutional validity or could be explained on the basis of the constitutional power to regulate the territories. What Monroe was doing through his memorandum was providing what was, for him, a sound constitutional basis for the measures that had been enacted and, at the same time, using those measures as legislative precedent in favor of the interpretation that he was postulating, in essence the only practicable legal approach available to him. In this vein, he gave a shorthand version of his conclusion. "My idea is that Congress have an unlimited power to raise money, and that in its appropriation they have a discretionary power restricted only by the duty to appropriate it to purposes of common defense and of general, not local, national, not State, benefit."[33]

While emphasizing that the General Welfare Clause conferred a mere power to appropriate, Monroe also touted the advantages of national control and jurisdiction over a system of internal improvements, a goal that could be achieved only by constitutional amendment. Monroe described the military and economic advantages of roads and canals. He stressed as well their impact on what he called "the bond of union" as affording "an inducement for them more powerful than any which have been urged or all of them united." Moreover, he observed that "it can not be doubted that that improvements for great national purposes would be better made by the National Government than by the the governments of the several States." These considerations, however, did not move him away from his central legal conclusion and the central distinction between the federal government's assuming jurisdiction and merely appropriating.

If the federal government were to assume overarching power over internal improvements, Monroe opined that a constitutional amendment was necessary to achieve that end. Nor could the states assent to such an assumption of jurisdiction. With these points in mind, Monroe again recommended the adoption of such an amendment as preferable to the option which his legal memorandum supported, that of "merely appropriating" funds: "If it is thought proper to vest this power [that of a national system of internal improvements with federal jurisdiction over them] in the United States, the only mode in which it can be done is by an amendment to the Constitution. . . . The States through which this road passes have given their sanction only to the route and to the acquisition of the soil by the United States, a right very different from that of jurisdiction, which can not be granted without an amendment to the Constitution. . . ."[34] He therefore recommended one.

Monroe's Post-Memorandum, Post-Veto Spending Policy in Light of Congressional Failure to Adopt an Amendment

Congress, however, proposed no such amendment. The reasons for its failure to do so are complex. For some members of Congress, plenary power in the United States to construct roads and canals was assumed. For others, the guidelines in the Monroe Memorandum that countenanced appropriations to the states for the purposes of constructing such improvements under state jurisdiction were deemed sufficient. Moreover, the reluctance of Congress to concede that it lacked authority to appropriate broadly for the general welfare doomed Monroe's amendment proposal and gave credence to the prediction of John Quincy Adams that it was a "moral certainty" that such an amendment would never be adopted.

In his sixth annual message, in December of 1822, Monroe was obliged to recognize this reality and to recommend the lesser alternative. He used the occasion to sum up where things stood in the framework of the memorandum that he had sent to Congress in May: "It is understood that the Cumberland road, which was constructed at a great expense, has already suffered from the want of that regular superintendence and of those repairs which are indispensable to the preservation of such a work." He recited the advantages of the work: it was "an ornament and honor to the nation." Then he recapitulated the essence of his memorandum, reiterating the need for constitutional amendment should Congress wish to exercise "a competent power to adopt and execute a system of internal improvement."[35]

Monroe then came to the congressional action that he thought justified by the analysis in his memorandum: "Should Congress, however, deem it improper to recommend such an amendment, they have, according to my judgment, the right to keep the road in repair by providing for the superintendence of it and appropriating the money necessary for repairs. *Surely if they had the right to appropriate money to make the road they have a right to appropriate it to preserve the road from ruin.* From the exercise of this power no danger is to be apprehended. Under our happy system the people are the sole and exclusive fountain of power."[36]

When Congress produced legislation providing for the repair of the road in the form of an appropriation that satisfied Monroe's prescription, he signed it without the constitutional amendment he had requested. In his seventh annual message, in 1823, Monroe touted the success of the repair legislation mentioned in his earlier message as a basis for the recommendations he made in the later one. He noted that sums had been appropriated for repair of the Cumberland Road and had been applied to "good effect," about which he promised a report.[37] In his final message, the president did not dwell at length on the internal-improvement issue but reported to Congress on a survey of roads and canals that might be deemed of national importance from a commercial or military point of view. Legislation providing for such a survey had been enacted in 1824.[38] On the final day of his presidency, Monroe signed legislation that appropriated $150,000 for extending the Cumberland Road from Wheeling, West Virginia, to Zanesville, Ohio.[39] Today this is essentially the route of Interstate 70.

With respect to the issue of internal improvements, Monroe's administration ended quite differently from that of his predecessor. Rather than vetoing an internal-improvement measure, Monroe signed one. The Monroe memorandum had intervened, and a pattern of appropriations legislation under the General Welfare Clause was beginning to unfold. The fifth president had given his legal blessing to that pattern, if confined to mere appropriation rather than an assumption of national jurisdiction. The compromise may have been gossamer-like, but it was the stuff of governing under the new Constitution. Further progress and clarification would be the domain of Monroe's successors.

Historical Perspectives on the Monroe Memorandum

Harry Ammon, who has given us a most comprehensive and authoritative biography of James Monroe characterizes his legal memorandum as "an ungracious work on an ungrateful subject." Ammon's assessment of Monroe's labor is mixed: "Monroe's pronouncement did nothing to stimulate the amending process, but at least it established clear guidelines for future measures relating to internal improvements. In the next year Monroe approved a bill appropriating $25,000 for repairing the Cumberland Road and another measure providing funds for a survey of a general system of internal improvements."[40]

Whatever its relative adequacy in terms of argumentation, the Monroe Memorandum represents the first recognition by a sitting president of the potential role of the General Welfare Clause as the basis for broad exercise of the congressional power of the purse. Monroe's specific contribution was the identification of Article I, section 8, clause 1 as the constitutional underpinning for congressional appropriations for internal improvements (albeit devoid of jurisdiction over them).[41]

How does this history fit into our thesis? The fifth president forthrightly maintained that Congress could appropriate for purposes that fell within the ambit of the "general welfare" and that Congress had broad discretion in determining the scope of the general welfare. He hastened to add, however, that such discretion was not without limit and that federal appropriations must be for initiatives that were national in scope. Monroe did not abandon his predecessors' quest for a constitutional amendment. Such an amendment was needed, Monroe thought, if the central government were to play a lead role in the construction of internal improvements and assume appropriate jurisdiction over individual projects, a result that he favored as a matter of policy. To authorize a national system of internal improvements, Congress would be obliged to pursue a constitutional amendment. Doing so, however, became less and less necessary with the alternative that the Monroe Memorandum left open: appropriate for the road and let the state construct and maintain jurisdiction. Cooperative federalism would suffice to move the nation along toward growth in those areas where the states had a major and primary role but needed financial assistance from the federal government as well as the leadership inherent in an overall framework. This assistance could be provided under the General Welfare Clause as interpreted by Monroe. With his memo drafted and presented, Monroe felt comfortable in approving legislation providing for a survey of internal improvement possibilities. As Kelly, Harbison, and Belz put it, "This resolution of the question [through Monroe's action] and the consistent rejection of exclusively federal projects may be said to have vindicated the states'-rights-strict-construction point of view. But the more important point is that a national policy took shape under federal sponsorship in a way that respected the sensibilities of states' rights advocates."[42] Of equal importance is the fact that Monroe's analysis, emanating from a Jeffersonian Republican administration, provided a basis for freeing General Welfare Clause application from the limitations of the strict doctrine of Madison and Jefferson that confined its reach only to those purposes embraced within the enumerated powers. In future policy development this was to be of enormous significance, not only for internal improvement projects but for a whole range of social policy initiatives.

The broad outlines of the Monroe Memorandum and the conclusions as to the scope of the General Welfare Clause contained in it were to be embraced more than a decade later by Justice Story in his *Commentaries.* Indeed those commentaries formed a basis for the Supreme Court's decision in the *Butler* case that essentially affirmed the Hamiltonian view as to the scope of the clause and the spending power embraced within it. History records that Monroe provided Story with a copy of his memorandum. Story declined to comment on the merits, but it seems clear that he had a considerable period during which to reflect on Monroe's analysis. When he came to write his own commentaries on the taxing power, Story appropriately cited Monroe. Monroe, it is recorded, also sent a copy of the memorandum to John Marshall who observed that the views contained therein seemed "generally just."[43]

The theory that Monroe expounded 1822, in an effort to justify his veto of a bill that would have provided for tolls on the Cumberland Road, extended by Story, adopted by the courts, and enhanced through various incidental judicial doctrines, became in part a legal foundation for the modern benefit state. Monroe, who began his political life as a partial anti-Federalist and ended it as an explicator of the Constitution, helped to formulate the theory that embodies an extension of the Constitution into many areas of national life. His memorandum was a bridge between the early founders—he was among the last of a group that had fought for or led the nation during the Revolutionary period—and the modern nation that they helped to found. His doctrine, born of the practical necessities of governing a great and growing nation, became a basis for relating the modern spending power to the Democratic-Republican, as well as to the Federalist, tradition.

IV
John Quincy Adams and the Jacksonians: A Clash of Visions

8
John Quincy Adams's "Spirit of Improvement"

Adams's Role

EXPERIENCE, BIRTH, OUTLOOK, AND ABILITY EQUIPPED JOHN QUINCY Adams well for the office of the presidency. He was the son of John Adams, founding father and second president. His mother, Abigail Adams, had a profound influence on his outlook and his deep commitment to the cause of improvement and the nation's role in fostering it. He had served as United States senator, minister to various European courts, and as James Monroe's very successful secretary of state. He was blessed with a profound intellect, a scholarly disposition, and an all-pervasive sense of duty. He carried to the office a broad vision of where he wanted to take the country. In articulating that vision, he was far ahead of his time. Nevertheless, history has generally consigned John Quincy Adams to the ranks of the unsuccessful presidents. With that assessment, Adams did not disagree. A modern-day biographer of the sixth president, who concludes that for Adams the presidency was an unrequited "misery," devotes but a chapter to that period of his life.[1] To some degree this assessment is attributable to Adams's failings as a practical politician. As Samuel Flagg Bemis, perhaps the most renowned Adams biographer, has observed: "No man has ever been better fitted, as professional public servant, for the Presidency. No man has had less aptitude or inclination for the organization and command of political cohorts."[2]

The single term of John Quincy Adams was fatally marred at its inception by the manner of his selection. The election of 1824 was thrown into the House of Representatives when none of the candidates, Adams, Henry Clay of Kentucky, the Speaker of the House of Representatives, William H. Crawford of Georgia, Monroe's Secretary of the Treasury, and General Andrew Jackson of

Tennessee, received a majority of the electoral college votes, the requirement for election. Of the high three, Jackson received ninety-nine. Adams placed second with eighty-four, and Crawford was third with forty-one. Under the procedures established by the twelfth amendment to the Constitution, the election was decided by the House of Representatives, with the House voting by state delegation. The candidate who won the majority of the states in the House vote became president.

The House was obliged by the Constitution to select among the three candidates receiving the greatest votes. Clay was thus excluded from the contest. Adams was selected by the House with the support of Clay, who mustered the Kentucky delegation, among others, in support of Adams, although he had not received any electoral votes in Kentucky and the Kentucky legislature had instructed its delegation to support Jackson. Adams was elected by a vote of thirteen of the twenty-four state delegations, a bare majority. After the election, Adams appointed Clay as secretary of state. The appointment spawned charges of a "corrupt bargain" that haunted the new president throughout his administration and ensured that much of his program would never be implemented. The status of minority president and the aura of corruption and political bargain tainted his policies in the public mind and largely doomed them, whatever their merits.[3]

Once in office, Adams was unable to organize the supporters that he did have. Nor was he able to organize sympathetic members of opposing factions into an effective bloc that would convert his policies into legislation. His initiatives were largely stymied by the opposition of a pro-Jackson coalition that ultimately formed the Democratic Party to counter Adams and the National Republicans in the election of 1828. Because Adams was widely perceived as a proponent of the business and privileged classes, he was unable to command the allegiance of the common man, notwithstanding his devotion to the nation, his honesty, and his profound dedication to its general welfare. He was regarded as distant, temperamental and aloof. A second term was easily denied him by Andrew Jackson, who was identified as the champion of a new brand of democracy. His unhappy tenure as chief executive was generally regarded as a failed presidency.[4]

The contribution of President John Quincy Adams to the evolution of an effective expression of general welfare spending authority at the federal level must, however, be considered in a somewhat different light. In his approach to the active use of the General Welfare Clause to support a program of nationally financed and designed internal improvements, Adams must be considered as far more than a transitional figure, despite the limited number of projects that he was able to sign into law. He was determined not to let the constitutional doubts that had prompted his predecessors to limit their advocacy of such a program preclude his own initiatives. Adams used the General Welfare Clause, explicitly or implicitly, to recommend the appropriation of federal funds for the planning, laying out, and construction of a wide range of internal-improvement projects, while strongly urging that Congress authorize further initiatives in the area of education, science, and exploration.

Jefferson, Madison, and Monroe had been absorbed with the issue of the constitutionality of a system of federally financed internal improvements. Adams, on the other hand, emphasized the national benefits to be derived from such a system. Rather than urging a constitutional amendment, as had the Virginia presidents, Adams identified the legal support for his recommendations in the precedents that the Virginia presidents had approved, notably federal financial assistance for the design and construction of the Cumberland Road. The constitutional foundation for the Cumberland Road initiative and thus for Adams's policies on internal improvements had been identified as residing in the General Welfare Clause. Monroe, after his 1822 veto, had approved legislation extending the Cumberland Road and a number of other internal-improvement measures, including the survey legislation of 1824. In his annual messages touting the advantages of internal improvements, Adams relied heavily upon Monroe's legislative precedents. While he did not cite it, had taken a dim view of its unveiling, and after his presidency was to criticize its limiting role, Adams necessarily relied on the reasoning in the Monroe Memorandum of 1822, to the extent that it affirmed a reading of the General Welfare Clause that supported appropriations for purposes that went beyond the confines of the enumerated powers. However, given the opportunity, Adams clearly would have approved enactments that surpassed the limits of the Monroe Memorandum. The sixth president did not observe its "nice distinctions" as binding.[5]

Although he did not define publicly his constitutional theory during his presidency, Adams invoked Monroe's record in promoting his own program. Adams, however, did not use his messages to agonize over where the line was drawn between an appropriation to the states and an assumption of national jurisdiction or between a local and a national project. The legislation that he did sign included such items as river or harbor improvements primarily of local benefit. He recommended new projects and emphasized their advantages to the nation without mentioning the need for constitutional change or brandishing the threat of a veto. In this, he represented a measure of significant change from his predecessors. His avowed aim was to have the government embark upon a national system of internal improvements without insisting that it first obtain popular assent through a constitutional amendment to authorize or regularize such a system. He privately regarded such an amendment as impracticable and unnecessary because he believed that the Constitution already afforded such authority and that regularization could be achieved through legislation.[6]

The position that Adams took on internal improvements and the constitutional authority to support them with federal funds was in harmony with the philosophy of his coalition partner, Henry Clay. Adams had been elected with the support of Clay who was the principal proponent of the American System under which high tariffs would promote American manufactures and would at the same time generate substantial federal revenues that could be used for internal improvements to enhance economic growth and open up the country. That Clay threw his support to Adams rather than Jackson, while bitterly criticized as antirepublican, may have in part reflected Clay's conclusion that his thinking and that of Adams on major issues of domestic policy, particularly internal improvement, were closely aligned.[7]

Adams's subsequent adoption, in his annual messages, of a high-profile program in favor of internal improvements was thus consistent with Clay's approach and with the understanding that both partners presumably had reached. Indeed, Adams was often ahead of Clay in favoring recommendations for internal improvements in education and scientific exploration—proposals that Clay would have subordinated.[8]

It would be a mistake, however, to conclude that the pro-internal-improvement stance based upon a broad reading of the General Welfare Clause was, for Adams, primarily a matter of political expediency and a desire for high office. Adams did not suddenly become a proponent of internal improvement just to gain Clay's support in the election of 1824. As far back as 1806, when Adams was a United States senator from Massachusetts, he had supported a program of federally financed internal improvements. During the Monroe Administration, despite Clay's opposition to the government, Adams had expressed sympathy for Clay's internal-improvement policies. During the campaign of 1824, Adams had reiterated his strong support for internal improvements in transportation, education, science, and geographic exploration, without a prior constitutional amendment. This was the product of his own long-held vision. In turn, Adams's expression of that vision during his presidency, despite the unwillingness of Congress to adopt his program fully, established an Executive-Branch precedent that could be deferred or put aside by the Jacksonians who followed but could not be totally destroyed or eradicated.[9]

The primary goal of John Quincy Adams as president was to lead the nation in an ambitious program of internal improvement that would benefit future generations. He brought to the task more religious zeal than political skill. His inability to achieve that goal and his fall from office at the hands of the Jacksonians galled him immeasurably. He took it to be the signal failure of his life. At times, bathed in self-pity, Adams ruminated about how his efforts to gain approval for internal-improvement legislation had failed. At other times, he reasoned that, if the union survived, his views would prevail. After his presidency, he ran for and was elected to the House of Representatives. There he turned his energies to opposing slavery and the infamous gag role, but even in these undertakings, he kept his philosophy of the general welfare foremost in mind.

The way of John Quincy Adams on internal improvements, deprecated by Jefferson and Madison as heresy and partially rolled back by the Jacksonians, ultimately became the way of Lincoln and later the way of the Democratic Party that had been founded by Jackson to counter the Adams policy and reverse his election. Under Wilson, Franklin Roosevelt, Truman, Kennedy, and Johnson, the twentieth-century Democratic Party in effect embraced the Hamiltonian view of a vigorous federal spending power that Adams sought to promote and extend. It enhanced that view through the adoption of federalized programs in such diverse areas as social security and health and scientific research, as well as through the extension of state-administered formula programs in transportation and education. That view found recent expression in the 1990s in the Clinton administration's emphasis on public investment in education and the environment, the preservation of social and health insurance programs, and the reform of the income-maintenance safety net within a context of an overall budget surplus.[10]

THE ADAMS INAUGURAL

John Quincy Adams's inaugural address heralded his position on internal improvements and telegraphed the high priority that he accorded them. His emphasis on those themes reflected his own views. They may also have been designed to engender support and enthusiasm for an administration that had come to office despite a popular election that had favored Andrew Jackson. Perhaps he thought a pro-internal-improvement policy that created jobs for working people and opened up distant western farms and towns to markets would help to overcome the charges of "corrupt bargain" and anti-republicanism that swirled around the capital and isolated the new president.

The inaugural ceremony, as Adams described it in his diary, was restrained and straightforward. Andrew Jackson compared it unfavorably to the simplicity of Jefferson's first inaugural. As Adams wrote in his diary on March 4, 1825, the inaugural entourage solemnly wended its way by carriage to the Capitol and its Senate chamber and thence to the House chamber. Adams added: "[A]fter delivering from the Speaker's chair my inaugural address to a crowded auditory, I pronounced from a volume of the laws held up to me by John Marshall, Chief Justice of the United States, the oath faithfully to execute the office of President of the United States."[11]

Adams declined to spare his audience a long address. Bemis characterizes it as "a sober, sensible appeal for national unity—always the Washingtonian compass of Adams's continental outlook." Adams began by reviewing the progress of the nation in the thirty-six years since the adoption of the Constitution, received "as a precious inheritance from those to whom we are indebted by its establishment." It had "promoted the lasting welfare" of the country. Despite the "wrongs and injustices" of other nations and "dissensions among ourselves," the great "experiment upon the theory of human rights" had "been crowned with success equal to the most sanguine expectations of its founders." He pointed to the key elements of its success: "Union, justice, tranquility, the common defense, the general welfare, and the blessings of liberty—all have been promoted by the Government under which we have lived." In this context of affirmation and hope, he alluded to the dark period when the nation had been affected by the French Revolution. "Ten years of peace, at home and abroad," had, however, "assuaged the animosities of political contention and blended into harmony the most discordant elements of public opinion." Imbued perhaps with more hope than expectation in light of the bitterness of the recent election, the president's apparent aim was to preserve this era of good feeling and "[t]he harmony of the nation."[12]

A System of Internal Improvements as an Instrument of Harmony

Within this framework Adams freely acknowledged his debt to his predecessor and proudly enumerated Monroe's accomplishments. Not the least of these was "to proceed in the great system of internal improvements within the limits of the constitutional power of the Union" and to prepare "by scientific researches and surveys for the further application of our national resources to the *internal improvement* of our country." Adams took great comfort in the framework of the 1824 survey legislation and found there the "promise and performance" of Monroe that clearly delineated his own "line of duty." Within that framework, he believed that the subject of internal improvements warranted the highest priority. As he himself said, "To pursue to their consummation those purposes of improvement in our common condition instituted or recommended by [Monroe] will embrace the whole sphere of my obligations."

He continued, "To the topic of internal improvements emphatically urged by [Monroe] at his inauguration, I recur with particular satisfaction." He was "convinced that the unborn millions of our posterity who are in future ages to people this continent will derive their most fervent gratitude to the founders of the Union; that in which the beneficent action of its Government will be most deeply felt and acknowledged." In this he took his cue not only from Monroe but from ancient history. "The magnificence and splendor of their public works are among the imperishable glories of the ancient republics. The roads and aqueducts of Rome have been the admiration of all after ages . . ."[13]

The Constitutional Divide

Within the framework of this emphasis on the benefits of a bold public improvement program, Adams turned briefly to the constitutional issue that had bitterly divided Hamilton from Jefferson and Madison and Federalist from Republican since the earliest days of the Republic. The new president sought to deal with it through conciliation rather than confrontation. "Some diversity of opinion," he observed by way of understatement, "has prevailed with regard to the powers of Congress for legislation upon objects of this nature." The "most respectful deference" was due to "doubts originating in pure patriotism and sustained by venerated authority." The views of Madison and Jefferson were thus invoked but respectfully put aside on the strength of the actual precedent that had been established in the years of their administrations. Adams observed: "[N]early twenty years have passed since the construction of the first national road was commenced. The authority for its construction was then unquestioned." It had proven beneficial to thousands and had injured no one. "Repeated, liberal, and candid discussions in the Legislature have conciliated the sentiments and approximated the opinions of enlightened minds upon the question of constitutional power."[14]

Adams concluded this part of the discussion by expressing hope that the spirit of good feeling in which he had enveloped his inaugural would sweep away any further disputation. "I can not but hope that by the same process of friendly, patient and persevering deliberation all constitutional objections will ultimately be removed. The extent and limitation of the powers of the General Government in relation to this transcendently important interest will be settled and acknowledged to the common satisfaction of all, and every speculative scruple will be solved by a practical public blessing."[15] Thus, Adams urged a pragmatic, nonconfrontational, nonamendment-based solution to the old battle over the scope of the General Welfare authority.

Adams ended his address with an allusion to the "peculiar circumstances" of his own election that had left him "[l]ess possessed of your confidence in advance than any of my predecessors." This was his attempt to put the best face on the difficult situation that confronted him and enraged his opponents. The admission may help to explain his posture on internal improvements and their constitutional basis. While that posture was rooted in the accomplishments and thinking of Monroe, the Adams stance was clearly different.

Unlike Monroe, Adams did not announce in his inaugural that he would veto certain internal-improvement measures. Nor did he urge the adoption of a constitutional amendment. Instead, he relied upon the precedent of the Cumberland Road and on the unquestioned benefit that that project and others like it would have. Even if Adams had been inclined to recommend an amendment in order to clarify the constitutional situation, conciliate his opposition, and line up with his venerated predecessors, the circumstances of his election would have practicably precluded the adoption of such a course. His observations on the circumstance of his election in this context may have reflected his own recognition that, if his predecessors, elected by large majorities without the intervention of the legislature, had been unable to sway Congress on the need for a constitutional amendment, he would be unlikely to do so.

But Adams was not inclined to call for the adoption of such an amendment even if he had been elected with the highest popular or electoral vote. His position reflected more than political reality. During the Monroe Administration, Adams, then a member of the cabinet, had strongly questioned the wisdom of the constitutional amendment policy. In 1819, when Monroe first unveiled his memorandum on internal improvements, with its recommendation for a constitutional amendment that would express the government's authority to construct or finance internal improvements, Adams had counseled against sending it to Congress. At the time, Adams had felt that the proposal would exacerbate tensions between Congress and the Monroe Administration. On that occasion, Adams had noted in his diary his belief that it was a "moral certainty" that no amendment would ever be proposed to the states by Congress. Moreover, he regarded it as questionable statecraft for the president to recommend a course of action that he knew Congress would oppose. Finally, Adams himself did not believe such an amendment to be necessary or useful, even if it could be secured. He believed that the Constitution as written contained the necessary authority. His visceral reaction was based not so much on close legal analysis as on his conclusion that if the Constitution could, without amendment, support the Louisiana Purchase, it could, without amendment, sustain the construction of roads and canals to bind together a nation doubled in size by that acquisition.[16]

Nothing had changed since 1819 to warrant a reversal of Adams's thinking on the subject. Indeed, in 1822, Monroe had vetoed an internal-improvements measure with a recommendation for an amendment, accompanied by his memorandum, described above. Congress had declined to propose one. Instead, in the absence of an amendment, Monroe had signed appropriation measures and survey legislation within the framework of the distinctions worked out in his memorandum. Thus Adams had the experience, as well as the pro-internal improvement precedents of the Monroe years, to bolster his thinking. In his 1825 inaugural address, he used his pro-internal improvement/post-veto experience from the Monroe administration to reinforce two central propositions: (1) his own enthusiastic support for internal improvements as a matter of policy and (2) his belief that the constitutional issues could be worked out by Congress without an amendment. From the perspective of his own political weakness, as well as a matter of his own policy preference, Adams adopted a stance favorable to internal improvement, unaccompanied by a recommendation for constitutional change. Like Monroe, Adams believed that the General Welfare Clause authorized appropriations for purposes beyond the strict bounds of the enumerated powers; unlike Monroe, he believed that the Constitution authorized Congress to establish a national system of internal improvements. To the extent that the Monroe Memorandum denied such a power, its limitations were superfluous. As Bemis has stated, Adams believed that the Constitution "gave the General Government the right to build and maintain internal improvements within the states for the general welfare of the whole nation." This Adams implied, but did not assert directly, in his momentous, first annual message.[17]

By relying on the precedents of the Monroe Administration and implicitly, but not expressly, on the Monroe Memorandum, which had explained and justified those precedents, Adams may have believed that he could maintain some kind of faith with his predecessors and patrons in the Republican party. He could at least avoid offending them by openly declaring his own adherence to a broad reading of the General Welfare Clause that authorized a national system, even though that might be his private view. That these feeble efforts at conciliation failed may not have been attributable to lack of vision as much as flawed execution, fierce political opposition, and the firm adherence of Jefferson and Madison in their retirement to their long-held doctrine that the General Welfare Clause was confined by the enumerated powers.

Adams's diary fills us in on the balance of his inaugural day following the delivery of his address, a review of the military companies in front of the Capital, the procession's return to his house, his receiving there a throng of well-wishers, his visit to Monroe at the President's House, and his attendance at the ball at Carusi's Hall. The new president's day concluded with an activity more in keeping with his personality than the crowded hours that had preceded. "Immediately after supper I withdrew, and came home. I closed the day as it had begun, with thanksgiving to God for all His mercies and favors past, and with prayers for the continuance of them to my country, and to myself and mine."[18]

THE FIRST ANNUAL MESSAGE:
THE "SPIRIT OF INTERNAL IMPROVEMENT"

The formulation of Adams's first annual message did not go smoothly. Its preparation, Adams regarded as "a task of deep anxiety." His cabinet pondered over the early drafts and took issue with the new president as to specific sections. Members worried, with considerable justification, over whether its proposals, some far-reaching in terms of federal activity, would be rejected. John Quincy Adams chafed at these constraints. He wanted to send a message not only to Congress but to posterity.

The message, essentially as Adams wished it, was transmitted to Congress in December 1825, hand-carried by his son, John. The message was not an exercise in pussyfooting. As the inaugural address had suggested, Adams's emphasis was on internal improvements. He began by reporting on legislation enacted during the Monroe administration. He first invoked the Act of April 30, 1824, which Monroe had signed and which enabled the government to procure surveys, plans and estimates for roads and canals. Adams saw this statute as ground-breaking legislation under the General Welfare Clause authority, and he reported in detail on the progress that had been made under it.

The Board of Engineers appointed under this measure had, Adams explained, completed the surveys needed to determine the practicability of building a canal from the Chesapeake Bay to the Ohio River. The new president devoted considerable space to this Chesapeake and Ohio Canal project. He told Congress that the company formed to arrange for the work was organizing and receiving subscriptions. Three commissioners for the United States and a like number for the participating states, Maryland and Virginia, had been appointed to perform these acts, presumably in recognition of the federal-state nature of the project. Adams also reported on progress in implementing the Act of March 3, 1825. Signed by Monroe on his last day in office, it directed the secretary of the treasury to subscribe for shares of the stock in the company.[19]

Other projects which had occupied the Board were also mentioned, including the building of a "national road" from Washington to New Orleans and a navigation project in Connecticut. The continuation of the the Cumberland Road, "the most important" project, as Adams characterized it, had, "after surmounting no inconsiderable difficulty in fixing upon the direction of the road," "commenced under the most promising auspices. . . ."[20]

For John Quincy Adams, the spirit of internal improvement was not confined to bricks and mortar or roads and canals. On the contrary, the president unashamedly extended it to the subject of education. A compelling aspect of the message was Adams's recommendation that Congress consider the subject of internal improvement in "a more enlarged extent." In making it, Adams conveyed the central tenet of his general welfare philosophy and his vision of the core role of government in "improving the condition" of the governed through public investments:

> The great object of the institution of civil government is the improvement of the condition of those who are parties to the social compact, and no government, in whatever form constituted, can accomplish the lawful ends of its institution but in proportion as it improves the condition of those over whom it is established. Roads and canals, by multiplying and facilitating the communication and intercourse between distant regions and multitudes of men, are among the most important means of improvement. But moral, political, intellectual improvement are duties assigned by the Author of Our Existence to social no less than to individual man. For the fulfillment of those duties governments are invested with power, and to the attainment of the end—*the progressive improvement of the condition of the governed*—the exercise of delegated powers is a duty as sacred and indispensable as the usurpation of powers not granted is criminal and odious.[21]

Adams conceived of himself as reviving the Washington legacy. His enlarged view of the scope of government responsibility for internal improvement led him to an appeal on behalf of Washington's recommendation for federal assistance for a seminary of learning in the nation's capital. "Among the first, perhaps the very first, instrument for the improvement of the condition [of the governed]," wrote Adams, "is knowledge, and to the acquisition of much of the knowledge adapted to the wants, the comforts, and enjoyments of human life public institutions and seminaries of learning are essential." Adams referred to Washington's proposal for the formation of a national university and a military academy. The latter had been adopted; the nation's capital as a site of a university, Adams observed, was still "bare and barren."[22]

In sum, Adams clearly connected support for transportation projects and educational assistance, the first as a means of enhancing human communication, the second, as a means of providing for intellectual, moral, and political development. Adams did not reach beyond Washington's proposal for federal aid to a seminary of learning in the nation's capital, an initiative that could be supported constitutionally through the express power of Congress over the seat of government. However, in terms of rationale and public policy, it seems evident that he connected the two as species of initiatives that enhanced the general welfare. He regarded both as initiatives that it was his duty to propose rather than as potentially useful proposals for which authority must first be found. His predecessors had supported them with equal enthusiasm but had taken care to draw lines about authority; Adams focused on the benefits and subordinated the constitutional issues.

Adams's fervor for internal improvements moved him to yet another recommendation—extending the federal government into the area of scientific exploration. Here he was courting difficulty for he, or members of his cabinet, could foresee the probability of congressional criticism from those who favored a limited federal role. Nevertheless, Adams added to his annual message a recommendation for federal support of the pursuit of "geographical and astronomical science" and for outfitting a "public ship" for the exploration of the northwest coast of the continent. He further called for the establishment of an astronomical observatory, either in connection with the establishment of the university or separate from it. He believed that the United States should not be dependent upon Europe for astronomical discoveries. Here, his florid language got him in trouble. He observed: "It is with no feeling of pride as an American that the remark may be that on the comparatively small territorial surface of Europe there are existing upward of 130 of these *light-houses of the skies*, while throughout the American hemisphere is not one." His opponents would repeatedly and derisively refer to his "light houses of the skies" as a mark of how disconnected he was with the needs of the common man.[23]

The ambitious program announced in this message required Adams again to address the yet-unresolved question of whether Congress had the constitutional power to finance internal improvements. He did so in a way that, on the surface, paid deference to Congress but made clear the thrust of his own thought. The Constitution was a charter of "limited powers." If the Congress should conclude that his recommendations fell outside those powers, he urged Congress not to adopt them: "[S]hould you come to the conclusion that, however desirable in themselves, the enactment of laws for effecting [his recommendations] would transcend the powers committed to you by that venerable instrument which we are all bound to support," he solemnly cautioned, "let no consideration induce you to assume the exercise of powers not granted to you by the people." Then he added this admonition which discloses the essence of the constitutional interpretation that he believed would permit the government to play the core role that he had expounded: "[I]f the power to exercise exclusive legislation in all cases whatsoever over the District of Columbia; if the power to lay and collect taxes, duties, imposts and excises, to pay the debts and provide for the common defense and general welfare of the United States [and other powers listed in Article I, section 8].... if these powers and others enumerated in the Constitution may be effectually brought into action by laws promoting the improvement of agriculture, commerce, and manufactures, the cultivation and encouragement of the mechanic and of the elegant arts, the advancement of literature, and the progress of the sciences, ornamental and profound, to refrain from exercising them for the benefit of the people themselves would be to hide in the earth the talent committed to our charge—would be treachery to the most sacred of trusts."[24]

Adams would, for the record, defer to Congress on the constitutional issue. He would not announce a veto in advance and would not argue for a particular position. On the other hand, he did not, as had his predecessors, call for a constitutional amendment as a necessary prelude to the legislation he was recommending. Again, it was for Congress, not the president to decide. If they decided to enact legislation, he would assume its validity and would not interpose the veto. This, in and of itself, was a significant step. It was, in effect, the position that Clay had urged on Monroe in 1819.

However, Adams appeared to be moving beyond mere neutrality. In recommending a flood of public works legislation without calling for an amendment, Adams was saying implicitly that he thought the Constitution authorized his program without amendment. In citing specific provisions of the Constitution that a proponent of such a position might look to, Adams was describing his own position. The constitutional power over the seat of government could justify the national university and astronomical observatory; indeed, since 1787, this power had been put forward as a basis for a national seminary of learning. As for the broader road and canal legislation, it is significant that Adams cited the General Welfare Clause in Article I, section 8, clause 1 as the most available indefinite authority. In effect, if not directly, Adams was adopting (and extending) the analysis of the General Welfare Clause in the Monroe Memorandum as a plausible basis or underpinning for his ambitious program.

In concluding his message, Adams put aside his own constitutional analysis and portrayed the adoption of his policies as a national moral imperative. He bravely announced: "The spirit of improvement is abroad upon the earth." He followed it with a restatement of his own political creed: "While dwelling with pleasing satisfaction upon the superior excellence of our political institutions, let us not be unmindful that *liberty is power*; that the nation blessed with the largest portion of liberty must in proportion to its numbers be the most powerful nation on earth, and that the tenure of power by man is, in the moral purposes of his Creator, upon condition that it shall be exercised to ends of beneficence, to improve the condition of himself and his fellow-men." The reference to "liberty is power" is one of the most quoted of Adams's expressions.

Adams's enthusiasm did not permit him to stop there. He added: "While foreign nations less blessed with that freedom which is power than ourselves are advancing with gigantic strides in the career of public improvement, were we to slumber in indolence or fold up our arms and proclaim to the world that *we are palsied by the will of our constituents*, would it not be to cast away the bounties of Providence and doom ourselves to perpetual inferiority?"[25]

Despite Adams's invocation of democracy, elsewhere in the message, the use of the word "palsied" seemed to suggest that Congress should ignore the "will" of its constituents. It played into the hands of those who opposed Adams as a president who, elected against the popular will, would ignore the popular will. This phrase, in the context of the message as a whole, contributed to the emergence of an opposition coalition that would ultimately take the form of Jackson's Democratic Party. Jackson and his partisans seized upon it to portray Adams as asking Congress to exercise enormous power that it did not possess. Jackson's biographer, Robert Remini, describes the phrase as "[a]n incredible blunder."[26]

PREPARATION AND PUBLIC REACTION: ADAMS AND BAILEY CONVERSE

Preparations for the first annual message were far from stress-free. During the weeks prior to its December 1825 transmission, Adams and his cabinet anticipated the potentially adverse reaction it might evoke. Adams had formulated his recommendations with considerable effort and confessed to his diary that he suffered profound anxiety about them. Several cabinet sessions were devoted to discussing content, particularly the passages on internal improvements and education. Some cabinet members advised against including controversial recommendations, such as the need to establish a national university, on the ground that Congress would not adopt them. Others urged that the message be confined to recommendations that needed presidential support.

The greatest dispute centered on the final paragraphs that focused on internal improvements, presumably those about support for education, science, and constitutionality. Clay and James Barbour, steeped in knowledge about congressional reaction, were inclined to delete these proposals. Adams noted in his diary for November 25, a day on which a cabinet meeting addressed the draft message: "Mr. Clay was for recommending nothing which, from its unpopularity, would be unlikely to succeed; Governor [James] Barbour, [the secretary of war and a former governor of Virginia] nothing so popular that it may be carried without recommendation. Clay good-humoredly remarked this alternate stripping off from my draft; and I told them I was like the man with his two wives—one plucking out his black hairs, and other the white, till none were left."[27]

Clay objected to the national university recommendation which he thought "entirely hopeless." Moreover, he found it more constitutionally objectionable (to Congress) than internal improvements. Adams wrote in his diary that he agreed that impracticable projects should not be recommended but explained that he "would look to a practicability of a longer range than a simple session of Congress." He pointed to the ten years that had elapsed between Washington's recommendation of a national military academy and its adoption: "The plant may come late, though the seed should be sown early."[28]

Adams had no illusions about the likelihood that his recommendations would be adopted by Congress, but he felt duty-bound to propose them for posterity early in his term. "There is this consideration for offering them now—that of the future I can never be sure." Some cabinet members supported the message. Clay favored the content on policy grounds and was convinced of the powers of Congress but doubted that they would be exercised. With these divisions Adams concluded: "Thus situated, the perilous experiment must be made. Let me make it with full deliberation, and be prepared for the consequences."[29]

When Attorney General William Wirt, who had apparently been absent from the earlier session, heard Adams read the draft portion on internal improvements, he sagely observed that they were "excessively bold." Wirt approved the message in principle but correctly predicted that it would be used by Adams's opponents in Virginia to charge him with "grasping for power." Adams again made some alterations. By the second of December, the revised message was ready for printing. On December 6, when Adams sent his son John to carry the message to Congress, he observed in his diary: "The delivery of this annual message is one of the principal duties of the President of the United States, and there is deep responsibility attached to it."[30]

It seems evident from these passages in the diary that the cabinet's concerns regarding the internal improvements and other spending power initiatives in Adams's first message centered on their political acceptability rather than their constitutionality. It also appears that Adams was ahead of his cabinet in desiring to present progressive proposals that he thought the country needed, even though he recognized that they might not be adopted and that even suggesting them might adversely affect his popularity.

Adams's fears and those of his cabinet were justified. The impact of the word "palsied" has been suggested above. Not only the Jacksonians, but the Radicals in Congress, strict constructionists in the tradition of Jefferson, reacted strongly. The effect of Adams's first State of the Union message was the fostering of a coalition of Van Buren Radicals, Calhoun, and the Jacksonians. This coalition ultimately became the Jacksonian Democratic Party and crushed Adams in the 1828 election. As Lynn Parsons puts it in his modern biography of John Quincy Adams, "The annual message was the first element in the undermining of Adams' presidency."[31]

The opposition to Adams's first annual message was not universal. Some Adams supporters hailed it. Representative Hemphill of Philadelphia, for example, commended Adams for the "lift" that Hemphill's internal improvements bill had received. Another congressman assured Adams of his agreement with "every part" of the message.[32]

In one of these sessions, Adams candidly shared his views on the constitutional issue, the views that were somewhat shrouded in the message, presumably for political reasons. Representative John Bailey of Massachusetts, a friend of Adams, visited the president on December 14, following the transmission of the message. He told the president of several resolutions that he had offered in the House concerning roads and canals, as well as an amendment of the Constitution on internal improvements. Bailey's initiative constituted an alternative to the broad program proposed in the message because it included the element of a constitutional amendment that the Virginia presidents had called for. It might provide a basis for conciliation with the Radicals. Despite its possible political appeal, Adams stood on principle and flatly declined to support it. The president recorded in his diary: "I told him that the discussion of his resolutions might be useful, but I must in candor say that my opinions did not concur with them. *I thought the power of making roads and canals given by the Constitution; and then an amendment, asking the grant of that which was already granted, equally impracticable and useless.*"[33]

Here Adams is at his most revealing. He had recommended internal improvements but had not directly expressed or explained his view as to their constitutionality in either his inaugural address or his State of the Union message. However, he was willing to share with Congressman Bailey of Massachusetts his personal belief that Congress had the authority to build roads and canals and that an amendment was not necessary, even harmful. Clearly Adams had traveled beyond the confines of the Madison limitations and the Monroe Memorandum, which limited federal assumption of jurisdiction over roads and canals. He did not reveal to Bailey—at least not so far as his diary indicates—the basis for his constitutional view. However, in his annual message, he had invoked the General Welfare Clause as a potential support for internal improvements. It therefore seems evident that in 1825 Adams was relying on Article I, section 8, clause 1 as sufficiently broad to cover internal-improvement appropriations. It also seems evident that he did not insist upon the jurisdictional limitations that Monroe had discussed and on the basis of which Monroe had proposed a constitutional amendment. For Adams an amendment to overcome these limits was unnecessary. Adams as president, and prior to that as senator and cabinet member, was postulating a broad authority under the General Welfare Clause, on the part of Congress, to finance internal improvements on a large scale, with or without state participation.

Thus December and the first year of John Quincy Adams's term as president came to a close. Through a difficult and bitterly resented election process, the nation had acquired its first president totally committed to internal improvements and possessed of a belief that the General Welfare Clause of the Constitution, as framed by the Philadelphia Convention, gave Congress complete power to assist them with financial resources obtained through the taxing power. How his policy and philosophy on the issue would play out became the subject of his other messages and of the give and take of politics during the balance of his brief administration. However, it was clear at the outset that his position put him at odds with the venerated, retired but still active previous presidents, Jefferson and Madison.[34]

Writing to Madison from retirement in Monticello, evidently in reaction to Adams's first annual message, Jefferson proposed that Virginia issue a formal declaration of protest in order to "save" the Constitution.[35] The document Jefferson conceived would have invoked unequivocally the interpretation of the General Welfare Clause that he and Madison had observed since the advent of the *Report on Manufactures*. Pending the adoption of an appropriate constitutional amendment, Jefferson's proposed declaration would have had the Virginia assembly acquiesce in the internal improvement measures that might be passed, while declaring them of no precedential force.[36]

While he did not disagree with Jefferson's views, Madison coolly counseled restraint in the use of a declaration or protest by the Virginia General Assembly. He believed that such a declaration might bring negative attention to the state. He also calculated that the internal-improvement initiative might founder on practical difficulties when states understood that they would receive less from the federal government in appropriations than they contributed in taxes. Further, he questioned the practical effect of enacting federal legislation into state law.[37]

Madison ended by enclosing a letter that he written to Thomas Ritchie some ten days earlier. Ritchie had first asked whether Virginia should propose an amendment to the Constitution "giving to Congress a power as to roads and canals." Madison responded: "Those who think the power a proper one, and that it does not exist, must espouse such an amendment; and those who think the power neither existing nor proper, may prefer a specific grant, forming a restrictive precedent, to a moral certainty of an exercise of the power, furnishing a contrary precedent." It was apparent that Madison still favored such an amendment but that his thinking had matured on its purposes. Significantly, Madison did not include in his enumeration a third category: those who believed that the power existed and was proper and that an amendment was unnecessary and perhaps dangerous, a category that included the president.

Ritchie had also sought Madison's views on a "proposed amendment to comprise a particular guard against the sweeping construction of the terms, 'common defence, and general welfare.'" Madison cautioned that the experiment might backfire unless there were a strong likelihood of success. Then Madison turned to the doctrine that, under the General Welfare Clause, appropriations could be made for purposes beyond the enumerated power—the doctrine that he had opposed throughout his public life. This was the doctrine of the Monroe Memorandum, although Madison did not so characterize it to Ritchie. On this he disclosed his strategic thinking in full and his belief that a narrowly framed amendment authorizing only internal improvements, might be a solid weapon to defuse the broad, Hamiltonian vision of the General Welfare Clause:

> The doctrine presenting the most serious aspect is that which limits the claim to the mere "appropriation of money" for the general welfare. However, untenable or artificial the distinction may be, its seducing tendencies, and the progress made in giving it a practical sanction, render it pretty certain that a constitutional prohibition is not at present attainable; while an abortive attempt would but give to the innovation a greater stability. Should a specific amendment take place on the subject of roads and canals, the zeal for this appropriating power would be cooled by the provision for the primary and popular object of it; at the same time that the implied necessity of the amendment would have a salutary influence on other points of construction.[38]

Both Jefferson and Madison, in their separate ways, expressed their disapproval of what they regarded as the movement of the nation, during the Adams administration, toward a broad construction of the General Welfare Clause to support internal improvements. In their presidencies, they had not opposed federal aid for such improvements as a matter of policy, as long as accompanied by a constitutional amendment. Time, it appears, had not altered their views. Both former presidents appeared to recommend constitutional amendments to sanction federal involvement in road and canal construction, in part as a means of limiting the broad construction of the General Welfare Clause. The area-by-area specification of authority through discrete constitutional amendment was, as it had been during their presidencies, a route to authorize their desire for federal involvement in internal improvements in a way that did not suggest that Congress had appropriation authority in areas that transcended the enumerated powers.

On the other hand, for President Adams, carving the General Welfare Clause to the limits of the Monroe Memorandum would have been overly confining. Quite apart from the issue of jurisdiction and the question of roads and canals, implementation of the Adams program depended on a reading of the Constitution that permitted appropriations to be administered at the federal level for purposes relating to education, science, and exploration. Because these purposes did not fall within the enumerated powers, the construction that Jefferson and Madison preferred would have precluded the bold program that Adams advocated. Moreover, the federal system that Adams contemplated, if implemented, may have required freedom from the constraints of state jurisdiction and administration that Monroe maintained. Fear of such a limitation may have been implicit, if not explicit, in Adams's admonitions to Representative Bailey regarding an amendment strategy. There was thus an inherent conflict between Adams's persuasion and that of his venerated predecessors—a conflict that Monroe's compromise could partially but not fully bridge.

Adams did not respond specifically to the former presidents on the subject. Nor does it appear that Jefferson or Madison expressed particular animus against John Quincy Adams himself. The focus was on the substantive issue. Indeed, Jefferson was at pains to mask his personal involvement in a potential protest by Virginia.[39]

On July 4, 1826, both Jefferson and John Adams, the second president of the United States, died. John Quincy Adams paid appropriate tribute to Jefferson, left Washington, and returned to

Quincy to spend 100 days in mourning for his father and looking after his affairs. When he returned to Washington, he took up the burden of office again and his efforts to promote an internal-improvement policy.[40] But the fate of his program was largely in the hands of Congress. His ability to influence that body was constrained by his political weakness and by the growing strength of the Jackson and Van Buren adherents. Despite these limitations, Adams dutifully continued to send annual messages that emphasized the importance of internal improvements and that proposed no amendment that would specify congressional authority over them.[41] This stance separated him from the legacy of his Virginia predecessors and his Jacksonian successors and marked his administration as distinct.

Despite Adams's political weakness and the increased strength of his opposition in the twentieth Congress, that Congress enacted several measures which partially reflected the president's position on internal improvements on a piece meal basis and which he readily signed. In May 1828, he signed an omnibus appropriation bill providing funds for a number of projects to clear river obstructions, erect piers, complete interstate or intrastate roads, and preserve lighthouses. Congress in that bill also appropriated $175,000 for the continuation of the Cumberland Road to Zanesville, Ohio. Other bills that Adams signed in that session of Congress provided for a breakwater near the mouth of the Delaware Bay and for numerous other public works in the form of river and harbor improvements.

By an Act of May 24, 1828, Congress also authorized an additional subscription by the federal government to the stock of the Chesapeake and Ohio Canal Company, which had been the subject of a number of Adams's earlier messages. The legislation provided that the secretary of the treasury would have, on behalf of the United States, the right of a shareholder in the company, suggesting a more than passive federal role. The legislation enabled the company to break ground for the project on July 4, 1828, a ceremony in which Adams enthusiastically participated.

While the ceremony may have represented a highlight of the Adams internal-improvement program, the initiation of the Chesapeake and Ohio Canal was not the sole public-works project of the Adams presidency. Notwithstanding the antipathy of many of its members to the administration, Congress continued to approve discrete internal-improvement measures that fell well short of a national system but constituted individual legislative precedents for the exercise of the federal spending power beyond the limits of strict construction. That Adams readily signed these was consistent with his philosophy. That he signed them without objecting to their constitutionality established and extended Executive Branch precedents in favor of the adoption of internal-improvement legislation under the Constitution without the amendments that Jefferson and Madison had sought.[42]

Shortly after his fourth State of the Union message, necessarily subdued because it was transmitted after his defeat in the election of 1828, Adams left the White House. His contributions to the "spirit of internal improvement" as president were at end. He was, however, shortly to return to public service as a member of the House of Representatives where he served until his death in 1848, continuing in that role to support projects of public improvement, not the least of which was the establishment of the Smithsonian Institution.[43]

Madison's Draft Constitutional Amendment

For the surviving partner, James Madison, preserving the Jefferson-Madison legacy of strict enumeration was an important objective in retirement, as it had been in public life. Adams's program presented a real threat, for he was the first president willing to accede to a national system of internal improvements without the authority of a constitutional amendment.[44] It is not surprising, therefore, to find Madison providing advice to those in the Congress who would act as a brake on the Adams agenda. In September 1826, he responded to Senator Martin Van Buren, who asked his counsel on the issue of a constitutional amendment authorizing internal improvements. Madison made clear that his retirement had not dimmed his political acumen as he pursued the strategy that he had propounded to Jefferson and Ritchie during the preceding December.[45]

To implement it, Madison offered his own constitutional drafting skills, as he had done so often in 1787. If the object was merely to "obtain the aid of the Federal Treasury for roads and canals, without interfering with the jurisdiction of the States," Madison proposed the following amendment to the Constitution, presumably as an addition to the enumerated powers: "'Congress may make appropriations of moneys for roads and canals, to be applied to such purposes by the Legislatures of the States within their respective limits, the jurisdiction of the States remaining unimpaired'" This exchange suggests that, as of 1826, Madison still did not share Monroe's view that the power to appropriate merely for internal improvements was contained in the General Welfare Clause. To establish even that limited power on a sound constitutional footing required an amendment of the basic charter; Madison had offered the language to Van Buren as one who would be sympathetic to this view. No formal change to the Constitution emerged from the process.[46]

The Constitutional Thought of John Quincy Adams

Madison's draft amendment when compared to Adams's position against an amendment reflect the polarities of the day on General Welfare philosophy. In effect, Adams's position constituted a third approach. Jefferson and Madison advocated the view that no financial assistance for internal improvements or other initiatives could be based on the General Welfare Clause unless within the enumerated powers. Thus, a constitutional amendment was necessary to extend the reach of the spending power to internal improvements. Monroe, in his memorandum, had argued that a mere appropriation was constitutional as long as it did not involve an assumption of federal jurisdiction with respect to the improvement. For that an amendment was needed. Adams's third course was to support the power of the federal government generally to construct (or help construct) roads and canals without an amendment. To that end, he approved the range of project-oriented appropriation measures that were presented to him. In this sense, John Quincy Adams was the first president to take a modern, broad view of the General Welfare Clause as conferring within its own terms an adequate, full-blown federal spending power.

Adams revealed more of his constitutional analysis in his funeral oratory after his presidency than he did in his official papers during his tenure in that office. When Adams eulogized Madison after his death in 1836, the aging former president politely refrained from airing his differences with Madison over the issue of internal improvements or from complaining that Madison's views may have bolstered opposition to the program of the Adams Administration in the 1820s.[47]

However, five years earlier in 1831, when he was asked by the Corporation of Boston to deliver a eulogy on his predecessor and patron James Monroe, following the death of the fifth president, Adams jumped at the chance. It gave the ex-president an opportunity to venerate his old chief and at the same time critique his successor's shortcomings. In so doing, Adams exposed the basis of his own General Welfare Clause thinking to a greater degree than he had during his presidency, when he had muted his analysis in his annual messages and deferred to Congress on the question of constitutional authority.

Adams introduced that part of his eulogy by expressing regret at Monroe's reluctance to embrace the doctrine that Congress possessed power to construct roads and canals, as evidenced by Monroe's 1822 veto of that year's internal-improvements legislation providing for the repair and maintenance of the Cumberland Road, through the establishment of tolls, and by the memorandum that accompanied that action. Adams characterized this action in a way that revealed his own view on the subject: "Firm and consistent in the constitutional views which he had taken, [Monroe] deemed it his duty to apply to this act his Presidential arresting power; and in returning the Bill to the House where it originated justified his exercise of prerogative in an able and elaborate exposition of the reasons of his opinions. This work, probably, contains whatever of argument the intellectual power of man can eviscerate from reason against the exercise, by Congress, of the contested power. It arrested, to a considerable extent, the progress of Internal Improvement; and succeeded by similar scruples in the mind of one of his successors [presumably a reference to Jackson], has held them in abeyance to this day."[48] Thus, Adams dismissed the Monroe Memorandum, described in the preceding chapter, as a largely negative influence.

However, when he turned to Monroe's actions in 1823, approving the power of Congress to appropriate for internal improvements, Adams had fulsome praise. The manner in which he described this transition again discloses his own perspective and his particular understanding of the role of the Monroe Administration in formulating a progressive interpretation of the General Welfare Clause:

> In his Annual Message to Congress, on the 2d of December 1823, he announced his belief that Congress did possess the power of *appropriating money* for the construction of a canal to connect together the waters of the Chesapeake and the Ohio (the jurisdiction remaining to the States through which the canal would pass). This of course included the concession of the same right of appropriating money for all other like objects of national interest. . . .[49]

Adams then recounted how Monroe's message had recommended an appropriation for surveys by the Corps of Engineers which led to the enactment of the Act of April 30, 1824, that Monroe had signed and that appropriated $30,000 for surveys of roads and canals. Adams employed Biblical language and evangelical fervor in describing his praise for this legislation. "Rise!" he exclaimed. "Rise, before your forefathers here assembled, ye unborn ages of after-time! Rise! and bid the feeble and perishing voice which now addresses them proclaim your gratitude to your and their Creator, for having disposed the hearts of that portion of their Representatives, who then composed their Supreme National Council, to the passage of that Act." Adams then summarized his assessment of Monroe: "The system of Internal Improvement, then, though severely checked by the opinion that the people of this Union have practically denied to themselves the power of bettering their own condition, by restraining their government from the exercise of the faculties by which alone it can be made effective, was commenced under the administration of James Monroe: commenced with his sanction; commenced at his earnest recommendation."[50]

While Adams went to lyrical lengths in lauding Monroe's role in establishing useful precedents to support internal-improvement legislation, Adams went beyond Monroe in believing that the Constitution afforded power to establish a national system. Thus, Adams was apparently unwilling to embrace fully the Monroe Memorandum. That document created an underpinning for congressional involvement through "mere appropriation," but it denied congressional authority to establish a national system with national "jurisdiction." Adams signed the C and O Canal legislation that envisaged a directory role for the Executive Branch in the project. Adams's policy leadership also contemplated wholly federalized programs in science, programs that would not be based upon mere appropriations to the states. This readiness to promote and sign into law federalized programs of assistance distinguishes Adams's contribution. His advocacy anticipated by more than 150 years today's mix of wholly federally administered and state-administered formula programs, all based upon the General Welfare Clause.

The closest that Adams came to a brief or legal argument on the scope of the General Welfare Clause was an 1832 letter to Andrew Stevenson, Speaker of the House. The letter was a response to Stevenson on a position that Adams maintained (in his capacity as chair of the House Committee on Manufactures) to the effect that the General Welfare Clause could be read to support legislation protective of manufactures. Although its focus was on the authority to lay tariffs, the letter sheds light on John Quincy Adams's constitutional views respecting the General Welfare Clause. Stevenson and others had characterized those views as "latitudinarian," citing Madison's interpretation of the clause in an 1830 letter to Stevenson.

Adams conceded that the General Welfare language did not confer a separate substantive power but modified the taxing power in Article I, section 8. As such, Adams contended this language was not "harmless," as Madison argued, but conferred upon Congress broad taxing (and presumably spending) authority. Adams's argument was largely an exercise in self-vindication. He relied primarily on the Louisiana Purchase and the legislative enactments accompanying it, and here he made reference to his own role in their enactment. He recalled at length that, as a young Senator, he had voted against legislation to implement the purchase that gave the president strong executive authority over the territory in question. Adams then believed that the president lacked such authority under the Constitution. The Jefferson Administration had, however, rejected his constitutional qualms, citing the General Welfare Clause.

In his 1832 letter, Adams positively relished the opportunity to expose what he saw as the hypocrisy of strict constructionism. For him, the Louisiana Purchase legislation was the arch-precedent. If it was constutional under the General Welfare Clause, so was the protection legislation in question. That precedent, along with the Cumberland Road legislation, also justified his prointernal improvement stance as president. It was absurd to suggest, Adams had noted in the Monroe eulogy, that Congress could, without constitutional change, annex Louisiana but was "incompetent to the construction of a post-road, the opening of a canal, or the diffusion of the light of Heaven upon the minds of afterages, by the institution of seminaries of learning." Earlier, in 1824 before his election, sharing with Senator Barbour his opinion on the power of the purse, Adams had observed: "Since the Act of Congress establishing the Cumberland Road, there had been no constitutional question worth disputing about involved in the discussion."[51]

JOHN QUINCY ADAMS'S LEGACY

Adams shared his own assessment of his role in this evolution of General Welfare thought in a letter in February of 1837, to his friend, Reverend Charles Upham. The letter was replete with self-pity and bitterness. Adams reflected on his aspirations as president, on their frustration in his defeat by Jackson, and on their gloomy prospects in the future: "The great effort of my administration was to mature into a permanent and regular system the application of all the superfluous revenue of the Union to internal improvement which at this day would have afforded high wages and constant employment to hundreds of thousands of laborers, and in which every dollar expended would have repaid itself fourfold in the enhanced value of the public lands. With this system in ten years from this day the surface of the whole Union would have been checkered over with railroads and canals...."[52] Adams lamented that with the "fall" of his presidency had come the fall of the system of internal improvement that he had so warmly championed. The "great object of [his] life" had therefore "failed."

In the light of the more than 160 years that have transpired since John Quincy Adams penned this gloomy self-evaluation, a more rounded view may be appropriate. It is true, as Nagel points out and as Adams lamented, that his his legislative program was largely ignored or rejected by Congress, led by a coalition of Jackson, Van Buren, Calhoun and Crawford forces. His education initiative—the national university—was never acted on, an unsurprising result since the same proposal by Washington, Madison, and Monroe, presidents elected by wide margins, also failed to be reflected in legislation. His proposal for federal financial assistance for scientific or astronomical studies was never taken seriously in his administration, but in his postpresidential public life he was able to convince Congress to accept the Smithson bequest. Moreover, he played an important role in the crafting of the legislation authorizing the establishment of the Smithsonian Institution.[53]

His effort to establish a truly national system of internal improvements in the form of roads and canals was largely stymied. At the same time, it should be noted that during his administration, Congress enacted a number of appropriation measures or took a number of actions that did expand the national body of roads and canals, including extending the Cumberland Road and initiating the Chesapeake and Ohio Canal. Moreover, during his administration the Executive Branch broadly exercised the survey powers under the 1824 legislation that Monroe had signed. Adams thus made the fullest possible use of the internal-improvement precedents that his predecessor left him and that he praised so fulsomely in his eulogy of 1831. His legacy was to leave, or leave undisturbed, a body of precedent that could not be easily erased by successors with different views.[54]

Perhaps, more importantly, Adams's internal-improvement policies and recommendations, for friend and foe alike, constituted an indelible marker of General Welfare Clause philosophy and approach. Adams's legacy was to forge a position, however maligned, in which the chief executive would, without benefit of constitutional amendment, strongly recommend and promote a coherent program of internal improvement, in transportation, education, and science and posit that program on the basis of the General Welfare Clause as a source of broad authority to meet the nation's needs. The circumstances of his election and his own political ineptitude in failing to organize his own supporters, as well as his occasional overzealous oratory, were unquestionable self-made barriers. But the mark he laid down was, following his administration, to be picked up briefly and fitfully by the Whigs, and more effectively and definitively by Lincoln; that mark can be regarded as an antecedent of the New Deal and Great Society and as a precedent for modern presidents of both parties who, in varying degrees, embraced a policy of improvement, national investment, and human betterment. As Lynn Parsons has aptly observed, "[Adams's] vision of a federal government capable of guiding and directing the economic and intellectual development of the nation through internal improvements and the subsidization of investigation and learning was at least a generation, perhaps a century, ahead of its time."[55]

In 1998 President Clinton paid just tribute to the unique aspect of Adams's service but focused on that part of it that succeeded the sixth presidency:

> John Quincy Adams, a man who was a one-term President, got the living daylights beat out of him for reelection by Andrew Jackson, an American hero, and then was humble enough and dedicated enough to go back and serve nine terms in the House of Representatives, where he died in service in his early eighties—a unique American story. John Quincy Adams was the embodiment of the Nation's opposition to slavery and to something called the gag rule which, believe it or not, was imposed by the Southerners in Congress before the Civil War so that you weren't even supposed to be able to bring up petitions opposing slavery on the floor of Congress.
> Now, at that moment, Adams was the symbol for our country of the idea that the National Government ought to take a stand against

slavery, to strengthen the Union and to, in effect, apply the guarantees of the Constitution to the present moment . . .[56]

The aspect of Adams's contribution to which President Clinton alluded is probably the best remembered period of his service. At the time, Adams observed in his diary how much satisfaction he derived from his election to the House: "My election as President was not half so gratifying to my inmost soul." J. David Greenstone observed in his excellent and absorbing book, *The Lincoln Persuasion*, that Adams's successful fight against the gag rule "secured his place in American political history" and made him an "American institution." However, Adams's campaign against slavery would seem to be related to his advocacy, while president, of a strong role for the federal government in promoting internal improvement. Both were aspects of the same broad effort to enlist government in the improvement of the human condition. Both implicitly recognized the relationship between the use of the spending power and the use of civil-rights guarantees in the Constitution to confront our most intractable social issues.[57]

Adams himself reflected on that relationship—in a negative way—in identifying for Reverend Upham the causes of his "fall." He believed that the desire of the South to preserve the institution of slavery had contributed to the opposition that had been mounted against his internal-improvement program in the southern states, opposition that was reflected in his total loss of the electoral votes of that section of the country in the 1828 election: "When I came to the presidency the principle of internal improvement was swelling the tide of public prosperity, till the Sable Genius of the South saw the signs of his own inevitable downfall in the unparalleled progress of the general welfare of the North, and fell to cursing the tariff, and internal improvement, and raised the standard of free trade, nullification, and state rights."[58]

Thus, for Adams, the resistance to his program and the perpetuation of slavery were inextricably bound up in the collective mind of the South. Slavery was a barrier to the full expression of a prointernal-improvement policy. This was hardly surprising. If the central government had, as Adams contended, the constitutional power to construct roads and canals, might it not also have the power to restrict, and ultimately eliminate slavery? To address this concern, antebellum Democratic presidents who followed Adams and who depended on the South for political support, would work to restrict the power of Congress to enact internal-improvement measures and to conform them to state rights doctrine. Conversely, Adams—the champion of that power both in and out of office—would work to restrict the extension and ultimately set the stage for the abolition of slavery. In the last years of his life Adams increasingly came to see a negative relationship between slavery and the full pursuit of general welfare principles. The former was a brake upon the latter. He told his constituents as much in an 1842 speech: "Slavery stands aghast at the prospective promotion of the general welfare, and flies to nullification for defense against the energies of freedom, and the inalienable rights of man."[59]

Adams thus recognized that as long as slavery survived, the promotion of the general welfare according to his own vision could not proceed. He may also have recognized that once slavery was expunged, the nation would inevitably turn to general-welfare initiatives as a means of meeting the needs of a newly emancipated minority. That positive nexus between emancipation and the "promotion of the general welfare" would ultimately be reflected in the modern day interaction between progressive programs under a General Welfare Clause, read broadly as Hamilton, Adams, Story, and, later, Lincoln, would have it, and the civil rights guarantees of the Constitution, notably the fourteenth amendment that Adams in a sense anticipated and for which Lincoln laid the foundation. As Greenstone notes: ". . . Adams's role in American politics remained largely negative; his was a continuing opposition to the claims and demands of the slave-holding interests. The positive articulation and affirmation of doctrine was to be left to Lincoln."[60]

Largely because of the political failure of his presidency and in part because of the more dramatic quality of his years in the House and his opposition to slavery, witness the *Amistad,* his post–White House years have tended to overshadow the role of John Quincy Adams as a spokesperson for the energetic use of federal power and resources to foster internal improvements without the necessity of the ever-elusive constitutional amendment.

The two strands of Adams's thought—opposition to the interests of the slave-holding states during his years in Congress and his internal-improvement advocacy in the presidential years—are interrelated and mutually reinforcing. Both were reflected in Lincoln's ultimately successful resolution of the tension that increasingly gripped the nation in the years between Adams's departure from the White House and Lincoln's entry into it.

9

Internal Improvements in the Age of Jackson

Jackson's Role in Brief

ANDREW JACKSON'S ROLE IN THIS ACCOUNT IS ONE OF SYNTHESIS AND ambivalence. On the one hand, he sought to limit the application of the General Welfare Clause to justify internal improvements that had characterized the administration of John Quincy Adams. On the other hand, he understood the size of the nation's appetite for internal improvements and wisely articulated the need for a pragmatic approach to constitutional interpretation that would, in the main, satisfy it, while maintaining fiscal discipline and pursuing his goals for decentralization. His most dramatic confrontation with the issue took the form of the Maysville Road veto message. It rejected a congressional appropriation for an internal improvement within a single state as violating the national-local distinction that Jackson saw as an imperative in the application of the General Welfare Clause. In the same message, Jackson reluctantly accepted the doctrine that years of practical construction under preceding administrations had moved the interpretation of the clause beyond the constraints advocated in 1798 by Jefferson and Madison. The Maysville Road veto and Jackson's subsequent pronouncements in light of it constitute a vital bridge between the framing and the modern application of the clause in the twentieth (and now the twenty-first) century.

Inaugural Address and First State of the Union Message

Andrew Jackson's inaugural ceremony is remembered not for the content of the general's inaugural address, although the address was well received, but for the nature of the festivities that followed. Historians relish the recording of it. A White House crowded with average citizens. Orange punch flowing or overflowing. Guests in the White House standing on the upholstered furniture to catch a glimpse of their hero. The new president standing, muddy boots and all, on the portico greeting the throngs and then escaping to his lodging at Gadsby's tavern. It was in all respects a people's inaugural—an event that would be cherished through the ages. Certainly, it was in stark contrast to the solemn inauguration of Jackson's predecessor four years earlier.[1]

Insofar as it touched upon the issue of internal improvements, Jackson's inaugural address was also a marked departure from that of John Quincy Adams. The latter had tried to usher in an era of federally financed internal improvements under the umbrella of an unamended General Welfare Clause. In a terse and guarded sentence, Jackson observed: "Internal improvement and the diffusion of knowledge, so far as they can be promoted by the constitutional acts of the Federal Government, are of high importance."[2]

Jackson's first State of the Union message telegraphed somewhat more extensively his thinking and his antipathy to the nationally oriented general welfare policies of John Quincy Adams. The new president began by holding out the promise of a surplus. He told Congress and the nation that it could look forward to the day when the Government had extinguished its public debt. One effect would be to increase the fiscal capacity of the states to finance education and other public objects, "while ample means will remain in the Federal Government to promote the general weal in all the modes permitted to its authority."[3] Jackson thus stirred up the long simmering internal-improvement debate. He called for the adoption of "some plan which will reconcile the diversified interests of the States and strengthen the bonds which unite them." At the same time, he observed that the mode previously adopted for internal improvements (a thinly veiled reference to Adams's advocacy of a federally financed national system of internal improvements) had been "deprecated" by many citizens as "an infraction of the Constitution" and viewed by others as "inexpedient."[4]

Jackson's proposed solution was a more decentralized, state-based approach than Adams had followed: an "apportionment [of the surplus] among the several States according to their ratio of representation, and should this measure not be found warranted by the Constitution . . . a [constitutional] amendment authorizing it." He added to this a warning against "overstrained constructions" of the Constitution and "all encroachments upon the legitimate sphere of State sovereignty."[5]

Congress failed to take full heed of Jackson's message. It did not adopt the president's state apportionment idea. It did, however, send Jackson a number of internal-improvement measures involving funds for particular projects within individual states. Several of these he vetoed. One of the vetoes rejected a measure to aid a private corporation in the construction of a road from Maysville to Lexington, Kentucky. In a comprehensive message, Jackson seized the opportunity to drive home to the nation his intent to retrench and reform in the area of internal improvement.

THE MAYSVILLE ROAD VETO

The Maysville Road project was designed to join Maysville, Kentucky, on the Ohio River, with interior points in the state. Arthur Schlesinger Jr., in his history of the Jackson era, ascribes the Maysville Road veto to Jackson's ready acceptance of Martin Van Buren's argument that legislation providing financial aid to private corporations should be rejected by the administration. This was not the sole reason for the veto. Jackson's explanation of his action in the accompanying veto message was meant to communicate his understanding of the constitutional posture of internal improvements at the time and to establish a comprehensive framework for his administration's approach to the spending power. It was at root a political document of great importance to the new administration. Jackson pitched the veto, not on the Madisonian ground of lack of an enumerated power in the Constitution to make roads and canals but rather on the ground that the Maysville measure involved assistance to a local rather than a national project.

As Schlesinger describes it, Jackson's veto disappointed not only the backers of the American system but some of Jackson's Western supporters as well, including Richard M. Johnson of Kentucky, who urged that Jackson's friends in Kentucky would be crushed by the action. Jackson firmly rejected his plea. He cited the depleted state of the treasury and asked whether Johnson would favor new taxes or new borrowing to pay for the road. On the morning of the transmission of the message, Martin Van Buren approached Jackson, concerned that political considerations might stay the president's hand. Jackson confidently assured him that "the thing" was in his pocket.

Jackson had urged Van Buren to look out for legislation that would provide a likely target for an internal-improvement veto that would signal the administration's intent to retrench and reform. Van Buren regarded the Maysville Road bill as affording just such an opportunity. When it came time to write the message, Van Buren, as well as Representative James Knox Polk, contributed to its text. Opposition to the bill, largely from members of Congress in the southeast, was sufficient to sustain the veto. The bill's proponents regarded the road as an appropriate part of a national system extending the National Road to the South; opponents regarded it as local legislation. Jackson's modern presidential biographer, Donald B. Cole, sees the veto as an attack by Jackson on "a federal 'system' of roads and canals, not all internal improvements."[6]

After reminding Congress of the recommendations that he had made in his first annual message about the apportionment of tax funds among the states as an alternative to ill-advised internal improvement legislation, Jackson, in his veto message, turned to an assessment of the constitutional posture. If the question were whether the United States could establish jurisdiction over the territory occupied by an internal improvement, the president's answer was simple and concise. Such a power had not been granted. Jackson would veto any measure that attempted to exercise it. The matter was less clear if the question were whether Congress had a "simple right to appropriate money from the National Treasury in aid of such works when undertaken by State authority." To be sure, Madison's precept of 1798 was attractive. "The symmetry and purity of the Government would doubtless have been better preserved if this restriction of the power of appropriation could have been maintained. . . ." But symmetry and purity could not overcome history. "[E]very subsequent Administration of the Government . . . [had] adopted a more enlarged construction of the power," Jackson declared.[7]

In this context, Jackson treated Congress to a recapitulation of the spending power records of his predecessors to prove his point. Jefferson's approval of appropriations for the Louisiana Purchase and the Cumberland Road were cases in point. The latter involved "[n]o less than twenty-three different laws" and $2.5 million with the support of every president since the commencement of the project. In contrast, Madison had vetoed the internal improvement legislation in 1817. Monroe's views had not been left to surmise. Jackson cited the conclusion of Monroe's memorandum, specifically that Congress had an *unlimited* power of appropriation for the "'general, not local, national, not State benefit.'" To Adams, his political foe, Jackson gave short shrift. He observed: "It is well known that the appropriating power, to the utmost extent which had been claimed for it, in relation to internal improvements was fully recognized and exercised by [that administration]."[8]

Having given this historical recapitulation, Jackson concluded that history, if not constitutional principle, had settled the matter: "This brief reference to known facts will be sufficient to show the difficulty, if not impracticability, of bringing back the operations of the Government to the construction of the Constitution set up in 1798, assuming that to be its true reading in relation to the power under consideration. . . ." While there was a duty to resist loose construction, "it is not less true that the public good and the nature of our political institutions require that individual differences should yield *to a well-settled acquiescence of the people and the confederated authorities in particular constructions of the Constitution on doubtful points.* Not to concede this much to the spirit of our institutions would impair their stability and defeat the objects of the Constitution itself." Jackson's reference to 1798 invoked the Virginia Resolutions of that year into which Madison had engraved his narrow interpretation of the General Welfare Clause, as reflected in "Federalist No. 41."[9]

In sum, at this stage in his explanation, Jackson had reached the same conclusions as had Monroe. Jackson would not veto *nationally oriented* internal improvement measures in the form of mere appropriations that did not seek to assert federal jurisdiction over the projects. He had declined to adopt as his own, however reluctantly, Madison's reading of the General Welfare Clause as confined to spending to carry out the enumerated powers. Like Monroe, Jackson, no doubt reinforced by the wily Van Buren, had pragmatically left himself some operational room. This may constitute the most significant aspect of the veto message. The approach enabled the president to sign into law measures to extend existing projects—such as the Cumberland Road—that he favored and regarded as clearly national in scope, while claiming credit for controlling "improvident" appropriations.

This nod to pragmatism did not, however, save the Maysville Road. Quoting Monroe, Jackson claimed that grants to aid works of internal improvement "have always been professedly under the control of the general principle that the works which might be thus aided should be of 'of a general, not local, national, not State' character." He sternly lectured Congress on the significance of this distinction and on the imperative of rejecting all appropriations that could be categorized as local:

> A disregard of this distinction would of necessity lead to the subversion of the federal system. . . . [This distinction] is . . . sufficiently definite and imperative to my mind to forbid my approbation of any bill having the character of the one under consideration . . . I am not able to view [the bill] in any other light than as a measure of purely local character; or, if it can be considered national, that no further distinction between the appropriate duties of the General and State Governments need be attempted, for there can be no local interest that may not with equal propriety be denominated national. It has no connection with any established system of improvements; is exclusively within the limits of a State, starting at a point on the Ohio River and running out 60 miles to an interior town, and even as far as the State is interested conferring partial instead of general advantages.[10]

Thus, Jackson explained where he would draw the line with respect to his approval of internal improvements and, accordingly, where he would draw the line with respect to the exercise of congressional authority under the General Welfare Clause. He readily conceded that the distinction would involve "an inquiry which is often extremely difficult of solution." That the bill provided for aid through the means of a private corporation did not help in the solution. The fundamental inquiry would remain: "Is [the measure] national and conducive to the benefit of the whole, or local and operating only to the advantage of a portion of the Union?"[11]

Jackson's Maysville Policy

At this point Jackson felt it necessary to go beyond the legal niceties of his veto justification and provide a rationale or framework for his general welfare/internal improvement philosophy—to explain the political basis for internal improvement policy under Jacksonian democracy. He therefore devoted the balance of his observations in the Maysville Road veto message to a lengthy discussion of a proposal about how his administration might handle the issue. He started with the constitutional point—his accord with Monroe. "[A]lthough I might not feel it to be my official duty to interpose the Executive veto to the passage of a bill appropriating money for the construction of such works as are authorized by the States and are *national* in their character, I do not wish to be understood as expressing an opinion that it is expedient at this time for the General Government to embark in a system of this kind." He earnestly wanted his constituents to know his views on the subject. In this regard, two aspects of the situation seemed paramount. The first was fiscal, the second programmatic.

Fiscal Imperatives

As Jackson indicated in his first state of the union message, Treasury estimates foretold that internal improvements already enacted, or likely to be enacted during the current session, would require appropriations substantially in excess of Treasury receipts. "Without a well regulated system of internal improvement," Jackson noted, "this exhausting mode of appropriation is not likely to be avoided, and the plain consequence must be either a continuance of the national debt or a resort to additional taxes."[12] Adams's "spirit of improvement" was beginning to have its budgetary and fiscal consequences.

Support for internal improvement might be a worthy goal, but Jackson saw other objects as also demanding the "fostering care" of the federal government. The attachment of the people to the government would, Jackson declared, depend upon the "comparative lightness of their public burthens," as well as the success of its operations. Taxes collected through imposts had for a time been onerous and been borne by the "laboring and less prosperous classes" of the community. These had been cheerfully borne because they were thought to be necessary to the support of the government and the payment of debts "incurred in the acquisition and maintenance of our national rights and liberties." But this same "cheerful acquiescence" in taxation might not be forthcoming, Jackson predicted, when the taxes attributable to the "irregular, improvident, and unequal appropriations of the public funds" that would result from unsystematic internal improvement legislation.[13]

Jackson then declared what he believed to be the fiscal precondition for such legislation in the framework of Jacksonian democracy: "When the national debt is paid, the duties upon those articles which we do not raise may be repealed with safety, and still leave, I trust, without oppression to any section of the country, an accumulating surplus fund, which may be beneficially applied to some well-digested system of improvement."[14] In effect, the high tariff policies of the American System must give way.

Only with the debt paid and imposts reduced as much as possible, consistent with appropriate canons of protectionism, could the nation contemplate devoting a surplus in the Treasury to internal improvements and then only those pursuant to a "well-digested" system. Only in this context could Jackson contemplate a proper role for internal improvements, consistent with his concept of a vigorous democracy. Jackson also invoked his moral antipathy to an unchecked internal-improvement policy. It would breed corruption, favor speculators, and undermine the integrity of the government. He contrasted his utopian picture to the "scramble for appropriations that have no relation to any general system of improvement, and whose good effects must of necessity be very limited."[15] Such appropriations were no more than "artful expedients" to shift to the Government losses of "unsuccessful private speculation."[16]

Programmatic-Constitutional Considerations

After describing the fiscal conditions that he considered necessary for a sound foundation for legislation related to internal improvements, Jackson turned to programmatic concerns. Like his Jeffersonian predecessors, he proposed a constitutional amendment, but in a somewhat different framework. For Jackson, adopting an amendment that defined the government's power with respect to internal improvements was a matter of expediency, if not jurisprudence. As Jackson wrote, "Assuming the right to appropriate money to aid in the construction of national works to be warranted by the contemporaneous and continued exposition of the Constitution, its insufficiency for the successful prosecution of them must be admitted by all candid minds."[17]

Even if one admitted constitutional authority to enact appropriations, without a constitutional amendment there could be no adequate framework for carrying out a successful program of internal improvements. Usage would not suffice; it was too confusing. "In most, if not all, other disputed questions of appropriation the construction of the Constitution must be regarded as unsettled if the right to apply money in the enumerated cases is placed on the ground of usage."[18]

Shifting to less gloomy apprehensions, Jackson set forth his own vision for the constitutional change that he proposed. He offered a prescription for a constitutional and policy framework for the effective exercise of the national spending power, which he recognized that the people then desired or would in some future day desire.

> If it be the wish of the people that the construction of roads and canals should be conducted by the Federal Government, it is not only highly expedient, *but indispensably necessary*, that a previous amendment of the Constitution, delegating the necessary power and defining and restricting its exercise with reference to the sovereignty of the States, should be made.... The right to exercise as much jurisdiction as is necessary to preserve the works and to raise funds by the collection of tolls to keep them in repair can not be dispensed with.... If it be the desire of the people that the agency of the Federal Government should be confined to the appropriation of money in aid of such undertakings, in virtue of State authorities, then the occasion, the manner, and the extent of the appropriations should be made the subject of constitutional regulation. This is the more necessary in order that they may be equitable among the several States, promote harmony between different sections of the Union and their representatives, preserve other parts of the Constitution from being undermined by the exercise of doubtful powers or the too great extension of those which are not so, and protect the whole subject against the deleterious influence of combinations to carry by concert measures which, considered by themselves, might meet but little countenance.[19]

History to the contrary, Jackson regarded the "supposed impracticability of obtaining an amendment" as unfounded.[20]

On the surface, the Maysville veto message may seem like an exercise in obfuscation and circumlocution. On the one hand, we find Jackson conceding that he was not obliged by the Constitution to veto internal-improvement measures of a national dimension. On the other hand, we find him urging a constitutional amendment to regulate Congress in the exercise of its legislative authority over internal improvements, especially with respect to the distribution of funds. Beneath the surface is an artful political compromise. Like Monroe, Jackson felt the need to leave constitutional room to sign internal-improvement measures that he favored or that he believed the country required. If Congress did not propose, or the states did not ratify, an amendment, it seems clear that he did not wish to be forced to veto all improvement measures.

At the same time, a major segment of his reform was to limit the appetite of Congress for internal improvements. Moreover, he had to distance himself from the Adams-Clay faction that supported broad appropriations for internal improvements—a national system. What better way to do this than to insist upon a constitutional amendment to regularize the process of appropriations for state-administered projects? Such an amendment would serve the purpose that Madison had suggested to Van Buren in 1826. It would establish a precedent that federal spending for internal improvement must be accompanied by a constitutional amendment, even if the General Welfare Clause could be read as authorizing mere appropriations for that purpose. Thus, Jackson called for an amendment, whether the people wished the federal government to assume the role of constructing internal improvements or whether they wished the federal government to continue to appropriate money to the states for this purpose. In the former case the amendment was needed to confer power not possessed; in the latter case, it was intended to regularize power already available. Either way, the call for an amendment would permit the Jackson administration to retrench while still affording it a basis upon which to approve those appropriations that were regarded as essential, if no amendment were proposed.

If anyone could have convinced Congress to adopt such an amendment, it would have been Jackson, caricatured in some quarters as "King Andrew." His hold over Congress was so strong that John Quincy Adams in retirement remarked enviously about the degree to which Congress deferred to the new president.[21] But Jackson could not persuade Congress to propose to the states the constitutional amendment that he sketched out in the Maysville Road message. Part of the difficulty may have been the inherent contradiction that John Quincy Adams had recognized in his conversation with Bailey. If the Constitution afforded the power—and Jackson conceded that it did—then an amendment was not necessary. It was also dangerous, because it would tie the hands of Congress by implying that a constitutional amendment was needed to support each new spending mission.[22]

Post-Maysville Reflections

Despite the premonitions of some of Jackson's supporters, the Maysville veto was a political success. It played well among the

Radicals of the strict constructionist stripe. It did not erode Jackson's following in the West to the degree that had been predicted. Jackson himself was pleased with the reception that it received and believed that it gained him adherents in the West. He had broken with the Adams tradition and established a framework that placed a limit upon improvident improvements. That Congress did not respond with an amendment immediately was clearly not fatal, because Jackson could approve or veto spending measures as he saw fit.

Not all applauded. John Quincy Adams expressed apprehension about the Maysville message but conceded that it would be popular. "I suppose that the sacrifice of the Indians and of the interest of internal improvement and domestic industry will strengthen, rather than weaken the popularity of the present Administration," he wrote, leaving us this interesting and prophetic insight into the history of the federal spending power:

> I have cherished the principle and the system of internal improvement, under a conviction that it was for this nation the only path to increasing comforts and well-being, to honor, to glory, and finally to the general improvement of the condition of mankind. This system has had its fluctuations from the time of the establishment of the present Constitution of the United States. . . . The combination in Congress became by their means so strong that it overpowered the resistance of Mr. Monroe and produced the Act of Congress of April, 1824. The slave-holders of the South have since discovered that it will operate against their interests. Calhoun has turned his back upon it, and Jackson, who to promote his election and obtain Western support truckled to it for a time, has now taken a decided stand against it. . . . The cause will no doubt survive me, and, if the Union is destined to continue, will no doubt ultimately triumph. At present it is desperate.[23]

In a similar vein, Adams's former political partner, Henry Clay, attacked Jackson for inconsistency and for abandoning pledges that Clay asserted Jackson had made in the 1828 campaign. For Clay, Jackson's application of Hamilton's local-national distinction was fundamentally flawed: "If the road facilitates, in a considerable degree, the transportation of the mail to a considerable portion of the Union, and at the same time promotes internal commerce among the several states and may tend to accelerate the movement of armies and distribution of munitions of war, it is of national consideration. Tested by this, the true rule, the Maysville road was undoubtedly national."[24]

Jackson's message had focused upon a fundamental weakness in the exercise of the spending power, a weakness that Adams's enthusiasm could not obviate. If the distribution of funds was seen as inequitable, and the regular appropriation of funds for initiating repairing, or extending internal improvements or other spending measures was dependent solely on the vicissitudes of the annual project-by-project appropriation process, then a coherent national system could never develop. The nation, in planning projects that would stimulate growth, would be hampered by doubt and the absence of a clear and rational guide. At the same time, the very limited interpretation of the General Welfare Clause that Monroe had announced, and that Jackson seemed to be embracing, precluded federal financial participation in a national system of internal improvements. The project must be national in scope, but it could not be part of a national *system*. The approach seemed to be internally incoherent. Jackson's way out was a constitutional amendment, not to cure the limitation that Madison perceived but the potential incoherence that characterized Monroe's effort to overcome that limitation.

The constitutional amendment that Jackson sought never arrived. Ultimately Congress was forced to adopt another strategy to rationalize the appropriation of federal funds for internal improvements. This took the form of enacting authorizing legislation. Such legislation empowered Congress to make future appropriations for projects of federal interest and established a national framework within which appropriations would be enacted. It also established standards for the equitable distribution of funds to the states, the purposes for which the funds could be used, and the conditions imposed on the grant of funds. Such a measure would address some of the needs that Jackson had portrayed in his Maysville Road message, so important for an understanding of the evolution of the spending power. Although it lacks the force of a constitutional amendment adopted under Article V of the Constitution, the modern authorizing process has come to provide a measure of coherence in the practice of making federal appropriations to support state projects of national consequence, a practice that Jackson recognized as constitutional even in the absence of such an amendment.[25]

Following the delivery of the Maysville message, Jackson continued to preach the central philosophy of that message in succeeding state of the union addresses but vacillated as to the means to implement it. During his first term, he promoted a formula that would have allowed the federal government to distribute to the states surplus funds remaining in the Treasury after the national debt was paid. At the end of his second term, he backed away from this proposal. He explained that it had been introduced to control the profligate exercise of the spending power to finance internal improvements. That goal accomplished, he had come to believe that his revenue sharing proposal exceeded constitutional authority and was, in any case, unwise. It would convert the federal government into a taxing mechanism for the entire country. For Jackson, the General Welfare Clause could be exercised only through the appropriation of funds for general welfare purposes of a national dimension.[26]

Within the constraints of the policy he had taken great pains to explain, the national-local distinction in the Maysville message enabled Jackson to sign into law measures that allowed the Cumberland Road to be extended from Zanesville, Ohio (where Adams had left it), to Indiana, and from there to Illinois. Responsibility for administering the extension was left to the states affected. This important national road to the west was the product of two administrations with sharply different philosophies about exercising the power conferred by the General Welfare Clause.

Donald B. Cole assesses the General Welfare Clause record of the Jackson presidency from a somewhat different vantage point, that of the appropriation legislation that it produced. His observations reinforce the thesis that an interpretation of the clause sufficiently broad to justify at least a moderate level of federal support for internal improvement was inevitable, once one granted the indefinite quality of the language that the framers crafted and once one accepted, as Jackson did, the limited, but powerful conclusions of the Monroe Memorandum. Cole notes that "Jackson had said no to a comprehensive national program—not to internal improvements in general. In 1830 he vetoed four of the six major internal improvement bills, but he accepted the two most important ones, the survey bill and the bill for extending the National Road. . . . By the time he had left office his administration had spent $10 million on internal improvements, twice as much as all previous administrations combined, even when adjusted for inflation." Jackson's expenditures doubled those of John Quincy Adams, "who had already spent far more annually than any previous president." Jackson spent almost $4 million on the road, compared with $1.6 million spent on the road prior to the Maysville veto. By the time Jackson left office, this first major federally assisted internal improvement almost had reached the Mississippi. All this had been done within the strictures that he had laid out in the Maysville Road veto message.[27] The exercise of the General Welfare Clause for the general improvement of the nation could be constrained, but it could not be totally stifled, even in an administration highly conscious of the limitations of federal authority.

10

Madison's Testament, Story's Commentary, and the Postulates of the Antebellum Presidents

THE LABORING OAR IN THE DEVELOPMENT OF GENERAL WELFARE doctrine in the early nineteenth century had been that of Congress in tandem with the Executive Branch. There remained a need for the judiciary to clarify and resolve the matter. No case, however, came before the Supreme Court to afford a basis for a definitive decision. Instead, a surrogate appeared early in Jackson's second term. It took the form of a comprehensive set of commentaries on the Constitution delivered by Supreme Court Justice Joseph Story in 1833. The commentaries were written by Story, not in his capacity as a justice of the Supreme Court but in his role as a professor of law at Harvard University. Story, a Federalist turned National Republican, contradicted what Madison had proclaimed throughout his public career and reinforced strongly during retirement, most notably in an 1830 letter to Andrew Stevenson in the nature of a legal brief.

Story opined that the General Welfare Clause did not confine Congress to use tax revenues only for appropriations to carry out the enumerated powers in Article I, section 8 of the Constitution. He saw the General Welfare Clause as conferring "a distinct, substantive, and independent power" to spend or appropriate for "the general welfare," unconstrained by the enumerated powers. His commentary constituted a legal bridge between the framers and succeeding generations that served until the Supreme Court came to adjudicate the controversy. It is appropriate to compare Story's analysis to that in Madison's last public testament.[1]

MADISON'S TESTAMENT: THE 1830 STEVENSON LETTER

As the sage of Montpelier, James Madison continued to be drawn into the constitutional controversies of the day. The battle over internal improvement was no exception. Martin Van Buren consulted him on various aspects of the Maysville veto message. Others sought to ascertain whether the construction placed on his 1817 internal-improvements veto message was correct. Toward the end of 1830, Andrew Stevenson, a Virginian, Speaker of the United States House of Representatives, and "a defender of the rights of states," visited Madison at Montpelier and conversed with him about the meaning of the clause. At Stevenson's request, Madison agreed to commit his analysis to writing. His response constitutes the most comprehensive statement of his views on the subject during his retirement. Drew McCoy, in his chronicle of Madison's retirement years, *The Last of the Fathers,* has observed that Madison "loathed" the General Welfare Clause and what he regarded as its broad construction. McCoy portrays Madison as "actually eager to publicize his views" on the subject. Madison's letters to Stevenson afforded the retired president an opportunity to do so. One can imagine him, at the age of 79, ensconced in his copious but cluttered library at Montpelier, warming to the defense of a lifelong cause.[2]

Turning to the proceedings of the Philadelphia Convention of 1787, Madison, in his 1830 letter, noted that the terms "common defence and general welfare" did not figure in the debates during the period from May 30 to August 6, 1787 and that the Committee of Detail did not include language referring to the general welfare when, on August 6, it reported out a draft giving the legislature of the central government the power "to lay and collect taxes." Madison then related the events of the August sessions of the Constitutional Convention which had focused on the issue of the payment of the public debt. He noted that on August 21, the Committee of Eleven had reported a clause empowering the Congress, *inter alia,* "'to discharge . . . the debts of the United States as the debts incurred by the *several* States *during the late war,* for the *common defence* and *general welfare.*'" Madison underlined the key terms in his letter to Stevenson, and noted that this language conformed to comparable language in the Articles of Confederation. The retired president then noted that on August 23 the clause relating to the discharge of the debt was amended to read: "The Legislature shall fulfill the engagements and discharge the debts of the United States, and shall have the power to lay and collect taxes, duties, imposts, and excises." Madison observed that the two powers relating to taxes and debts had been "merely transposed."[3]

Madison then interpreted the actions of August 25, 1787. On

that day, as Madison related it to Stevenson, the clause was altered to provide that debts contracted by the Revolutionary Congress would be valid under the Constitution. This amendment was followed by "a proposition, referring to the powers to lay and collect taxes, 'for the payment of *said* debts and for defraying the *expenses that shall be* incurred *for the common defense and general welfare.*'" This was the amendment proposed by Roger Sherman, although Madison did not attribute it to him in the Stevenson letter. Madison noted that the August 25 amendment was rejected but that on September 4, the Committee of Eleven (the Committee on Unfinished Parts) had reported the following language: "The Legislature shall have power to lay and collect taxes, duties, imposts and excises to pay the debts and provide for the common defense and the general welfare." To Madison, this action amounted to "retaining the terms of the Articles of Confederation, and covering, by the general term 'debts,' those of the old Congress."[4]

Madison framed his interpretation of the General Welfare Clause from this history as he had recounted it: Special provision would not have been needed for the debts of the new Congress. The power to provide money and carry out certain powers would have implicitly contained the power to pay the debts. Therefore, Madison tied the General Welfare Clause to the power relating, not to the new debts and to the new taxing power, but to the old debts: "[B]ut for the old debts, and their association with the terms 'common defence and general welfare,' the clause would have remained as reported in the first draught of a Constitution [presumably the August 6 draft], expressing generally, 'a power in Congress to lay and collect taxes, duties, imposts and excises' without any addition of the phrase 'to provide for the common defense and general welfare.'" Madison believed that the terms "would not have been introduced but for the introduction of the old debts." Once introduced, however, they "passed undisturbed through the subsequent stages" of the framing process.[5]

This said, Madison felt compelled to respond to the argument that if the framers had intended the General Welfare Clause to be a mere reference point having no general effect they would have said so. "It may be asked," he observed in the 1830 letter, "why the terms 'common defence and general welfare,' if not meant to convey the comprehensive power which, *taken literally*, they express, were not qualified and explained by some reference to the particular powers subjoined." Madison then responded to his own question: "although it might easily have been done, and experience shows it might be well if it had been done, yet the omission is accounted for by an inattention to the phraseology, occasioned doubtless by its identify with the harmless character attached to it in the instrument from which it was borrowed," namely, the Articles of Confederation.

McCoy has noted that Madison "emphatically rejected," as a proper approach to constitutional interpretation, relying solely "on textual exegesis, or simple analysis of the meaning of the language of the Constitution." McCoy further reinforces this point: "[Madison] believed that history must take priority over the arguments of present-day theoreticians who scrutinized text alone, because history provided, in addition to legitimacy, the only viable basis for stable government under the Constitution."

At the same time, the former president must have recognized that this argument was not fully persuasive, as indeed it was not to be to Joseph Story, for he made the further argument that, if the framers had intended the General Welfare Clause to authorize the broad power that had been claimed for it, they also would have said so expressly. "May it not be asked" wrote Madison in the 1830 letter, "with infinitely more propriety, and without the possibility of a satisfactory answer, why, if the terms were meant to embrace not only all the powers particularly expressed, but the indefinite power which has been claimed under them, the intention was not so declared?"

In sum, Madison dismissed the initiative of Roger Sherman on August 25 because it had not been agreed to by the states and drew the following conclusion in his letter to Stevenson: "The obvious conclusion to which we are brought is, that these terms, copied from the Articles of Confederation, were regarded in the new as in the old instrument, merely as general terms, explained and limited by the subjoined specifications [the enumerated powers], and therefore requiring no critical attention or studied precaution." To augment Stevenson's understanding, Madison launched into a long discussion of the practice of the Revolutionary Congress.

The absence of any meaningful debate in the Convention, Madison argued, suggested that the General Welfare Clause could not be read broadly to support appropriations for internal improvements and other public works of an educational or scientific nature. He concluded: "That the terms in question were not suspected in the Convention which formed the Constitution of any such meaning as has been constructively applied to them, may be pronounced with entire confidence; for it exceeds the possibility of belief that the known advocates in the Convention for a jealous grant and cautious definition of Federal powers should have silently permitted the introduction of words or phrases in a sense rendering fruitless the restrictions and definitions elaborated by them."[6]

More than once, Madison came back to this central argument. He asked his reader to "[c]onsider . . . the immeasurable difference between the Constitution limited in its powers to the enumerated objects, and expounded as it would be by the import claimed for the phraseology in question." He regarded the difference as "equivalent to two Constitutions . . . the one possessing powers confined to certain specified cases, the other extended to all cases whatsoever; for what is the case that could not be embraced by a general power to raise money, a power to provide for the general welfare, and a power to pass all laws necessary and proper to carry these powers into execution; all such provisions and laws superseding, at the same time, all local laws and constitutions at variance with them?" To Madison it was impossible that such a Constitution would have been presented by the framers to the ratifying conventions.[7]

Finally, Madison turned to the actions of the first session of the First Congress in which the Bill of Rights had been debated. He noted that the General Welfare Clause had not been the subject of any discussions in the First Congress. Nor had it been the subject of the amendments that comprised the Bill of Rights. "Such a forbearance and silence on such an occasion, and among so many members who belonged to the part of the nation which called for explanatory and restrictive amendments, and who had been elected as known advocates for them, cannot be accounted for without supposing that the terms 'common defence and general welfare' were not at that time deemed susceptible of any such construction as has since been applied to them."

Madison concluded his letter to Stevenson with a plea for his vision of the "middle ground." He expressed the "hope" that, "as our Constitution rests on a middle ground between a form wholly national and one merely federal, and on a division of the powers of Government between the States in their united character and in their individual characters, this peculiarity of the system will be kept in view, as a key to the sound interpretation of the instrument, and a warning against any doctrine that would either enable the States to invalidate the powers of the United States, or confer all power on them."[8]

Madison's analysis was advanced in reasonable and cogent

terms. It was set forth in a highly professional and well-crafted legal brief that surely conveyed the writer's public advocacy stance. His purpose was to preserve the integrity of the enumerated powers that he had helped to draft in 1787, a cause for which he felt a special guardianship, particularly because his lifetime political partner and ally on this issue had passed in 1826. Yet Madison's analysis was open and transparent, and its author candidly confronted a number of the considerations that arguably ran counter to it.

- First, as Madison conceded, the language of the General Welfare Clause literally conveyed a broad spending power not limited by the enumerated powers.
- Second, as Madison recognized, the framers easily could have made clear that the general welfare language was intended as no more than a reference to the enumerated powers. This they did not do.
- Third, Madison's principal contention was that the Philadelphia framers were deeply suspicious of broad federal power and could never have intended the General Welfare Clause to convey a virtually unlimited grant of the power to appropriate, as was contended by those who supported Hamilton's reading. However, there is evidence that the framers were not of a single mind on this issue. A number of delegates favored an indefinite grant of legislative authority to Congress. Hamilton, Gouverneur Morris, and James Wilson seem clearly in this camp. Other delegates, such as James McHenry, were ready to seize upon broad language in order to support their internal-improvement aspirations. Governor Randolph in the Virginia ratifying convention denied that the General Welfare Clause conferred a general power to regulate to provide for the general welfare but did not urge that the clause confined appropriations to purposes within the limits of the enumerated powers. In short, despite Madison's affinity for history as a sure guide to constitutional interpretation, the historical record was itself susceptible to varied interpretations. Former framers could be found on either side of the issue, sometimes both. Under these circumstances, a resort to textual reading, despite Madison's distaste, would be an attractive alternative, particularly for those with a policy ax to grind or a strong appetite for federally financed internal improvements.
- Fourth, Madison ingeniously proposed that the phrase "to provide for the general welfare" was merely intended to identify the old debts that Congress would now be authorized to pay under Article I, section 8, clause 1. If the August 21 language from the Committee of Eleven had been adopted, there would have been textual support for this. However, the proposal of Roger Sherman, upon which the

General Welfare Clause was based, was not so confined. Its terms differed from that of the August 21 formulation. Moreover, it appears that Sherman's purpose was to limit the scope of the spending power rather than merely identifying the old debts that could be paid pursuant to it.
- Fifth, Madison's contention that the General Welfare Clause was intended to invoke language used in the Articles of Confederation is consistent with Sherman's stated intent. However, as Madison himself conceded, the practice of the Confederation Congress was not uniformly consistent with a narrow reading of the phrase.
- Sixth, Madison perhaps dismissed too readily the difference between a power to appropriate for the general welfare and a plenary power to provide for the general welfare independent of the spending power.

Monroe had seized upon a number of these points in his 1822 memorandum, and it was along these lines that the response to Madison's letter was formulated in a set of commentaries by Joseph Story several years after Madison wrote to Stevenson. Notwithstanding the homage genuinely due Madison as the father of the Constitution, Story's work took issue with Madison's analysis and posed an alternative reading of the General Welfare Clause, consistent with that of Hamilton and Monroe.

In a subsequent private letter and perhaps in a more mellow mood on the matter, Madison recognized some of the practical considerations at play respecting the internal-improvement issue. In January 1831, he wrote from Montpelier, responding to a writer's request for his comments on a manuscript relating, among other things, to internal improvements. On that subject, the former president referred to the Bonus Bill veto as denying the "constitutionality" of the "appropriating" power. Madison observed that his opinion remained, "subject, as heretofore, to the exception of particular cases, where a reading of the Constitution different from mine may have derived from a continued course of practical sanctions an authority sufficient to overrule individual constructions." Madison added that it was not surprising that "doubts and difficulties" should arise with respect to constitutional interpretation, given the distribution of governmental power among coordinate branches with the "lines of division obscure." Madison observed: "A settled practice, enlightened by occurring cases and obviously conformable to the public good, can alone remove the obscurity." In the legislative branch, Madison mused, the Constitution was "read by some as if it were a Constitution for a single Government, with powers coextensive with the general welfare, and by others interpreted as if it were an ordinary statute, and with the strictness almost of a penal one."

The former president advocated an "intermediate course" to be prescribed by a constitutional amendment. He perceived such a course to be most "desirable" in the case of internal improvements and recalled that he had always believed that vesting the federal government with the power to construct canals would have been appropriate. Here he laid out the public policy considerations that favored a federal role in such internal improvements in terms of money and national interest. "If I err or am too sanguine in the views I indulge," he concluded, "it must be ascribed to my conviction that canals, railroads, and turnpikes are at once the *criteria* of a wise policy and causes of national prosperity; that the want of them will be a reproach to our republican system . . . ; and that the exclusion, to a mortifying extent, will ensue, if the power be not lodged where alone it can have its due effect." Thus, Madison in retirement seemed to be striking the same notes as his seventh annual message: authority to appropriate for internal improvements was lacking in the Constitution; it would be eminently wise as a matter of policy for the federal government to have a role in advancing such improvements; and a constitutional amendment should be adopted as an "intermediate" means of resolving the issue. At the same time, while restating an interpretation which he had devoutly maintained throughout his lifetime, he was able to recognize the force of continued application by Congress—the people's representatives—as part of the framework of constitutional growth and development, even though it ran counter to his own view. That perspective and detachment were leavened by his own unwavering commitment, as a matter of policy, to a meaningful federal role in achieving national growth and prosperity through an effective and well-devised system of internal improvements.[9]

Story's Commentaries: Another Perspective

Joseph Story was a gifted American politician, jurist and law teacher, who served for over thirty years on the Supreme Court. For most of those years, Story's service coincided with that of Chief Justice Marshall, and he joined in or wrote a number of the landmark opinions of the Court in the Marshall era. He graduated from Harvard, quickly distinguished himself as a member of the bar and served in the Massachusetts legislature. From December 1808 to March 1809, Story served in the United States House of Representatives. Although a member of Jefferson's Democratic-Republican party, Story led the rebellion against Jefferson's embargo. Jefferson wished the embargo to continue until he left office in March of 1809, but Story and others in the Massachusetts delegation were determined to end it sooner. Jefferson, Madison, and other cabinet members urged Congress to stand firm and maintain the embargo until June 1809; Story and his northern Republican colleagues thought that New England could no longer suffer the embargo and that immediate repeal would prevent war. Repudiation of Jefferson's leadership and policies at the end of his term was a significant part of the mix.

This history did not prevent Madison from appointing Story to the Supreme Court in 1811, a post that he retained until his death in 1845. He participated in the remarkable series of judicial decisions during the twenty year period from 1812 to 1832 when the Court produced a body of precedent that established the full scope of judicial review. In addition to his duties on the Court, Story became Dane Professor of Law at Harvard in 1829 and, with prodigious industry and energy, continued to produce respected treatises on various areas of the law including bailments, conflict of laws, and equity. His most influential work was his three volume *Commentaries on the Constitution of the United States*, first published in 1833 during Andrew Jackson's second term as president. The commentaries were enormously influential and remained persuasive into the twentieth century. They have been characterized by Professors Rotunda and Nowak as a "vital force advocating nationalism and supplying the theoretical framework to attack the theories of state rights, reserved powers, and dual sovereignty. . . ." These scholars further point to Story's belief "that the best hope for the country to flourish as a nation and as a place where republican principles could thrive was a strong central government."

Story intersected with both John Quincy Adams and Jackson. Adams had consulted Story during his presidency about his personal difficulties regarding the Hartford Convention. Both Adams and Story were active in Harvard University affairs, and Story was among the party of justices who visited Adams after the end of his presidency. Adams was predisposed in favor of opinions of the court during the Marshall era, in many of which Story had joined. On the other hand, Jackson declined to name Story chief justice on the death of Marshall. He turned instead to

Roger Brooke Taney, a move that history attributes to Jackson's displeasure with Story's judicial philosophy. How much this perspective influenced Story in the positions that he took in the *Commentaries* on sensitive constitutional issues, particularly those regarding the spending power, is a matter of mere speculation. However, it seems fair to note that Story came down on the question of the breadth of the General Welfare Clause in a manner consistent with the views of Hamilton, Monroe, and John Quincy Adams and contrary to the views of Jefferson and Madison. This would have put him at odds with the Jacksonian view that caution should be exercised in making General Welfare expenditures although, as has been noted, Jackson was willing to sign appropriation bills for national internal improvements, particular those begun before his term.[10]

In his chapter in the *Commentaries* on the powers of Congress and on the taxing power, Story sought to deal definitively with three questions:

(1) Did the General Welfare Clause state an independent power to legislate for the "general welfare" separate from the power to tax and appropriate?
(2) Did the General Welfare Clause constitute a limitation or qualification on the power to appropriate federal funds secured through taxation?
(3) Was the power to tax (and appropriate) limited, as Madison and Jefferson had argued, to purposes that fell within the enumerated powers in Article I, section 8, or was that power available for any purpose determined to fall within the purview of the term "general Welfare of the United States?"

These questions were, of course, at the heart of the debate that had raged over the scope of the General Welfare Clause since the formation of the nation, questions that had divided Federalist from Jeffersonian Republican, president from Congress. Although Story addressed them as an academic, his role as a member of the Court insulated him from the legislative and administrative battles that swirled around these issues, and his stature made his observations on these sensitive questions in the *Commentaries* particularly significant and compelling.

The General Welfare Clause as a Qualification of the Taxing Power

In commencing his discussion of Article I, section 8, Story invoked the "controversies and discussions to which it has given rise." He relished the dramatic aspect of this highly charged area of constitutional law on which he was about to opine. Section 8 of Article I, he continued, "has been in the past time, it is in the present time, and it will probably in all future time continue to be the debatable ground of the Constitution, signalized at once by the victories and the defeats of the same parties. Here the advocates of State rights and the friends of the Union will meet in hostile array."[11]

Story could not resist a gentle poke at the inconsistencies of politicians on the spending power issue both in and out of office. More than likely he had Jefferson in mind when he observed in the *Commentaries*: "Nor ought it all to surprise us . . . that the opposing parties shall occasionally be found to maintain the same system, when in power, which they have obstinately resisted when out of power." Somewhat tongue-in-cheek, Story continued his jibe: "Without supposing any insincerity or departure from principle in such cases, it will be easily imagined that a very different course of reasoning will force itself on the minds of those who are responsible for the measures of government, from that which the ardor of opposition and the jealousy of rivals might well foster in those who may desire to defeat what they have no interest to approve."

With these preliminaries behind him, Story turned to the language of clause 1 of Article I, section 8. He found it necessary, as a threshold matter, "to settle the grammatical construction of the clause." Story then posed the central question: "Do the words, 'to lay and collect taxes, duties, imposts, and excises,' constitute a distinct substantial power; and the words, 'to pay the debts and provide for the common defence and general welfare of the United States,' constitute another distinct and substantial power? Or are the latter words connected with the former so as to constitute a qualification upon them?" Story recognized that this question had been "a topic of political controversy" and that it had "furnished abundant materials for popular declamation and alarm."

Moreover, the national stakes were high. "If the former be the true interpretation, then it is obvious that under color of the generality of the words, to 'provide for the common defence and general welfare,' the government of the United States is, in reality, a government of general and unlimited powers, notwithstanding the subsequent enumeration of specific powers." On the other hand, if the latter interpretation was correct and the General Welfare Clause was a mere qualification of the taxing clause, "then the power of taxation only is given by the clause, and it is limited to objects of a national character, 'to pay the debts and provide for the common defence and the general welfare.'"

Story devoted a number of paragraphs to support his conclusion that the latter, more limited reading, was the correct one. He conceded that the former opinion had been maintained by some "minds of great ingenuity," but he refuted what he regarded as Jefferson's perception that the Federalists, as a party, had maintained the former, broader doctrine. Story insisted that the latter, narrower doctrine had been maintained by the "some of the most strenuous federalists."[12]

Irrespective of the historical notes, Story concluded that the latter reading—the reading that Article I, section 8, clause 1 gives only a power of taxation, limited or qualified by the General Welfare Clause—"has been the generally received sense of the nation, and seems supported by reasoning at once solid and impregnable." Accordingly, the reading that he would maintain in the commentaries is "that which makes the latter words a qualification of the former." He then restated Article I, section 8, clause 1 supplying the words necessary to make it properly understood: "'The Congress shall have power to lay and collect taxes, duties, imposts, and excises *in order* to pay the debts, and to provide for the common defence and general welfare of the United States." The words "in order" were italicized by Story. This was the way that he understood the provision, and this is the way that posterity has come to understand the provision.

Story then underscored the significance of this key interpretation. "In this sense, Congress has not an unlimited power of taxation; but it is limited to specific objects,—the payment of the public debts, and providing for the common defence and general welfare [of the United States]. A tax, therefore, laid by Congress for neither of these objects, would be unconstitutional as an excess of its legislative authority."

By what reasoning did Story reach this result? He argued that a broad reading in this respect would be inconsistent with the notion of the constitutional structure of the national government as one of enumerated powers: "If the clause, 'to pay the debts and provide for the common defence and general welfare of the United States,' is construed to be an independent and substantive grant of power, it not only renders wholly unimportant and unnecessary the subsequent enumeration of specific powers, but it plainly extends far beyond them and creates a general authority in Congress to pass all laws which they may deem for the common defence or general welfare." Under such a reading, the

Constitution would "practicably create an unlimited government." In concluding that no such reading was intended, Story cited President Monroe's memorandum of May 1822 issued in connection with his internal improvement veto of that year. Both Story and Monroe had reached the same conclusion.[13]

Further, Story reasoned, to give the enumeration of powers a "sensible place" in the Constitution, it was necessary to construe them "as not wholly and necessarily embraced in the general power [to provide for the common defence and general welfare]." Moreover, to give every part of the Constitution meaning, it was necessary to avoid the broader construction of the General Welfare Clause. "For what purpose could the enumeration of particular powers be inserted, if these and all others were meant to be included in the preceding general power? . . . [T]he idea of an enumeration of particulars which neither explain nor qualify the general meaning, and can [have] no other effect than to confound and mislead, is an absurdity which no one ought to charge on the enlightened authors of the Constitution. It would be to charge them either with premeditated folly or premeditated fraud." Here, Story appropriately cited Madison's "Federalist No. 41," in which the same conclusion was reached.

The reading that Story selected avoided all these pitfalls. "[C]onstruing the [General Welfare] clause in connection with and as a part of the preceding clause giving the power to lay taxes, it becomes sensible and operative. It becomes a qualification of that clause, and limits the taxing power to objects for the common defence or general welfare. It then contains no grant of any power whatsoever; but it is a mere expression of the ends and purposes to be effected by the preceding power of taxation." Again, Story relied upon the Monroe Memorandum as well as Madison.

At this stage, Story had interpreted Article I, section 8 in what he regarded as a reasonable manner. It contained an independent taxing power qualified by the General Welfare Clause. It also contained a number of separate enumerated powers relating to defense, interstate and foreign commerce, and other Article I, section 8 fields. The taxing power so construed was one of a number of enumerated powers. However, as read by Story, the General Welfare Clause did *not* constitute a regulatory power, independent of the spending power, authorizing Congress to enact whatever measures it wished, with or without appropriation, under an unlimited power to legislate for the general welfare of the United States. The structure of the Constitution as conferring a set of enumerated legislative powers, rather than one general power, was maintained. His interpretation was consistent with both Madison and Monroe, as well as Jackson, as expressed in the Maysville veto message. It put Story in the moderate, traditionalist camp on the issue.

There remained for Story, however, the important task of addressing Madison's long-standing interpretation, which Jefferson had shared, that the General Welfare Clause, rather than constituting a qualification of the taxing power, was no more than a reference to a touchstone in the Articles of Confederation. It was therefore "harmless" and of no significance. The enumerated powers themselves constituted the true limitation on the taxing power, to the end that any appropriation must fall within the ambit of those powers. Story devoted the next portion of his discussion of the taxing power to this issue.[14]

REFUTING MADISON: MORE THAN A "FINGERBOARD"

Story's analysis addressed the Madison reading as it had been stated or reflected in various epochs of the fourth president's life—in the "Federalist No. 41," in the Virginia Resolutions, in the 1817 Bonus Bill veto, and, finally, in the 1830 letter to Andrew Stevenson. It is important to note that in crafting his analysis, Story had before him Madison's most comprehensive postretirement dissertation on the subject.

Story's response was at once incisive and unyielding. He expressed absolute certainty that Madison's interpretation was unsound, whereas his own was founded on the following points:

- First, Madison's reading gave no effect to the General Welfare Clause. If taxing and spending were confined to the enumerated powers, there would have been no need for an explicit spending power because the Necessary and Proper Clause would have afforded the authority to spend for enumerated power purposes.
- Second, under traditional maxims of interpretation, all provisions of an instrument must be given meaning. This was especially true of the Constitution. Madison's reading denied the General Welfare Clause any meaning.
- Third the framers, if they so intended, could have easily included in the General Welfare Clause a specific reference to the enumerated powers, but they did not. Madison was in effect reading language into Article I that was not there.
- Finally, Story disputed Madison's contention that the practice of

the Confederation Congress under the Articles of Confederation, from which the General Welfare language arguably was drawn, supported the strict view. On the contrary, Story contended, the Confederation Congress under the Articles had spent (or tried to spend) for General Welfare purposes that went beyond the enumerated powers in the Articles.[15] In this part of his analysis, Story was responding to Madison's 1830 letter to Andrew Stevenson.

Story began by restating the proposition that he sought to refute. "An attempt has been sometimes made," he observed, "to treat [the General Welfare] clause as distinct and independent, and yet as having no real significance *per se* but . . . as a mere prelude to the succeeding enumerated powers." He dismissed the notion that this interpretation was supported by the punctuation; in some copies a semicolon separated the two clauses. Story also noted that the General Welfare Clause was first "introduced as an appendage" to the taxing power, an apparent reference to Roger Sherman's amendment of August 25, 1787. Presumably this fact overcame any inferences to be drawn from the punctuation.

However, Story's fundamental objection to Madison's view was that "it robs the [General Welfare] clause of all efficacy and meaning. No person has a right to assume that any part of the Constitution is useless, or is without a meaning." Moreover, no person "has a right to rob any part [of the Constitution] of a meaning, natural and appropriate to the language in the connection in which it stands." Since the clause had a "natural and appropriate meaning" as a qualification of the taxing power, it was, improper to "rob" (to use Story's word) it of a meaning "natural and appropriate" to that setting. Here, he again cited Monroe's Memorandum.

With this general principle as a foundation, Story responded to Madison's contention in the Stevenson letter that the General Welfare Clause was confined by the enumerated powers and therefore required no particular attention. This, to Story, assumed the very point in controversy: was the clause limited by the enumerated powers? Story emphasized that the General Welfare Clause did not state "to provide for the common defence, and general welfare, *in manner following*." Such a formulation would have been the natural way to express the intent that Madison attributed to the clause. Moreover, if the Madison interpretation were correct, there would have been no need for the Necessary and Proper Clause, because that clause surely would have afforded the power to lay taxes to carry out the enumerated powers. In short, the Madison interpretation made either the General Welfare Clause or the Necessary and Proper Clause surplusage.[16]

At this stage, Story digressed to refute the frequently stated argument that Madison's interpretation was supported by the Articles of Confederation, that the articles contained a general welfare clause that was confined in the way Madison regarded the taxing power. This, Story suggested, was the gravamen of Madison's argument in "Federalist No. 41" and the Virginia Resolutions. In contrast, said Story, the general welfare language in the Articles of Confederation limited the power of the Confederation Congress to expend funds resulting from requisitions upon the states, a point that supported Story's theory that it limited the taxing power of the Constitution. Moreover, Story contended that, in practice, the Confederation Congress never construed the articles to limit spending to the enumerated powers specified in that document. On the contrary, the Confederation Congress had "construed their power on the subject of requisitions . . . exactly as it is now contended for, as a power to make requisitions on the States . . . for the general welfare." Moreover, Story argued that Madison, in the Stevenson letter, had conceded the point by admitting that the Confederation Congress had frequently departed from the rule for which he contended. Story's final argument was that the practice of the Confederation Congress squared with the language of the Articles of Confederation.

For Story, however, resorting to the Articles of Confederation to interpret the General Welfare Clause was but a useless and improvident diversion. The key to understanding that provision was to be found in the language of the Constitution itself. To this Story turned in the summation of his analysis. "[T]here is no ground whatsoever," he insisted, "which authorizes any resort to the confederation, to interpret the power of taxation which is conferred on Congress by the Constitution. The clause has no reference whatsoever to the confederation, nor indeed to any other clause of the Constitution."

Story summed up his position on the clause: "[The taxing power] is, on its face, a distinct, substantive, and independent power. Who, then, is at liberty to say that it is to be limited by other clauses, rather than they to be enlarged by it; since there is no avowed connection or reference from the one to the others? Interpretation would here desert its proper office, that which requires that 'every part of the expression ought, if possible, to be allowed some meaning and be made to conspire to some common end.'"[17]

To reinforce his conclusion, Story directly confronted the central proposition of the Jeffersonian Republicans. He quoted at length from the Virginia Resolutions of 1798 to the effect that a broad reading of the spending power would "'[destroy] the import and force of the particular enumeration of powers. . . .'" As Madison and Jefferson had argued, almost anything could be related to the appropriation power. If Congress had so broad a power of the purse, there would have been no reason for a careful enumeration of powers, the national government would have been a government of unlimited rather than limited powers by virtue of that very power of the purse. Story reiterated the central conclusion of the Virginia Resolutions: "'Where, therefore, money has been raised by the general authority, and is to be applied to a particular measure, a question arises, whether the particular measure be within the enumerated authorities vested in the Congress. If it be, the money requisite for it may be applied to it; if it be not, no such application can be made.'" This same reasoning, Story reminded his readers, had been applied by Madison in his famous internal-improvements veto of March 3, 1817, and it had been restated even more forcefully in the Stevenson letter of 1830.

Story emphatically rejected this central tenet of the Democratic Republican party, the party of Jefferson and Madison. For Story, Madison's argument rendered the General Welfare Clause meaningless:

> Stripped of the ingenious texture by which this argument is disguised, it is neither more nor less than an attempt to obliterate from the Constitution the whole clause, 'to pay the debts, and provide for the common defence and general welfare of the United States,' as entirely senseless, or inexpressive of any intention whatsoever. Strike them out, and the Constitution is exactly what the argument contends for. It is, therefore, an argument that the words ought not to be in the Constitution; because if they are, and have any meaning, they enlarge it beyond the scope of certain other enumerated powers, and this is both mischievous and dangerous. Being in the Constitution, they are to be deemed . . . an empty sound and vain phraseology, a finger-board pointing to other powers, but having no use whatsoever since these powers are sufficiently apparent without.[18]

For Story, this view was totally untenable: "Now, it is not too much to say, that in a constitution of government framed and adopted by the people, it is a most unjustifiable latitude of interpretation to deny effect to any clause, if it is sensible in the language in which it is expressed, and in the place in which it stands." For emphasis, he continued in this vein: "If words are inserted, we are bound to presume that they have some definite object and intent; and to reason them out of the Constitution upon arguments *ab inconvenienti*.... is to make a new constitution, not to construe the old one. It is to do the very thing which so often complained of, to make a constitution to suit our notions and wishes, and not to administer or construe that which the people have given to the country."

In the 1833 one-volume abridged version, Story included a number of arguments in response to Madison's view that were also included in the 1891 two-volume version. Among other things, he took note of Madison's contention that the convention could not possibly have intended to confer so broad a spending power on the Congress, given its careful enumeration in Article I. Story then pointed to the "constant and decided maintenance" of the contrary position by "the government and its functionaries, as well as by many of our ablest statesmen from the very commencement of the constitution." Story's answer to Madison's central point was thus "the actual practice." To reinforce his argument, Story cited at length from the pertinent passages in Hamilton's *Report on Manufactures* and noted that Congress had not limited appropriations to matters falling within the specific enumerated powers.

On the contrary, Story maintained that appropriations for internal improvements, as well as for "destitute foreigners," buttressed his case. On the basis of such arguments, Story emphatically concluded that Congress could appropriate federal funds for the construction of internal improvements such as roads and canals, the same conclusion that Monroe had reached some ten years earlier. However, Story limited the power "directly to initiate and carry out a system of internal improvements" to cases where "such improvements fell within the scope of enumerated powers," such as a military road. Such authority he derived from an implied power under the enumerated power in question. On the executive-legislative battle over whether there was a general power to construct, as distinguished from appropriating for, internal improvements, Story wisely deferred. The important point is that Story strongly supported Monroe's thesis that the power of appropriation was not limited to the legislative fields spelled out in the enumerated powers. It took the Supreme Court over one hundred years to affirm that conclusion. When it did so, it relied strongly upon Story who had, in turn, relied upon Hamilton and Monroe.[19]

In the main, Story's response to Madison was one of *literal* interpretation. His reading gave effect to all the relevant provisions of Article I, section 8. Article I, section 8, clause 1 contained a taxing power, modified or qualified by the General Welfare Clause. The taxing power was an independent power, not confined by the enumerated powers. The enumerated powers were, on the other hand, distinct and independent powers, not swallowed up by an overall power to regulate for the general welfare. All the relevant provisions had an appropriate place in the analysis, and the General Welfare Clause was not read out or relegated to a "finger-board" by reference to the Articles of Confederation. Story rested his argument on what Madison had reluctantly conceded in the Stevenson letter—that the General Welfare Clause *literally* conferred the power in question.

Except by invoking the contrary practice and Hamilton's observations, Story's analysis did not directly respond to Madison's central objection that it made no sense to interpret the clause as furnishing Congress with a broad, unrestricted spending power when the Philadelphia Convention had taken such pains to craft the enumerated powers. Story did not attempt to respond to Madison's point in the Stevenson letter that if the Convention had intended a broad power of the purse, it would have thoroughly debated the issue rather than inserting the General Welfare language into the document virtually without debate. To Story, the answer was that the General Welfare Clause was *in* the Constitution. Those who interpreted the Constitution were obliged to give effect to the General Welfare Clause rather than read it out, notwithstanding the absence of meaningful debate or full reflection.

Indeed, if Story had relied upon the legislative history of the clause, he would have found, as discussed above, no clear message. Instead, he set up the internal-improvement legislation and other evidence of continued legislative practice as a counterweight to Madison's arguments in the Virginia Resolutions. It was this practice that had convinced Story's fellow Harvard alumnus, John Quincy Adams, that the Constitution gave Congress the power over internal improvements and had persuaded Jackson that he could sign nationally focused internal-improvement measures. However, Story declined to grapple with the implications that Madison drew from the legislative record. In so doing, Story did not fully address Madison's central point. For Story the textual analysis was controlling; for Madison, this history, or his view of this history, was.[20]

Story's analysis left Congress with a broad power of appropriation and specified enumerated fields which it might regulate or act upon, without regard to spending. With respect to the enumerated powers, Congress could regulate in the specified areas without resort to the spending power. It could regulate interstate and foreign commerce and its regulations would be controlling, whether or not attached to appropriation legislation. With respect to the General Welfare Clause, Congress was confined to the spending power which was in turn limited by the capacity of the Congress to tax and, in many cases, further restricted by the transitory nature of appropriations.

In explaining the scope of the General Welfare Clause, Story did not deal with the relevance of recipient choice. When Congress properly exercises its regulatory authority under an enumerated power, the regulatee has no choice but to comply. When Congress exercises the spending power through the formulation of program and appropriation legislation, the recipient, by declining to participate in the program, may avoid adhering to the applicable grant conditions. Because participation in the program is voluntary, submission to the regulatory scheme inherent in the conditions attached to the program is likewise voluntary. Moreover, as the Supreme Court has decided, the conditions themselves must be unambiguous and reasonably related to the purposes of the program.[21]

These distinctions were well beyond the scope of Story's analysis and would be considered decades later. He did not consider it necessary to explore them in his commentaries. Instead he relied on the language of the Constitution. He apparently believed that distinctions based upon the nature of the spending power and the enumerated powers would detract from the force of the literal argument. In so doing, Story had given legal weight to Hamilton's theory about the spending power.

Insofar as they affirmed the power of Congress to appropriate for internal improvements, the *Commentaries* must have provided comfort to those of John Quincy Adams's persuasion who believed that a program of federally financed internal improvements was central to the growth of the nation and who wished to extend Adams's spirit of internal improvements. Most importantly, the *Commentaries* provided future sympathetic chief executives with a well reasoned alternative to the view of Madison and Jefferson, an alternative that would justify more internal improvement and other public investment legislation when the political climate warranted. Thus, the friends of internal improvements could continue to build over the decades, as they had done during the administrations of Monroe and Adams, a body of precedent that would be impossible to ignore when the courts finally came to rule on the issue. At that juncture, Story's analysis would reemerge as a compelling starting point for a judicial decision incorporating the Hamiltonian view into the authoritative judicial interpretation of the General Welfare Clause.[22]

In sum, Story provided a constitutional continuum respecting the General Welfare Clause. On one end of the continuum is the proposition that Congress may appropriate tax revenues in order to provide for the general welfare, a general welfare that is not confined to the legislative fields assigned to Congress in the enumerated powers contained in Article I, section 8. At the other end of the continuum is the proposition that Congress may not legislate to provide for the general welfare, independent of federal spending. To use Monroe's example, it may assist states in the construction of roads (subject to reasonably related grant conditions) but may not supersede state jurisdiction over the roads in question. By the same token Congress may not, in the absence of constitutional authority separate from the General Welfare Clause, wholly federalize areas committed to state authority which it is authorized to assist under the spending power.

THE GENERAL WELFARE WISDOM OF THE ANTEBELLUM PRESIDENTS

The period before the Civil War was characterized by a continuation of the rift over the scope of the spending power. Democratic presidents who looked to the South for political support—including James K. Polk, John Tyler, Franklin Pierce, and James Buchanan—followed Jacksonian philosophy and vetoed internal-improvement legislation as a means of preventing the restoration of the American System and maintaining perceived constitutional constraints. For these men, Madison's testament was the paramount starting point. In contrast, Whig presidents, especially Zachary Taylor and Millard Fillmore, were proponents of Clay's American System and more tolerant of internal-improvement legislation. Their time on the stage was, however, of such short duration that they were unable to install policies that endured.

Although he had been one of the Maysville Road's major architects during the Jackson administration, as president, Martin Van Buren did not play a major role in extending it as a precedent. His administration was preoccupied with the financial panic of 1837 and with a continuing effort to persuade Congress to adopt its subtreasury proposals—a mechanism for the receipt and disbursement of federal funds that is essential to the administration of federal spending programs.[23]

Van Buren was defeated by William Henry Harrison in the election of 1840. Harrison, a Whig, survived only a month after his inaugural address, which was a long disquisition on the constitutional role of the executive. It fell to John Tyler to carry out the policies of the administration. Tyler, a Democrat, followed Jacksonian principles with regard to internal improvements. Tyler had supported Jackson's Maysville Road veto. His annual messages encouraged river and harbor improvements on the Great Lakes or the Mississippi that Tyler believed would enhance trade and therefore would be justified as national in scope. However, in 1844, he vetoed a river and harbor measure because it contained appropriations for local projects that he believed could not be justified.[24]

Polk's Vetoes

Tyler's successor, James Knox Polk, was explicitly Jacksonian in his actions on the internal improvements issue and, if anything, less compromising than his mentor from his native state. Polk vetoed several internal improvement bills and carefully explained his views in the accompanying messages. In his final state of the union message, he also gave the nation an unyielding brief in opposition to Clay's American System, in which federally financed internal improvements were portrayed as an unmitigated evil.

Polk's second internal-improvement veto, which took place toward the end of 1847, was accompanied by a statement of his views on internal improvements and, more broadly, on the spending power. The measure in question appropriated over 500 thousand dollars for the improvement of rivers and harbors lying within the individual states. Polk stated his objection at the outset. The bill would set a precedent for further appropriations for the improvement of rivers and harbors. Without an immediate resort to taxation, it would be difficult to maintain the credit of the United States at a time when the nation was engaged in a war with Mexico.[25]

Polk then undertook to review the history of the internal-improvement movement, as he saw it. He attributed the policy of "embarking the Federal Government in a general system of internal improvement" to the Adams administration twenty years earlier. Applications for projects had then reached the sum of $200 million. Polk's predecessor, Andrew Jackson, had confronted the crisis by vetoing the Maysville Road bill. This, to Polk, had checked the policy of placing the cost of local improvements on the federal government and had led to the reduction of the debt. Polk maintained that he could not distinguish the legislation involved in Jackson's vetoes from that before him.[26]

Polk's alternative for financing internal improvements was to propose that Congress permit the states to lay tonnage duties in order to finance them. As an alternative, he proposed adopting a constitutional amendment. Despite his commitment, he was no more successful than the Virginia presidents he had cited in convincing Congress to forward such an amendment to the states.[27]

In his farewell message, Polk warned the people of the perils of the American System. As he described it, the system involved three elements: (1) a national bank; (2) a high protective tariff; and (3) "a comprehensive scheme of internal improvements." What Polk termed "a comprehensive scheme of internal improvements" was a "convenient and necessary adjunct" of the high protective tariff. It was "capable of indefinite enlargement and sufficient to swallow up as many millions annually as could be exacted from the foreign commerce of the country." Internal improvements for Polk were thus, not a means of opening up the country and expanding trade, but a pretext for higher taxes in the form of protective duties.[28]

Zachary Taylor, Millard Fillmore, and the Brief Revival of Internal Improvements

The Whig Party acquired the habit of nominating for president military heroes who died early in their terms. They were succeeded by vice presidents who were not reelected and have been little remembered. Such was the case with Zachary Taylor, elected as the twelfth president in 1848 under the Whig banner. He died on July 9, 1850, having served little more than a year after his March 1849 inauguration, and was succeeded by his vice president, Millard Fillmore of New York. Taylor had little opportunity to demonstrate his fidelity to the American System and other Whig principles, including those pertaining to internal improvements. However, support for internal improvements had been an issue in Taylor's 1848 campaign against Lewis Cass, the Democratic candidate. Abraham Lincoln and other Whig supporters expressed their belief that Taylor favored internal improvements by voicing their preference for him.[29]

While Taylor's death cut short his opportunity to pursue internal-improvement initiatives, his successor, Millard Fillmore, amplified the internal-improvement themes that Taylor had sounded. As J. D. Richardson observed, "[Fillmore's] political career began and ended with the birth and extinction of the Whig party." He had served in Congress during the Jackson and Van Buren years and in 1848 had been nominated by the Whigs for vice president. Fillmore's philosophical leanings were entirely consistent with the resumption and extension of the internal-improvement movement, as he made abundantly clear in his first annual message at the end of 1850.

Fillmore began by laying out the constitutional markers. "I entertain no doubt," he said, "of the authority of Congress to make appropriations for leading objects in that class of public works comprising what are usually called works of internal improvement. This authority I suppose to be derived chiefly from the power of regulating commerce with the foreign nations and among the States and the power of laying and collecting imposts." Presumably, the latter reference was to the spending power under the General Welfare Clause.[30]

Like Adams in 1825, Fillmore was using the precedent of past legislative support for the infrastructure as a basis for asserting that federal appropriations for this class of public works were constitutional. He cited previous federally funded projects such as lighthouses, buoys, and beacons.[31] By removing the states' power to collect imposts, Fillmore argued, the Constitution made it necessary for Congress to aid the states by subsidizing internal improvements. As Fillmore so cogently put it: "By the adoption of the Constitution the several States voluntarily parted with the power of collecting duties or imposts in their own ports, and it is not to be expected that they should raise money by internal taxation, direct or indirect, for the benefit of that commerce the revenues derived from which do not either in whole or in part go into their own treasuries."[32]

The practice of supporting internal improvements, in the tradition if not with the zeal of John Quincy Adams, had been resumed. Fillmore's place in the sun was, however, fleeting, and the resumption expired with his presidency. As the Whig president who served longest (almost three years), Fillmore's actions on behalf of internal improvements and the federal spending power may be taken to reflect the Whig persuasion in its most well developed form as expressed by a sitting Whig president. But Fillmore's lack of stature, his status as a nonelected president, the brevity of his tenure, and the absence of any comprehensive constitutional analysis or decision law did not permit great weight to be given to his views. As a reward for his steady, if less than passionate, advocacy of Whig views on the subject, the Whig party declined to renominate him in 1852, turning instead to yet another military hero, General Winfield Scott, who was in turn defeated by the Democrat Franklin Pierce.[33]

Franklin Pierce and James Buchanan: Strict Construction in the Shadow of Secession

In 1854, Pierce vetoed two legislative measures. His explanation for so doing made clear his understanding of the limits of the spending power, as well as his understanding of the scope of that power under the broad, alternative construction of the Constitution. The first bill, vetoed in May 1854, would have granted public lands to the states on the basis of an apportionment formula. Each state was to place the proceeds from the sale of these lands in an interest-earning fund, and the interest was to be dedicated to maintaining the indigent insane within the state. States without public lands would be issued scrip for the same purpose. In essence, the measure constituted a state administered, formula driven, categorical federal-aid program to assist states in better serving a specific, needy population.[34]

Pierce saw this initiative as flatly unconstitutional and profoundly dangerous. The breadth of the proposition alarmed him. If Congress could make provision for the indigent insane in the states, he correctly forecast, it would also have the power to provide for the noninsane indigent and "thus to transfer to the Federal Government the charge of all the poor in all the States." He turned to the General Welfare Clause and rejected it as a source of that power. He took it as settled construction that Article I, section 8, clause 1 was "not a substantive general power to provide for the welfare of the United States, but it is a limitation on the grant of power to raise money by taxes, duties, and imposts."

The government could lay taxes in order to provide for the general welfare. To construe it otherwise would, as Jefferson and Madison had argued, eradicate the enumerated powers, invade states' rights, and dry up local spending for charitable purposes.[35]

In his analysis of the General Welfare Clause as not conferring a power to provide for the general welfare, separate and apart from the power to apply tax revenues, Pierce was consistent with the views of Monroe and Story on the precise point. However, the president did not address the proposition clearly announced by Monroe and Story, and strongly supported by Adams, that the spending power contained in the General Welfare Clause conferred the power to appropriate for the general welfare, unconfined by the enumerated powers. That jump was apparently too great for Pierce's political convictions. Those convictions were rooted in Democratic tradition and deference to its strict construction doctrines.

Pierce declined to apply the analysis that Monroe and Story had formulated, an analysis that might have permitted him to sign the indigent-insane measure before him. For the same reasons, he declined to place any stock in Article IV, section 3 of the Constitution which affords Congress the power to "dispose of and make all needful rules and regulations respecting the territory or other property belonging to the United States." If the bill exceeded the power of Congress under the spending power, it exceeded it under the power to dispose of lands. As a constitutional matter, for Pierce, it was "wholly immaterial whether the appropriation be in money or in land." He applied the same strict constructionist philosophy to federal assistance measures, whether in the form of direct appropriations under Article I or dispositions of public lands under Article IV.[36]

Pierce's successor, James Buchanan, was forced to report, in his final annual message, that the state of the union was disunion. He had begun his administration by identifying himself as a "strict constructionist" of the Constitution. He concluded that a state had no right under that Constitution to secede. His strict stance precluded him, however, from finding in the Constitution a power that would authorize him to use force to stop a state from seceding. He urged compromise and constitutional conventions, steps that did nothing to stem the slide toward national dismemberment.

Using Polk's 1847 veto message as a starting point, Buchanan vetoed a number of internal improvement measures that he believed to be lacking in constitutional authority. He vetoed as well a bill that would have donated land to the states in exchange for their promise to devote the proceeds of the sale of the land to establish agricultural colleges. This bill was a precursor of the Morrill Act of 1862.[37]

The land-grant college bill in question donated 20,000 acres of land for each Senator or Representative in Congress. Over 6 million acres with a valuation of over $6 million would be distributed. States with public lands would receive their quota in the form of land grants. The remaining states would receive land scrip which they might sell on the market. In both cases, proceeds had to be used by the grantee states for the endowment, support and maintenance of at least one college where the primary purpose would be the teaching of agriculture and mechanic arts "in order to promote the liberal and practical education of the industrial classes in the several pursuits and professions in life." Each state was obliged to provide for at least one college within a five year period or the grant would cease and proceeds of the sales revert to the United States.

Buchanan pitched his veto on both questions of expediency and constitutionality but made clear that his constitutional concerns were controlling. He began this part of his message by avowing that it was "undeniable that Congress does not possess the power to appropriate money in the Treasury of the United States for the purpose of educating the people of the respective States." He could not find the power in the Necessary and Proper Clause. He did not discuss the spending power and the General Welfare Clause extensively. When he did turn to that provision, he complained that admitting a constitutional power under that language in favor of the bill in question would involve taxation for state, as well as federal, purposes. "This," he observed, "would be an actual consolidation of the Federal and State governments so far as the great taxing and money power is concerned, and constitute a sort of partnership between the two in the Treasury of the United States, equally ruinous to both." Evidently, for Buchanan, encouragement for education did not come within the purview of the phrase, "the general Welfare of the United States." Or, if it did, the General Welfare Clause was an insufficient prop because the spending could not be justified as within the ambit of a discrete enumerated power.[38]

That the bill in question related to the disposition of the public lands, rather than a direct appropriation, did not persuade Buchanan of its constitutionality. The Constitution provided Congress with "power to dispose of and make all needful rules and regulations respecting the territory or other property belonging to the United States." The defenders of the bill had pointed to this language as justifying their contention that Congress could make a gift of the public lands for the purpose of education. Buchanan, like Pierce, saw this as exceeding the enumerated powers. The framers would not have carefully limited these powers, while leaving Congress the power to use funds from the disposition of lands to carry out any domestic policy. Lands could be disposed of only to carry out duties corresponding to the enumerated powers. In short, dispositions of land must, for constitutional purpose, be subjected to the same test as the appropriation of funds.[39]

Nor could the term "dispose of" be used to convey the power to "give away." Because the lands were purchased with the proceeds of federal taxes, Congress was confined, in applying the lands or money derived from their sale, to the purposes for which money could be appropriated. Buchanan said: "The inference is irresistible that this land partakes of the very same character with the money paid for it, and can be devoted to no objects different from those to which the money could have been devoted." In short, Buchanan, like Pierce, treated the issue as a question about the constitutionality of an appropriation of federal funds. In answering that question, Buchanan declined to apply the General Welfare Clause as justifying the appropriation. For him, assisting higher education in the states was not tantamount to providing for the general welfare of the United States.[40]

The reasoning behind Buchanan's veto of the 1859 homestead bill was similar to that behind the land-grant college bill. The homestead bill gave every adult citizen who was the head of a family, and every adult of foreign birth residing in the United States who declared the intention of becoming a citizen, the privilege of obtaining 160 acres of federal land so long as the settler resided upon it continuously for five years. At the end of the five-year period, the settler would receive a land patent in exchange for the payment of twenty-five cents per acre, or one-fifth of the government price. The bill also provided for a cession of certain public lands to the states. In vetoing the bill, Buchanan invoked constitutional considerations similar to those raised earlier when he vetoed the land-grant college legislation.[41]

The internal improvement vetoes of Polk, Pierce, and Buchanan represent the high-water mark of resistance to a broad, Hamiltonian construction of the General Welfare Clause. They represent the efforts of antebellum Democratic presidents to hold the line against what they saw as constitutional derogation. But their policies were not equal to the times or to the crises that they posed, any more than were the temporizing efforts to address the all-consuming sin of slavery. To those crises, Lincoln brought a different set of starting points than his immediate predecessors, points that he had developed and formulated throughout his political career and ones to which he would give significant effect, if without explicit rhetoric, during his presidency despite his consuming preoccupation with the Civil War.

V
Lincoln's Role

11
Lincoln's General Welfare Clause

ABRAHAM LINCOLN DID NOT ENTER THE WHITE HOUSE AS A STRANGER to the question of internal improvements or their constitutional dimensions. His career in the Illinois House of Representatives centered on local internal-improvement measures. Long before he reached the White House, Lincoln the Congressman had committed himself politically on the issue of federal assistance for internal improvements and the scope of the federal spending power. He was not to deviate from the position when he became president. Despite his concentration on preserving the Union, he found time to focus on the significance of internal improvements and to include a general-welfare component in his overarching political philosophy. The progressive legislation that he signed into law during wartime established a set of significant precedents in the history of the General Welfare Clause that would reverberate in peacetime. Those precedents ensured that a broad reading of the General Welfare Clause would be the prevailing philosophy for those presidents who advocated its application to the challenges of the late nineteenth century.[1]

CONGRESSMAN LINCOLN'S 1848 INTERNAL IMPROVEMENT SPEECH

In August 1846, Lincoln was elected to the U.S. House of Representatives from his congressional district in central Illinois. He served in the Thirtieth Congress as a member of the Whig Party from December 1847, when the Congress convened, to March 1849, when Zachary Taylor was inaugurated. Lincoln was not a candidate for reelection to the House, and his post in that body was the last federal public office that he held until assuming the presidency in 1861.[2] Few historians regard Lincoln's single term in the House as a high point in his political career. On the other hand, Paul Findley, who represented Lincoln's district in the House in modern times and who wrote a book on Lincoln's service in that body, regarded that period as having catapulted Lincoln to national prominence in his party and ultimately into the White House.[3] Findley's study, however, gives little prominence to Lincoln's speech on internal improvements, delivered on the floor of the House in June 1848, in response to President Polk's veto of the rivers and harbors bill during the prior year. Far more attention has been paid to Lincoln's views on the Mexican War and slavery.[4]

Notwithstanding this dearth of attention, Lincoln's speech on internal improvements represents more than a routine address expressing the stock Whig reaction to Jacksonian internal-improvement policy. It reflected the most explicit and comprehensive discussion of internal improvements that Lincoln produced prior to assuming the presidency. More importantly, Lincoln's 1848 speech discloses the evolution of his thinking on the scope of the constitutional spending power and of the General Welfare Clause. His approach to those concepts, as presented in the speech, was contrary to the Jacksonians. He advocated a broad reading of the Constitution to support federal assistance for internal improvements. He denied the need for a constitutional amendment to justify this type of legislation despite the fact that it put him—at least on this issue—outside the camp of Jefferson, Madison, Monroe, Jackson, and Polk. At the same time, it aligned him philosophically with John Quincy Adams.

Polk's second veto, later in 1847, gave Lincoln an opportunity for a greater exposition of his views. On June 20, 1848, he took the floor of the House during the debate (in Committee of the Whole) on the civil and diplomatic appropriation. He explained to the chair that he intended to deliver a speech on "the general subject of internal improvements." He refuted Polk, arguing in favor of the expediency of internal-improvement legislation and rejecting the "general-local" distinction that Democratic presidents had used to veto internal improvement measures.[5]

Polk's constitutional concerns had been the centerpiece of his 1847 veto message. In his effort to rebut Polk's constitutional arguments, Lincoln began with a note of modesty. He conceded that, "in any attempt at an original constitutional argument," the House should not hear him "patiently." He noted that the "ablest" men had covered the "whole ground." He would merely take notice of what they had said. Polk had relied upon Jefferson. Lincoln readily conceded that Jefferson had called for a constitutional amendment to warrant federal aid for internal improvements. However, Lincoln correctly noted that "on the question of *expediency*," Jefferson's opinion was in favor of internal improvements and thus contrary to that of Polk.[6]

As to the merits of the constitutional issue, Lincoln relied not on the views of the current president or his predecessors, but rather on the views of respected legal scholars. This was appropriate for one of Lincoln's leaning, since few presidents had supported the constitutionality of a general system of internal improvements. Lincoln therefore cited Chancellor James Kent in his *Commentaries on American Law*. On the question of the power to appropriate for internal improvements, Lincoln related that Kent's 1826 treatise had discussed the issue in terms of the Executive-Legislative branch dialogue in which the Executive generally opposed the power, at least until the administration of John Quincy Adams.

At this stage, it is appropriate to provide the full text of Lincoln's argument on the constitutional issue as it reflects the most comprehensive statement of his views on that subject:

> But to the constitutional question—In 1826, Chancellor Kent first published his Commentaries on American Law. He devoted a portion of one of the lectures to the question of the authority of congress to appropriate public moneyes for internal improvements. He mentions that the question had never been brought under judicial consideration, and proceeds to give a brief summary of the discussions it had undergone between the legislative, and executive branches of the government. He shows that the legislative branch had usually been *for*, and the executive against the power, till the period of Mr. J.Q. Adams' administration, at which point he considers the executive influence as withdrawn from opposition, and added to the support of the power. In 1844, the chancellor published a new edition of his commentaries, in which he adds some notes on what had transpired on the question since 1826. I have not time to read the original text, or the notes; but the whole may be found on page 267, and the two or three following pages of the first volume of the edition of 1844. As what Chancellor Kent seems to consider the sum of the whole, I read from one of the notes:
>
> "Mr. Justice Story, in his commentaries on the Constitution of the United States . . . has stated at large the arguments for and and [sic] against the proposition, that congress have a constitutional authority to lay taxes, and to apply the power to regulate commerce as a means directly to encourage and protect domestic manufactures; and without giving any opinion of his own on the contested doctrine, he has left the reader to draw his own conclusions. I should think, however,

from the arguments as stated, that every mind which has taken no part in the discussions, and felt no prejudice or territorial bias on either side of the question, would deem the arguments favor of the congressional power vastly superior."[7]

This passage indicates that Lincoln shared Kent's conclusion and readily extended it to the question of internal improvements. Lincoln continued: "It will be seen, that in this extract the power to make improvements is not directly mentioned, but by examining the context, both of Kent and Story, it will be seen that the power mentioned in the extract, and the power to make improvements are regarded as identical." Lincoln may have been defending the authority of Congress to authorize a national system of improvements as well as its authority to appropriate for internal improvements (the distinction discussed in the Monroe Memorandum). Because he favored the broader authority, he necessarily must be taken to have believed that the lesser authority was constitutionally proper.

At this point Lincoln rendered his conclusion: "It is not to be denied that many great and good men have been *against* the power; but it is insisted that quite as many, as great and as good, have been *for* it; and it is shown that, on a full survey of the whole, Chancellor Kent was of opinion that the arguments of the latter were *vastly* superior." Thus, did Lincoln encapsulate and resolve sixty years of spending power disputation that had resounded in the highest councils of the nation. While the passage he quoted did not discuss Story's analysis of the spending power (described above), Kent's analysis, which favored federal financing for internal improvements, is generally consistent with Story. As to choosing between Polk and Kent on a constitutional issue, Congressman Lincoln recommended that the House should follow Kent whose reputation he extolled. As to choosing between the views of a politician and a lawyer, Lincoln believed the views of the lawyer should prevail: "Can the party opinion of a party president on a law question, as this purely is, be at all compared . . . to that of such a man, in such an attitude, as Chancellor Kent?"

Finally, Lincoln correctly divined that the matter was for the courts. In the meantime, the government should move forward. "This constitutional question will probably never be better settled than it is, until it shall pass under judicial consideration; but I do think no man, who is clear on the question of expediency, needs feel his conscience much pricked upon this." In fact, Lincoln was right on his prediction that the question would ultimately be taken up by the Supreme Court, and he was right on his legal prediction as to how the Court would come out with respect to the scope of the General Welfare Clause. As to the need for a constitutional amendment, Lincoln regarded it as unwise and unnecessary. In sum, it seems evident that, in his congressional years, Lincoln had become comfortable with Joseph Story's conclusion that the Constitution authorized Congress to appropriate for internal improvements and other general welfare objectives and that, in so doing, Congress was not confined to the legislative fields expressed in the enumerated powers. Although Lincoln did not give the legal issue substantial attention in the speeches and writings that have come down to us, he was involved in exercising the power many times.[8]

THE ROAD TO THE WHITE HOUSE

The year 1848 appears to have been the high-water mark of Lincoln's internal-improvement advocacy. After 1848, the issue disappeared from his political lexicon as a defining issue, or at least as a compelling subject of his public oratory. An examination of his writings suggests that it was replaced by a far more controversial and divisive one: the extension of slavery. To be sure, there are occasional references to internal improvements. For example, in an 1852 campaign speech in Peoria, Illinois, he attacked the Democrats on this question and voiced his profound opposition to the election of Franklin Pierce on the basis of Pierce's antagonism to internal-improvement legislation.

With the demise of the Whig party in the 1850s, Lincoln sought a new political alignment. In May 1856, he helped frame a call to his fellow citizens in Sangamon County, requesting them to join in a county convention to appoint delegates to the state convention of the recently formed (1854) Republican Party later that month in Bloomington, Illinois. Those signing the call characterized themselves as "opposed to the Repeal of the Missouri Compromise . . . opposed to the present [Pierce] Administration, and . . . in favor of restoring the administration of the General Government to the policy of Washington and Jefferson."[9]

The "Duty of Providing for the General Welfare"

In this period prior to receiving the Republican nomination in 1860, Lincoln also sought to create a balance between the containment of slavery and his perception of the government's proper role in providing for the general welfare. That relationship went beyond a definition of constitutional limitations applicable to the spending power. It encompassed an early effort to articulate a nexus between the concepts of civil rights and general welfare, a nexus that would increasingly characterize Lincoln's thinking. In a speech in Cincinnati, Ohio, in September 1859, the future president told his listeners: "This government is expressly charged with the duty of providing for the general welfare. We believe that the spreading out and perpetuity of the institution of slavery impairs the general welfare."

Was Lincoln here asserting that the Constitution in Article I, section 8, clause 1 afforded the federal government a power to "provide for the general welfare" through regulatory legislation apart from the exercise of the spending power—the proposition that had been attributed to Gouverneur Morris in the Constitutional Convention and later discussed and rejected by Monroe and Story? It is doubtful that Lincoln, the careful student of the Constitution, would have casually embraced such a proposition. He did not assert that the general welfare provision overcame what he conceded was a constitutional limitation on congressional interference with slavery in the states. He continued: "I say that we must not interfere with the institution of slavery in the states where it exists, because the constitution forbids it, and the general welfare does not require us to do so.... But we must prevent the outspreading of the institution, because neither the constitution nor general welfare requires us to extend it." Thus, in this passage, the "general welfare" becomes a rationale for a policy direction. Because extending slavery impairs the general welfare, containing slavery is an imperative policy direction that may be pursued because the Constitution does not preclude that policy. The same philosophy governed Lincoln's approach to the spending power as it related to internal improvements. The Constitution did not preclude its exercise, and the general welfare justified it. Accordingly, internal-improvement spending was warranted without a constitutional amendment. Later as president, when he came to realize that providing for the general welfare also meant extinguishing slavery in the states where it existed, Lincoln favored doing so through a constitutional amendment. He believed the Constitution's formal amendment process should be invoked only when absolutely necessary to effect imperative change.

On his road to the White House, Lincoln was attempting to articulate a nexus between general welfare doctrine and civil rights that would later be employed to justify progressive legislation under the spending power, even if the duty to provide for the general welfare was not a constitutional warrant for regulatory legislation independent of the spending power. Moreover, by converting the general welfare concept into a duty Lincoln was in effect emphasizing the gulf between his views and those of the Democratic occupants of the White House who were striving to put as narrow a gloss as possible on the general welfare concept as it appeared in Article I, section 8, clause 1. For them, the duty was to insist that the General Welfare Clause was confined to the enumerated powers, as Madison had argued, and therefore was not a fit constitutional basis for the homestead and college aid legislation that Buchanan vetoed.[10]

By the time Lincoln arrived in the White House, his experience as a state and federal legislator and as a prominent political figure had given him a perspective on the scope of the federal spending power that prepared him for the crises that he would face as president. It had also armed him with a deep hostility to the policies of the Democratic presidents, Polk, Pierce, and Buchanan, whom he had opposed in one capacity or another, including, no doubt, their policies of vetoing or constraining internal improvements and related legislation.[11]

Lincoln's Presidency and the General Welfare Clause

In a series of messages early in his first term, Lincoln articulated three concepts that underpinned his response to the threatened dissolution of the Union. They included the nature of federalism, the role of the central government in elevating the human condition, and the implications of a free labor society. Taken together, the three provide a framework for the broadened exercise of the spending power during and after the Civil War.[12]

Federalism Restated

In his special session message of July 4, 1861, after the attack on Fort Sumter, the president called upon Congress to supply manpower and financial resources to address the crises of secession.[13] In so doing, Lincoln felt it essential to respond to the arguments of the seceding states that their action was legal. The constitutional foundation of the antisecession policy must be made plain if the policy were to be implemented by a call for the sacrifice of human and financial resources. The president flatly rejected the right of state secession and the doctrine of state rights on which it was based. He decried the "assumption that there is some omnipotent and sacred supremacy pertaining to a *State*—to each State of our Federal Union."[14]

"Our States," he said, "have neither more, nor less power than that reserved to them in the Union by the Constitution, no one of them ever having been a State *out* of the Union. . . . Having never been States, either in substance or in name, *outside* of the Union, whence this magical omnipotence of 'State rights,' asserting a claim of power to lawfully destroy the Union itself? . . . The States have their status in the Union, and they have no other legal status. If they break from this, they can only do so against law and by revolution. The Union, and not themselves separately, procured their independence and their liberty."[15]

From this conception of the nature of the Union and the relationship of the states to it, Lincoln turned to restating the nature of federalism. While that conception was expressed in the context of a call to arms to preserve and protect the Union, it provides a perspective on the role of the federal government in the exercise of its constitutional powers, including the spending power, as Lincoln saw them at the beginning of the nation's greatest constitutional crisis. It provides perspective as well on the context in which the spending power was exercised during his administration, for domestic purposes as well as for the prosecution of the Civil War. It also conveys his mind-set in favor of a broadly stated federal power to address national problems through national legislation. "This relative matter of national power and State rights, as a principle, is no other than the principle of *generality*, and *locality*. Whatever concerns the whole should be confided to the whole—to the General Government—while whatever concerns *only* the State should be left exclusively to the State. This is all there is of the original principle about it. Whether the National Constitution in defining boundaries between the two has applied the principle with exact accuracy is not to be questioned. We are all bound by that defining, without question."[16]

Lincoln was enunciating a different notion of federalism than his Democratic predecessors, one that presumably, when applied to domestic issues, would permit greater flexibility in applying federal resources to meet general needs or the needs of the whole. The emphasis of the Jacksonians, at least in their rhetoric, was on avoiding the overly vigorous exercise of the spending power for projects that might have only local benefit out of a concern that the federal authority would overwhelm state interests. Lincoln's special session message replaced it with a counteremphasis. An unduly expansive view of state rights and state sovereignty cannot be taken to permit the destruction of the Union and the national interests that it might promote.

Lincoln's restatement of federalism for the purpose of sustaining his anti-secessionist measures could be equally well applied to domestic program use, when it came to examining the scope of the General Welfare Clause to sustain federal financial assistance for internal improvements, education, or scientific exploration. Such a redefinition was a fitting end to a long historical controversy. The shift in emphasis from state rights-strict construction to the constitutional position of the Union has relevance when the question becomes one of national growth as well as national preservation. Significantly, it came from a president rooted in Whig doctrines of internal improvement whose public stance on that subject had itself been a factor in his selection as a candidate in 1860 and who was reflecting some of the same themes that he had sounded as a congressman in 1848.[17]

The "People's Contest": Equal Opportunity and the Role of Government

The threat to the Union posed by secession—and the rationale for preserving the Union—transcended legal arguments drawn from the text of the Constitution. The dissolution of the Union that the doctrine of secession demanded would destroy the opportunities for human progress that the Constitution promised. While a more realistic conceptualization of federalism was necessary to establish the legal basis for challenging the seceding states, it would not alone serve as a rallying cry for citizens who would bear the cruel burden of that challenge. The underlying issues were human rights and individual growth. Lincoln's challenge was to dramatize this. He did so skillfully by portraying the advances that had been made by the American experiment and the benefits that it conferred upon its citizens.[18]

Lincoln sought to depict the gulf between the value system of the Union and that of the secessionists and, in so doing, to define the central character of the war. Lincoln regarded the war as a "people's contest," in which the the improvement of the human condition was a central focus. "On the side of the Union it is a struggle for maintaining in the world that form and substance of government whose leading object is to elevate the condition of men; to lift artificial weights from all shoulders; to clear the paths of laudable pursuit for all; to afford all an unfettered start and a fair chance in the race of life. Yielding to partial and temporary departures, from necessity, this is the leading object of the Government for whose existence we contend."[19]

In his first annual message at the end of the year, Lincoln returned to the theme of the people's contest in what his biographer, David Herbert Donald, calls an "oddly incongruous disquisition" on the relationship of capital and labor. In it Lincoln went to the defense of the free laborer, dependent neither on capital nor slave labor: "The prudent penniless beginner in the world labors for wages awhile, saves a surplus with which to buy tools or land for himself, then labors for his own account for awhile, and at length hires a new beginner to help him. This is the just and generous and prosperous system which opens the way to all, gives hope to all, and consequent energy and progress and improvement of condition to all." Lincoln saw the insurrection as threatening such advancement, the Union as promoting it. Its cause would elevate the condition of free labor by emphasizing opportunity.

If the special session message was Jacksonian in its rejection of the right of secession, it was like Adams in its effort to enlist the purpose of government in the national effort to save the government. In reviewing the annual messages of Lincoln's predecessors, one must to go back to the administration of John Quincy Adams to find comparable content. Indeed, Lincoln's invocation of the role of government in elevating the "condition of men" recalls Adams's first annual message. There, in support of his internal-improvement policy, the sixth president had observed: "The great object of the institution of civil government is the improvement of the condition of those who are parties to the social compact." Lincoln's special-session message, taken with these earlier precedents and delivered as an instrument of war policy, provided a fresh framework for the exercise of the General Welfare authority when peace would permit it. Both in terms of its redefinition of federalism and in its restatement of the central aim of government—a preserved and strengthened Union—that framework would have lasting impact in the years to come. Just as Adams had recognized, that framework necessarily involved the broad exercise of the spending power as a means of vindicating its promise of opportunity and progress.

Lincoln defined the task before him on July 4, 1861. He was convinced the people had settled two points with respect to popular Government, "the successful *establishing* and the successful *administering* of it." "One still remains—its successful *maintenance* against a formidable internal attempt to overthrow it." After that point had been established through the successful prosecution of the Civil War, Lincoln assured Congress that his course toward the Southern states would be "guided by the Constitution." All present must have known, however, that the relationship would be structured within a new framework. That framework would serve as a reference point for the future exercise of federal powers, including the spending power.[20]

DOMESTIC INITIATIVES IN THE ANNUAL MESSAGE OF 1861

In his first annual message, sent to Congress in December 1861, as in the other three, Lincoln's focal point was the prosecution of the Civil War. The president wove into the account references to domestic initiatives in such areas as agriculture, communication, and transportation that provide some insights into his thinking on the use of federal assistance to support these enterprises. However, it would be a mistake to conclude, because of his early political and legislative role, that Lincoln's principal preoccupation was with internal improvements. So absorbed was he in the prosecution of the war and so frequent and profound were the reverses and frustrations that he faced, particularly in 1861 and 1862, that it would have been astonishing if he had given the subject much reflection, despite his experience during his state and federal legislative days. Moreover, Lincoln brought to the presidency the Whig tradition of Executive Branch deference to Congress on legislative matters. In general, he did not see his role as that of an active lobbyist for a legislative program. Nor did he consider it his duty to telegraph his intent to veto legislation in advance.

Consequently, the president's references to internal improvements or other potential objects of federal assistance were sporadic and suggest no effort to frame a cohesive program. In a sense, the references are more significant for what they did not say than for what they did. Unlike his Democratic predecessors, Buchanan, Pierce, Polk, Tyler, and Jackson, Lincoln did not agonize about internal improvements and almost took it as a given that the federal government had an appropriate role in their advancement to the extent that the war and fiscal constraints permitted. From this perspective, his administration represents a clear break with the past on General Welfare Clause issues.

Of greater significance are the allusions in Lincoln's annual messages to his own concept of the general welfare. Often interwoven into his reports on the progress of the war, or discussions of his efforts to shorten the war by various proposals, was a return to the theme he had sounded in his special session message: the particular role of government in ensuring equal opportunity and the significance of the great civil struggle for the average working man. Coextensive with that theme as well, one gains from a reading of Lincoln's messages a better sense of his approach to the constitutional authority of the federal government to deal effectively with the crises that faced it. Lincoln conceived of that government as having sufficient authority to confront those crises. He did not shrink from asserting that authority. While he often alluded to Jefferson, whom he regarded as something of a touchstone, the nation, which he could visualize as containing 250 million citizens by 1930, had moved beyond the constitutional qualms that Jefferson had sometimes expressed but had, in practice, overcome, during his presidency.

Several of these elements can be seen in play in the more traditional internal-improvement recommendations in Lincoln's first annual message, which is characterized in David Herbert Donald's contemporary biography as a "perfunctory document." Lincoln began it with a discussion of foreign policy and the failed efforts of the Confederacy to enlist the support of foreign nations to its cause. He followed with a discussion of the status of various states in their allegiance to the Union and interlaced it with a recommendation for the construction of a railroad to connect east Tennessee, western North Carolina, and Kentucky with other "faithful parts of the Union." Lincoln recommended the construction of such a railroad as a military measure but looked to its future benefit as well: "Kentucky and the General Government cooperating, the work can be completed in a very short time, and when done it will be not only of vast present usefulness, but also a valuable permanent improvement, worth its cost in all the future." Lincoln's ability to advocate federal appropriations and cooperative federalism as a military expedient, while simultaneously recognizing the railroad's long-term benefit to the nation, brings to mind his 1848 speech about internal improvements and his practical approach to matters before the Illinois legislature.[21]

Lincoln followed this recommendation by advocating forming an organization within the government to handle agricultural issues: "Agriculture, confessedly the largest interest of the nation, has not a department nor a bureau, but a clerkship only, assigned to it in the Government. While it is fortunate that this great interest is so independent in its nature as to not have demanded and extorted more from the Government, I respectfully ask Congress to consider whether something more can not be given voluntarily with general advantage." This recommendation resulted in the establishment of the Department of Agriculture the following year, the first step in a long chain of events leading to the greater participation of the federal government in the agricultural life of the nation. Under Lincoln's leadership the federal government was taking on the character that Gouverneur Morris had contemplated in 1787 when he proposed to the Philadelphia Convention that it provide for a secretary of domestic affairs.[22]

First Steps toward Emancipation: The Role of the Spending Power

At the root of disunion and the Civil War was the question of slavery. A redefinition of federalism or the federal role would not resolve that question. Nor would the shaping of a progressive domestic program. As John Quincy Adams had observed perceptively some forty years earlier: "[I]f the dissolution of the Union must come, let it come from no other cause but this. If slavery be the destined sword in the hand of the destroying angel which is to sever the ties of this Union, the same sword will cut in sunder the bonds of slavery itself." These lines make it clear that Adams recognized both the need for reform and the obstacles to achieving it. Lincoln must have understood as well, although he did not immediately express himself on the subject. He knew that ultimately he would have to address the issue of emancipation in order to preserve the Union—and that amending the Constitution in order to repair its fundamental defect, its failure to ban slavery, was the only way to achieve that goal.

In 1820, at the time of the adoption of the Missouri Compromise, Adams, then secretary of state to President Monroe, had declared in his diary: "The fault is in the Constitution of the United States, which has sanctioned a dishonorable compromise with slavery. There is henceforth no remedy for it but a new organization of the Union, to effect which a concert of all the [free] States is indispensable...." Indeed, while he supported the 1820 compromise as the best that could be accomplished under the Constitution, Adams mused in his diary at the time that it might have been "wiser" and "bolder" to have insisted on a restriction for Missouri and forced "a convention of the States to revise and amend the Constitution. This would have produced a new Union of thirteen or fourteen States unpolluted with slavery, with a great and glorious object to effect, namely, that of rallying to their standard the other States by the universal emancipation of their slaves." Adams would then have convened such a convention for reasons other than slavery: the need to reform the banking system and to affirm a positive spending power: ("[T]hree subjects ... produce a state of things issuing in a necessity [for a convention]. One was the regulation of the currency, banks, and paper money; another, the impotence of the National Government to make internal improvements by roads and canals; and the third was slavery." It would be Lincoln's legacy to address effectively all three in his pervasive effort to save the Union but to address only one—slavery—through the change agent of a constitutional amendment.

Adams had fully recognized the difficulty of revising the Constitution to resolve the issue of slavery: "It is a contemplation not very creditable to human nature that the cement of common interest produced by slavery is stronger and more solid than that of unmingled freedom. In this stance the slave States have clung together in one unbroken phalanx, and have been victorious by the means of accomplices and deserters from the ranks of freedom. Time only can show whether the contest may ever be with equal advantage renewed."[23]

Forty years later Lincoln, called upon to lead the nation in the "contest" that Adams predicted, recognized the need to reform the Constitution and the inevitability of emancipation. Like Adams, he appreciated fully the difficulty and sensitivity of the task, realizing that change must be achieved in a way, and with a timing, that did not further erode the power of the North by driving out of the Union the border states. Accordingly, in his first annual message, in a special message in March of 1862, and later in the second annual message, Lincoln floated three proposals for emancipation that manifested his gradualist approach to the issue and his hope that such an approach might forge a basis for confining or ending secession and for reuniting the Union without further bloodshed and within the existing constitutional framework. All of these proposals were basically flawed, inequitable, rejected by the states to which they were addressed and finally abandoned. However, in the aggregate, they formed a bridge to abolition through immediate, mandatory, uncompensated emancipation, effected by executive authority or constitutional amendment, depending on the status of the state in question with respect to the Union.

All three depended upon a radical and unprecedented application of the spending power. They signaled that Lincoln and his administration were prepared to use the spending power, without dwelling on its scope, in a bold and novel way to address the fundamental issues that confronted the nation. Faced with most excruciatingly difficult challenge of his presidency, Lincoln began with the carrot approach afforded by the spending power, reserving for later the stick of mandatory emancipation through resort to the war power or constitutional change. The first of these three initiatives (in the first annual message) proposed a program of "colonization" for consenting emancipated slaves; the second a program of federal financial aid to states that would embrace voluntary state-wide emancipation, the third a program of gradual, constitutionally prescribed "compensated emancipation," effected over an extended time period.[24]

In March of 1862, in a separate message to Congress, Lincoln recommended that Congress adopt a joint resolution to the effect that the United States cooperate with any state which "may adopt gradual abolishment of slavery." The resolution would further provide for giving such a state "pecuniary aid" to be used by the state at its discretion to compensate for public and private "inconveniences" produced by the change in systems. The proposal evidently called for federal financial assistance to states that adopted a program of gradual emancipation with the funds going to the states for use in their discretion. Participation by the state in a program of "abolishment" would presumably be a condition of receipt of the funds; what other conditions would be imposed in terms of education, provision of civil rights and like were not stated.

The avowed purpose of this scheme was to induce border states to stay in the Union and, at the same time, move voluntarily toward emancipation. Lincoln feared that border states, notably Kentucky and Missouri, might be lured into the Confederacy by its military success and by a desire to maintain slavery within their borders. If they could be induced to remain in the Union and at the same time to abandon slavery, the hope of an expanding Confederacy would be denied the seceding states. Consequently, these states would abandon the rebellion and would embrace federally compensated emancipation as well. As Lincoln expressed it: "To deprive them [the seceding states] of this hope substantially ends the rebellion, and the initiation of emancipation completely deprives them of it as to all the States initiating it."

The inducement for all this was the federal financial assistance program that Lincoln proposed. The intent was to balance state choice and state interest in a way that would not engender hostility in the border states and would move them toward the goal of gradual emancipation. This would be done within the framework of the Constitution, which Lincoln believed precluded interfering with slavery in states that remained in the Union. "Such a proposition on the part of the General Government," urged Lincoln in his March message, "sets up no claim of a right by Federal authority to interfere with slavery within State limits, referring as it does, the absolute control of the subject in each case to the State and its people immediately interested. It is proposed as a matter of perfectly free choice with them." It is significant that Lincoln saw no need to defend this proposed exercise of the spending power on constitutional, General Welfare Clause grounds. All "indispensable means" to preserve the Union must be available. Such means included the bold use of a spending power, unconfined by specific enumerations, to encourage emancipation through pecuniary assistance to loyal slave states. This was first proposal to abolish slavery submitted to Congress by an American president.[25]

Lincoln followed up on the March 1862 proposal with a number of implementing steps. On July 12, 1862, he invited border state representatives in Congress to the White House and read to them an urgent appeal to give favorable consideration to the initiative. He touted his plan as a "swift means of ending" the war. "Let the states which are in rebellion see, definitely and certainly, that, in no event, will the states you represent ever join their proposed Confederacy, and they can not, much longer maintain the contest." He argued that time was running out and confided that the pressures on him to issue an immediate proclamation of emancipation were growing. He "begged" their attention to the March resolution message and pleaded with them to discard "maxims adapted to more manageable times." The majority of representatives rejected the proposal, arguing that it would reinforce the spirit of rebellion in states that had seceded and fan the flames of secession in the border states. A minority of the representatives supported Lincoln. It does not appear that there was any objection on constitutional grounds to this use of the spending power.

Undeterred, Lincoln submitted a draft bill to Congress in July 1862 that would implement his proposal. He earnestly recommended its passage. The bill would have directed the president, whenever he found that a state had lawfully abolished slavery throughout the state, to deliver to that state United States bonds based on a formula determined by the number of persons emancipated. The bonds would bear interest at six percent. If any state that received the bonds later reintroduced or tolerated slavery, the bonds would become null and void, and the state would be required to refund the interest it received. It is difficult to conclude that the constitutional basis for this proposal could be other than the federal spending power under Article I, section 8, clause 1 of the Constitution. If it was, the proposal depended on a broad reading of the General Welfare Clause in the fashion of Joseph Story's *Commentaries*. No one who took the view of the Constitution advocated by Lincoln's predecessors, Polk, Pierce, and Buchanan, could have advocated such pecuniary assistance. Indeed, if this proposal was authorized under the General Welfare Clause, and Lincoln in pressing it must have believed that it was, then the more conventional initiatives in the fields of education, transportation, and agriculture were also authorized.

Congress subsequently adopted the suggested resolution by large votes in both Houses, despite constitutional objections raised by some, but Lincoln's draft bill was not enacted, although the relevant House committee reported it favorably. Despite Lincoln's strenuous lobbying efforts and some consideration of the matter in Delaware and other states, no state came forward definitively to claim the benefits and trigger implementing legislation, appropriations, or the like. The initiative was abandoned. It was flawed on many fronts, not the least of which is that it would have precluded the civil rights protections embraced in the fourteenth and fifteenth amendments. The episode, however, does illustrate the extent to which Lincoln and Congress, during the early years of the war, were prepared to use the spending power to achieve national aims that otherwise seemed elusive. Moreover, with no action taken by the border states, the initiative led to, or evolved into, a more effective step to address the antislavery sentiments of those who had supported the administration: immediate, uncompensated emancipation for those held in servitude in the states that had renounced the Union.[26]

In June of 1862 Lincoln—perhaps satisfied that he had tried a carrot strategy and that it would not work—began drafting an emancipation proclamation. He had become committed to such a course, convinced not only that it was a political and moral imperative but also a "military necessity absolutely essential to the salvation of the Union." The version of the document that he read to his cabinet in July of 1862 would have, as of January 1, 1863, freed all persons held in servitude in states where the authority of the United States Constitution was not recognized. It would also have made known Lincoln's intention to renew his compensated emancipation ("pecuniary aid") proposal in the succeeding session of Congress, presumably to embrace the border states. After considering the divided counsel of his cabinet, Lincoln held back this preliminary proclamation, declaring that he must first have a military victory.

One came in the fall of 1862 in the form of the bloody battle of Antietam. Lincoln issued the preliminary proclamation in September of 1862. That proclamation declared that emancipation would take place as of January 1, 1863. It marked a sea change in the affairs of the nation, the beginning of a reframing of the Constitution, and the initiation of the "universal emancipation" that Adams had written of in the privacy of his diary. In issuing the 1862 proclamation, however, Lincoln did not totally abandon his spending power initiative; he referred to compensated emancipation in the September proclamation presumably as an option for the border states (or returning seceding states) to which the proclamation did not apply.[27]

Paludan suggests that Lincoln's constitutional amendment proposal of December 1862 was a last effort on his part to look back to the pre–Civil War era and address slavery through a gradual process of constitutional change and possibly shorten the war: "The most satisfactory rational explanation of Lincoln's plan is that it spoke to many audiences and thus was intentionally vague perhaps even intentionally confusing." In formulating these proposals, Lincoln was seeking to steer a balanced course between the radical Republicans and abolitionists who sought immediate emancipation and the conservative Democrats who, initially at least, were seeking to preserve, to the extent possible, pre–Civil War norms. As the war progressed, events moved Lincoln toward a more immediate, less graduated end to slavery, effected under federal, rather than state, timing, control, and conditions, including conditions relating to civil rights.

Ultimately, there was no occasion for using the spending power as a means of effecting emancipation. The Thirteenth Amendment, whose proposal to the states Lincoln embraced and urged upon the Congress in 1864 would resolve the issue of the status of slavery through the requisite constitutional change on an immediate basis. However, in these first tentative steps from December 1861 to December 1862, Lincoln attempted to invoke a broadly defined spending power in a manner that paved the way for an effective and more satisfying resolution, cleansing the Constitution of the imperfection that John Quincy Adams had noted in 1820. In the years following Lincoln's tenure, the use of that authority would increase and would embrace efforts to address effectively and lastingly searing problems rooted in the corrosive institution of slavery. It would be used, not as an alternative to definitive civil rights measures, but as an instrument for reinforcing them.[28]

12
Lincoln's General Welfare Legacy

IN SUCCEEDING ANNUAL MESSAGES, LINCOLN CONTINUED TO REINforce his interest in internal improvements and to lend his support to other progressive legislation. The Homestead Act, which Lincoln signed and promoted, and the Morrill Land Grant College Act, which he approved, represented landmark enactments. The executive branch support for this legislation represented a significant break with the constitutional position of Lincoln's immediate Democratic predecessors. While based on land grants, it, nevertheless, paved the way for a more open approach to general welfare spending legislation by Republican presidents who followed during Reconstruction and who were faced with the task of implementing the "new birth of freedom" that Lincoln initiated. Lincoln himself recognized the importance of education in such implementation in the course of advocating his own policies for reconstruction, a perspective that anticipated education's central role in the promotion of civil rights.

INTERNAL IMPROVEMENTS AND THE SECOND ANNUAL MESSAGE

Lincoln's second annual message was delivered at the end of 1862, a year which had seen no quick resolution of the crisis that confronted the Union. The message contained a mixture of domestic initiatives, reflections on the course of the war, and the proposal to end it by adopting a constitutional amendment to provide for compensated emancipation discussed above. On the domestic front, despite the national preoccupation with the war, Lincoln focused on steps that would make a preserved Union a better habitat for the free laborers that he had portrayed in the preceding year's message. Accordingly, he presented proposals to connect Europe, Russia, and the United States through telegraphic communication; to enhance progress on the construction of the Pacific Railroad; and to expand the functions of the newly established Agriculture Department.[1]

The president related his support for the railroad to a broader set of internal improvement proposals, submitting a statement of the proceedings of the railroad commissioners which demonstrated the progress that had been made in the construction of the Pacific (transcontinental) Railroad, a project which Lincoln had encouraged since gaining office. "[T]his suggests," he observed, "the earliest completion of this road, and also the favorable action of Congress upon the projects now pending before them for enlarging the capacities of the great canals in New York and Illinois, as being of vital and rapidly increasing importance to the whole nation, and especially to the vast interior region...." He gave favorable mention to the enlargement of the Illinois and Michigan Canal and improving of the Illinois River, projects that he had championed earlier in his poiitical life. Employing traditional Whig deference to the legislature, Lincoln respectfully but unmistakably asked Congress to give attention to the matter. As G. S. Boritt puts it, Lincoln "maintained a very large measure of confidence in the ability of the United States, both the government and the economy, to underwrite improvement works while engaged in a great war."[2]

Finally, the president mentioned his organization of the Department of Agriculture and pointed to that department's establishment of exchanges that would enhance knowledge of improvements in agriculture and the introduction of new products. The department, he promised, would soon be prepared to distribute seeds, cereals, plants, and cuttings. "The creation of this Department was for the more immediate benefit of a large class of our most valuable citizens, and I trust that the liberal basis upon which it has been organized will not only meet your approbation, but that it will realize at no distant day all the fondest anticipations of its most sanguine friends and become the fruitful source of advantage to all our people."[3]

The connection that Lincoln did draw for his modest internal improvement measures was not to the past constitutional battles that had concerned his predecessors but to the crisis that then absorbed the nation and threatened the dissolution of the Union. Internal improvement symbolized an element of the struggle for unity that gripped Lincoln's America. The improvements he recommended made sense for *one* nation not two. "That portion of the earth's surface which is owned and inhabited by the people of the United States is well adapted to be home of one national family, and it is not well adapted for two or more. Its vast extent and its variety of climate and productions are of advantage in this age for one people, whatever they might have been in former ages. Steam, telegraphs, and intelligence have brought these to an advantageous combination for one united people."[4] With this bridge, Lincoln came to the basic point of his annual message. Disunion was an inadequate remedy for the sectional differences between what should properly be a united people. Indeed, the president astutely recognized that trade and commercial interests required union. These considerations he predicted "would ere long force reunion, however much of blood and treasure the separation might have cost." Federal financial assistance for internal improvements was not only justified on grounds of legality and expediency; it was a reunionizing force.[5]

THE THIRD ANNUAL MESSAGE: TOWARD THE "NEW BIRTH OF FREEDOM"

In the Gettysburg Address, delivered in November 1863, Lincoln gave voice to the "new birth of freedom" that ennobled the war. To the preservation of the Union, he added equality as a major purpose of the war. In this context in the third annual message, Lincoln could begin to focus not only on measures to improve the nation and the condition of its people, but also on a framework for reconstruction and for reconciliation with the seceding states.[6]

The Homestead Legislation

In the former category, one such measure had already been enacted into law through passage by the Thirty-Seventh Congress and the signature of the president in 1862. This was the Homestead Act. It called for the wider use of public lands to achieve general welfare-equal opportunity purposes. Earlier in his career Lincoln had favored the grant of public lands (or the proceeds of their sale) to the states to support internal improvements. Therefore it is not surprising that Lincoln as president favored efforts to expand the use of public lands to foster other general welfare goals. The Homestead Act involved such a use. It provided that a certain portion of the unoccupied public lands would be set aside for transfer to homesteaders for a nominal fee. By maintaining residence for five years, the homesteader became entitled to the land. The act represented a break with early practice under which public lands had been sold in order to obtain revenue. Heather Cox Richardson, in her comprehensive study of Republican economic legislation during the Civil War, assesses the impact of the Homestead Act as follows: "With the passage of the Homestead Act, the Republicans demonstrated their commitment to a policy of government-sponsored economic development to increase the nation's prosperity and expand the wartime tax base." Richardson further describes its impact on farm settlement and the growth of independent farmers: "Republican agricultural legislation did much to settle the West and provide homes for farming families, but it did not ultimately create the thriving expanses of small farms the Republicans had envisioned."[7]

The Homestead Act was one of a series of legislative measures passed by the Thirty-Seventh Congress and signed by the president that David Herbert Donald characterizes as "an impressive body of legislation." The body of laws included, in addition to the homestead legislation, the National Banking Act, the transcontinental railroad legislation, the legislation creating the Department of Agriculture mentioned above, the Morrill Land Grant College Act, and an important revision and reform of the internal revenue legislation. Despite the acrimony and friction between Lincoln and various elements in Congress, this record reflected, as Donald puts it, "the cooperation of all factions of the Republicans acting with the President."[8]

In his 1863 annual message, Lincoln took note of this achievement, commenting favorably on the progress made since the enactment of the Homestead and other public land legislation: "It has long been a cherished opinion of some of our wisest statesmen that the people of the United States had a higher and more enduring interest in the early settlement and substantial cultivation of the public lands than in the amount of direct revenue to be derived from the sale of them. This opinion has had a controlling influence in shaping legislation upon the subject of our national domain." Lincoln cited as evidence "the liberal measures adopted in reference to actual settlers," the grant to states of "overflowed lands" within their borders for reclamation, and the grants to railway companies. The policy had received "its most signal and beneficent illustration in the recent enactment of legislation granting homesteads to actual settlers." This was a reference to the Homestead Act which Lincoln had earlier signed. He reported with great satisfaction that over 1.4 million acres (out of a total of 3.8 million) had been taken up under the act. "This fact and the amount of sales furnish gratifying evidence of increasing settlement upon the public lands notwithstanding the great struggle in which the energies of the nation have been engaged...."

The president then urged a modification of the law to benefit those who had engaged in military or naval service—a veteran's preference amendment. "I doubt not," he said, "that Congress will cheerfully adopt such measures as will, without essentially changing the general features of the system, secure to the greatest practicable extent its benefits to those who have left their homes in the defense of the country in this arduous crisis." The granting of federal lands to individuals is a forerunner of federal transfer payments to individuals under the spending power to achieve general welfare objectives, avoid poverty, improve national health, or other aims. The program reflects Lincoln's belief that government should have a role in improving the condition of individual citizens and providing equal opportunity.[9]

Neither in his 1863 message praising the legislation nor in approving it did Lincoln dwell on the constitutional ramifications of using the federal government's authority over the public lands to achieve such objectives. His immediate predecessors, Pierce and Buchanan, had viewed such legislation as tantamount to the appropriation of funds and therefore subject to the constraints advocated by Madison regarding the exercise of power under Article I, section 8, clause 1. Buchanan had vetoed homestead legislation passed by Congress in 1859 on the basis of such thinking. Accordingly, in supporting the transfer of public lands to homesteaders, in signing legislation to effectuate that policy, and in proposing to extend the policy to veterans, Lincoln was implicitly countenancing and supporting a vigorous exercise of the spending power that would have been antithetical to his Democratic predecessors and represented a break with that history.[10]

To be sure, Lincoln did not explain whether his action in support of the homestead legislation merely represented a rejection of Buchanan's view that disposal of public land was subject to the same test as applied to the appropriation of funds and was therefore sustainable under a broad reading of the power over public lands, irrespective of how one read the General Welfare Clause. However, it is unlikely that Lincoln would have felt himself obliged to rely upon such a narrow distinction when he was simultaneously lending his support to transcontinental railroad legislation and other conventional internal improvements that involved direct appropriations. If the issue was considered at all, it is likely that Lincoln, had he applied Buchanan's principles, would have concluded that the General Welfare Clause embraced this species of legislation as "providing for the general welfare," whether aid was in the form of land grants or direct appropriations.

Lincoln's approval of and praise for the Homestead Act constitutes one more example of the importance of the combination of a forward-looking president who gently pressed for equal opportunity with the advent of a Republican Party that favored internal improvements and the diminution of influence of a Congress consisting of legislators with state-right views. This combination shifted the nation toward a more vigorous use of the federal-spending and public-land powers. If the public lands could be used to assist, for example, economically disadvantaged individuals willing to settle and work the land, then they could be used for other General Welfare initiatives. Put in spending power terms, if the grant of authority to Congress under Article I, section 8, clause 1 of the Constitution extended to financial assistance for homesteaders, clearly a purpose beyond the scope of the enumerated powers, it could be used for other general welfare purposes, including improving education, health research, and public benefits for the aged or less advantaged.[11]

In the 1863 message, Lincoln followed his observations on the Homestead Act with some more traditional lobbying on behalf of internal improvements. He noted that the preceding session of Congress had considered but not adopted propositions designed to enlarge water communication between the Mississippi and the northeastern seaboard. He reminded Congress that a convention had been held in Chicago regarding the same subject, the report of which he submitted to Congress with his message and a supportive statement of his own: "That this interest is one which ere long will force its own way, I do not entertain a doubt, while it is submitted entirely to your wisdom as to what can be done now. Augmented interest is given to this subject by the actual commencement of work upon the Pacific Railroad, under auspices so favorable to rapid progress and completion. The enlarged navigation becomes a palpable need to the great road." The bridge between the Lincoln of the Illinois legislature, Lincoln as a member of Congress, and Lincoln as president seems evident in this passage.[12]

LOBBYING FOR THE REFRAMING OF THE CONSTITUTION

Lincoln's fourth and last annual message, delivered in December of 1864 after his reelection, returned to the themes of the first three. It was delivered to the third (lame duck) session of the Thirty-Eighth Congress that would come to support most of Lincoln's aims. The war had not come to a close. The disbursements for the War and Navy Departments dominated the budget. It was hardly a time for vast domestic initiatives. Nevertheless, Lincoln could note with pride that "the steady expansion of population, *improvement,* and governmental institutions over the new and unoccupied portions of our country have scarcely been checked" by the "great civil war."[13] He largely deferred to the Interior Department report on issues related to the public lands and the progress of the Pacific Railroad but noted that "[t]he great enterprise of connecting the Atlantic with the Pacific States by railways and telegraph lines," spending power initiatives that he had steadfastly supported throughout the war, "has been entered upon with a vigor that gives assurance of success, notwithstanding the embarrassments arising from the prevailing high prices of materials and labor." He commented favorably on the progress of the newly formed Agriculture Department. He regarded it as "peculiarly the people's Department, in which they feel more directly concerned than in any other." While a war president, Lincoln seemed satisfied that his administration had been able to initiate a progressive domestic program.[14]

He turned again to abolition and permanent emancipation, this time with greater assurance as to purpose and strategy. The House had failed to approve, for submission to the states, a proposed amendment to the Constitution to abolish slavery throughout the United States. While often disinclined to press Congress to approve measures he favored—a throw-back to the Whig heritage—Lincoln urged Congress to propose to the states for ratification what would become the Thirteenth Amendment. "I venture to recommend the reconsideration and passage of the measure at the present session," he said, and he predicted that the new Congress (which would convene in 1865) would pass the amendment on to the states if the present one did not. "It is the voice of the people now for the first time heard upon the question ... In this case the common end is the maintenance of the Union, and among the means to secure that end such will, through the election, is most clearly declared in favor of such constitutional amendment."

Following the fourth annual message, Lincoln was deeply involved in pressing Congress to approve the resolution calling for state ratification of the Thirteenth Amendment. His efforts were successful. In February 1865, the session to which his final annual message was delivered approved the resolution. The ratification of the Thirteenth Amendment by the states after Lincoln's death, but during the second term to which he had been elected, effected the reframing of the Constitution and the reversal of the compromise with slavery that the original framers had made in 1787. It accomplished the imperative constitutional corrective that John Quincy Adams had contemplated as inevitable at the time of the Missouri Compromise.[15]

The election of 1864, Lincoln observed in his fourth annual message, had also established that, despite the war, the nation was not approaching the exhaustion of the "most important branch of national resources, that of living men." He explained: "The national resources, then, are unexhausted, and, as we believe, inexhaustible. The public purpose to reestablish and maintain the national authority is unchanged, and, as we believe, unchangeable." Choice remained as to the "manner of continuing the effort." Negotiation with "the insurgent leader" would do no good; "He cannot voluntarily reaccept the Union; we cannot voluntarily yield it." Those individuals in the seceding states who wished peace could obtain it under the terms for individual pardons that Lincoln had specified in earlier messages: "They can at any moment have peace simply by laying down their arms and submitting to the national authority under the Constitution."[16]

In recapitulating these wartime provisions, Lincoln recognized that there were limits on his own authority and that the end of the war might bring more formal and rigorous terms for pardon and reconstruction. On the central point, however, he remained clear. "In presenting the abandonment of armed resistance to the national authority on the part of the insurgents as the only indispensable condition to ending the war on the part of the Government, I retract nothing heretofore said as to slavery." And he carefully repeated his admonition in the 1863 message regarding the immutability of the Emancipation Proclamation. "In stating a single condition of peace," he observed in concluding his message, "I mean simply to say that the war will cease on the part of the Government whenever it shall have ceased on the part of those who began it."

When it did, the General Welfare Clause embraced, as it had not before, the aspirations and the needs of the three million *per-*

sons in the United States who had been emancipated. The interpretation of the constitutional concept contained in that clause had itself been freed from prior constraints that had held it in check. In time that clause would be become an increasingly powerful instrument for giving effect to the "new birth of freedom" of which Lincoln spoke at Gettysburg and which he helped institute by promoting the Thirteenth Amendment. It remains so to this day. Lincoln's most important contribution to the growth of the spending power may be connected to his role in ending slavery and in thus confronting the nation with the challenge of dispensing social justice to an oppressed minority. Whatever it might have meant prior to Lincoln's time, it was inevitable that the General Welfare Clause would be seized upon as a prime instrument for responding to that challenge. The nexus between civil rights and spending power actions at the federal level has been a close one ever since.[17]

LINCOLN, EDUCATION, AND THE SPENDING POWER: THE MORRILL ACT

Despite Abraham Lincoln's recognition of the importance of education in a reconstructed state, the reader of his annual messages during the period of his presidency finds little reference to education and to the role of the federal government in promoting it. In fact, there are fewer references to that subject in Lincoln's presidential papers than in the annual messages of Washington, Jefferson, Madison, Monroe, and John Quincy Adams. Lincoln, as we have seen, had taken a positive approach to a national role in financing internal improvements, particularly through financing canals and railroads, in assisting agriculture, and in authorizing homestead grants, all expressions of the spending power. During his earlier political life he had argued eloquently and persuasively for a broad reading of that power. Yet, it does not appear that he gave the same emphasis to education, as an object of an energetic application of the federal spending power, in his public statements, notwithstanding his apparent recognition of the important role of education in postwar reconstruction.

The legislation that Lincoln signed into law during his administration represents a marked departure from this pattern. That departure took the form of Lincoln's approval of the Morrill Land Grant College Act. The Morrill Act provided for the donation of public lands to states and territories to assist them in establishing and maintaining colleges that would offer education in agriculture and the mechanic arts. Lincoln signed it into law on July 2, 1862, without, as far as research reveals, any fanfare, in the form of a signing statement or accompanying address.[18] Nor did Lincoln mention the legislation in his December 1862 annual message, or in later messages. The president's silence on the issue attracted the attention of Phillip Paludan in his account of the Lincoln presidency. "Interestingly enough, the president apparently paid little attention to this bill. He did not mention it in his annual message to Congress in 1863, which did refer to the homestead and banking bills." Paludan attributes this to the "ambiguity about formal education in a man who had had little of it himself."[19]

The Morrill Act in effect constituted a simple but classic program of federal assistance to the states involving cooperative federalism. The federal government provided financial assistance in the form of land grants. The statute provided an apportionment formula for allocating the assistance (the land or land scrip) among the states. The law directed the state to use the funds in question (the proceeds of the land or scrip sales) for a general purpose set forth in the law, to endow, support, and maintain institutions of higher education. The law specified the role of the instrumentality of the participating state that would carry out duties under the act, here the state legislature. Participation by the state was voluntary. The state would have to signify its assent by legislation before the law's provisions came into play for that state. The law specified the conditions upon which the grants were made. The law also described the consequences of failure to comply with the conditions, here, return of the grant funds. An agency or department of the federal government was named as the administering agency: the Department of the Interior. The state was required to submit an annual report to the administering department, presumably as a means of facilitating evaluation and fostering accountability. In sum, Congress had passed, and Lincoln signed into law, a federal education program statute. By providing a framework for such assistance, the statute in effect provided for a national system of aid to land grant colleges, without any semblance of national jurisdiction over the institutions themselves. Thus, through authorizing legislation, the concept of appropriation to the states under the General Welfare Clause was gradually being transformed into a workable instrument without the need for a constitutional amendment.[20]

Lincoln's role and its significance

What is significant is not what Lincoln said about this legislation. He signed the land grant college bill without an accompanying statement, at least without one that has been passed down to posterity. His subsequent annual messages are silent about it. What is significant is that he signed the bill. His predecessor, Buchanan, had vetoed similar legislation. In explaining his veto, Buchanan had complained that the legislation represented an expression of the spending power beyond the authority of Congress under the Constitution. Buchanan had also feared that the measure would draw the federal government into a wide range of domestic matters not, in his view, appropriate for its attention.

Buchanan's predecessor, Pierce, had vetoed legislation that would have granted public lands to states to enable them to serve indigent persons who were mentally ill. Pierce's veto had urged constitutional and policy concerns similar to those voiced by Buchanan when he vetoed the land grant college bill. Pierce had expressed his own apprehension that if the bill before him were enacted, it would set a precedent for undue expansion of the role of the federal government. Both Pierce and Buchanan regarded the bills they vetoed as efforts to exercise the constitutional spending power in ways that exceeded that power, rather than proper expressions of the congressional power over the public lands. They had insisted that a disposition of the public lands must meet the same test as an appropriation of funds under the General Welfare Clause.[21]

Lincoln and his advisors were doubtless aware of these precedents. Lincoln had predicted that Pierce would veto this type of legislation in the period prior to the latter's election in 1852. In reversing the Buchanan land grant college veto policy, President Lincoln took a very different course than that of his northern Democratic predecessors. That course implicitly recognized an appropriate role for the federal government in assisting activities at the state level that fell within the ambit of the general welfare. In signing the Morrill bill, Lincoln moved the Executive Branch in a new direction regarding such legislation and paved the way for future enactments providing federal aid to education or other endeavors that came within the broadly encompassing general welfare ambit.

In making the Morrill Act a public law, for all that the record shows, Lincoln declined to raise the objections, legal or policy, that his predecessors had raised. He even declined to give them credence by discussing and rejecting them. In the three-year span that separated Buchanan's veto from Lincoln's signature, a great change in the constitutional landscape had taken place, a change that both the Executive and Legislative branches understood and that required no explication. In this respect, Lincoln's approval of the Morrill Act marks a new approach toward spending-power legislation, one that reflected the earlier stance of John Quincy Adams but that at the same time had moved beyond it.

One can, of course, argue that Lincoln's approval of the measure was pro forma and reflective of the traditional Whig view that presidents should not employ the veto to frustrate congressional action. In other words, in signing the Morrill Act, Lincoln was arguably following the course that William Henry Harrison or Zachary Taylor would have followed regarding domestic legislation to come before them had they survived to serve out their terms. Lincoln's signature on the Morrill Act is, on this basis, nothing more than a Whig president's deferential nod to the Legislative Branch rather than a thoughtful expression of support for the law and policy inherent in the legislation.

On the other hand, Lincoln's signature on the bill arguably represents more than Whigish deference. While Lincoln did generally practice Whig restraint in his dealings with Congress on legislation, his action in approving the college bill is wholly consistent with the constitutional and policy positions that he had taken before he reached the White House, the platform on which he ran in order to get there, and the other domestic policies that he supported during the time he occupied that office. His failure to articulate his support for this higher education legislation more likely reflects his preoccupation with the war than his indifference to the policy of federal support for higher education.

As a state legislator, Lincoln had advocated a governmental role in internal improvements. As a congressman during the Polk administration, he had eloquently opposed that president's veto of federal internal improvement legislation, a veto pitched on much the same grounds that moved Buchanan in his comparable veto of the 1859 version of the Morrill Act. Lincoln had supported both the constitutionality and expediency of the legislation that Polk vetoed. In his speech criticizing the Polk veto Lincoln had expressed not only the standard Whig position of deference to the legislative branch but his own conclusions on the constitutionality of internal-improvement legislation under the General Welfare Clause. On that occasion he had counseled his congressional colleagues that their constitutional consciences should not be "pricked" unduly if they supported such legislation.

Moreover, the Morrill Act was consistent with legislation that Lincoln actively promoted during his presidency and discussed in his annual messages, including grants of public lands for railroads, federal assistance for internal improvements such as canals and waterways, and the homestead legislation discussed above. Representative Justin Smith Morrill of Vermont, who proposed and managed the college bill, argued during the debates on the legislation that it would enhance national prosperity by increasing agricultural production and efficiency. Morrill tied his legislation to the Homestead Act; if land was being given freely, farmers would have to learn how to use it. All of the legislation— for the railroad, for internal improvements, and for education— shared a common theme: their constitutional support ultimately depended upon a broad, Hamiltonian reading of the General Welfare Clause.

In providing expanded higher-education opportunities for the industrial classes, Lincoln was implementing a theme that he had sounded throughout his administration: the role of government in supporting equal opportunity. At the time he signed the legislation, Lincoln was calling upon the "industrial classes" to bear the burdens of the war he was waging to preserve the Constitution. It would have been completely incongruous for him to have invoked that same Constitution as a reason for denying them opportunities for education, especially since he had earlier referred to them as a "national resource."

As Paludan correctly observes, "Lincoln clearly believed . . . that one of the contrasts between free labor and slave labor was that free laborers were thinking people whose labor was improved by their inventiveness and whose thought was sharpened and enlivened by their labor. The Morrill Land Grant Act exemplified that image." Paludan's point appropriately identifies the Morrill Act's ties to free labor expressed in Lincoln's first annual message. Lincoln's 1859 speech in Milwaukee reinforces this conclusion. There Lincoln had pointed out the contribution of education to the successful pursuit of agriculture. The 1862 education act was thus integrated into and interlocking with other components of the Lincoln administration's domestic program and Lincoln's overall political and economic philosophy.

One may speculate that, in signing the bill, Lincoln saw no need for calling attention to a move that was consistent with both his own prior positions, with the platform of his own party and with other bills that he had signed. While he did not, except in rare occasions, intervene in the legislative process, his overall support for his party's program and his general encouragement of the Congress to implement it presumably embraced the Morrill Act as well as other progressive legislation during the first two years of his administration.

To be sure, in defending the constitutionality of his legislative proposal in 1858, Morrill had relied upon the power of Congress under the Constitution to dispose of public lands rather than General Welfare Clause. He had supported this argument by ample reference to public land grants under various administrations for purposes such as agriculture and education. In his remarks in 1862 prior to the congressional debates on the legislation, he did not return to the constitutional issue. Thus, there is no specific indication that the General Welfare Clause was specifically before the Congress during the debate.

However, the relationship to the General Welfare Clause issue could not so easily be avoided. In vetoing the legislation in 1858, President Buchanan had raised a reasonable question. If appropriations could not be made for educational purposes under the spending power, how could public lands be donated for that purpose? The purpose for appropriations or dispositions of tax revenues and public lands must be on the same footing. Otherwise, the general welfare limitation on the spending power could be avoided by using land proceeds for purposes that exceeded the limitations on the spending power.

The answer to Buchanan's question was that both tax revenues and land grants could be used for educational purposes because the General Welfare Clause limitation was not confined to areas or fields embraced within the enumerated powers. Therefore both the spending and land powers were available for such purposes. While the 1862 debates in Congress regarding the Morrill Act did not specifically focus on this point, that answer was implicit in congressional passage of that legislation on the basis of broad educational considerations. Indeed, while the senators who debated the Morrill Act were reminded of Buchanan's veto, none of those who supported the legislation defended their votes on the ground that the public lands power was broader than the spending power.

Moreover, the Morrill Act soon became a convenient precedent for direct appropriation of funds under the spending power. If land grants could be made for the support of institutions of higher education, proponents of federal aid to education argued, appropriations of tax revenues could also be made available for college aid, as well as for elementary and secondary schools. Republican presidents who followed Lincoln, most notably, Rutherford B. Hayes, made this relationship specific. It was reinforced by the enactment of the Second Morrill Act in 1890 which provided appropriations from land sale revenues for the use of college aid under the 1862 legislation. Later, when the Supreme Court came to consider the scope of the spending power, the Second Morrill Act was cited by the government as a precedent for the Court's approval of the Hamiltonian reading of the clause.

In signing the 1862 Morrill Act, Lincoln was taking an important step down the road to a broader view of the constitutional authority of Congress to enact progressive spending power legislation in aid of education and other general welfare missions, a more progressive step than his prewar Democratic predecessors had been willing to countenance.

Lincoln transmitted to Congress territorial legislation for New Mexico that enabled it to receive the benefits of the Morrill Act. The report of his Interior Department, attached to one annual message, described the progress that had been made in securing the adherence of other states to the act. It has its counterparts in subsequent legislation of assistance to higher education under the Higher Education Act of 1965, through aid to developing institutions, aid for international activities, and aid for construction of academic facilities. The 1862 act can be seen as paving the way for the massively significant participation of the federal government in student financial aid under Title IV of the Higher Education Act, a development that has had an enormous, positive impact in increasing the numbers of college graduates in the United States. Moreover, its enactment and interpretation were to figure in the Supreme Court's analysis, when it finally came to adjudicate the scope of the spending power in 1936 in *United States v. Butler*. The great dissent by Justice, later Chief Justice, Harlan Fiske Stone in that case relied in part on the precedent established by the Morrill Act and the implications that could be drawn from it. Lincoln himself had correctly predicted that such an adjudication would come to pass in his 1848 speech.[22]

Lincoln's signature on the Morrill Act, despite the absence of an explanation when he affixed it, is a profoundly important bridging event. The Morrill Act constituted major federal legislation giving effect to the pleas of Washington, Jefferson, Madison, and John Quincy Adams that Congress make provision for "seminaries of learning." It implemented in part Lincoln's stated commitment to the role of government in elevating the human condition, a theme that he had sounded in his July 1861 message to Congress in response to the secession of the states that had joined the Confederacy. That commitment in turn aligns Lincoln, in the context of this study, with John Quincy Adams, who had briefly been Lincoln's colleague in the Thirtieth Congress, and who, as president, had advocated a concept of internal improvement that went beyond roads and canals. The Morrill Act was one of the most significant manifestations of that concept in the first "fourscore and seven years" of the nation's history.[23]

Lincoln's General Welfare Legacy: A Bridge to the Twentieth Century

Lincoln's contribution to the evolution of the spending power must be regarded as salient. In some measure, that contribution takes the form of the policies that he advocated in his annual messages and elsewhere, such as assistance for internal improvements in transportation and communications, for agricultural benefits, and for homesteading assistance. It also takes the form of the body of progressive legislation that he signed providing for assistance to railroads, aid to land-grant colleges, homestead legislation, and the establishment of the Department of Agriculture. That legislation contributed to the emergence of a set of legislative precedents reflecting spending for general welfare purposes that would not have been possible had the thinking of Polk, Pierce, and Buchanan continued to prevail. The juxtaposition of a Republican president with Whig leanings on internal improvements and a Republican Congress with whom he cooperated reversed the constitutional pattern that had been characterized by prewar Democratic presidents extending Jacksonian philosophy. The Lincoln-congressional combination, through the legislation it produced, effected a sea change in the scope of the exercise of the spending power that can be seen as a significant aspect of Lincoln's "new birth of freedom."

In a larger sense, however, Lincoln's greatest contribution to this evolution lies in the forces that he set in motion: emancipation, enfranchisement, reconstruction, recognition of the important role of the central government in securing equal opportunity, and finally in his successful labor to preserve the Union and transform it from a house divided into a single nation. Lincoln's administration thus represents a transformation in the development of the concept of providing "for the general welfare" under the Constitution that he labored so valiantly to preserve. Engaged in the throes of a great civil war, he lacked the time, and possibly the inclination, to engage in comprehensive constitutional analysis of the course he implicitly pursued under the General Welfare Clause, as had Madison, Monroe and Jackson. However, that clause was the only reliable constitutional authority for the pursuit of that course. Accordingly, the constitutional implications of the "Lincoln persuasion" in the use of the spending power are clearly consistent with the more analytical approach of Hamilton, Monroe, John Quincy Adams, and Joseph Story and, ultimately, with the position taken by the Supreme Court in *United States v. Butler* adopting the Hamilton-Story interpretation. Lincoln's contribution to that evolution and to the events that followed it is undeniable.

Finally, Lincoln's general welfare legacy embraces the extension of the benefits of the General Welfare Clause to all Americans, including African Americans. Emancipation and the accompanying civil-rights amendments meant freedom. Freedom included the right to travel at will on the roads, canals, and railroads that had been financed in whole or in part with federal assistance, not as a fugitive but as a citizen. Equal protection of the laws became a guaranty ensconced in the Fourteenth Amendment that itself grew out of the experience over which Lincoln presided. Equal protection extended to laws enacted pursuant to the spending power. It meant in theory, for example, protection against discrimination in the enjoyment of the benefits of education legislation enacted under the authority of the spending power. Freedom and equal protection ultimately meant the right of all Americans to share, in accordance with statutory formulas, in the tangible benefits of the massive social insurance and income maintenance programs that were enacted generations later on the strength of the General Welfare Clause.

It might require a century for court determinations and subsequent legislation to vindicate those rights through such decisions as *Brown v. Board of Education* and such enactments as Title VI of the Civil Rights Act of 1964. Indeed, those rights are not fully vindicated to this day. The steps taken during the tenure of Abraham Lincoln, however, were the initial ones. The opening of the Constitution, that included a more broadly applied General Welfare Clause, to these new citizens constitutes one of the most significant elements of Lincoln's role. The implicit recognition of education as falling within the purview of the "general welfare of the United States" and therefore a just target of assistance constitutes another. The juxtaposition of an adequate and vigorous spending power under Article I, section 8 and Fourteenth Amendment jurisprudence in securing social justice has been essential to a successful transition from antebellum America in the decades since the Lincoln presidency.

VI
Reconstruction, Realignment, Revolution, Resolution

13
Reconstruction, T. R., and Wilson's Realignment

THE REPUBLICAN PRESIDENTS WHO FOLLOWED IN THE WAKE OF THE Civil War were not reluctant to propose the bold use of the spending power to accomplish commercial aims, make internal improvements, and, most importantly, reinforce the goals of the newly adopted Fourteenth and Fifteenth Amendments through supplementary federal funding for public elementary and secondary education. At the same time, they found it necessary to caution against extravagant spending for public works and to veto, on occasion, particularly egregious internal-improvement measures. The era from 1869 to 1885, roughly from the beginning of the Grant Administration to the end of the Arthur Administration, was characterized by a concern that had confronted Thomas Jefferson: how best to use a growing surplus. The election of Grover Cleveland, the first Democrat to hold the White House since James Buchanan, did not mark a return to the latter's limited view of the spending power. However, while accepting the scope of that power, Cleveland sought to constrain its extravagant use and declined to propose broad expansion of its exercise. Benjamin Harrison, sandwiched between Cleveland's two terms, took up the stance of his Republican predecessors in favor of federal aid to education. The last of the nineteenth century Republican presidents, William McKinley, did not bring substantial change to their spending-power philosophy.

The twentieth century opened with a far more energetic presidency, that of Theodore Roosevelt. Increasingly committed to progressive reform, Roosevelt's primary focus was on regulating business. However, Roosevelt also sought appropriations to support his bold conservation and reclamation initiatives. Moreover, he promoted key reinforcement for the vigorous exercise of the spending power through his support for the income tax amendment, a reform largely effected by the administration of

Roosevelt's successor, William Howard Taft. The election of 1912 brought to the White House Woodrow Wilson, who regarded the government as an instrument of progressive reform and who represented a clear break with nineteenth century Democratic presidential tradition in favor of a restrained exercise of federal authority to promote internal improvements and social welfare policies. Wilson saw the Constitution as a living document, to be interpreted creatively in order to secure fair play and achieve social justice in contemporary America. His stance on the spending power must be taken as consistent with that framework.

RECONSTRUCTION, THE SPENDING POWER, AND FEDERAL AID TO EDUCATION

Grant

Their support for federal aid to education reveals something of the constitutional leanings of the Republican Reconstruction presidents who succeeded Andrew Johnson. The first of these, Ulysses S. Grant, saw such assistance as a corollary to the constitutional revolution represented by the Fourteenth and Fifteenth Amendments. In notifying the Congress of the adoption of the latter amendment in 1870, Grant observed that it "completes the greatest civil change and constitutes the most important event that has occurred since the nation came into life."[1] Because Grant recognized that public education was essential to making the amendment effective, he urged Congress "to take all the means within their constitutional powers to promote and encourage popular education throughout the country, and upon the people everywhere to see to it that all who possess and exercise political rights shall have the opportunity to acquire the knowledge which will make their share in the Government a blessing and not a danger." In so doing, he also invoked the memory of Washington's plea for aid to "seminaries of learning"—offered at a time when the population of the country numbered only a few million—while also underlining the importance of educating the more than 40 million citizens of post–Civil War America. Grant knew that only through aid to education could the benefits implicit in the Fifteenth Amendment be secured. Congress, however, declined to heed the president's recommendation, thereby demonstrating the difficulty of obtaining legislative approval for educational reform proposals during the late nineteenth century.[2]

Hayes

Following a bitterly contested election, Grant's successor, Rutherford B. Hayes, took up the same theme with renewed vigor and, perhaps, greater personal commitment, albeit with no greater legislative success. The Hayes inaugural address proclaimed that '[u]niversal suffrage should rest upon universal education." To achieve this end, the new president recommended that "liberal and permanent provisions should be made for the support of free schools by the State governments, and, if need be, supplemented by legitimate aid from [the] national authority." In his first annual message, in December of 1877, Hayes strongly reinforced the same proposal, emphasizing his deep belief in the soundness of the policy: "The wisdom of legislation upon the part of Congress, in aid of the States, for the education of the whole people in those branches of study which are taught in the common schools of the country is no longer a question." He appended his own view as to the constitutional propriety of such a measure, grounding it on the basis of "general welfare" considerations in the framework of Lincoln's land grant college precedent: "The intelligent judgment of the country goes still further, regarding it as also both constitutional and expedient for the General Government to extend to technical and higher education such aid as is deemed essential to the general welfare and to our due prominence among the enlightened and cultured nations of the world."

Noting that one-seventh of the voting population of the country was illiterate, Hayes extended the land grant college precedent to the elementary and secondary level. He pledged his approval for "any appropriate measures which may be enacted by Congress for the purpose of supplementing with national aid the local systems of education in those States [in which slavery formerly existed] and in all the States. . . ." Like Grant before him, Hayes expressed support for a national university. That Hayes was personally invested in his federal to aid to education proposals, reiterated in subsequent annual messages, is amply reflected in his diary.[3]

While his rhetoric did not produce actual legislation, it is clear that Hayes had adopted the conclusion, implicit in Lincoln's approval of the Morrill Act, that under the Constitution, Congress could aid education at elementary, secondary, and postsecondary levels. The needs of Reconstruction gave force to that conclusion; the adoption of the civil rights amendments (the Thirteenth, Fourteenth, and Fifteenth Amendments) to the Constitution lent urgency to the cause.

The inaugural and annual message pleas of President Hayes for federal aid to education were matched by the policies that he pursued during his presidency and the causes he supported during his retirement. As chief executive, Hayes presided over a Department of Interior (headed by Carl Schurz) that included a small body of civil servants organized as a Bureau of Education and dedicated to collecting information and statistics about education, an early forerunner of the present Center on Education Statistics within the present United States Department of Education. The head of that bureau, John Eaton, was an advocate of federal aid for states developing school systems. Hayes, along with Eaton, lent his support to proposed legislation introduced in 1881 that would have distributed federal funds to states on the basis of relative illiteracy. The bill passed the Senate but was blocked in the House.[4]

Hayes's support was apparently a product of his firm conviction that in education lay the foundation for the preservation of the constitutional rights of African Americans and for their full participation in political life and public administration. "Appropriately for a man who favored civil-service reform, Hayes believed that the meritorious should govern, but he also believed that through public education everyone should have access to public office." In keeping with this philosophy, Hayes continued to press for federal aid legislation after he retired.[5]

In his presidential speaking tours and, most notably, in his valedictory message of December 1880, Hayes reinforced his proeducation stance and his enduring commitment to making federal school aid, as Morton Keller puts it, "an active issue in the postwar years." If anything, it had grown stronger. Early in the message, while affirming the duty of the executive to prosecute "unsparingly" those engaged in the denial of constitutional rights, Hayes proclaimed the role of education (including federal aid therefor) as a primary means of advancing civil rights. He also set forth a reasoned argument for federal participation in improving education. He remained convinced that state resources were inadequate to the task, particularly when the education of the African American population had been ignored during the period of slavery. "Firmly convinced that the subject of popular education deserves the earnest attention of the people of the whole country, with a view to wise and comprehensive action by the Government of the United States, I respectfully recommend that Congress, by suitable legislation and with proper safeguards, supplement the local educational funds in the several States where the grave duties and responsibilities of citizenship have been devolved on uneducated people by devoting to the purpose grants of the public lands and, if necessary, by *appropriations* from the Treasury of the United States."[6]

While the presidency of Rutherford B. Hayes is identified with the removal of federal troops from the South, a step which led to the massive deprivation of civil rights in that region, Hayes's regard for the importance of education in the struggle for civil rights is a counterweight. He devoted his private energies to that same cause, serving on the boards of several foundations and pursuing educational progress for disadvantaged populations. He linked his presidency with that of John Quincy Adams, whose election was also sharply contested and who shared with Hayes an affinity for promoting the bold exercise of the general welfare authority in the interest of education and other initiatives to improve the human condition. Ari Hoogenboom, Hayes's presidential biographer, observes, "Hayes admired Washington's integrity and Lincoln's commitment to equality of opportunity, but he identified with John Quincy Adams in his struggles with Congress, his patronage policies, and his desire to use national policy to foster education."[7]

Garfield, Arthur, and Harrison

Hayes's successor, James A. Garfield, elevated the subject of education to an important place by mentioning it in his inaugural address. He first traced the history of the nation, insisting that "the most important political change" since the adoption of the Constitution was the end of slavery and subsequent enfranchisement of millions of African Americans. Garfield, like his predecessors, warned of the dangers of illiteracy and recognized the nation's obligation to remove it: "All the constitutional power of the nation and of the States . . . should be surrendered to meet this danger by the savory influence of public education." Garfield did not survive to pursue this vision.[8]

Chester Arthur, who assumed the presidency following Garfield's death, dutifully took up the slain president's education agenda, but with less enthusiasm. In his first annual message, in

December 1881, Arthur recommended a program of supplementary federal aid to education, "as can be constitutionally afforded by the National Government," supporting this recommendation on the basis of the need to increase the literacy of those eligible to vote, particularly the "many who had just emerged from a condition of slavery." Arthur reiterated this recommendation in subsequent annual messages but without the passion of his predecessor, Hayes, who, from retirement, complained that Arthur harbored constitutional doubts on the subject. On that score Hayes observed that there was "no ground for hesitation." Apart from constitutional considerations, practical considerations contrary to Hayes's enthusiastic support ran counter to adopting a federal aid program. They included what Keller describes as "localism, diverse interests and hostility to active central government," as well as opposition from Democrats and educational organizations.[9]

Arthur's particular General Welfare cause lay in rivers and harbors legislation. He opposed extravagant bills but otherwise supported such needed projects as strengthening levees on the Mississippi, noting that "the constitutionality of a law making appropriations in aid of these objects can not be questioned."[10] Although he vetoed legislation emerging from this proposal that he deemed local and not general, it appears that Arthur, like his other elected Republican predecessors who succeeded Lincoln, took a broad, non-Madisonian view of the General Welfare Clause.

The point was made explicit by President Benjamin Harrison, who succeeded to the presidency in 1889 after the expiration of Grover Cleveland's initial term. Harrison revealed his thinking on the issue in his first annual message in December of that year, observing: "National aid to education has heretofore taken the form of land grants, and in that form the constitutional power of Congress to promote the education of the people is not seriously questioned. *I do not think it can be successfully questioned when the form is changed to that of a direct grant of money from the public Treasury.*"[11] Harrison had in mind not only the precedent of the 1862 Morrill Land Grant College Act, but also grants of public land in new states for the purpose of establishing primary and secondary schools.

Harrison posited his recommendation on the same rationale as that of his predecessors—the Fifteenth Amendment. "The sudden emancipation of the slaves of the South, the bestowal of the suffrage which soon followed, and the impairment of the ability of the States where those new citizens were chiefly found to adequately provide educational facilities presented not only exceptional but unexampled conditions." Harrison suggested supplementary, time-limited aid directed at this problem that would not "supplant local taxation for school purposes." Anticipating the juxtaposition of spending power and civil liberties legislation in the 1960s, Harrison accompanied these exhortations with strong pleas for civil-rights legislation to protect the right to vote. During his administration, Congress afforded the president an opportunity to extend the federal role in higher education and to apply the philosophy that he had promoted in his earlier annual message. Harrison signed into law the Second Morrill Act, which provided for federal appropriations for land grant colleges, making plain the conviction of both the Executive and the Legislative branches that authority was available for allocating federal appropriations to education, an area not specified in the enumerated powers.[12]

In sum, the Reconstruction Republican presidents, with respect to both education and traditional internal improvements, were prepared, implicitly or explicitly, to read Article I, section 8, clause 1 broadly and support remedial federal legislation based on the spending power, while asserting the role of the president to use the veto power to prevent extravagance and waste in the exercise of the General Welfare authority. Thus, by the end of the Civil War, the Executive Branch, when in Republican hands, had abandoned the posture of the antebellum Democratic presidents who had opposed such general welfare legislation on constitutional grounds. The battle over the scope of the clause that characterized early nineteenth century national politics faded in the late nineteenth century. In part, the Republican stance was consistent with its Reconstruction policy in favor of high protective tariffs that favored home industry but at the same time led to substantial Treasury surpluses that could be used for limited general-welfare spending programs such as those proposed for education. The policy had its roots in Henry Clay's American System, which Lincoln had admired so greatly.

The Cleveland Perspective

Grover Cleveland, the first Democrat to enter the White House since Buchanan, manifested a substantially different perspective. His objective was to root out waste and extravagance in government spending. Standing between Buchanan and Wilson in the pantheon of Democratic presidents, Cleveland is, in some respects, a throwback to the pre–Civil War Jacksonians. He championed lower tariffs and diminished revenues as a response to the growing surplus. He carried out a personal campaign for pension reform. His volume of vetoes on that and other measures greatly surpassed that of his predecessors.

Not surprisingly, neither in his first term, following Arthur, nor in his second, following Harrison, did Cleveland renew his predecessors' recommendations regarding federal supplementary aid to education. This may have been due to his own policy preferences and his belief in frugal, nonpaternalistic government rather than a conviction that such aid was unconstitutional. (It may have also reflected his own conservative perspective, as well as the conservative leanings of his party with its strong southern base.) No suggestion has been found that Cleveland regarded traditional aid to internal improvements as squarely unconstitutional, as Madison had, although Cleveland did veto a revenue-sharing bill as contrary to the basic charter. He took a similar position in vigorously opposing the distribution of seeds by the Department of Agriculture, whose sole role he saw as a provider of research and information. In his second inaugural address, in March 1893, Cleveland solemnly warned his fellow citizens against government paternalism and the "prevalence of a popular disposition to expect from the operation of the Government especial and direct individual advantages."[13]

Cleveland's first-term energies were directed at high tariffs and excessive surpluses. His third annual message in December of 1887, blessedly short and lacking the usual summaries of departmental reports, was deliberately devoted to a disquisition on the evils of Treasury surpluses. "The public Treasury," he declaimed, "which should only exist as a conduit conveying the people's tribute to its legitimate objects of expenditure, becomes a hoarding place for money needlessly withdrawn from trade and the people's use, thus crippling our national energies, suspending our country's development, preventing investment in productive enterprise, threatening financial disturbance and inviting schemes of public plunder." In his final message, he also criticized the excessive use of the general welfare authority as a basis for unwarranted appropriations.[14] His solution to the evils he described was substantial tariff reduction.

Defeated by Harrison in the election of 1888, despite winning the popular vote, but returned again to the White House in 1892 on the basis of a platform calling for lower tariffs, Cleveland sought to put his beliefs in place through tariff-reform legislation. His second term was marred by the financial depression of 1893 and controversy over silver purchase legislation.[15] Thus beset with financial and economic issues, and philosophically disinclined to support government spending programs, Cleveland did not advocate substantial spending for general welfare purposes during the balance of his second administration. The financial crisis did lead to decreased revenues and a deficit in the last two years of Cleveland's term.

During the succeeding administration, that of William McKinley, the country returned to favoring high tariffs and reciprocity. Confidence in business grew and economic growth resumed. McKinley proposed no major government programs posited on the general-welfare authority. He did not revive the aid to education proposals of his Republican predecessors. The country was instead focused on an expression of national energy different from that characterized by internal improvement in the Monroe or John Quincy Adams sense of the concept—expansion beyond its borders and the acquisition of new territories, a trend that Cleveland had resisted. Hawaii was annexed by treaty and became a territory. The successful conclusion of the Spanish-American War brought with it American responsibility for Puerto Rico and the Philippine Islands.[16]

THEODORE ROOSEVELT—ENERGY IN THE EXERCISE OF FEDERAL POWER

With the assassination of President McKinley in 1901, there entered the White House a president devoted to the application of energy and activism in both domestic and international arenas. While accretions to the exercise of the spending power were not the major priority of the Theodore Roosevelt years in office, his presidency is characterized by increasing resort to that source of power where needed to advance his initiatives. During his two terms, he advocated federal aid for water conservation, forest preservation, land reclamation through irrigation projects, workmen's compensation, and enhanced appropriations for the Bureau of Education in the Department of the Interior, along with traditional federal spending for rivers and harbors improvements. There is little doubt that he held the constitutional view that such expenditures were within the purview of the Constitution. During his second term, as he became increasingly progressive, he proclaimed in a 1907 speech that the Constitution should be interpreted liberally. On that occasion, Roosevelt observed: "... I hold that [the Constitution] must be interpreted not as a straitjacket, not as laying the hand of death upon our development, but as an instrument designed for the life and healthy growth of the Nation."[17] While not specifically directed at the General Welfare Clause, Roosevelt's affirmation can certainly be seen as a rationale for its broad interpretation.

Roosevelt's first annual message, delivered three months after McKinley's death, sounded a number of general-welfare themes. Written in an arresting and vivid style, the message was designed to be read. Departing from the practice of his predecessors, Roosevelt put domestic concerns first, painting a picture of a progressive nation that faced immense challenges. For Roosevelt, the challenges were an elixir; he addressed each with a few deft sentences. The monopolies, or trusts, could be dealt with by solid federal regulation of business posited on the interstate commerce power: "[I]n the interest of the whole people, the Nation should, without interfering with the power of the States ..., also assume power of supervision and regulation over all corporations doing an interstate business."

For Roosevelt, the Constitution was flexible; clearly times had changed. He predicted that an appropriate law could be framed but continued: "If, however, the judgment of the Congress is that it lacks the constitutional power to pass such an act, then a constitutional amendment should be submitted to confer the power." Roosevelt was not shy about suggesting a resort to "higher lawmaking." Similarly, the Constitution could support efforts to improve the lot of the working man through maximum hours legislation, workmen's compensation, and other initiatives. The Interstate Commerce Act, adopted in 1887 during the Cleveland presidency, could be tightened.

The message was focused primarily on government regulation of business, the major issue of the day. However, Roosevelt devoted some attention to such initiatives as forest and water conservation and land reclamation. As to the latter, Roosevelt recommended the appropriation of federal funds for building reservoirs and carrying out reclamation projects, activities that implicated the spending power, even though the president did not specifically invoke that authority in his request.

To all this there was a practical cast. "The preservation of our forests is an imperative business necessity," Roosevelt wrote.

And again, "[t]he western half of the United States would sustain a population greater than that of our whole country to-day if the waters that now run to waste were saved and used for irrigation." Roosevelt reinforced the critical nature of these imperatives: "The forest and water problems are perhaps the most vital internal questions of the United States."[18]

In George Mowry's account of the era of Theodore Roosevelt, this first message is described as having been hailed as a "safe document." But Mowry quickly clarifies this impression: "[O]n careful reading Roosevelt's first message does not appear as conservative as either his contemporaries thought or as subsequent historians have judged." Many of the "seeds of his future legislative program" can be found in the message.[19]

Federal legislation authorized the president to set aside tracts of public lands for forest preservation, immune from settlement. Following his message, Roosevelt proceeded to do so in a series of executive proclamations. While strictly speaking not the exercise of the spending power through federal grants to states, these actions are akin to such an exercise; federal environmental resources were set aside by federal executive action; federal appropriations for salaries and other costs were necessary to maintain the tracts so reserved. The public interest of the nation, as well as the needs of "wild forest creatures" would be served.[20]

With respect to water conservation, the nexus to the General Welfare Clause is more apparent. "Great storage works" would be needed. Roosevelt made the traditional spending power arguments for the application of federal funds. The construction of such works was "an undertaking too vast for private effort." Like his predecessors who had advocated federal spending to address national problems, Roosevelt emphasized the inability of states to meet reclamation needs without federal help. "Nor can it be best accomplished by the individual States acting alone." The vast undertaking was "properly a national function, at least in some of its features." The analogy to traditional internal improvements was, moreover, clear. "It is as right for the National Government to make the streams and rivers of the arid region useful by engineering works for water storage as to make useful the rivers and harbors of the humid region by engineering works of another kind. The storing of the floods in reservoirs at the head waters of our rivers is but an enlargement of our present policy of river control. . . ." The General Welfare Clause was invoked implicitly to justify the expenditure of funds for a class of internal improvements that could be built and maintained with federal funds; the reach of the spending power was extended to another government mission, in our day embraced within budget function 350. Land reclamation was on the same footing.[21]

In recommending this extension, Theodore Roosevelt did not raise constitutional considerations, as he had in the case of the extension of the interstate commerce clause. By then, it was clear that the General Welfare Clause could support federal spending for internal improvement. Nor did Roosevelt find it necessary to resurrect the ancient Madison-Hamilton feud. He merely made the case for the proposition that the general-welfare considerations reflected in his policies would serve "the broadest public interest."

Land reclamation stood on the same footing, but here the co-operation of the states would be particularly essential. The extension of irrigation must improve the condition of those on irrigated land. In this cause, the states must be enlisted. A study by both nation and states was needed. "Ultimately," Roosevelt said, "it will probably be necessary for the Nation to co-operate with the several arid States in proportion as these States by their legislation and administration show themselves fit to receive it." In 1902, Congress responded positively to these recommendations by passing the Land Reclamation Act of that year, providing for federally subsidized construction of large-scale irrigation works. The legislation, sponsored by Senator Francis J. Newlands of Nevada, was enacted with "Roosevelt's substantial help." It involved using the receipts of public land sales for constructing the reclamation projects. To the extent that federal funds were in play, some constitutional purpose for that use was necessary. The General Welfare Clause is the only available source of that authority.[22]

In sum, along with a broad federal spending initiative came the need for a policy of cooperative federalism to achieve the general welfare objectives. States would be aided by the vigorous, but prudent, exercise of the spending power; the aid and active participation of the states, through legal and implementing action, was essential if the policy were to work. The formula, here enlisted on behalf of environmental concerns, would be extended later in the century to a multitude of other national problem areas.

In succeeding annual messages, Roosevelt continued to make clear his view that the Constitution (or constitutionalism) presented no bar to his program. In his fifth annual message, in December 1905, he wrote: "The makers of our National Constitution provided especially that the regulation of interstate commerce should come within the sphere of the General Government." "[A]dequate regulation of these great corporations" could not be secured by state action. It could be "effectively exercised" only by the National Government. Such regulation and supervision, Roosevelt believed, could be obtained by the enactment of a law. "If this proves impossible," he wrote, "it will certainly be necessary ultimately to confer in fullest form such power upon the National Government by a proper amendment of the Constitution."[23]

That Roosevelt's later messages may not have emphasized spending power initiatives should not suggest a trend toward increasing conservatism on his part. On the contrary, his stance became increasingly progressive as his second term moved to its conclusion. After the mid-term election of 1906, he moved in the direction of the progressives who had been newly elected to Congress, and his requests for reform legislation increased. During this period Roosevelt also exercised the executive veto to stave off impediments to the progress of his conservation program. During his term, the president succeeded in adding 150 million acres to the government reserves, an achievement which Mowry assesses as "among his most impressive and enduring."[24]

However, the enactment of spending-power based programs was not the source of Roosevelt's major General Welfare Clause legacy. It was rather his contribution to the adoption of the Sixteenth Amendment, which provided constitutional authority for the federal income tax. In his seventh annual message, Roosevelt declared, "[A] graduated income tax of the proper type would be a desirable feature of Federal taxation, and it is to be hoped that one may be devised which the Supreme Court will declare constitutional."[25] The constitutional concern lay in the clause of the Constitution requiring apportionment of all taxes among the states in proportion to population as required by Article I, section 9, clause 4. The Supreme Court had previously struck down income tax legislation on this basis. In 1909, in a special message to Congress, Taft lamented that the Court's decision had "deprived" the nation of an important power that the "National Government ought to have" and one that would be "indispensable to the Nation's life in great crises."[26]

Recognizing the impracticability of further litigation, Taft recommended that Congress propose an appropriate amendment to the states. Congress did so in the form of the Sixteenth Amendment, which was ratified by the requisite number of states a week before Woodrow Wilson took office. The amendment read simply: "The Congress shall have power to lay and collect taxes on incomes, from whatever sources derived, without apportionment among the several States, and without regard to any census or enumeration."[27]

Taft's recommendation may have been the product of his own reluctance to support the enactment of a federal income tax law during his administration. Opposed to outright enactment of a measure that he thought necessary only in emergencies, Taft proposed a compromise that involved a constitutional amendment authorizing the graduated income tax without regard to the apportionment provisions of the Constitution. Taft also lobbied the Ohio legislature to ratify the amendment. His effort, along with the earlier support of Roosevelt, contributed to the project's implementation by 1913.[28]

The income tax amendment paved the way for future exertions of the spending power later in the twentieth century. By affording the government a new and substantially enlarged base of revenue, it effectively permitted the extension of the power into bold new areas like social insurance, public welfare, aid to agricultural and commercial sectors, and, later, aid to training and education. Thus the General Welfare Clause, crafted in 1787 and adopted in 1788, can be considered to have been enlarged in 1913 by the adoption of the Sixteenth Amendment. As Mowry correctly observes, "It is almost impossible to see how most of the social legislation passed since 1912 could have been financed without the income tax. . . . The modern democratic social service state, in fact, probably rests more upon the income tax than upon any other single legislative act."[29] The combination of a broadly interpreted spending power under Article I, section 8, clause 1 and the income tax legislation grounded on the Sixteenth Amendment constitutes the underpinning of such a state.

WOODROW WILSON AND THE DEMOCRATIC REALIGNMENT

Woodrow Wilson entered the White House proclaiming that he had come to the presidency to preside over a "change of government." First the House and then the Senate had come under the control of the Democratic Party. Now a Democratic President had been elected, the first since 1892. Only one other Democrat had been elected to that office since 1860.

"What does this change mean?" Wilson asked those assembled to hear his inaugural address. For the new president it transcended the "mere success of a party." It reflected a profound change in the nation's "plans and point of view." "We have been refreshed," Wilson proclaimed, "by a new insight into our own life." He amplified this concept: "Great" in wealth, in industrial power, "in the diversity and sweep of its energy," endowed with "a great system of government," the nation had, nonetheless, come to confront the dark side of its success—the failure to conserve "the exceeding bounty of nature" and the uncounted "human cost" of "industrial achievements." These shortcomings profoundly troubled Wilson: "With the great Government went many deep secret things which we too long delayed to look into and scrutinize with candid, fearless eyes."

But Wilson recognized that a new "vision" had "been vouchsafed" the nation. Under his presidency, its work would be "a work of restoration." Restoration meant not only reducing tariffs, reforming banking and currency laws, establishing better rural credit facilities, and fostering water conservation and land reclamation; it meant forging a new role for government in securing social justice in new areas of endeavor. The federal government must "be put at the service of humanity, in safeguarding the health of the Nation, the health of its men and its women and its children, as well as their rights in the struggle for existence." "The firm basis of government," Wilson insisted, is "justice, not pity." "There can be no equality or opportunity, the first essential of justice in the body politic, if men and women and children be not shielded in their lives, their very vitality, from the consequences of great industrial and social processes which they can not alter, control, or singly cope with."[30]

This restoration would be accomplished by law, because "[t]he first duty of law is to keep sound the society it serves." Sanitary laws, pure food laws, and laws concerning the condition of labor were among the specifics that Wilson invoked. They were followed by more in the first annual message, delivered by Wilson in person before a joint session of Congress—today's tradition. Enhanced facilities of rural credit and more explicit anti-trust legislation were among the major recommendations.[31]

With respect to the specific application of the spending power, there was little that was dramatic in these proposals. Water conservation and land reclamation had been promoted by Theodore Roosevelt and legislation had been enacted during his administration. Later messages or speeches expanded Wilson's recommendations to include vocational or industrial education, a proposal broached during the president's 1916 defense-preparedness campaign across the nation. But these proposals, and the legislation that followed, are fairly limited when one considers the landmark education legislation that was to come fifty years later.

What seems more significant is the extent to which Wilson's vision and energy represent a *realignment* in the posture of his party and in the political thought of Democratic presidents. Approximately one hundred years before Wilson sounded his call for social justice via federal action, Madison had insisted that a federal role in internal improvement, however desirable, required a constitutional amendment. Jackson and the antebellum Democratic presidents who followed, Polk, Pierce, and Buchanan, had exercised the veto to hold the spending power at bay. Cleveland, the first post–Civil War Democrat in the White House had stressed frugality, self-reliance, presidential independence from the legislative branch, and the "negative use of presidential power" through the veto rather than using the power of the purse for munificent public programs. By calling for a new and active role for government, both in his inaugural address and subsequent messages, Wilson effected a major realignment in Democratic political thought that established the foundation for the broader application of the General Welfare Clause that was to come later.

The actual initiatives that Wilson proposed, while not dramatic, clearly relied upon a broad reading of the General Welfare Clause. In his third annual message, again before a joint session of the Congress in December 1915, while urging that the industries and resources of the country be ready for defense mobilization, Wilson advanced a specific recommendation: "[W]e should give intelligent federal aid and stimulation to industrial and vocational education, as we have long done in the large field of our agricultural industry." In making this proposal, Wilson, the scholar president, offered no constitutional explanation or apologia. It was assumed that the Constitution warranted such an expenditure, as it had in the case of the Morrill Act. Wilson had implicitly bought into the Hamilton-Monroe-Adams-Story view of the spending power, but offered no exegesis to explain his reasoning. The same, of course, could be said for his conservation and reclamation recommendations.[32]

In passing the Smith-Hughes Vocational Education Act of 1917, Congress converted Wilson's recommendation to legislation, a result that eluded Hayes and other earlier proponents of federal aid in the late nineteenth century. A framework had been established for activist government in the twentieth century by a Democratic Party that had arisen in the nineteenth, in part in suspicious counterreaction to the spending power policies of John Quincy Adams. The twentieth century version and the Wilson realignment were to come into play with much greater force with the election of Franklin Roosevelt and the advent of the New Deal.[33]

The Contribution of Theodore Roosevelt and Woodrow Wilson to the Growth of the Spending Power

The era of Theodore Roosevelt and Woodrow Wilson laid the foundation for the broadly read and energetically applied federal spending power during the twentieth century. It anticipated the dramatic growth spurts in the exercise of that power during the administrations of Franklin Roosevelt and Lyndon Johnson. It paved the way for the formulation and conduct of the New Deal and the Great Society during those administrations and the landmark social legislation that they collectively advocated still affects the lives of millions of Americans today.

This was not because both presidents teamed up for a common cause. On the contrary they were ardent political foes. Roosevelt and Wilson vied for the presidency in 1912. Wilson's election and early legislative success infuriated Roosevelt; only the latter's death ended the conflict. Yet despite their differences, both presidents promoted and nourished a brand of progressivism in the administration of federal affairs and the formulation of programs that depended largely upon a broad interpretation of the constitutional spending power and led to an activist role for the federal government. Neither president focused only on that power or on the ancient controversy between Hamilton and Madison as to its scope. Both appeared to operate on the belief or assumption that the contest had been (or should be) resolved in Hamilton's favor; certainly one must so conclude from the tenor of their legislative proposals, as well as their overarching progressive orientation.[34]

Roosevelt's tilt in favor of a flexibly read Constitution has been cited above. His advocacy of conservation and reclamation programs that depended on the generous application of federal financial resources is a rich part of his legacy. As leader of the reform-oriented Progressive Party in the 1912 election, he embraced a forward-looking legislative program under the rubric of the New Nationalism that included such reforms as government-backed pensions and unemployment insurance, initiatives that depended on a Hamiltonian reading of the General Welfare Clause.[35]

For his part, Wilson's New Freedom proposed a broad role for government, not a return to the conservative ways of the pre–Civil War Democratic Party that had looked askance at a broad reading of the General Welfare Clause, a role that differed from the constraints of the Cleveland era. Wilson campaigned on a platform that embraced aid to individual workers and farmers. His administration saw the passage of aid to education legislation and health-related reforms. As president, Wilson openly characterized his administration as "progressive." In his first term, he governed as an effective party leader, coaxing Congress, through collaboration and consultation, to enact large portions of his reform program, trying where he could to make progressive appointments.[36]

Theodore Roosevelt and Wilson have been characterized by John Milton Cooper as "twentieth century analogues" of Hamilton and Jefferson, with Roosevelt closer to Hamilton and Wilson to Jefferson. But in so characterizing them, Cooper is quick to note that: "Unlike Hamilton and Jefferson, they did not differ over governmental power and centralization, despite Roosevelt's assertions to the contrary."[37] Wilson himself provided evidence of this. In the 1912 campaign, in refuting Roosevelt's political attacks, Wilson, despite his Jeffersonian leanings, assured his audience that he rejected Jefferson's dictum that the "best government is that which does as little governing as possible." Wilson insisted that he did not fear "the utmost exercise of the powers of the government of Pennsylvania, or of the Union, provided that they are exercised with patriotism and intelligence and really in the interest of the people who are living under them."[38]

Wilson's *The New Freedom* (a collection of essays drawn from his 1912 campaign speeches) amplifies his thought about applying the Jeffersonian tradition to the modern age. In an essay entitled "The Liberation of A People's Vital Energies," Wilson speculated on how Jefferson might have approached the realities and complexities of American life in 1912 and the government's role in addressing them:

> You know that one of the interesting things that Mr. Jefferson said in those early days of simplicity which marked the beginnings of our

government was that the best government consisted in as little government as possible. And there is still a sense in which that is true. It is still intolerable for the government to interfere with our individual activities except where it is necessary to interfere with them in order to free them. But I feel confident that if Jefferson were living in our day he would see what we see: that the individual is caught in a great confused nexus of all sorts of complicated circumstances, and that to let him alone is to leave him helpless as against the obstacles with which he has to contend; and that, therefore, law in our day must come to the assistance of the individual.[39]

Neither in this essay nor in the others included in *The New Freedom* is there specific discussion of the controversy over the scope of the spending power to which Jefferson, along with Madison, devoted a considerable measure of his energies. Nor does one find in Wilson's *The New Freedom* essays a litany of federal programs in the manner of more modern state of the union messages. Wilson's focus is on the relationship of government to the individual and to its role in the preservation of liberty in a complex world characterized by large aggregations of private power. In such a context, government must be seen as capable of a new and more positive role, different from that of the hands-off concepts of an earlier age. That Jefferson himself in his own presidency contemplated an active role for government in helping to finance internal improvements and education lends credence to Wilson's speculation.

Although Wilson's essay contains no erudite discussion of the spending power or of social programs that might be based on its authority, neither does it include a clarion call for a constitutional amendment to implement the New Freedom. Wilson simply appears to have assumed that the Constitution as written—including the soon-to-be-adopted Sixteenth Amendment—was flexible enough to allow government to meet the needs of its twentieth-century citizens. Indeed, Wilson insists that the document must be so interpreted if the nation is to survive. Despite his sharp repudiation of Hamilton's alleged aristocratic leanings in other portions of the *The New Freedom*, Wilson's essay adopts (without attribution) the Hamiltonian concept of constitutional flexibility via the General Welfare Clause, along with Jefferson's invocation of individual liberty. If those energies can be liberated by aid to education or by special help to the farmer, Hamilton's understanding of the Constitution, as reflected in the *Report on Manufactures*, anticipates Wilson's own persuasion. Wilson's

The New Freedom, in the passage quoted above, thus represents a fusion of both Jefferson's and Hamilton's thinking in the context of twentieth-century America: liberty promoted by a watchful and "positive" government, that government operating within the framework of a Constitution flexibly interpreted to address exigencies that the framers could not contemplate but for which they wisely made ample provision.[40]

These dynamics in the 1912 essays in turn reflect the flavor of Wilson's earlier set of lectures arranged in his celebrated 1908 book, *Constitutional Government*. Despite the title, there is again no specific discussion of the spending power or the contest over its meaning. Wilson's more all-encompassing take on constitutional change is, nonetheless, consistent with the Hamiltonian concept of that authority. Wilson's unmistakable bias is in favor of a flexible reading of the Constitution to comport with the realities of each age, rather than a painstaking effort to discover original intent. "Undoubtedly the powers of the federal government have grown, have even grown enormously, since the creation of the government," Wilson notes approvingly. He continues: "[T]hey have grown for the most part without amendment of the Constitution." The process of adaptability by which this has happened Wilson describes as "normal and legitimate." He reinforces this concept of constitutional interpretation attuned to contemporary needs. "As the life of the nation changes so must the interpretation of the document which contains it change, by a nice adjustment, determined not by the original intention of those who drew the paper, but by the exigencies and the new aspects of life itself." For Wilson, this is a perfectly sufficient rationale for the growth of governmental power attributable to the General Welfare Clause. This is so even though the broad application of that clause can be read as consistent with original intent, at least if one accepts the Hamiltonian interpretation and Joseph Story's widely accepted textual analysis in support of it.[41]

The New Deal and the Great Society's debt to the Theodore Roosevelt–Woodrow Wilson era is thus in part grounded on overall policy posture and attitude of both presidents toward the scope and desirability of governmental power to solve social problems—on an overarching philosophy regarding the proper role of government, rather than a close parsing of constitutional language and history. At the same time, that debt is also grounded on the practical contribution of both presidents (and of Taft who served between them) to the adoption of the centrally important Sixteenth Amendment. The adoption of that amendment, together with the reform orientation of the first two decades of the twentieth century, were steps along the road toward Hamilton's way. As the century proceeded, the Republican party became more conservative. The Roosevelt influence was felt most decidedly in the Northeastern wing of the party and in the administrations of Dwight Eisenhower and Richard Nixon. Wilson's legacy was advanced more extensively by Franklin Roosevelt who had served in Wilson's administration and who led the Democratic Party in forging coalitions that supported the enactment of progressive legislation, in part on the strength of the General Welfare Clause as it finally came definitively to be interpreted by the Supreme Court in the course of the Constitutional Revolution of 1937.

The contribution of the Roosevelt-Wilson era to this account of the evolution of the spending power does not rest on their erudite pronouncements on the scope of the General Welfare Clause. Rather, both Roosevelt and Wilson, each in his own way, expressed—from the bully pulpit of the White House and the presidential campaign trail—a new constitutional mood for the twentieth century, a mood that befitted their progressive notion of what government could and should do for the common man, the newcomer, and the vulnerable. In later years, amplified vigorously by the Executive Branch and, embraced after some reluctance by the Judicial Branch, this mood profoundly affected American policy, law, government, and life for a century. It promises do so as well in the century that is just beginning.

14
The New Deal and Judicial Resolution

THE GREAT DEPRESSION THAT BROUGHT FRANKLIN ROOSEVELT TO power in the election of 1932 confronted the United States with unprecedented levels of economic dislocation. With it came a massive dose of personal misery. Millions were unemployed and without subsistence. National production tumbled. The stock market crashed. Confidence in the government unraveled. The future of the experiment begun in 1787 was threatened. Following his 1933 inauguration, Roosevelt swiftly proposed to Congress a series of programs collectively known as the New Deal. One of these was designed to ease economic distress in agriculture. For years farmers had been receiving depressed prices for their crops, substantially reducing their purchasing power and subjecting them to foreclosure and loss of their farms. This had contributed the economy's devastation and the onset of the Depression. To restore farm prices as well as stability to the sector, the Roosevelt Administration had conceived and sent to the Congress a proposal for an Agricultural Adjustment Act, which Congress passed in 1933.

The tests of the constitutionality of that measure, and of the Social Security legislation that followed in 1935, provided the framework for the first definitive interpretation of the General Welfare Clause by the Supreme Court. The 1936 *Butler* case produced the first judicial affirmation that Hamilton's reading of the clause, rather than Madison's, was correct. Nevertheless, the Court struck down the AAA on Tenth Amendment grounds. The following year, however, the same Court upheld the Social Security Act's unemployment compensation and old-age retirement programs under the General Welfare Clause, read Hamilton's way. This application of the clause to sustain key social programs cleared a constitutional path for the New Deal's other social legislation, for Truman's Fair Deal, for the Great Society, and for the survival, growth, and refinement of the benefit state during the presidencies of Nixon, Ford, Carter, Reagan, George H. W. Bush, and Clinton.[1]

THE BIRTH OF THE AGRICULTURAL ADJUSTMENT ACT

To recount that story one must begin with the process that give rise to the Agricultural Adjustment Act. The conceptualization of that legislation was the product of a group of Roosevelt advisers under the leadership of Henry Wallace, Roosevelt's secretary of agriculture. In his vivid portrayal of the process, Arthur Schlesinger, Jr. characterizes the man: "The concrete and utilitarian mingled in Wallace with much that was vague and dreamy," but no vague and dreamy task confronted either him or the farmers. Farm income had plummeted by one-third; farmer purchasing power had declined substantially. Wallace saw the problem as one of oversupply. The solution was a "domestic allotment plan." It "proposed in effect to offer the farmer a price subsidy in return for his tacit agreement to limit output."[2] A bill encompassing the plan had been introduced in Congress in 1932. Four major surplus crops—wheat, hogs, cotton, tobacco—were impacted. "Every farmer agreeing to regulate his production in accordance with the government plan would receive payments; noncooperating farmers would gain from the general price increase, but, if benefit payments were properly calculated, the co-operators would get a larger income from reducing production than than the noncooperator would get from increasing it."[3]

This was the essence of the plan that Wallace and his colleagues proposed to President Roosevelt in 1933. Stanley Reed (later Roosevelt's solicitor general at the time of the Butler argument and still later a Roosevelt appointee to the Supreme Court) insisted that the plan must be based upon the spending power to ensure constitutionality. An excise tax at the point of processing to provide revenue for the proposed benefit payments would serve to invoke that power.[4] The bill drafted for Roosevelt by Wallace and his associates (Jerome Frank and Rexford Tugwell, among others) embraced this core notion of "agricultural adjustment." As Schlesinger characterizes it, "The agricultural adjustment bill was essentially a leadership measure, devised by farm economists, sold by them to farm organization leaders, sold again by economists and farm leaders in combination to the President, but lacking any basis in public understanding."[5]

Opponents of the measure countered that inflationary strategies rather than limits on farm production constituted the proper response. Pressure mounted for congressional action as the farm economy continued to dwindle. Against a backdrop of intense farmer frustration and discontent—occasionally punctuated by violent protest—the legislation was passed by Congress in May 1933 and presented to Roosevelt who signed it. It contained the agricultural adjustment provisions, as well as discretionary authority to adopt inflationary measures. An Agricultural Adjustment Administration was promptly established in the Department of Agriculture. Cotton became the first target for application of the new subsidy program in view of the large surplus of prior year stocks.[6] It was the act's application to cotton that gave rise to the litigation that came before the Supreme Court when cotton processors declined to pay the processing tax.

United States v. Butler

The Statutory Scheme

Justice Roberts's majority opinion for the Court faithfully described the pertinent terms of the new legislation clothed in its solemn statutory language. An "economic emergency" had arisen "due to disparity between the prices of agricultural and other commodities, with consequent destruction of farmers' purchasing power and breakdown in orderly exchange." The act's purpose was "to establish and maintain such balance between the production and consumption of agricultural commodities . . . as will reestablish prices to farmers at a level that will give agricultural commodities a purchasing power with respect to articles that farmers buy, equivalent to the purchasing power of agricultural commodities in the base period" (generally August 1909 to July 1914).[7]

To make this policy effective, the secretary of agriculture was authorized, among other things, to make agreements with individual farmers for a reduction of acreage or production upon such terms as he deemed reasonable. In exchange for the farmer's agreement to reduce acreage, the secretary was authorized to make rental or benefit payments. The proceeds of the payments would be derived from a processing tax on the commodity in question, in this case, cotton, to be levied and collected on the first domestic processing of the commodity with respect to a marketing year. The receivers of a cotton mill resisted the taxes so levied; the district court sustained them; the circuit court of appeals reversed. The matter was now before the high court.[8]

The Supreme Court first disposed of a threshold procedural issue. It determined that the receivers of the mill had standing to contest the tax in court. The Court treated the suit not as a mere challenge to the use of public moneys but as a challenge to a tax that was part of the overall program to reduce agricultural production.[9]

The Administration's Brief

The Roosevelt Administration had claimed that, even if the processors had standing to question the propriety of the appropriation, the contemplated expenditure was authorized by Article I, section 8 of the Constitution. Mr. Justice Roberts, writing for the majority, saw this contention as "present[ing] the great and the controlling question in the case." In its brief, the Roosevelt Justice Department had indeed mounted a strenuous and comprehensive argument in support of Hamilton's reading of the General Welfare Clause. While Franklin Roosevelt, perhaps reflecting the "living document" philosophy of his former superior and White House predecessor, Woodrow Wilson, had termed the Constitution an "eminently practical" document authorizing novel solutions to current problems, his lawyers carefully made the case that the original intent of the clause was consistent with Hamilton's, not Madison's, reading.[10]

The brief took the justices at length through the framing, the arguments in favor of a broad reading during ratification, Hamilton's interpretation in the *Report on Manufactures*, the Monroe Memorandum, the broad interpretation of John Quincy Adams, Story's commentaries, and much else. It argued that an earlier Supreme Court in the Marshall era had informally approved Monroe's reading. Not content with history, the Roosevelt Justice Department urged that congressional application of the clause over the decades confirmed the Hamiltonian reading and compelled its affirmation. Among other enactments, the brief cited education precedents, among them, the Second Morrill Act of 1890. It was this comprehensive argument as to the meaning of the clause that the *Butler* Court confronted as it came to its decision.[11]

Power to Appropriate, not Regulate

In addressing the government's contention that the Agricultural Adjustment Act was constitutional, the Court quickly put aside the Interstate Commerce Clause; the act in question did not purport to regulate interstate or foreign commerce, and the government had not sought to justify it on that basis. Agreeing with the Roosevelt administration's analysis, the Court concluded that the clause of Article I, section 8 that was in play was the first, that which conferred upon Congress power "to lay and collect Taxes . . . to pay the Debts and provide for the common Defence and general Welfare of the United States." It is what we have here called the General Welfare Clause.[12]

In its analysis of that clause, the Court initially addressed a question that had divided framers and founders since the earliest days of the nation: did it merely confer a power to tax for the purposes described or did it confer a power generally to regulate activity in order to provide for the general welfare. (This was the issue posed by Gouvernor Morris's attempt to change the punctuation of the clause in the dying days of the 1787 convention.) The Court adopted the narrower option, observing that the government did not contend "that this provision grants power to regulate agricultural production on the theory that such legislation would promote the general welfare." Justice Roberts noted that the Roosevelt Administration "concedes that the phrase 'to provide for the general welfare' qualifies the power to lay and collect taxes." The view that the General Welfare Clause "grants power to provide for the general welfare, independently of the taxing power, [has] never been authoritatively accepted," the Court opined. Citing Story on the point, it therefore concluded: "The true construction undoubtedly is that the only thing granted is the power to tax for the purpose of providing funds for the payment of the nation's debts and making provision for the general welfare."[13]

This analysis obliged the justices to address the government's central contention: The Agricultural Adjustment Act was constitutional because Congress was authorized under the clause to appropriate funds for the "general welfare," meaning "anything conducive to national welfare," a determination within the discretion of Congress, and because the appropriation in question (to provide a farmer with benefits for reducing production) was for the general welfare of the United States.[14]

In confronting this contention, the Court first decided that the General Welfare Clause could properly be read to authorize *appropriation* for the general welfare of the United States: "Funds in the Treasury as a result of taxation may be expended only through appropriation (Article I, section 9, clause 7). They can never accomplish the objects for which they were collected unless the power to appropriate is as broad as the power to tax. The necessary implication from the terms of the grant [in the General Welfare Clause] is that public funds may be appropriated 'to provide for the general welfare of the United States.'"[15]

Hamilton v. Madison: The Contest Resolved

Having come this far, the Court finally faced the ancient controversy that had divided Hamilton from Madison, Federalists from Jeffersonians. The Court so described it in these terms: "Since the foundation of the Nation sharp differences of opinion have persisted as to the true interpretation of the phrase." It then took up Madison's contention first: "Madison asserted it amounted to no more than a reference to other powers enumerated in the subsequent clauses of the same section; that, as the United States is a government of limited and enumerated powers, the grant of power to tax and spend for the general national welfare must be confined to the enumerated legislative fields committed to the Congress."

The Court, however, objected to this view on the basis of an argument that Joseph Story had advanced more than one hundred years earlier. Said the Court: "In this [Madison's] view the phrase is mere tautology, for taxation and appropriation are or may be necessary incidents of the exercise of any of the enumerated legislative powers." Story, it will be recalled, had argued that the Necessary and Proper Clause already gave Congress power to tax and appropriate to carry out the enumerated powers. Reading the General Welfare Clause as Madison read it gave it no effect; reading the clause Madison's way in effect expunged it from the Constitution.[16]

The Court in *Butler* then turned to Hamilton. "Hamilton, on the other hand, maintained the clause confers a power separate and distinct from those later enumerated, is not restricted in meaning by the grant of them, and Congress consequently has a substantive power to tax and to appropriate, limited only by the requirement that it shall be exercised to provide for the general welfare of the United States."[17]

The Court then came quickly to its choice in resolving the contest in favor of Hamilton: "Each contention has had the support of those whose views are entitled to weight. This court has noticed the question, but has never found it necessary to decide which is the true construction. Mr. Justice Story in his Commentaries, espouses the Hamiltonian position. We shall not review the writings of public men and commentators or discuss the legislative practice. Study of all these leads us to conclude that the reading advocated by Mr. Justice Story is the correct one."

Having chosen Hamilton's way, Mr. Justice Roberts summarized the Court's conclusion in two definitive sentences: "While, therefore, the power to tax is not unlimited, its confines are set in the clause which confers it, and not in those of [section] 8 which bestow and define the legislative powers of the Congress. It results that the power of Congress to authorize expenditure of public moneys for public purposes is not limited by the direct grants of legislative power found in the Constitution."[18]

Thus, without extensive citation of authority beyond Story's commentaries and without extensive analysis, the Court's opinion had resolved a constitutional controversy that had divided framer from framer, president from president, president from Congress, and party from party since the inception of the Republic. The broad, Hamilton reading had prevailed. While the Court's opinion on the subject was spare, the copious recitation of the constitutional history in the government's brief gives it some foundation in history and precedent. The stage was set to use the power the clause afforded to support other New Deal spending initiatives, as well as those of the Great Society.

However, for the Court's majority, the Tenth Amendment barred such a result. Despite its broad interpretation of the General Welfare Clause, the Court in *Butler* did not sustain the Agricultural Adjustment Act under the Hamiltonian reading. It struck it down on the ground that the regulation of production inherent in the legislative scheme constituted an invasion of the Tenth Amendment, which left agricultural production to the states, as the majority saw it. Congress could not, said the majority, use the spending power, broadly defined as it was, to purchase from grantees compliance with conditions that Congress could not impose directly. Because the production of cotton was a local matter, Congress could not use the spending power to extract from a farmer a promise to limit its production. Such a scheme was seen to violate the Tenth Amendment.[19]

The Stone Dissent

That conclusion in turn prompted a stinging dissent from Justice Stone, joined by Justices Cardozo and Brandeis. Stone began his analysis by recasting the majority's position from his own perspective: "Although the farmer is placed under no legal compulsion to reduce acreage, it is said that the mere offer of compensation for so doing is a species of economic coercion which operates with the same legal force and effect as though the curtailment were made mandatory by Act of Congress." To this contention, Stone bitterly objected; the farmers did not so contend; there was no basis for it in the record. "Threat of loss, not hope of gain, is the essence of economic coercion." Farmers who participated in the program expected higher return for their effort.[20]

With equal fervor, Stone denounced the conclusion of the majority that "the expenditure of public funds to induce the recipients to curtail production is itself an infringement of state power, since the federal government cannot invade the domain of the states by the 'purchase' of performance of acts which it has no power to compel." Stone turned this argument on its head, insisting that the conditions in question were not only authorized but necessary to sustain the constitutionality of the provision at issue. In so doing, he announced the dissenters' vision of the scope of the power to condition the grant to a recipient of funds appropriated under the spending power: "The Constitution requires that public funds shall be spent for a defined purpose, the promotion of the general welfare. Their expenditure usually involves payment on terms which will ensure use by the selected recipients within the limits of the constitutional purpose. Expenditures would fail of their purpose and thus lose their constitutional sanction if the terms of payment were not such that by their influence on the action of the recipients the permitted end would be attained. The power of Congress to spend is inseparable from persuasion to action over which Congress has no legislative control."

To illustrate the point, Stone selected an example based on both Morrill Acts: "Congress may not command that the science of agriculture be taught in state universities. But if it would aid the teaching of that science by grants to state institutions, it is appropriate, if not necessary, that the grant be on the condition, incorporated in the Morrill Act [citations omitted], that it be used for the intended purpose."[21]

For Stone and his fellow dissenters, imposing such a condition was a mere incident of the spending power, sustainable under principles announced by Chief Justice Marshall in *McCulloch v. Maryland*. If the act were struck down for this reason, Stone protested, the spending power would be subject to limitations imposed on no other power. "It is a contradiction in terms to say that there is power to spend for the national welfare, while rejecting any power to impose conditions reasonably adapted to the attainment of the end which alone would justify the expenditure."[22]

This brought Stone to his inevitable conclusion. In the exercise of the spending power, Congress may impose conditions that it cannot directly command: "If appropriation in aid of a program of curtailment of agricultural production is constitutional, and it is not denied that it is, payment to farmers on condition that they reduce their crop acreage is constitutional."[23] Stone conceded the breadth of the power of the purse. "That the governmental power of the purse is a great one is not now for the first time announced." But this was no basis to curtail it judicially. "'The power to tax is the power to destroy,' but we do not, for that reason doubt its existence, or hold that its efficacy is to be restricted by its incidental or collateral effects upon the states."[24]

While the Agricultural Adjustment Act was struck down, the constitutional future of the spending power was not to be confined by the Tenth Amendment analysis conceived by the *Butler* majority. By the end of the year following that decision, the vision of the spending power portrayed in the Stone dissent had become in effect the majority view. In a series of cases involving challenges to the constitutionality of the Social Security Act of 1935, the Court used Hamilton's reading of the spending power, now at least ostensibly Supreme Court blessed, to sustain the programs in question despite the presentation of Tenth Amendment arguments designed to overturn those programs.[25]

THE BIRTH OF THE SOCIAL SECURITY PROGRAM

Arthur Schlesinger's *The Age of Roosevelt: The Coming of the New Deal* presents a vivid portrait of the formulation of the Social Security Act of 1935 and of the programs that came before the Court in 1937. The central figure in the battle to achieve adequate social insurance protection was Frances Perkins, Roosevelt's resolute secretary of labor. The 1932 Democratic platform had promised an old-age insurance program, and Roosevelt had identified himself with that cause, a cause that owed a debt to the Progressive Platform of 1912 under the banner of which Theodore Roosevelt had sought another term in the White House.[26]

The Depression had made unemployment insurance a priority. At least one state, Wisconsin, had adopted a prototype state program, and there was considerable force behind a state-based federal program. It was Louis D. Brandeis who suggested the basic scheme: a progressive tax on employers with a credit against the tax where employer contributions had been made to a state program. In the case of insurance for the aged, a number of states had enacted legislation, but the state programs were considered inadequate.[27]

Faced with bills in Congress in late 1934, Roosevelt sought time to formulate an administration program. He appointed a cabinet committee with Perkins as its chair. Roosevelt's preference was for a state-based unemployment program. Some staff members of the cabinet committee, on the other hand, wanted a stronger federal role than a state-based program involved. Ultimately, the committee opted for the state-program approach. One of the considerations that led to this decision was a concern over constitutionality. If the national features of the program were struck down by an unsympathetic court, at least the state features would survive. In December 1934, the committee put its weight behind the Wagner-Lewis, state-based bill.[28] As for social insurance for the aged, the committee recommended a national system given the absence or inadequacies of state programs, as well as the influence of the universal pensions advocated by Dr. Francis E. Townsend. The committee recognized, moreover, that an actuarily based program required a national scope that took into account beneficiary mobility.[29]

In January 1935, Roosevelt requested legislation along the lines suggested by the committee. Despite opposition from conservatives, both houses of Congress passed the legislation by lopsided votes. The nation had adopted broad-gauge unemployment and old-age insurance programs, and Roosevelt signed them into law in 1935.[30] It thus became the duty of the Supreme Court to assess the constitutionality of these programs. In a pair of cases, the Court again confronted the age-old controversy over the scope of the spending power. This time it again affirmed the Hamiltonian reading, but this time the justices also affirmed that reading in a context in which the constitutionality of the programs at issue was sustained.

Steward Machine Co. v. Davis and *Helvering v. Davis*

Unemployment Compensation

The first of these cases, *Steward Machine Co. v. Davis*, involved the unemployment compensation program authorized by the Social Security Act of 1935. Title IX of that act was the focal point of the constitutional attack. That title imposed an excise tax on every employer of eight or more persons, with certain exceptions. The tax was measured by a prescribed percentage of the wages payable by the employer during a calendar year. The tax revenues were not earmarked and were paid into the Treasury.[31]

A key element of the program was a credit for state taxes paid. An employer who contributed to an unemployment compensation fund established under state law was authorized to credit the contributions against the federal tax, up to a level of 90 percent of the tax. The federal statute established certain minimum criteria which a state program was required to satisfy before the credit would be recognized. These criteria were designed to insure that the state program was one of substance and that contributions would be protected against loss after payment to the state.[32]

The program was challenged by Charles C. Steward Machine Co., an Alabama corporation, that paid the tax and then sued to recover on the ground that the statute violated the Federal Constitution. Both lower federal courts sustained the statute. In the Supreme Court, Justice Cardozo characterized "the assault on the statute" as proceeding "on an extended front." But two prongs of that assault concern us here. First, Steward Machine Co. challenged the statute as involving the coercion of the states in contravention of the Tenth Amendment or of restrictions implicit in federalism. Second, it contended that the statute required the states to surrender powers "essential to their quasi-sovereign existence."[33]

For Cardozo, the core of the first challenge to the statute was the coercion argument. It was grounded on the 90 percent credit that the statute afforded. Did this provision, taken with the tax, *coerce* states into adopting their own unemployment compensation laws thus destroying their autonomy? To answer this question, Cardozo first considered the national problem to which the program was addressed. During the depression, the rolls of the unemployed had "mounted to unprecedented heights." States were "unable to give the requisite relief." Because the problem was national in scope, it could be properly addressed under the General Welfare Clause. "It is too late today," Cardozo wrote, "for the argument to be heard with tolerance that in a crisis so extreme the use of the moneys of the nation to relieve the unemployed and their dependents is a use for any purpose narrower than the promotion of the general welfare " In so ruling, Cardozo relied upon *Butler* for authority.[34]

From this point, Cardozo inquired whether the expedient adopted by the Congress in the Social Security Act (using tax funds to promote the general welfare) "overlept the bounds of power" by "driv[ing] the state Legislatures under the whip of economic pressure into the enactment of unemployment compensation laws at the bidding of the central government." Or, was the statute to be seen as seeking "the creation of a larger freedom, the states and nation joining in a co-operative endeavor to avert a common evil"? Cardozo saw it from the latter perspective. He noted that a few states had adopted unemployment compensation laws; those that had declined to do so were not unsympathetic to the problem but feared that they would be put at an economic disadvantagage in competing for industry if they imposed such a tax. The result was a greater burden for the nation. In consequence of this, Congress could adopt a program to encourage states to lessen that burden. Accordingly Cardozo concluded, "If Congress believed that the general welfare would better be promoted by relief through local units than by the system then in vogue, the co-operating localities ought not in all fairness to pay a second time."[35] For Cardozo and those who joined in the majority, neither the taxpayer nor the state was coerced by this scheme. Indeed, the state was not before the court complaining that in passing her unemployment compensation law "she was affected by duress." Alabama had made a choice with which she was satisfied.

"The difficulty with petitioner's contention," Cardozo observed, "is that it confuses motive with coercion." A rebate from a tax when conditioned on conduct was in some measure a temptation. "But to hold that motive or temptation is equivalent to coercion is to plunge the law in endless difficulties. The outcome of such a doctrine is the acceptance of a philosophical determinism by which choice becomes impossible." In short, the point at which pressure becomes compulsion had not not been reached when Alabama made her choice. "We cannot say that she was acting, not of her unfettered will, but under the strain of a persuasion equivalent to undue influence, when she chose to have relief administered under laws of her own making, by agents of her own selection, instead of under federal laws, administered by federal officers, with all the ensuing evils, at least to many minds, of federal patronage and power."[36]

This analysis brought Cardozo to the second prong of the assault: in imposing conditions on the credit or rebate relative to the state program, had Congress violated the Tenth Amendment by undermining the sovereignty of the state? Did the state have to pay too much in order to participate? In answering these questions in the negative, Cardozo, as had Stone in *Butler*, recognized the practical necessity of imposing reasonable conditions as the price of state participation in a federal spending-power program: "A credit to taxpayers for payments made to a state under a state unemployment law will be manifestly futile in the absence of some assurance that the law leading to the credit is in truth what it professes to be. An unemployment law framed in such a way that the unemployed who look to it will be deprived of reasonable protection is one in name and nothing more. What is basic and essential may be assured by suitable conditions." Moreover, the state did not bind itself to keep the law in force.[37] For the Court's majority, none of this constituted "abdication" of sovereignty in violation of the Tenth Amendment: "The inference of abdication thus dissolves in thinnest air when the deposit is conceived of as dependent upon a statutory consent, and not upon a contract effective to create a duty."[38]

In so concluding, the majority in *Steward Machine Co.* had put a judicial imprimatur on the essence of a federal spending program. Once it was clear that Congress was addressing a national problem within the scope of the General Welfare Clause, read Hamilton's way per *Butler*, its effort to encourage states to participate in the program through financial inducements did not constitute coercion and its efforts to maintain the integrity of the program by imposing reasonable conditions did not require the state to abdicate its sovereignty. These conclusions reached, a foundation was established for extending these principles to many other areas of national life.

The four dissenters recognized the far-reaching quality of the decision. Justices McReynolds and Butler dissented; Justices Sutherland and Van Devanter dissented in part. In his separate opinion, Mr. Justice Sutherland took issue only with the Court's conclusion as to abdication and sovereignty. The sweeping dissent of Justice McReynolds invoked the veto messages of Franklin Pierce.[39]

Social Security: Retirement Benefits

In *Helvering v. Davis*, the second of the two cases, Title II of the Social Security Act was before the Court. It provided for pay-

14: THE NEW DEAL AND JUDICIAL RESOLUTION 317

roll taxes familiar to those who either participate in today's Old Age Survivors and Disability Insurance (OASDI) program or employ individuals in their homes or businesses. It established an income tax on employees, to be deducted from wages by the employer, and an excise tax on employers. The income tax was measured by wages paid during a calendar year. The excise tax was paid on individuals in the employ of the employer. Both taxes were at identical rates. Starting at one percent in 1937, the rate rose to 3 percent in 1948. All remuneration was to be counted up to $3,000, and the proceeds of the taxes were to be paid into the treasury.

The act's principal benefit was a monthly pension payable to persons attaining the age of 65, who had worked for a specified period and earned at least a specified amount and were not then receiving wages as a result of regular employment. Benefits could not exceed $85 per month and were to be measured by a percentage of the wages earned during a specified period, the "percentage decreasing at stated intervals as the wages became higher." The program was thus comparable in many respects to present day Old Age and Survivors Insurance program under current Title II of the Social Security Act.[40] The program came under challenge when a shareholder of a corporation sued to restrain the corporation from making the required payments and deductions on the ground that the statute was unconstitutional. The Court of Appeals had held Title II void under the Tenth Amendment. The Supreme Court granted certiorari.

When he reached the merits of the controversy, Justice Cardozo, again writing for the majority, invoked the General Welfare Clause and its long history in a pithy passage: "Congress may spend money in aid of the 'general welfare' [citing Article I, section 8, *Butler*, and *Steward Machine Co*.]. There have been great statesmen in our history who have stood for other views. We will not resurrect the contest. *It is now settled by decision [citing Butler]. The conception of the spending power advocated by Hamilton and strongly reinforced by Story has prevailed over that of Madison, which has not been lacking in adherents.*"[41]

The Hamilton-Madison contest was at last resolved, but resolution left the Court with a difficult duty: "The line must still be drawn between one welfare and another, between particular and general." Cardozo described "a middle ground or certainly a penumbra in which discretion is at large." But the discretion was not that of the courts. "The discretion belongs to Congress, unless the choice is clearly wrong, a display of arbitrary power, not an exercise of judgment." All this was consistent with the Hamiltonian vision. It brought Cardozo to an examination of the Title II program within the framework he had laid out.

The root of the problem that Congress addressed in Title II of the Social Security Act was what Cardozo aptly termed "the purge of a nation-wide calamity that began in 1929." That calamity could not be geographically confined to one state or location. "Unemployment spreads from state to state, the hinterland now settled that in pioneer days gave an avenue of escape." Unemployment was thus "an ill not particular but general, which may be checked, if Congress so determines, by the resources of the Nation." *Steward Machine Co.* had put the matter to rest. Rescue became necessary whether men were thrown out of work "because there is no longer work to do or because the disabilities of age make them incapable of doing it." Cardozo encapsulated the statutory purpose. "The hope behind this statute is to save men and women from the rigors of the poor house as well as from the haunting fear that such a lot awaits them when journey's end is near."[42]

In support of this conclusion, Cardozo made brief reference to the findings of a Roosevelt cabinet commission. The "fate of workers over 65, when thrown out of work, is little less than desperate." The statistics, moreover, bore out the level of dependency. Approximately three out of four persons 65 or over were probably dependent wholly or partially on others for support. The problem was plainly "national in area and dimensions."

Moreover, the states could not be depended upon to solve it. Those states that established a social insurance system risked becoming a haven for the destitute. "Only a power that is national can serve the interests of all," Cardozo concluded. Having done so, he brushed aside policy arguments based upon values of self-reliance and frugality. "When money is spent to promote the general welfare, the concept of welfare or the opposite is shaped by Congress, not the states. So the concept be not arbitrary, the locality must yield [citing Article VI, par. 2 of the Constitution]."[43]

Cardozo did not, as he had done in *Steward Machine Co.*, devote considerable time to addressing explicitly the issue of the Tenth Amendment. Implicit in the Cardozo opinion is the proposition that once a case is made that a congressional enactment constitutes a proper exercise of the spending power under the General Welfare Clause, the Tenth Amendment objection is answered. Justice O'Connor, some fifty-five years after the decision in *Helvering v. Davis*, had occasion to note the relationship in a case captioned *New York v. United States*: "If a power is delegated to Congress in the Constitution, the Tenth Amendment expressly disclaims any reservation of that power to the States; if a power is an attribute of state sovereignty reserved by the Tenth Amendment, it is necessarily a power the Constitution has not conferred on Congress."[44]

Unlike the program involved in *Steward Machine Co.*, Title II of the Social Security Act had not attempted to engage the states in a scheme of cooperative federalism. States were not induced by the possibility of a grant of money to establish state programs and spend money granted for federally described services; states did not need to comport their law to federally established criteria in a spending-power-based statute. True, their citizens would now benefit from a federal program which attempted to address a need—the avoidance of destitution—that states had attempted to address by one means or another. But this was not a basis for invoking the Tenth Amendment. Indeed, the dissents did not attempt to articulate their lingering Tenth Amendment concern. Once the Hamiltonian threshold had been crossed in *Butler*, those concerns were, as a practical matter, largely irrelevant, at least in a wholly federalized program. That program in essence reflected an application of the principle that George Mason had eloquently described to his colleagues in the 1787 Convention: A national government may operate directly on the people and need not co-opt the state in that effort. If it could reach the people directly through taxation, it could reach them directly through a benefit program, such as the Social Security program involved.[45]

In the aggregate, the Supreme Court's work during 1936 and 1937 filled a judicial void in the history of the spending power that had existed since 1787. It created a judicial foundation for New Deal initiatives, grounded on the Hamiltonian theory of 1791, practiced partially or fully by James Monroe, John Quincy Adams, and Abraham Lincoln, and enunciated by several post–Civil War presidents including Ulysses S. Grant, Rutherford B. Hayes, and Benjamin Harrison, as well as Theodore Roosevelt and Woodrow Wilson. How that foundation was enhanced and built upon by those presidents who succeeded Franklin Roosevelt is the subject of the next chapters.[46]

THE SPENDING POWER AND THE
CONSTITUTIONAL REVOLUTION OF 1937

Renowned scholars, including Bruce Ackerman, Barry Cushman, Charles Leuchtenberg, and G. Edward White, have propounded a variety of theses to explain the Supreme Court's transformation between 1936 and 1937—and during the years that followed—from a high court prone to strike down as unconstitutional important New Deal legislative initiatives to one consistently inclined to uphold those initiatives. Leuchtenberg has described this transformation as the Constitutional Revolution of 1937. "The Constitutional Revolution of 1937 altered fundamentally the character of the Court's business, the nature of its decisions, and the alignment of its friends and foes. From the Marshall Court to the Hughes Court, the judiciary had largely been concerned with questions of property rights. After 1937, the most significant matters on the docket were civil liberties and other personal rights."[47]

This dramatic change in the pattern of decisions has been ascribed to the Supreme Court's reaction to Franklin Roosevelt's ultimately abortive effort to pack the Court through proposed legislation introduced in early 1937. "A switch in time saves nine," was the familiar refrain. Alternatively, the change has been attributed to the Court's recognition of Roosevelt's landslide victory in the election of 1936 as a mandate for New Deal change that the Court could not resist. The Court follows the election returns, it was said.[48] Cushman, suggests, on the contrary, that the constitutional change that characterized the New Deal was a product of evolution in the Court's own thinking. In effect, the Court abandoned long-standing constitutional theories that no longer seemed applicable to the problems it confronted.[49]

An analysis of these theories and the change in constitutional doctrine that took place in 1937 is beyond the scope of this study. However, in the context of an historical account of the spending power, it seems appropriate to note that the spending-power cases of 1936 and 1937 played a significant role in the saga that Leuchtenberg, Cushman, and others have so thoroughly analyzed. The Supreme Court's decision in *Butler*, to invalidate the Agricultural Adjustment Act, was one of a string of significant high-court decisions that prompted the Roosevelt administration to focus on confronting the Court, which was seen as an obstacle to implementing the New Deal. Indeed, the Supreme Court's rejection of the Agricultural Adjustment Act was a particularly telling blow, and Roosevelt—its principal architect and advocate—did not hesitate to blame the Court for striking it down. On the other hand, the Court's 1937 decisions in the Social Security Act cases upholding the landmark unemployment compensation and old age and survivors programs under that act on the strength of the General Welfare Clause were seen in some quarters as reducing the pressure to pack the court that had been introduced between the rendering of the *Butler* and Social Security decisions. To be sure, the court-packing legislation had lost considerable political steam by the time that the Cardozo opinions were handed down. However, had the Court's ruling been otherwise, one can speculate that the disposition of that plan—or alternatives to it—might have been different.[50] This said, the various theories discussed above to explain the New Deal constitutional revolution do not, in a fully satisfactory way, explain the evolution in spending power jurisprudence that occurred in 1936 and 1937. A number of factors were in play.

First, unlike the decision law developed under the Commerce Clause, the *Butler* decision was not preceded by a long line of spending-power decisions dating back to the nineteenth century. In *Butler*, as discussed above and as Mr. Justice Roberts noted in his opinion, the Court addressed the scope and meaning of the General Welfare Clause for the first time. In addressing the ancient controversy between Madison and Hamilton over that issue, Justice Roberts observed that it was the controlling question in the case, one that the Court had not previously directly confronted or been obliged to resolve. The Court did not engage its long-standing decision law on the central constitutional provision in question. There was none.[51]

Second, respecting the Hamilton-Madison controversy over the scope of the clause, the Court in *Butler* decided the matter as the Roosevelt Administration proposed. Roosevelt's Solicitor General, Stanley Reed, had posited the Agricultural Adjustment Act on the General Welfare Clause, had urged a broad reading of the clause in the fashion of Hamilton, and had conceded that the clause did not provide a grant of unlimited power to regulate for the general welfare but rather constituted a limitation on the taxing and spending power that was not itself constrained by the enumerated powers. The Court substantially adopted the Roosevelt administration's reading of the clause, relying heavily, not on Supreme Court precedent, but on the nonjudicial commentary of a former and long-respected justice, Joseph Story. While the Court's opinion on the subject was spare and did not reiterate the long account of constitutional history and legislative practice, Justice Roberts's opinion in *Butler* noted that these sources had been instructive to the majority. Indeed, the Hamiltonian reading that the court approved in this case created a foundation for decades of internal-improvement and education legislation during both Republican and Democratic administrations in the years leading up to *Butler*. Nevertheless when the Court stuck down the Agricultural Adjustment Act despite Stone's vigorous and eloquent dissent, it added an anomalous and curious gloss of the Tenth Amendment that ran counter to the majority's own Hamiltonian reading of the General Welfare Clause. However this emphasis on the holding and decision in the case should not shroud the significance of the *Butler* Court's having adopted—at least on the surface—the Hamiltonian reading.[52]

Third, the decisions in the subsequent Social Security cases, *Steward Machine Co.* and *Helvering v. Davis*, did not constitute outright repudiations or reversals of *Butler*, in which legislation that had been overturned in one case was then upheld in another. On the contrary, in both Social Security Cases, Justice Cardozo constructed his opinions sustaining the key New Deal social security programs on the foundation that had been nominally established in *Butler*. Cardozo used the *Butler* analysis of the General Welfare Clause—the broad Hamiltonian reading—to announce a solid, constitutional underpinning for the programs in question, grounded on that clause so read. Indeed, Cardozo took great pains to observe that the ancient contest over the scope of the Clause had already been resolved in favor of Hamilton's view. This conclusion left him free to devote the bulk of his opinion to the application of the General Welfare Clause to the programs in question. In *Helvering v. Davis*, he established, to the satisfaction of the Court, that Congress could address, under that clause, the nationwide problems that afflicted those unemployed as a result of old age. In both cases, Cardozo brushed aside the concerns that had served as a bar to the Agricultural Adjustment Act in *Butler*. In *Helvering*, Title II of the Social Security Act did not constitute an invasion of functions solely assigned to the states. In *Steward Machine Co.*, states were not coerced to adopt state unemployment compensation programs as a result of the federal legislation. In neither case did the state surrender sovereignty. Indeed, Cardozo carefully pointed out that the programs in question relieved those states that wanted to address the problems in question but were precluded from doing so by a fear that the relevant state taxation would put them at a disadvantage in competing with less progressive states. Far from being a burden, the General Welfare Clause benefited the states, notwithstanding the conditions that accompanied the grant of appropriated funds.[53]

With its concerns about the Tenth Amendment addressed, *Butler's* significance in resolving the Hamilton-Madison controversy has been institutionalized, while its force as a limitation on the exercise of the spending power (read Hamilton's way) has receded. As Laurence Tribe observes: "[S]ince its decisions upholding the Social Security Act, the Supreme Court has effectively ignored *Butler* when judging the limits of the congressional spending power."[54]

Fourth, in the first Social Security Act case the vaunted conservative four horsemen broke ranks. Justices Van Devanter and Sutherland agreed with the majority that the tax and tax credit were proper under the Constitution but objected to supervisory provisions of the act, presumably under the broadly read General Welfare Clause. Only Justices McReynolds and Butler joined in a dissent that resurrected Franklin Pierce's thinking on the scope of the General Welfare Clause, and that suggests that their concerns about the Tenth Amendment were grounded on a grudging acceptance of the breadth of that clause.[55]

In sum, these cases reflect a transition in the Court's thinking about the spending power over a two-year period. The precise extent to which that transition was driven by the Roosevelt administration's attempt to pack the Court or the 1936 election cannot be resolved here. Factors apart from these events also seem to have been in play. Having first identified in *Butler* the breadth of the General Welfare Clause as Hamilton and Story interpreted it, the Court, in the Social Security cases, could find no compelling reason to deny Congress the authority to address a national problem that involved the millions for whom journey's end was near. Its path to that result was eased because the spending power was being used to confer benefits upon eligible recipients as part of a national, social-insurance scheme rather than to control production or achieve economic regulation in a particular industry, let alone because the programs in question addressed social concerns that the states themselves had been struggling, without success, to address effectively and that clearly called for a national effort. In effect, after the drama of 1937 with its court packing and constitutional revolution, the nation had chosen progressive change through social insurance, a solution that the framers could not have contemplated. Moreover it had done so in a way that did not alter fundamentally the basic structure that the framers had adopted: social security, yes; court packing, no.

In adopting this equation, the New Deal forged constitutional change that was indeed revolutionary. In a sense, however, that change was attributable not only to the executives, and legislators and judges of the 1930s, but also to their predecessors: to Hamilton, Monroe, John Quincy Adams, and Story, who urged fidelity to the Constitution but who read it to countenance flexibility to address unanticipated problems in a way that would permit the country to grow and progress. As Bruce Ackerman has appropriately cautioned, the creative constitutional contribution of the New Deal may not be dismissed as a mere rediscovery of truths the framers first identified. They envisioned neither social security nor the constitutional problems it posed. At the same time, it should be recognized that they and those who followed had conducted a continuing, and at times intense, constitutional conversation over the scope of the power under which social security was ultimately sustained. With respect to the spending power, the "constitutional revolution" of 1937 is in part the product of a constitutional evolution that began in September 1787.[56]

VII
Modern Exercise

15
Truman to Ford—Toward Consensus

THIS SECTION PROVIDES A BRIEF SUMMARY OF THE PRACTICAL APplication of the General Welfare Clause by the presidents who followed Franklin Roosevelt. Post–World War II presidents, whether Democratic or Republican, proposed and—where Congress agreed—signed into law legislation that maintained, improved, or augmented the body of federal assistance programs. They made no serious attempt to repudiate the Supreme Court's 1936 and 1937 decisions about the scope of the General Welfare Clause. Their battles concerned the wisdom of the particular exercise of a broadly read spending power, proper canons of federalism, or fiscal impact. Out of four decades of executive and legislative activity arose a bipartisan consensus as to the availability of a broad, multidimensional spending power as a key element of modern American government.

HARRY S. TRUMAN

Harry Truman did not shrink from recommending the vigorous and progressive exercise of the spending power that had been judicially vindicated during the Roosevelt administration. He proposed that Social Security, unemployment compensation, and welfare programs inherited by his administration be maintained or strengthened. Undaunted by congressional opposition, Truman repeatedly proposed innovation and expansion in key general-welfare areas. He pushed, vigorously but unsuccessfully, for universal health insurance supported by payroll taxes, a move that would have extended the New Deal. His recognition of the need for a federal role in meeting the country's health care needs was well ahead of his time. In terms of actual legislation, the Truman administration succeeded in gaining the enactment of a number of major bills that built upon the New Deal legacy and laid the foundation for later initiatives. Notable among these were the Housing Act of 1949 and the Employment Act of 1946. The latter authorized a number of employment and manpower training programs in the wake of the war; the former provided for low-rent public housing projects in high poverty urban and rural areas.

Although Truman offered no new philosophical direction regarding spending power doctrine, the programs he advocated—notably in access to health care—were consistent with the prevailing constitutional jurisprudence as reflected in Justice Cardozo's opinion in *Helvering v. Davis*. Congress had power to address, through the expenditure of funds, economic problems of nationwide dimensions, such as those faced by aged or unemployed workers, particularly where states lacked resources or political will to deal with them effectively.[1]

DWIGHT D. EISENHOWER

Truman's successor, Dwight Eisenhower, was the first Republican to occupy the White House after the New Deal. If a change in constitutional course back to pre-*Butler* days were to be adopted, the Eisenhower administration would have been a logical place to start. Even if an administration accepted the Hamiltonian doctrine but wished to exercise the authority of the General Welfare Clause in a much more limited fashion, the Eisenhower Administration could have been a staging ground to roll back the New Deal and Fair Deal initiatives that had been adopted under that constitutional authority. However, Eisenhower did not repudiate the broad spending-power doctrine adopted by the Court. While he was generally modest in propounding his own spending programs, as Geoffrey Perret puts it, the president "didn't intend to try rolling back the New Deal." On the contrary, he proposed extensions of its safety net in such areas as Social Security, further aid to public housing, urban renewal, and assistance for vocational rehabilitation. These objectives, in some instances, collided with conservative interests in the Congress in a way that rankled the president. With regard to social insurance, the Eisenhower Administration's initial extension of Social Security to cover disability was a major change.

The Federal-Aid Highway Act of 1956 authorized the interstate highway system, a far-reaching system of modern, federally-funded, limited-access highways that has contributed enormously to America's economic growth and made distant regions more accessible. In so doing it extended the internal improvements approved by earlier president, including Jefferson, Madison, Monroe, and John Quincy Adams.

A principal mechanism launched by the Federal-Aid Highway Act of 1956 was the Highway Trust Fund. Under the basic arrangement, the Federal government would pay 90 percent of the costs of the interstate system. The states would be responsible for the remaining 10 percent. The roads would be funded, like social security, on a pay-as-you-go basis from dedicated taxes, including a gasoline tax that has been an underpinning of a stable system.

As proposed by the Eisenhower administration, the 1956 legislation constituted what has been described as "the largest highway construction program and, in fact, the largest single public works program ever undertaken by the United States." Putting to one side its dimensions and its obvious massive contribution to domestic transportation in twenty-first century America, the interstate system represents the Eisenhower Administration's implicit acceptance of the General Welfare Clause jurisprudence announced in *Helvering v. Davis*. While pitched in part on defense considerations, the massive federal-aid internal-improvement program authorized by the Federal-Aid Highway Act would not have been possible in the absence of the broad reading of the General Welfare Clause. A retreat from that reading would have precluded this aspect of the Eisenhower legacy. Eisenhower did not sound it. On the contrary, the Eisenhower years reflected bipartisan support for the constitutional doctrine that permitted the modern, multidimensional exercise of the spending power.[2]

Eisenhower fortified that reading in another context dear to the hearts of his early nineteenth-century predecessors: education. Following the Soviet Union's launch of Sputnik, which delivered a wake-up call to the United States, the Eisenhower administration proposed and Congress passed the National Defense Education Act of 1958. The act called for strengthening elementary and secondary education in the United States in a number of areas, including science education, teacher training, and scholarships that enabled thousands to go to graduate school. Because defense considerations also were advanced as a rationale for the legislation, the Common Defense Clause, as well as the General Welfare Clause, can be said to have afforded it constitutional support. In urging passage, Eisenhower cited the act's benefits both "to education and to national security." In the area of elementary and secondary education legislation, the NDEA represented a significant legislative precedent and constituted the most important federal aid to elementary and secondary education act prior to the adoption of the Elementary and Secondary Education Act of 1965. Thus, with respect to both transportation and education, two of the bedrock areas that had been the subject of the General Welfare Clause "contest" of the nineteenth century, the Eisenhower administration made positive contributions based upon the General Welfare Clause case law of the 1930s.

Both symbolically and administratively, Eisenhower helped continue the advent of the general welfare state. Out of a sometimes uncoordinated conglomeration of New Deal agencies responsible for various spending programs, he formed the Department of Health, Education, and Welfare and appointed Oveta Culp Hobby as its first secretary. The move had no constitutional significance, but in taking it he was obliged to recognize the prevailing constitutional framework. As Perret explains: "[t]he Republican leadership told [Eisenhower] the Constitution didn't say a word about the federal government being responsible for people's welfare or their education or their health." They suggested that the president first "push through" a constitutional amendment, but Eisenhower stood firm. Reorganization meant that Social Security, education, health, welfare, and children's and family programs now had a single home in the federal community, both constitutionally and organizationally. The new department's staff could conceive and draft new legislation that would—implicitly or explicitly—depend upon the General Welfare Clause in its Hamiltonian cast. In transmitting his plan, Eisenhower firmly reinforced these connections: "There should be," he said, "an unremitting effort to improve those health, education, and social security programs which have proved their value."[3]

JOHN F. KENNEDY

This constitutional legacy was part of John F. Kennedy's inheritance when he entered the White House on January 20, 1961, a bitter cold inauguration day following in the wake of a massive snowstorm. Kennedy's soaring Inaugural Address advanced progressive themes not unlike those posed by his Massachusetts predecessor 136 years earlier. He did not need to dwell upon any lingering doubts regarding the scope of the spending power; the intervening history had resolved them.[4]

Nestled within the less remembered passages of the Kennedy Inaugural were some programmatic ideas that signaled an active resort to the spending power and an intent to build on the New Deal legislative legacy. The New Frontier would propose to have the country "do" some things for the American people, invoking the spending power vigorously in order to effect them. Kennedy expanded on this in later addresses regarding greater health security, aid to the arts, and aid to education.

Kennedy's tragic assassination cut short the opportunity to transform the country through a body of new spending power programs. The list of what was enacted during his tenure fell short of the promise. However, that list contains a number of important initiatives that have survived the ensuing decades to the benefit of the nation. Moreover, Kennedy's unsuccessful legislative initiatives, particularly in education and health security for the aged, as well as some experimental executive actions, laid the foundation for the dramatically successful legislative record of the Johnson years.

The Mutual Educational, Cultural and Exchange Act of 1961 (Fullbright-Hayes) established a range of programs designed to finance educational and cultural exchange programs to serve foreign students and academics interested in studying in the United States as well as to promote study abroad programs for Americans. The benefit of this legislation in fostering international understanding and greater knowledge of the American system of government has been immeasurable. While the law might have been posited on the foreign policy powers of the United States, the exercise of spending power authority seems implicit as the constitutional foundation of the legislation.[5]

The Academic Facilities Act of 1963 broke new ground in invoking the spending power by providing assistance, in the form of grants and loans, to colleges and universities to help them in improving or constructing facilities to respond to new increases in enrollment following the war years. The law can be seen as an extension of the 1862 Morrill Act since it applied to colleges and universities irrespective of land-grant status. It also broke new ground by providing assistance for private, religiously affiliated institutions of higher education.[6]

Kennedy achieved success in persuading Congress to pass an Area Redevelopment Bill, as he had promised in West Virginia, that sought to address the needs of depressed areas in Appalachia and other regions of the country. While the program was phased out after its initial period of authorization, it helped to pave the way for later community development programs, including the Community Development Block Grant and the Empowerment Zone legislation.

The Kennedy Administration made a meaningful contribution to the evolution of spending power legislation with respect to housing through the passage of the Housing Act of 1961, which built upon the Truman legislation of 1949 and provided funds for urban renewal, public housing, housing for the elderly, and student housing. The Manpower Development and Training Act of 1962 (MDTA) broke new ground in the area of manpower training. Legislation to address perceived problems in confronting juvenile delinquency and mental retardation was also enacted in response to Kennedy's New Frontier initiative.[7]

Beyond the realm of immediate legislative enactments, the Kennedy Administration proposed a number of New Frontier initiatives that were to become law in the years after his 1963 assassination. Notable examples were elementary and secondary education and Medicare bills. In the case of elementary and secondary education, Kennedy presented a bold proposal calling for a more-than-$2-billion-authorization for elementary and secondary school aid that could be used for maintenance, teacher salaries, and school construction. The money was to be distributed to states on a formula basis. The bill foundered, in part because it failed to provide adequately for the needs of children in private schools, in part because it earned the enmity of a conservative coalition of Republicans and southern Democrats that bottled up considerable parts of Kennedy's domestic legislation program. The Medicare proposal offered to build on Social Security by imposing a payroll tax that would be used to provide hospitalization insurance for the elderly. This proposal, too, failed to pass. The introduction of both measures, and the confrontation of the obstacles to enactment that they posed, provided a basis for later success in the Johnson Administration, when congressional majorities were more in keeping with passage and when Johnson's legislative skills were creatively applied.[8]

In other significant areas, as well, Kennedy's initiatives constituted new beginnings. One such area was food security. Appalled by the notion that hunger gripped many Americans, the Kennedy administration initiated a new program. On January 21, 1961, the day after his inauguration, by executive order, Kennedy launched a pilot food stamp program addressed to six geographic areas. The program was expanded to additional areas in 1962, reaching over 200,000 individuals. In the year after Kennedy's death, the program was transformed into legislation through the enactment of the Food Stamp Act of 1964. In its present incarnation, following many amendments, that legislation offers income maintenance assistance to twenty million Americans and constitutes one of the most important of the Nation's means-tested income maintenance programs. Administered by the Food and Nutrition Service in the USDA, it presently faces the problem of diminished participation, attributable in part to the shift of milions of single parents from welfare to work, a problem that the government is seeking to address through an imaginative education and outreach campaign.[9]

John F. Kennedy, however, is not remembered in terms of legislative enactments or proposals. Few of his current admirers can recite a list of his administration's spending-power bills. His legacy lies rather in the eloquent expression of the proposition that government exists to serve the citizens and to improve the condition of the more vulnerable. In this sense, Kennedy was giving voice to an inherent conviction that "to provide for the general welfare of the United States" constituted a high purpose of the American polity. To this end, Kennedy, with infinite charm and style, attracted an army of young policy makers and civil servants to Washington who were imbued with the same conviction. It is upon that foundation that the more contemporary efforts to build a more equitable society within the framework of American democracy and constitutionalism are still going forward.[10]

Lyndon B. Johnson

Lyndon Johnson's administration represents a landmark in the resort to the federal spending power to address the host of economic and social problems plaguing the nation. 1965 was a seminal year of major initiatives posited in whole or in part on the General Welfare Clause. Still stunned by the death of John F. Kennedy, the nation rejected the unapologetically conservative Barry Goldwater and gave Lyndon Johnson a landslide victory in November 1964. With strong Democratic majorities in both houses of Congress, the stage was set for the Great Society and the second surge of federal programmatic creativity in the twentieth century.

The New Deal, which represents the first great surge, was sustained by the constitutional revolution described above. The Great Society, by contrast, did not need to overcome a hostile or skeptical Supreme Court. While Johnson at first worried about the constitutional obstacles his programs might face, his administration was not obliged to convince the Court that the broad spending power interpretation advocated by Hamilton reflected the correct reading of the General Welfare Clause. That had been resolved in 1936 and 1937. What faced the Great Society reformers of 1965 was the challenge of formulating workable and effective programs and persuading Congress to enact them.

In proposing the keystone programs of the Great Society—the poverty program in the form of the Economic Opportunity Act, aid to education in the form of the Elementary and Secondary Education Act, student financial assistance in the form of the Higher Education Act of 1965, greater health security for the elderly in the form of Medicare, and aid to the arts in the form of the National Foundation on the Arts and Humanities Act of 1965—President Johnson proposed initiatives constitutionally grounded on the Supreme Court's Social Security Act cases and the long legislative and executive evolution that had preceded them.[11]

Since the administration of George Washington, American presidents had given voice to the importance of education as a national concern, particularly higher education. Despite numerous proposals dating back to the post–Civil War era and a few statutory enactments, comprehensive federal aid to elementary and secondary education had eluded the nation prior to the Great Society. This Johnson proposed in the landmark Elementary and Secondary Education Act of 1965 (ESEA). A primary objective of the program was to aid in a new national effort to address or eradicate poverty. Equal educational opportunity was seen as a means, perhaps the primary means, of overcoming poverty grounded in decades of economic deprivation. If they were provided extra or remedial services to meet their special educational needs, educationally deprived children living in poverty could succeed in overcoming the obstacles that faced them and enter the economic mainstream via education. Johnson felt strongly that a federal assistance role was imperative "to avert disaster."

While primarily responsible for education, states lacked the resources to provide the extra services. The federal government could help by targeting federal funds by formula directly to school districts that had the highest concentrations of children from low-income families and within them to schools with the highest concentrations of such children. The school districts would have broad discretion in providing the services. The state educational agencies would administer the program, undertaking to target funds in accordance with the program legislation and to adhere to fiscal and other conditions designed to ensure that the services were supplementary. This was Title I of the legislation, posited initially in part on a national defense role; it survives today having been reauthorized many times.[12]

The Johnson administration intended that the new legislation would overcome an obstacle that had impeded previous legislation: the question of whether educationally deprived children attending private, parochial schools were eligible. President Kennedy had argued that providing funds to such private schools violated the prohibitions of the First Amendment. The lack of an opportunity for private school children to share in the legislation's benefits ensured its legislative defeat because significant numbers of Congressmen and Senators opposed enactment in the absence of adequate provision for such an opportunity. Johnson solved the problem by a deft compromise. Private schools would get no money. However, their students, if within the target population, would be assured the receipt of remedial and other *services* from participating local public school districts through an explicit grant condition binding on them.

Johnson threw himself into the legislative process, diligently cajoling reluctant legislators and directing the legislative strategies leading to passage. Once the House passed a bill, the Senate was persuaded to pass an identical bill. A conference was avoided and the legislation was signed in April 1965. The constitutional obstacle that had been overcome in its passage was not a dispute over the scope of the spending power. Even in the absence of a Supreme Court decision on the applicability of that power to education, such applicability was largely assumed. Opponents of the bill did not mount a serious constitutional challenge on that basis. Instead, dispute erupted over the principle of federal control of education and, here, the issue was solved by a statutory provision that forbade such control under the guise of federal program administration. In signing the legislation, Johnson struck an historical note, reflecting that since 1870 the nation had been trying to pass an elementary and secondary bill that would aid "all children of America." Thus, did he align his own effort with that of his post–Civil War Republican and twentieth-century Democratic, predecessors. The enactment of this legislation, as Dallek observes, is "an achievement for which Johnson deserves the country's continuing regard."[13]

But ESEA was not the only education legislation that Johnson managed through the legislative mill. Poverty could also be addressed by opening the doors of higher education to those with little or no resources. Improving elementary and secondary education would not succeed unless access to postsecondary education was enhanced. A precedent was available in the GI Bill, enacted during the Truman Administration, that had a substantial and positive impact on the society, opening the doors of colleges and universities to veterans. Title IV of the Higher Education Act enhanced this process by providing for need-based educational opportunity grants and low interest or interest-subsidized loans to all eligible students attending institutions of higher education.

The legislation was passed by Congress and signed by the president in 1965. It included, beyond student financial aid, a bundle of programs to support institutions of higher education, including aid to college libraries, aid to developing institutions (historically black colleges), aid to graduate education, and other supports that built on the precedent of Kennedy's Academic Facilities Act. As amended frequently over the decades that followed, the Higher Education Act, along with many other factors, has contributed to the more than doubling of the percentage of Americans (over twenty-five years of age) who graduate from colleges and universities and to the remarkable enhancement of gender equity in American higher education. These changes have greatly enriched late twentieth-century life in the United States. They represent a not-fully-appreciated American spending-power success story.[14]

Education was not the sole achievement. Through its poverty program, the Great Society dramatized one of its central theses: the federal power of the purse could be directly enlisted to combat one of the nation's most fundamental problems, searing, continuing, unrelenting poverty. Since the beginning of the nation, it had been assumed that economic growth and the vast territorial extent of the nation would address economic inequality. If the federal government had a role in the spending power, it was through aid to industry or by opening up the country through federally-assisted roads and canals, a proposition that was adopted through internal improvements of the nineteenth century. Americans could receive help in ameliorating their condition through individual low-cost land grants and, later, through the operation of the Homestead Act of 1862. Social Security and welfare aided particular segments of the nation's low-income population, the elderly, the temporarily unemployed, and single-parent families.

However, that the government constituted a force to combat poverty through the direct use of the spending power was not a generally accepted principle. Johnson transformed it into legislation through the Economic Opportunity Act of 1964, designed to address what he called "one of the most stubbornly entrenched social ills in America." It created a multitude of new programs under the rubric of the war on poverty, including neighborhood legal services, credit unions, neighborhood service centers, and the like, all administered by an Office of Economic Opportunity, and a structure of state and local offices. While ultimately terminated during the Nixon Administration, many of these services are reflected today in publicly or privately funded programs. Most important, a precedent was set for invoking the General Welfare Clause in a war against poverty. It was in a sense a manifestation, through specific programmatic responses, of John Quincy Adams's postulate that the highest role of government was to improve the condition of its citizens.[15]

In the same year that the Poverty Program became law, Johnson persuaded Congress to pass the Food Stamp Act originally proposed by President Kennedy to augment food security for the nation's disadvantaged. Today Food Stamps remain an important component of both the federal budgetary commitment to the nation's safety net and the body of means-tested, entitlement programs designed to effect income maintenance.

Educational equity and antipoverty programs, while landmark, were insufficient to address the problems of the nation as Johnson saw them. To complete Franklin Roosevelt's work of an adequate social insurance foundation for the nation's elderly, it was necessary to address their health-care needs. The growing cost and importance of health care made it clear that, even with Social Security, Americans over sixty-five would not be economically secure without a program of health care.

In 1965, Johnson proposed legislation to establish a Medicare program that would provide government-financed health insurance for those over sixty-five. As ultimately revised by Congress and presented to Johnson for signature, the legislation provided for hospitalization insurance (Part A) to be funded by a payroll tax, similar to the Social Security tax, on both employees and employers. Hospitalization, certain nursing home services following hospitalization, and hospice-care costs were to be covered for those insured. Physicians' services and related benefits were to be covered, financed in part by premiums paid by the insured and partially from general federal funds. To Medicare, in the last throes of legislative consideration, was added Medicaid, a federal-state matching program to cover health care costs for the economically deprived, including nursing-home based custodial care, to be available on a means-tested basis. Taken together, the two programs involved the federal government, again via the spending power, in the nation's health care system in a way that continues to create profound opportunities and profound health care and fiscal problems to this day.[16]

In addition to the programs discussed above, the Johnson Administration also passed the National Foundation on the Arts and Humanities Act of 1965. This legislation established the National Endowment for the Arts and the National Endowment for the Humanities. Through their discretionary grants these agencies were empowered to strengthen and diversify arts and humanities in America.

By building on the work of the New Deal and the General Welfare Clause legacy of previous administrations, Lyndon Johnson was able to move the federal government into augmenting welfare through instituting Food Stamps, aiding elementary and secondary education, providing financial assistance for postsecondary students, creating antipoverty initiatives, enhancing health security for the elderly and poor, and finally, establishing aid to the arts and humanities. All of these programs, in one form or another, remain vehicles of federal assistance today. As the Johnson administration became increasingly enmeshed in Vietnam, however, it was no longer able to focus only on the Great Society. The Vietnam conflict effectively muted the Johnson administration's formidable domestic record and veiled its massive contribution to the evolution of public, general welfare investment in the United States.[17]

RICHARD M. NIXON

Richard Nixon's *Memoirs* gives us a unique opportunity to assess, from his own perspective, his administration's contributions to the course of spending-power evolution during his six years in office. What is striking is how small a role spending power issues seemed to play in the overall panorama of his presidency. What is also of note is that those issues did not arise as constitutional concerns, as they had in the early history of the country; spending power considerations were important insofar as they enabled the administration to give effect to policy priorities or address major crises.

As he recalled in his *Memoirs*, toward the end of his first term and on the eve of the 1972 presidential campaign, Nixon cataloged the domestic accomplishments of that term: a major welfare-reform proposal, a new national health-insurance program, a major mass-transit bill; a reorganization of the education research functions of the government; and a new revenue-sharing measure were included in the list. Not mentioned was the water-pollution legislation he signed in 1972 or the establishment of the EPA.[18]

Nixon viewed a number of the New Deal and Great Society programs as "costly failures." Welfare was a top priority target. In 1969, with the help of Daniel Patrick Moynihan, then a domestic advisor, and the support of HEW Secretary Robert Finch and Secretary of Labor George Shultz, he proposed the Family Assistance Program (FAP). Receipt of welfare would have been tied to work, and the proposal was designed to make work more economically attractive. The proposal centered around the idea that federal financial assistance would be made available to the working poor, families in which fathers lived at home, as well as the traditional Aid to Families with Dependent Children (AFDC) constituency. Nixon recalled it as "revolutionary domestic legislation that required [him] to seek a legislative alliance with Democrats and liberals," a marriage that was never celebrated. However bold it may have been, FAP met resistance from the Democratic Congress and was finally dropped in 1972, when it failed to pass. Interestingly, one aspect of the proposal survived the congressional process. This was the initiative to bind into one program various measures to aid the aged, blind, and disabled with income-maintenance payments. President Nixon signed into law the authorization for the Supplemental Security Income Program (SSI) that remains on the books today as Title XVI of the Social Security Act, an important part of the nation's safety net.[19]

The other major priority that Nixon faced in the early years of his presidency involved the knotty problems growing out of the implementation of the Supreme Court's landmark school desegregation decision in *Brown v. Board of Education*. Considerable resistance to desegregation was being felt in the South and elsewhere. In 1969, the Supreme Court issued a further decision that required school districts to enhance the pace of compliance. Nixon opposed busing but knew that some effort to achieve compliance was essential. He reached for the spending power, and proposed what he later described as a "$1.5 billion [program] over two years for helping school districts desegregate." The result was the Emergency School Aid Act, which remained in effect for almost a decade.[20]

Nixon's other venture in education took the form of proposing and ultimately signing legislation to establish the National Institute of Education (NIE), the research arm of the federal Office of Education, then ensconced in the Department of Health, Education, and Welfare. The statutory reorganization gave the NIE greater flexibility, the opportunity to attract first-class researchers, and a focused charter. Nixon called it the "nation's first formal research institute for learning and education."[21]

Although Nixon's presidency focused primarily on Vietnam, foreign policy with regard to China and Russia, and Watergate, he did make some early efforts to address welfare and health reform. Nixon also made more modest changes in the architecture of existing New Deal or Great Society programs that his administration had inherited from its predecessors, notably SSI. Thus, a "moderate conservative" administration did not reverse the New Deal or wipe out the Great Society (the ESEA, for example, remained), but it was unable politically to put a major stamp in the priority area it identified, welfare reform. At the end of his first term, Nixon recalled with pride that he had reversed the percentage of national resources going to defense and domestic programs in favor of the latter. The growth of the entitlement programs enacted during previous administrations ensured that this would continue to be the case.[22]

Gerald Ford

Gerald Ford came to office in August 1974 as the result of Nixon's resignation in the face of near certain impeachment. Ford's presidential biographer, John Robert Greene, characterizes the president's domestic policy as "less an articulated agenda and more an exercise in crisis management." However, in his short tenure, Ford signed into a law a number of significant spending power measures, maintaining the growing tradition of modern bipartisanship with regard to the general welfare begun by Eisenhower. In 1975, Ford signed, albeit with reservations, the Education of All Handicapped Children Act. The EHA later evolved into the Individuals with Disabilities Education Act (IDEA), one of the most important keystones of federal elementary and secondary legislation. These measures have opened the doors of education to countless disabled children and ushered in a new chapter in federal aid to education. Ford's action is thus a landmark. In the 1976 primary campaign, Ford also demonstrated his commitment to another important general welfare mission, by promising not to revise Social Security.[23]

The General Welfare Clause authorizes, but does not require, Congress to appropriate, in order to provide for the general welfare of the United States; Article II of the Constitution authorizes the president to recommend to Congress "such Measures as he shall judge necessary and expedient." Accordingly, the president is authorized, but not required, to recommend spending-power measures that provide for the general welfare. Following the New Deal, six presidents, three Democrats and three Republicans, Truman, Eisenhower, Kennedy, Johnson, Nixon and Ford, recommended such measures to Congress, implicitly reflecting the broad reading adopted by the courts. The executive-branch consensus was that the modern exercise of the clause embraced such a reading, both as a matter of law and a matter of policy. But that consensus was broader.

By the mid-1970s, if not earlier, the exercise of the federal spending power and the recognition of its constitutional dimension, as first expressed by Hamilton, had become institutionalized in the legislative, executive, and judicial branches and in the practice of both major political parties. The exercise was all-pervasive. It profoundly affected many walks and seasons of American life: the schoolhouse, the college classroom, the library, the museum, the artist's studio, the physician's office and the hospital; the roads, railroads, airlines, and other means of transportation; the environment, forest preserves, and reclamation facilities; the dinner table and the school lunchroom; early childhood and retirement; disability, loss of spouse and financial need. All this was the result of judicial interpretation, of disputation among statesmen, great and less remembered, of legislative application, and of scholarly commentary. It was beyond demolition or serious retrenchment and had arisen as a response to the needs of the American people.

16
Carter to Clinton—Accommodating Budget and National Investment Imperatives

BUDGETARY RATHER THAN CONSTITUTIONAL CONCERNS HAVE COME to constrain the exercise of the spending power during the past twenty-five years. A compelling task of the new century will be to recognize the continuing importance of public investment in the general welfare while also recognizing other priorities, both domestic and international. The presidencies of Jimmy Carter, Ronald Reagan, George H. W. Bush, and Bill Clinton all reflect this tension. While the past quarter-century bears testimony to the durability of established programs, and while progress has been made in formulating and administering new programs, the twenty-first century has inherited a set of powerful spending-power challenges that will dominate efforts to continue to provide for the nation's welfare.

JIMMY CARTER

Jimmy Carter promised to break new ground in addressing the general welfare of his fellow Americans, but he was perceived, or perceived himself, as a Washington "outsider." The perception may have denied him support for many of his proposals despite a Congress in which his own party enjoyed a majority. Nevertheless, his administration promoted general-welfare legislation in a number of key areas. He was able to sign into law landmark bills that meaningfully affected education, the environment, and, most important, energy policy. At the same time, Carter deeply regretted his inability to obtain legislation implementing his ideas on welfare reform and national health.

While the Education Amendments of 1978 authorized innovations in federal programming to assist elementary and secondary education, Carter's major accomplishment was organizational. His administration proposed, and persuaded Congress to approve, the establishment of the United States Department of Education. The Department of Education Organization Act of 1979 furnished the statutory framework. It assigned the many individual education programs formerly administered by a variety of federal agencies, most notably the Department of Health, Education, and Welfare, to a single agency exclusively dedicated to education. Carter was satisfied with the result. "The new department," he wrote in *Keeping Faith,* his memoirs, "under the clear command of our first Secretary of Education, Shirley Hufstedler, was able to give much better service [and] to provide a consistent policy. . . ." The establishment of a cabinet-level department reinforced the high priority that Americans give to the education of their children and is an important part of Jimmy Carter's spending-power legacy.[1]

In the waning days of his administration, Carter enhanced the federal role in safeguarding and restoring the environment by signing Superfund legislation in response to the Love Canal disaster of the late 1970s. The Carter Administration proposed reform legislation that would give the government power to address chemical and oil spills. Industry opposition and division in Congress bottled up the legislation until a respite in partisanship after the 1980 election facilitated compromise and enabled Carter to approve the landmark legislation. Controversy over Superfund in the late 1990s and concern over the pace of its cleanup operations should not shroud the importance of this legislation in seeking to address environmental damage resulting from chemical spills. Today, Superfund expenditures constitute among the largest federal investments in the environment. Carter regarded it "as far-reaching and important as any accomplishment of my administration."[2]

Ronald Reagan

Ronald Reagan came to the White House with what he regarded as a mandate to abolish or trim many of the federal programs inherited from the New Deal and the Great Society and to reorganize the federal infrastructure that had grown up to administer them. To some extent, the Reagan Administration was successful in doing so. In many respects, however, the basic fabric of the New Deal-Great Society remained as intact when Reagan left office in January 1989 as it had been in January 1981 when he entered it. Indeed, some of the survivors gained new vitality. Social Security was financially fortified by the work of the Greenspan Commission of 1983 through such innovations as a graduated increase in the retirement age. The welfare programs in Title IV of the Social Security Act remained in place, slightly energized by the adoption of the Family Support Act of 1988 that stressed transition to work for welfare families.

Familiar Great Society landmarks, large and small, survived. Medicare stayed on the books, as did Medicaid, although both programs were subject to efforts at reform, cost containment, and restructuring effected in part through the budget reconciliation process. The Elementary and Secondary Education Act and the Higher Education Act, while significantly amended, were reauthorized. The Department of Education survived to administer them. Despite consideration of organizational alternatives, an attempt to abolish it did not receive substantial congressional support. The National Endowment for the Arts and National Endowment for the Humanities continued, despite efforts to cut or eliminate their funding. The very modestly funded Museum Services Program was retained, despite recommendations to zero it out, demonstrating the difficulty of terminating even the smallest programs enjoying local public support. Lou Cannon, in his comprehensive biography of the Reagan presidency, has observed: "[N]either the size nor the reach of the federal government receded on Reagan's watch... Spending as a share of the nation's gross domestic product increased during the Reagan years to an all-time high of 24.4 percent." It should be recognized, in assessing this observation, that much of the increase may have been attributable to natural growth in entitlement spending.[3]

In specific areas, the Reagan Administration achieved the goals of its consolidating or trimming efforts. For example, in 1981, at the behest of the administration, and with substantial Democratic support, Congress enacted the Education Consolidation and Improvement Act (ECIA) that consolidated some forty separate education categorical programs into a single education block grant, called Chapter 2, which gave state and local educational agencies greater flexibility in the use of federal education dollars and the purposes to which they would be put. The change was welcomed by those agencies and provided a valid test of the theory that greater flexibility was a positive factor in the administration of those programs. In its 1988 amendments, however, Congress receded somewhat on the flexibility afforded in the 1981 ECIA.

Respecting education, the administration pointed to new directions for maintaining the general welfare. During Reagan's watch and under the direction of Secretary Terrel H. Bell, an experienced, resolute and courageous champion of education, the government (through the National Commission on Excellence in Education) issued a 1993 report entitled, *A Nation at Risk*, which starkly identified shortcomings in the quality of elementary and secondary education nationwide and sparked a reform movement that contributed to positive local, state, and federal legislation to achieve educational excellence in the decades that followed. Cannon correctly regards it as "one of the most thoughtful documents to emerge from any government agency during the Reagan presidency."[4]

In his appointments to the Supreme Court, Reagan sought judges likely to "favor 'judicial restraint.' " However, there is no evidence that he also sought judges antagonistic to the rulings of the 1930s affirming a broad reading of the federal spending power, as interpreted by Hamilton and Story, if indeed any survived. On the contrary, during Reagan's administration, the Supreme Court essentially relied upon and applied these rulings in sustaining broad grant conditions established by Congress under the federal interstate highway program. The key case was *South Dakota v. Dole*. The opinion was written by Chief Justice Rehnquist. The decision effectively extended the reach of the spending power by affirming the authority of Congress to insist that South Dakota adhere to a minimum national drinking age as a condition for receiving its entire federal interstate highway allotment. In his opinion for the majority, the Chief Justice accurately summarized the thrust of the Court's spending power jurisprudence and the 150 year evolution that had preceded it: "[O]bjectives not thought to be within Article I's 'enumerated legislative fields' may nevertheless be attained through the use of the spending power and the conditional grant of funds." Justice O'Connor's dissent did not contradict this proposition but maintained that spending power conditions should be upheld only when related to the manner in which funds were to be spent. It was clear that retrenchment of the New Deal would not reverse the Supreme Court's 1937 spending power decisions.

Nor should this be surprising. Such a reversal would have overturned much of what the nation wanted, whatever the prevailing philosophy. Such a reversal would have, for example, jeopardized the Social Security Act, a keystone of the nation's social insurance system, and would have undermined other safety-net programs that Reagan recognized as necessary. Indeed, from a policy perspective, Reagan had been reluctant to appear to be reducing social security benefits when he rejected an invitation to support a congressional initiative to freeze cost-of-living increases under the program. A return to the General Welfare Clause concepts of the Virginia Resolutions would have had other troubling implications. While unstated, a narrow reading of the General Welfare Clause would have also presupposed a narrow reading of the Common Defense Clause which, like the General Welfare Clause, is found in Article 1, section 8, clause 1 of the Constitution. Accordingly, "morning in America" necessarily embraced the broad reading of the spending power that had come down from Hamilton, through Monroe, John Quincy Adams, Story, and Lincoln.[5]

A brake, if any, would have to be applied through nonconstitutional mechanisms. One of these was the budget process. Through a combination of tax cuts and increases in defense spending, the Reagan administration's decisions led to growing budget deficits. By the end of Reagan's second term, the national debt had risen substantially. The expectation had been that cuts in domestic programs would offset tax cuts and defense hikes. The offsetting cuts did not materialize. The result was deficit spending. While it might be justified by Cold War strategies, the long-term effect of institutionalized deficit spending on the economy and on public administration was alarming. The response of the administration and Congress was to create a system of budget controls and mandatory ceilings that would bring some discipline to the situation. Building on the Budget and Impoundment Control Act of 1974, an outgrowth of the Nixon impounding experience, Congress enacted and the President signed the Gramm, Rudman, Hollings legislation that imposed deficit-reduction targets and called for sequestration when they were not met. Budget controls had replaced Madisonian constitutional theory as a potent limit on the exercise of the federal spending power.[6]

George H. W. Bush

George Bush came to office pledging to extend the philosophy of the Reagan years in a "kinder and gentler" fashion. His years in the White House are characterized by decency, integrity, and support for public service. The milestones of his administration are generally thought to be in foreign policy and national defense and include the fall of the Soviet Union, Desert Storm, the buildup of the defense establishment, and the enhancement of the morale of the American military. In the 1988 campaign, Bush pledged that he would not raise taxes. Accordingly, massive expansion of federal spending-power programs or substantially greater outlays was not to be expected.

At the same time, the Bush years brought significant change. For example, Congress enacted and the President signed important reauthorizations of the nation's transportation and clean-air legislation. In reaching out to states on education matters, President Bush contributed to a new perspective in framing the federal role in education by pressing for national education goals. Most importantly, he promoted and signed into law the Budget Enforcement Act of 1990, which established the current framework for deficit control in federal spending.[7]

The Intermodal Surface Transportation Efficiency Act of 1991 (ISTEA) ushered in a new approach to federal aid for highway and related surface transportation spending. It was a 1990s approach to the age-old quandary about the infrastructure that began in the days of Thomas Jefferson. Indeed, the House report on the bill cited that early history in explaining the bill's provisions. That report described impressive progress over the centuries in establishing an infrastructure, but one demanding rehabilitation, repair, and renewal—a system "in jeopardy." ISTEA sought to respond through funds to complete the interstate system and effect repairs; it also sought to move the country in new directions: greater flexibility and intermodality in transportation; cross-program and cross-mission coordination; and responsiveness to globalization. Receiving states, for example, were given authority to spend some of their highway funds on mass transit. Greater emphasis was placed on safety, health, and environmental concerns.[8] The Clean Air Act, which President Bush called "the most significant air pollution legislation in our nation's history," represented a mixture of federal regulatory and financial assistance provisions, reflecting the tendency of modern legislation to invoke the commerce, as well as the spending, power.[9]

Respecting education, President Bush convened an education summit in Charlottesville, Virginia, in 1989. It brought together the nation's governors in an effort to plot strategies toward education reform and state-federal cooperation in education. The convocation launched a process that produced a document setting forth the national goals in education and an ambitious education reform initiative of the Department of Education, called America 2000. The six goals embraced key reform themes, including school readiness, high school graduation, student achievement, adult literacy, and safe schools. The strategies of renewed state-federal cooperation and national goal setting to achieve reform were to resonate in education for the balance of the decade.[10]

At the same time, after years of frustration and vacillation under Gramm-Rudman and succeeding iterations of that legislation, the nation had to confront rising budget deficits. The Omnibus Budget Reconciliation Act of 1990 attempted to address these persistent budget deficits, in part through tax increases and spending cuts, but also through a major revision of the 1974 congressional budget-control legislation. The revision took the form of the Budget Enforcement Act of 1990 (BEA). It introduced several new and important concepts: statutory limitations (or caps) on discretionary spending and a pay-as-you-go approach to entitlement or mandatory spending. Both of these mechanisms have imposed structural limitations on the extent to which the spending power may be exercised to address national problems or priorities. In an engaging postpresidential book of letters and other writings, President Bush characterized this legislation as "a major step in the direction of getting our deficit under control."[11]

BILL CLINTON

Bill Clinton's administration gives us a window on the modern exercise of the spending power, putting in bold relief its aspirations and its tensions. Clinton forcefully articulated a public investment strategy, posited on that power, to achieve progress in a range of critical areas of federal interest. They included education, income maintenance, health security, and crime prevention, to name but a few. He initiated a sweeping reauthorization of the nation's federal elementary and secondary programs in a way that tied them more closely to state reform efforts. The most significant revision of the nation's welfare programs became law during his administration. While his administration's attempt at massive change in the nation's health system was rejected by Congress, discrete health care reforms did become law. Crime prevention was the subject of new grant programs. The Earned Income Tax Credit was enhanced, and a new national service corps was established. However, Clinton's most significant contribution to prudent General Welfare Clause application may have been fiscal rather than programmatic. Large deficits of the previous years declined on his watch. In its last years, the nation achieved budget surpluses. Along with these accomplishments, the Clinton administration also left the nation with an unfinished agenda and a set of grave challenges in its pursuit of the general welfare that will occupy it in the twenty-first century.

Toward the end of his first term, Clinton sought to tie his administration's domestic objectives to three fundamental values: opportunity, responsibility, and community. His opportunity strategy was in turn driven by three basic objectives: "first, to put the nation's economic house in order so our businesses can prosper and create new jobs; second, to expand trade in American products all around the globe; and third, to invest in our people so that they all have the tools they need to succeed in the Information Age." Sharply reducing the deficits was a key strategy for achieving the first objective.

E. J. Dionne, in describing the administration's priorities, takes into account their embrace of public investment as well as their internal tensions: "The president had three priorities on taking office, and they were at odds with one another. He needed to cut the fiscal deficit. He needed to reduce the 'social' or 'investment' deficit—that is, to spend considerable sums on social programs and infrastructure improvements.... And he needed to close the 'fairness deficit' by providing some relief to a middle class that felt it was bearing an increasing share of the government's fiscal burden."[12]

The factors that generated fiscal deficit reduction in the Clinton years are the subject of dispute. President Clinton attributed it to the administration's 1993 decision to press for higher taxes for the highest income taxpayers and other reforms in that year's reconciliation legislation. The initiative passed narrowly. Interest rates declined on the expectation that budget deficits would decrease. Economic growth was stimulated. The resulting increased tax revenues helped to lower and then eliminate the deficit, despite continuing public investment in the later years of the administration. Others urge that the surplus was achieved through economic growth resulting from strict monetary and inflation control by the Federal Reserve Board, coupled with positive results from the 1990 reconciliation legislation. Causation aside, the transformation from a deficit to a surplus environment that occurred during Clinton's watch (and to which he contributed) had a positive influence on the exercise of the spending power in the 1990s. It demonstrated that a reasonable level of public investment actually could be accompanied by budget discipline. That said, budgetary considerations continued to constitute a far more powerful brake upon the exercise of the spending power in the 1990s than had constitutional considerations in the early part of the nineteenth century.[13]

One key component of the Clinton-investment-in-people strategy was the use of federal education funds (and the spending power authority to formulate reasonably related grant conditions) to encourage and strongly leverage state level education reform. In 1994, the Goals 2000: Educate America Act provided states and school districts with funds to encourage the adoption of challenging state standards, which Clinton called "clear standards for what we expect our teachers to teach and our children to know." The Improving America's Schools Act, enacted that year, made it a grant condition that states participating in Title I (the largest of the elementary and secondary programs) adopt such standards. By the close of the administration, all had done so and were in the process of developing aligned assessments and related accountability measures, another condition of the law.

The standards-based strategy was coupled with the adoption of specific, targeted spending-power programs to achieve related education goals such as class size reduction, smaller learning communities, after-school services, (21st Century Community Learning Centers), reading excellence, teacher training, and technology infusion. More traditional targeted programs, such as Bilingual Education and Indian Education, were reauthorized in light of the overarching goal of standards-based reform. As a useful counterweight to the addition of categorical programs, the administration encouraged cross-program integration and greater flexibility through such mechanisms as consolidated planning (submission of one state plan governing a multiplicity of programs) and authority to waive statutory and regulatory conditions determined to impede the achievement of program goals.

By the end of Clinton's tenure, measurable educational progress was recorded in terms of such indicators as mathematics achievement scores and enhanced high-school and college graduation rates, but achievement gaps between affluent and nonaffluent students persisted, posing a profound challenge for education policy makers in the new century. The progress that was made reflected the enduring commitment of Education Secretary Richard Riley, who gave the department extraordinarily caring, dedicated, and effective leadership during President Clinton's tenure.[14]

The income maintenance mission embraces a group of entitlement programs that (in addition to welfare) constitute the nation's safety net for the economically disadvantaged: Supplemental Security Income (SSI), Food Stamps, and the Earned Income Tax Credit. These Clinton bolstered. However, the greatest transformation in the Clinton years impacted the welfare program. The Personal Responsibility and Work Opportunity Reconciliation Act of 1996 (PRWORA) was the primary instrument of change. It reflected the conservative philosophy of the 104th Congress that passed it. In signing this legislation, Clinton noted both its promise and its shortcomings, expressing the hope that "welfare will no longer be a political issue." He characterized it as "bipartisan" and noted that he saw it as "significantly better" than measures he had previously vetoed, in its provisions for maintenance of health care benefits for welfare recipients transitioning to work, child care, and preservation of food stamp benefits.[15]

The PRWORA converted the former Aid to Families with Dependent Children program into the current Temporary Assistance to Needy Families (TANF) program. In place of an entitlement program which generally assured AFDC recipients of monthly payments of indefinite duration, TANF provided that assistance payments must, with some specific exceptions, terminate in five years. To keep benefits, recipients were required to secure work (as defined by the state) within twenty-four months of receipt of assistance. In addition, a state receiving federal funds under the program became subject to work-participation requirements that called for increasing percentages of the welfare caseload to be engaged in work (as defined by the federal statute) if the state were to retain the full amount of its grant. In turn, states were given greater flexibility in the use of funds in the form of a block grant.[16]

In addition to the changes made through the TANF program, the PRWORA, in its Title IV, undertook to limit the participation of legal, as well as undocumented, aliens in the nation's public benefit programs. For example, permanent resident aliens, were made ineligible for SSI, TANF, and Food Stamps. Clinton expressed "deep disappointment" at certain of the changes regarding legal aliens, and he promised to work to break down bureaucratic barriers to their becoming citizens.[17]

The early results of the PRWORA have been positive, within a discrete framework. The welfare rolls have been been reduced to record low levels. On the other hand, the transition to work has not been accompanied by a broad-based movement out of poverty. The jobs acquired have generally been entry level, minimum-wage jobs that often have not enabled former recipients to sustain families and leave poverty. The child poverty rate, while substantially decreased, remains unacceptably high. Moreover, welfare reform has focused on a category of hard core recipients, beset with multiple obstacles, whose movement from welfare has been more intractable. How to convert welfare reform into a true exodus from poverty and deprivation that will permanently reduce child welfare rolls and lower the ranks of the educationally deprived remains a formidable challenge for the exercise of the General Welfare Clause.[18]

That education and welfare are two General Welfare Clause areas in which the Clinton Administration brought substantial change should not go unnoticed. Both areas, representing two great budget functions, functions 500 and 600, are key to addressing a major general-welfare problem that plagues the nation: the substantial and, in some cases, growing gaps in income security and educational attainment between the economically affluent and disadvantaged—and in some cases, between minority and nonminority populations. The effective addressing of this issue in the twenty-first century will require a creative and effective juxtaposition and coordination of federal education and income-maintenance policies.[19]

The maturation of entitlement programs such as Social Security and Medicare—which serve large, middle-class constituencies and whose funding levels are fixed by the aggregate costs of serving all eligible beneficiaries rather than by discretionary appropriations decisions—presented the Clinton administration and the nation with another dilemma: How to maintain the level of benefits provided by these programs for future recipients without incurring intolerable deficits or impairing our ability to address other key priorities? The Social Security Trust Fund, it is estimated, will be unable to provide full benefit payments at some point in the 2030s. A similar fate, but one which will occur earlier, is predicted for Medicare. In the 1990s, a number of high-level federal commissions, including the 1994 Bipartisan Commission on Entitlement Reform (Kerry-Danforth Commission), addressed these issues. While it reached no conclusions, the resulting staff report posed a number of reasonable, but profoundly unattractive choices for reform—including raising the retirement age, reducing benefit payments by modifying the benefit formula at the upper income ends of the spectrum, increasing the taxation of benefits, and raising payroll taxes.

In its later years, the Clinton Administration proposed using the increasing budget surpluses to address the problem (either by paying down the existing debt or by additions to the trust fund) in a way that would enable the country to face higher benefit outlays in the future. However, proposals for structural reforms in the program were deferred, pending the development of bipartisan consensus. Nevertheless, if substantial portions of a surplus must be used as a surrogate for true structural reform, then much less is left for change-agent, financial-assistance programs to address income and achievement gaps in the coming decades.[20] Along with their domestic policy accomplishments, the Clinton years brought largely *incremental* change to such programs, or strategies to preserve them, rather than any major new programs in previously uncovered areas, in the fashion of the New Deal or Great Society.

One key area where the administration's early quest for major transformation was itself transformed into a policy of incrementalism concerned health care. On September 23, 1993, Clinton addressed Congress, calling upon it to enact a comprehensive and transcendent reform of the nation's health care financing programs, including Medicare and Medicaid. Health security would be enhanced by reliable health coverage for all Americans through a single, portable health security card linked to a single insurance form. Universal coverage and universal participation in the system were key aspects of the proposal. After months of hearings and debate, the program dramatically failed of passage, and comprehensive, universal health care reform was declared moribund for the duration of the Clinton presidency. E. J. Dionne sees this episode as part of the "failure of reform" in the first two years of the Clinton presidency and observes that "it can be argued that the Clinton plan foundered on the one issue that is so crippling to any sort of government innovation in the 1990s: Who pays?" At later stages of the administration, individual, incremental changes, many of considerable promise, were enacted into law, including expansion of Medicaid for children and the adoption of the Children's Health Insurance Program (CHIP), designed to extend insurance coverage to the poorest children.[21]

Despite the outcome on health care, the Clinton years witnessed significant growth, innovation, and change in the exercise of the spending power as an instrument for achieving national goals in a number of areas. The president regarded his administration as a bridge to the twenty-first century. That century will confront a set of excruciatingly difficult policy challenges that the Clinton administration struggled to resolve and which it bequeathed to subsequent administrations. Among them:

- Will we be able to pursue a vigorous and effective strategy of investing in human resources and still serve our other urgent priorities without incurring unwarranted deficit spending?
- Will we be able to maintain our obligations under widely cherished entitlement programs such as Social Security and Medicare while preserving fiscal integrity and sufficient resources to meet those priorities and sustain such a strategy?
- Will we be able to continue pursuing the goals of having all children learn to challenging content standards while also leaving no children behind?
- Will we be able to end welfare dependency while moving welfare recipients into jobs that provide an adequate income?
- How can we end poverty for children and families? For populations long here and those newly arrived?
- Will we be able to continue reforming our health-security system in order to provide all Americans with access to quality health care?

That we must address these and many other questions during perilous times heightens the challenge. In so doing, continued creative and prudent exercise of the General Welfare Clause will serve us well.

VIII
Constitutionalism and National Progress: The General Welfare Clause Contribution

17

The Spending Power, the Constitutional Amendment, and the Evolving American Presidency

Is THE STORY OF SPENDING POWER, AS DESCRIBED IN THE CHAPTERS above, isolated from and unrelated to the great strands of constitutional history that have been identified by constitutional scholars of our day? How does the evolution of the General Welfare Clause fit in with the various theses that have been propounded in modern constitutional scholarship to illuminate the great constitutional "transformations" that drive our contemporary public life?

These questions can be addressed from several perspectives.

First, it seems appropriate to consider the struggle—or contest—over the scope of the General Welfare Clause within the framework of the role of the constitutional amendment in the development of the federal Constitution. Doing so prompts one to recall the both the debate over "dualist democracy" and "higher lawmaking" that is explored fully in the works of Bruce Ackerman and the role of constitutional amendment that has been studied comprehensively by David Kyvig.

Second, it is also appropriate to view the spending-power story as it relates to the evolution of the role of the American presidency in enforcing constitutional limitations. That role has evolved from defender of the Constitution against the inroads of constitutionally questionable spending legislation to that of promoter of spending programs thought essential to national progress within a constitutional framework encompassing the Hamiltonian vision of the spending power.

These two perspectives are interrelated. The evolving stance of the American presidency with regard to the scope of the spending power has been central to a determination of whether that power shall be defined by express constitutional revision or by continuing legislative application and judicial interpretation.

"Dualist Democracy" and the Second Constitution

The role of the constitutional amendment in the structure of American democracy has been comprehensively and provocatively dealt with in Bruce Ackerman's set of works entitled *We the People*. The first volume, *Foundations*, explores the concept of "dualist democracy," in contrast to a number of conflicting theses. In brief, "dualism" supposes a two-track lawmaking system. "Normal lawmaking" takes place when an administration successful at the polls assumes responsibility for the machinery of government and produces, in conjunction with Congress, the body of statutes and regulations that constitute regular, "governmental" lawmaking within the framework of the prevailing constitutional norm. "Higher lawmaking," in its classic mode, occurs when a transcendent popular movement results in a formal amendment to the Constitution pursuant to its Article V procedures. Under our system, existing rights are not protected (or "entrenched") against higher order change. In theory, the Constitution could be amended to retract the First Amendment. If properly adopted, such an amendment would not be unconstitutional. "Higher lawmaking," accompanied and spurred by popular movements, has occurred rarely; the Founding, Reconstruction (and the Fourteenth Amendment it produced), and the New Deal were transcendent periods of higher lawmaking by the people.[1]

Various aspects of the spending-power story can be related powerfully to Ackerman's conception. Although they did not speak of "dualism" or "dualist democracy" in the above described terms, the major players in the early period of the General Welfare Clause contest implicitly embraced it. Madison argued that the Constitution framed in Philadelphia could not support a broad reading of the General Welfare Clause's spending power unconstrained by the enumerated powers. Jefferson joined him in advocating that position. For Madison and Jefferson, only an express constitutional amendment could expand the scope of the clause. To apply the spending power broadly in the absence of such an amendment was to transform the Constitution fundamentally from a government of limited powers to a government of indefinite powers—without a formal mark of approval from the people. This, for both Virginians, was rank heresy.

At the same time, both founders contemplated that transformation as acceptable and even desirable from a *policy* perspective, *if* accompanied by such an amendment formally adopted under the procedures set forth in the Constitution. They exhorted the legislature to propose such an amendment for ratification by the states. The people could alter their scheme, as long as they followed the proper "higher lawmaking" process, to use Ackerman's term. Madison reinforced this precept with the Bonus Bill veto of 1817, arguably a dramatic affirmation of "dualist democracy." In his 1830 letter to Andrew Stevenson, Madison argued that reading the Constitution in the broad fashion of Hamilton was akin to embracing a different or "second" Constitution.

During the succeeding presidency, that of Monroe, a founder who originally agreed with Jefferson and Madison, it became a "moral certainty," as John Quincy Adams put it, that such an amendment would not be forthcoming. The votes were not there for congressional action under Article V, proposing to the states an amendment for ratification. Monroe reluctantly turned to a compromise interpretation embodied in his Monroe Memorandum that partially accepted the Hamiltonian reading of the clause. While denying that Congress possessed a general power to construct and control a national system of internal improvements, Monroe maintained that the General Welfare Clause conferred upon Congress the authority to *appropriate* funds to the states for the purpose of constructing and repairing such improvements. This compromise was seized upon explicitly by John Quincy Adams and later, implicitly, by Lincoln to effect the constitutional transformation inherent in the broad reading of the spending power without a constitutional amendment. These presidents acted on such a view of the General Welfare Clause, signing internal-improvement and other spending-power legislation without waiting for the formal amendment that Jefferson and Madison advocated.

Following the Civil War, Reconstruction-era Republican presidents urged on Congress spending power legislation, notably in education. They defended its constitutionality on the basis of the General Welfare Clause or prior precedent, without calling for a constitutional amendment. Theodore Roosevelt advocated the application of the spending power to such matters as conservation and energy development; Wilson would have extended it to health care and applied it to vocational education. The New Deal Social Security Act cases decided by the Supreme Court applied the Hamiltonian view of the clause to sustain legislation on the basis of language in *United States v. Butler* approving that view, although striking down the legislation before it.[2]

One way to look at this evolution is through a "dualist" perspective. Hamilton, Monroe (in part, respecting mere appropriation), Adams, Story, and Lincoln thought (or acted as if) no amendment to the Constitution was needed to apply the spending power to a broad range of indefinite, "general welfare" purposes. The original Constitution crafted by the founders in 1787 explicitly provided for a broad spending power. To argue otherwise was to convert the General Welfare Clause into a "tautology," as Justice Roberts put it in *Butler*: language to authorize spending solely to implement the *enumerated* powers was superfluous. It was already inherent in the Necessary and Proper Clause. Accordingly, to confine the spending power as Madison proposed was to read the General Welfare Clause *out* of the Constitution, in effect to engage in "higher lawmaking" without license. Whether or not the framers specifically debated the implications of a broad reading of the clause, the original Constitution that emanated from the framing provided for it on its face. "We the People" spoke as to the spending power through Article I, section 8, clause 1 of the original Constitution of 1787. The Anti-Federalists plainly told the people what that clause meant (or could mean). The *people* ratified it with that knowledge. It was then that "higher lawmaking" took place with respect to the spending power.

More "higher lawmaking" via the amendment process was neither needed nor appropriate to confirm its broad meaning, as first announced by Hamilton. "Normal lawmaking" sufficed. So opined John Quincy Adams in 1825. For precedent, he relied upon the "normal lawmaking" that had preceded in the form of the legislation that had authorized the Louisiana Purchase and the Cumberland Road project. Joseph Story's effort was to ensure that the General Welfare Clause not be read "out" of the Constitution, rather than to advocate its insertion into the Constitution by amendment. "Normal lawmaking" confirmed his conclusion and confronted the Court with an impressive body of legislative precedent when it came to address the issue in 1936. It was this thesis that the "Old Court," embraced (at least partially) in *Butler*, relying for authority on the reading of Marshall's collaborator, the nationalist Story, to affirm the interpretation of Alexander Hamilton, the major proponent of "indefinite" legislative authority at the Philadelphia Convention. This evolutionary process has been the foundation upon which the 1930s judicial decisions and the New Deal, Great Society and post–Great Society modern legislative records have been built.[3]

17: THE SPENDING POWER, THE CONSTITUTIONAL AMENDMENT

What if—for the sake of argument—this reading of the Constitution is not wholly acceptable? After all, it does not fully answer Madison's central political point: the Philadelphia framers, wary of central authority, would not knowingly have endowed Congress with the vast and indefinite power that the General Welfare Clause, as interpreted by Hamilton, affords. Is the transformation from the Madison vision of the spending power in "Federalist No. 41" a violation of, or a departure from, "dualist democracy"? It seems reasonable to envisage a major evolution in constitutional thinking effected by usage, application and ultimately judicial interpretation—effected not by amendment but by presidents and Congresses working together to enact legislation. Is this an instance of "We the People" operating, not in one dramatic surge, as in the case of the adoption of the Fourteenth Amendment during Reconstruction or the New Deal experience but in a long continuum that spanned what Ackerman calls the Early, Middle, and Modern Republics? Can we accept this process of change by application and interpretation over a long span of time as a species of "higher lawmaking" and an exercise of "dualist democracy"? After all, the New Deal revolution was not codified by formal constitutional amendment but is, nonetheless, seen as a species of "higher lawmaking."[4]

This, coupled with the relevant "higher lawmaking" in the New Deal era, seems to represent a plausible alternative explanation of the history of the spending power and an alternative basis upon which to support the choice of Hamilton's theory, as reinforced by Story, in *Butler*, as well as the results in the Social Security Act cases. The Madisonian insistence on a formal amendment to signal the People's assent to the transformation of the original constitutional understanding (as expressed in "Federalist No. 41") is perfectly understandable from his perspective. But his insistent advocacy confronted the iron resistance of Congress to such a course. That in turn prompted John Quincy Adams's observation about moral certainty. Madison's veto of the Bonus Bill, while dramatic, did not move Congress to propose an amendment; and Monroe too was forced to compromise. To grow, the country needed—and still needs—roads; the federal fisc was—and is—the most logical means to help pay for them. Seen in this light, Monroe's compromise was an imperative.

The advent of progressive presidents who regarded internal improvement legislation as valid without such an amendment counters and ultimately overcomes Madison's precept. This makes the presidency of John Quincy Adams, largely maligned in history, so significant in this context. Adams was a president who was willing to sign broad internal-improvement legislation essentially on the strength of the General Welfare Clause without an amendment. to the Constitution.[5] While the states'-rights oriented Jacksonians gave pause to this development, they did not eradicate it. Indeed, it was Jackson who explicitly recognized in the revealing Maysville road veto message, that the Constitution had been *transformed* from what might have been its original, "pure" intent, as reflected in the Virginia Resolutions, transformed by successive presidential approvals of road legislation—by usage and application. It was Jackson who counseled that there could be no turning back from this informal mode of constitutional transformation. It was Jackson who confirmed that the Constitution is different from the document Madison described as the "received construction" in "Federalist No. 41" and the Virginia Resolutions. John Quincy Adams in effect blessed this approach in his 1832 letter to Andrew Stevenson and elsewhere when he grounded a broad reading of the General Welfare Clause on two precedents of the nominally strict constructionist Jefferson Administration: the Louisiana Purchase and the Cumberland Road legislation. Is this "higher lawmaking"—in the dualist democracy context made, not by formal amendment but, by the processes of application and day-to-day Executive Branch and legislative interpretation, ultimately confirmed by the courts? Tentatively, yes, but only because the language of the Constitution was, on its face, *susceptible* to the application and interpretation in question. In this case "the transformative statutes that challenge the fundamentals of the preexisting regime" (the internal improvement appropriations) were not repudiated by the nineteenth century courts but became the basis for a body of legislative precedent that became institutionalized in practice and produced, to use, Jackson's phrase, "a well-settled acquiescence of the people and the confederated authorities in particular constructions."[6]

In sum, "dualism" suggests alternative bases to support the Court's decision in the Social Security Act cases affirming the breadth of the spending clause. On the one hand, we can accept Hamilton's explanation in the *Report on Manufactures*: the framers deliberately intended to use the General Welfare Clause to afford a medium of broad flexibility in order to permit the Republic effectively to address unanticipated problems—education, manufacturing subsidies, agricultural needs. This understanding was incorporated into the Constitution as ratified. It is reflected in the plain language of the document which is the best evidence of its original intent.[7] For this author, there is substantial evidence to support that thesis.

On the other hand, we can recognize that there is no reliable original intent with respect to the issue. The framers never debated the matter and never arrived at an informed consensus as to the true meaning of the General Welfare Clause. Some, including Hamilton, Morris, and, probably, Wilson, embraced the broad reading; Madison obviously did not. Washington's policy recommendations were in keeping with a broad reading, although he did not indulge in constitutional interpretation. Sherman's vision is ambiguous; during ratification, he paraphrased the clause in a way that is consistent with Story's reading. The best that can be said is that the framers, deliberately or unconsciously, left a vague formulation that permitted future generations to make their mark. The collective action of the framing and succeeding generations in creating a body of legislative precedents (such as the Cumberland road appropriations) that depended on a broad reading constituted a legally supportable foundation that permitted Jackson—notwithstanding his states' rights perspective—to sign internal improvement legislation to his liking (national rather than "local," significant, and fiscally prudent) and thus outspend his predecessors. Arguably, this is "dualist democracy" at work.[8]

The formal interpretive work of the Court in explicating the scope of the Clause in *Butler* and in applying that thesis in the Social Security Act cases is consistent with both the plain meaning analysis that the Court used and with the long continuum of "informal" "higher lawmaking" posed above. David Kyvig has deplored the failure of the nation to seize this opportunity and convert the principles of the New Deal revolution into an express constitutional amendment. Such an amendment might have included a restatement of the broad spending power announced in *Butler* and the Social Security Act cases. Both Ackerman and Kyvig painstakingly explain why Franklin Roosevelt passed up the opportunity to press Congress to propose such an amendment and instead opted for the famous court-packing scheme. In a sense, such an amendment would have added clarity and perhaps softened the perennial, modern debate over the size and role of government.[9]

As to whether the scope and impact of the General Welfare Clause would be defined through formal "higher lawmaking" pursuant to the Constitution's Article V procedures, the Supreme Court drove the agenda. By sustaining the constitutionality of the New Deal's key Social Security Act programs under that clause in *Helvering* and *Steward Machine Co.*, the Court effectively halted whatever momentum existed for an Article V solution. Ackerman has observed: "in the American system, *the Supreme Court largely determines whether a constitutional revolution will be codified in Article Five terms.* Only if the Justices refuse to recognize the legitimacy of a transformation do the President and Congress have an incentive to take the Article Five path." Whether the Court that rendered the Social Security Act decisions was moved by the 1936 election or intimidated by the 1937 court-packing plan is a matter beyond the scope of this study. What is important for spending-power purposes is that the Court affirmed the "transformation" in the clause that Hamilton announced, if transformation it was, and applied the clause so transformed to uphold a set of major programs under its authority. In so doing, the Court insulated the process from Article V procedures. In so doing, the Court also legitimized the constitutional change in the General Welfare Clause that had resulted from successive internal improvement enactments. That process, as well as the Court's work in the 1930s, can be taken as elements of higher lawmaking as it relates to the spending power.[10]

This result was consistent with the history of the clause. Since at least 1806, the people, through their representatives had been earnestly invited to submit the question of the clause to those procedures by submitting an appropriate amendment to the states for ratification. The invitation had been delivered, eloquently and frequently, by presidents who had husbanded the revolution, Jefferson, Madison, Monroe and, later, by Jackson and his Democratic antebellum successors. Congress had rejected the invitation. That rejection had insured that the resolution of constitutional issues under the clause would take place through "normal lawmaking" procedures, interpretation by Executive Branch officers (Monroe, John Quincy Adams, Jackson and, ultimately, Lincoln) and application through successive, legislative enactment. The Court, by its 1937 decisions, gave its rather tardy blessing to the process by upholding major programs that affected a broad swath of the population. Those decisions came in the wake of a national election that, while it may not have represented a mandate for particular programs, strongly suggested the people approved the direction in which the New Dealers were taking the country. Thus "higher lawmaking," in the 1937 sense of that term, was part of a constitutional revolution and confirmed the work of "normal lawmaking." At least, this is one vantage point by which to view the effect of "dualist democracy" on the development of one of the most significant powers in the legislative arsenal. That there are many others is not to be doubted.[11]

This alternative higher lawmaking process for the General Welfare Clause can thus be summarized as follows in dualist terms: The transformation is Hamilton's interpretation in the *Report on Manufactures*. It was instantly recognized as such by Madison. Subsequent application and enactment institutionalized it. Popular mobilization and assent, however, occured only when Roosevelt and his New Dealers applied the transformed clause to support their invention and enactment of Social Security. The people swiftly affirmed it (and much more) in the transcendent election of 1936. In sustaining that application together with the programs in question, in *Steward Machine Co.* and *Helvering*, the Court obviated the need for resort to Article V. Today's massive popular support for Social Security is reinforcing. Whether all this would reconcile Madison to what he called the "second Constitution," as authorized by "a continued course of practical sanctions," is a matter for historical speculation.

When the Supreme Court approves a transformative statute (or interpretation), modern higher lawmaking affords no formal role to the state legislature, a role that it would otherwise play if Article V procedures were employed. A counterweight to this consideration, in the case of the spending power, was that states did not generally oppose the application of the General Welfare Clause to the Social Security Act programs in the 1930s litigation. In *Steward Machine Co.*, Cardozo noted that Alabama was not complaining about participating in the program. Moreover, since 1937, to my knowledge, no serious attempt has been mounted under Article V to reverse the Social Security decisions or Hamilton's reading of the General Welfare Clause, as affirmed by the Court. The states, which benefit from that reading profoundly through various forms of cooperative federalism, do not wish to expunge it. Moreover, if they wish to limit its reach, there are avenues available short of Article V, including the budget, appropriation, and reauthorization processes, as well as judicial review of particular applications. Nevertheless, these considerations raise concerns about the degree to which "modern" higher lawmaking can serve as a true surrogate for the classic form for all segments of the political spectrum. They make more attractive

Story's straightforward explanation, in 1833, of the General Welfare Clause. The plain language should be taken to mean what it says: Congress has the authority to tax (and spend) in order to provide for the common defense and general welfare of the United States. That authority is the product of the higher lawmaking that accompanied the founding.[12]

The impetus for constitutional amendment is the prospect of fundamental change that can not otherwise be accomplished. An amendment today that merely codified the Stone-Cardozo reading of the General Welfare Clause would preserve the status quo but effect no significant change; it would, moreover, revive a contest long since resolved on the basis of a number of reasonable theories sketched above. Had *Butler* announced that the spending power was limited to funding the enumerated powers rather than any "general welfare" purpose, the occasion for amendment would have been starkly presented. The time for an amendment regarding the General Welfare Clause passed; if one is to come in future generations, it will be in the context of an attempt to broaden the reach of that clause, not to confirm its present scope.[13]

With or without formal constitutional sanction through Article V amendment, the New Deal period provided the driving force for applying the spending power boldly to solve national problems and move the federal government into social insurance and income maintenance in a way that has fundamentally transformed its role, while simultaneously paving the way for later entrance into health, elementary and secondary education, housing, environmental protection, and other prime areas of national responsibility. In this view, the spending-power story is a distinct chapter in constitutional history and is an integral and important part of that history. It has been the instrument for conferring the "blessings," to use Edmund Randolph's term during the framing, at various stages of that history.[14]

THE ROLE OF THE PRESIDENCY: CONSTITUTIONAL SHIELD OR PROGRAM SWORD

The history of the spending power also represents an important chapter in the transformation of the role of the president and the presidency. It marks the evolution of the American president from defender of the Constitution against perceived legislative encroachment to promoter of legislation as a proper exercise of long accepted constitutional authority. Ackerman speaks of the emergence of the "plebiscitarian" presidency, of a president elected with a mandate to implement popular causes and thereby clothed with a "programmatic vision." Franklin Roosevelt is a twentieth century model. The Lyndon Johnson of 1965 is another prime example.[15]

The spending-power story provides a vantage point for examining changes in the presidential role. During the formative years—the first eighty from the founding through Lincoln's presidency—a subtle point-counterpoint was at work. Presidents typically used the veto to defend the Constitution from derogation by activist Congresses. At the same time they also chose *not* to use the veto power and *approved* internal-improvement legislation which they had previously promoted or with which they agreed.

Jefferson urged the adoption of a constitutional amendment to authorize internal improvement, thus hinting at a veto in the absence of one, but signed the Cumberland Road legislation without such an amendment. Madison, insisting on principle, vetoed internal-improvement legislation which he had encouraged in his seventh annual message because of the absence of the constitutional amendment he had intimated was necessary. John Quincy Adams, marking a new direction, readily signed spending power legislation without an amendment. Jackson, Polk, Pierce, and Buchanan returned to the exercise of what they saw as the Constitution reinforcing internal-improvement veto. To some extent, these vetoes may have reflected a perception by the presidents in question that they, rather than the courts, had primary responsibility for constitutional enforcement, particularly when Congress refused to transmit (via Article V) the constitutional amendments they proposed.[16]

It is Lincoln who made the significant transition. Lincoln, cooperating with a Congress reflecting the new "Republican nationalism," quietly signed the kind of legislation that Buchanan vetoed. Lincoln did so on the basis of a broad reading of the spending power that he, as congressman, had affirmed in his generally ignored internal-improvement speech of 1848. Lincoln's stance was to sign such legislation, leaving to the courts the task of constitutional interpretation, a strategy that Congressman Lincoln had advocated. This approach was echoed and extended by the Reconstruction Republican presidents who follow: Grant, Hayes, Garfield, and Benjamin Harrison. They advocated, for example, education legislation to vindicate or reinforce Reconstruction protections and urged its constitutionality. They did not call for a return to the spending-power veto policies of their antebellum Democratic predecessors. Indeed, even those nineteenth-century presidents decidedly lacking in a popular mandate were inspired to embark upon programmatic presidencies. John Quincy Adams made a national program of internal improvement, in the cause of ameliorating the condition of the governed, the defining characteristic of his presidency. Rutherford B. Hayes took up the banner of federal aid to education, along with civil service reform, as the defining issues in his presidency. Both invoked the General Welfare Clause, read Hamilton's way, as their constitutional foundation.[17]

The more activist presidents in the early twentieth century, Theodore Roosevelt and Woodrow Wilson, not only declined the use of the constitutionally enforcing veto for this purpose; they actively promoted and signed spending-power legislation that implemented their vision of the Constitution as a pliable and living document.[18]

Under Franklin Roosevelt, the twentieth-century "plebiscitarian" presidency came into full bloom. It was a striking contrast to the decentralizing, veto-prone Democratic tenures of the antebellum period. Roosevelt pushed through Congress spending-power legislation in the form of the Agricultural Adjustment Act and defended it vigorously in the Court through express resort to the constitutional spending power informed by the Hamiltonian vision of the General Welfare Clause, which the Court partially adopted. He then sought, unsuccessfully, to pack the Court when, despite its agreement with Hamilton, it struck down the act. Ultimately an accord was reached when the Court applied the broadly read General Welfare Clause to uphold the New Deal's Social Security programs. The "plebiscitarian" presidency, a willing Congress and a "constitutionally revolutionized" Court then joined forces to remake the federal landscape.[19]

The stage was then set for the modern programmatic presidency, characterized by presidents who (successfully or not so successfully) pushed spending-power programs through their annual messages, interstitial addresses, and all-consuming spates of legislative drafting at the departmental level followed by active lobbying in Congress. The administrations of Truman, Eisenhower, Kennedy, Johnson, Nixon, Ford, Carter, and George H. W. Bush can be characterized, to quite varying degrees, in this way. They relied upon (or assumed) the validity of the broadly read spending power; their success was based on the extent to which their domestic programmatic agenda was adopted, even when it involved consolidating or trimming prior legislative initiatives. The "Reagan revolution" sought in some respects to stem the tide. The result, however, was the preservation and strengthening of the major New Deal innovation, Social Security, as well as other landmarks. Program consolidation and budget control were instruments of limitation; the use of the veto against program legislation was to achieve fiscal, not constitutional objectives. Indeed, the *Dole* case in 1983, recognized the continuing validity of *Helvering v. Davis* and clarified the authority of the federal government under the spending power to frame far-reaching grant conditions to which the state must adhere as a condition of program participation.[20]

The Clinton era represented the programmatic presidency in full vigor. The spending power was invoked to support multiple programmatic initiatives in the interest of expanding opportunity in an environment of declining deficits. Moreover, Clinton used the veto power imaginatively, not to limit the broad exercise of the spending power in the fashion of the Democratic past, but to induce a reluctant Congress to provide more generous authorization and/or funding for favored presidential programs.[21]

Thus, in this context, the presidential veto has evolved from an instrument to reinforce perceived constitutional limitation to an instrument for reinforcing desired programmatic goals. A somewhat different perspective, reflecting less contrast across the historical landscape can be gained by looking chronologically at another constitutional tool afforded the presidency, the annual message. A central theme connects them across presidencies: the federal government has an appropriate role in providing support for initiatives that are critical to the unification, preservation, and advancement of the United States.

With some notable exceptions, Washington and his successors used their annual messages to advance such causes as education, improvements to the infrastructure, and commercial, industrial, and agricultural growth. This was as true of the presidents who took a broad, non-Madisonian view of the constitutional scope of the spending power, as it was of those who read the Constitution narrowly but also clearly saw the unifying force of a formally sanctioned internal-improvement authority. Even presidents who wielded the veto pen demonstrated their policy support for investment programs put forth in their annual messages. As two contrasting examples: Madison's Seventh Annual Message is a sunny, progressive document advocating the unifying value of supporting internal-improvement legislation and educational institutions; Monroe's 1822 veto message was coupled with a creative and courageous legal essay designed to rationalize his later signature on legislation providing for the repair of the Cumberland Road and the initiation of surveys of other improvements to the infrastructure. The use of the annual message as a bully pulpit to promote public investment has expanded exponentially since the New Deal. In his own way, each president has employed the message to define what is meant by "the General Welfare."

18
"Perseverance"

IN JULY OF 1828, PRESIDENT JOHN QUINCY ADAMS SAILED UP THE POTOmac to officiate at the ground breaking ceremony for the Chesapeake and Ohio Canal, one of the few internal improvements that Congress allowed him. At the first try, his spade hit a stump. He took off his coat and tried again, this time with success. The assembled crowd cheered. On the way back to the White House, Adams and his fellow dignitaries partook of a "light collation." The president was asked to make a toast. Reflecting on the years of effort to authorize a canal, Adams said simply: "The Chesapeake and Ohio Canal: perseverance."[1]

The legislative adoption of a serious spending power initiative typically requires decades, if not generations. It requires, as well, a large dose of perseverance. The long path to passage of federal aid to education affords an example.

During the Constitutional Convention, Charles Pinckney of South Carolina proposed an amendment to the draft Constitution that would have authorized federal funding for "seminaries of learning." In his annual messages, George Washington proposed a national university. Presidents Jefferson and Madison recommended federal assistance for higher education. John Quincy Adams renewed Washington's plea, accompanying it with his own proposals for federal funding of scientific research. Significant national legislation did not come until Abraham Lincoln signed the Morrill Act in 1862, an important early marker in the history of federal aid to higher education based upon the spending power. It was not until 1965 that a major federal role was carved out through the adoption of broadly encompassing student-aid legislation. That legislation has been revised many times through comprehensive reauthorization measures.

Federal aid to elementary and secondary education was proposed many times before its enactment in 1965. After the Civil War, Republican presidents advocated it as an essential corollary to the voting and other civil rights afforded under the Fourteenth and Fifteenth Amendments. President Rutherford B. Hayes made the cause a centerpiece of his administration. No substantial legislation emerged, however, until the Sputnik-inspired National Defense Education Act of 1958 enacted during the Eisenhower administration was followed by the Elementary and Secondary Education Act of 1965. In signing that act, President Johnson noted its debt to the earlier efforts in the nineteenth century. Proper timing, heavy legislative majorities, bipartisanship, and strong executive leadership had finally coalesced to produce this result. Perseverance was a requirement.[2]

Today's polity sees education as a major concern at the federal level. During his dedicated and effective stewardship of the United States Department of Education from 1993 to 2001, Secretary Richard Riley maintained that, while education is the primary responsibility of the states, it is also a national priority. That principle, well reflected in the history recited above, has taken root. This is no surprise. It reflects a realization that quality education is the key to securing and maintaining our national competitiveness in a global economy and to addressing many of the national challenges that confront twenty-first century America. Enhanced training and education will permit single mothers successfully to make the difficult transition from welfare to work to economic self-sufficiency. A better educated citizenry will embrace prevention programs that conserve health care outlays. Quality education is also essential to bind a pluralistic society characterized by an increase in the numbers and percentages of children whose primary language is other than English. The productive exercise of the spending and other constitutional power in twenty-first century America demands an increasingly strengthened focus on education as a centerpiece of a set of important national priorities.[3]

Perseverance is also required to bring about positive program results. At the turn of this century, the scores of all groups in mathematics and reading had increased. SAT scores, after a period of stagnation, had risen, particularly in mathematics. At the same time, the academic achievement gap between affluent and nonaffluent student populations remains persistently wide, particularly for affected African American, Hispanic American, and Native American children. As Secretary Riley has observed, "The achievement gap is persistent and intrinsically linked to the fact that millions of our nation's children still live in poverty." The present secretary of education, Rod Paige, has pointed out:

"[T]hough our nation is blessed with many excellent schools and many excellent educators, our system is still failing too many children." Unquestionably, closing the achievement gap remains the greatest challenge facing American education and the federal programs that assist it.[4]

For those who daily confront this issue, whether stewards of federal programs, state and local administrators, or teachers on the front lines, perseverance is therefore a professional prerequisite. It is as well required of the body of federal taxpayers who must patiently pay the bills while awaiting positive results. Solid effort and commitment over succeeding generations will be necessary for the full attainment of these goals.

The issue in the twenty-first century thus becomes not whether there should be federal aid to elementary and secondary education or whether such aid has a constitutional home but how it can be most effective in closing unacceptable learning gaps while raising educational attainment standards. The core federal program, Title I of the Elementary and Secondary Education Act, aid to states for the education of educationally deprived children, is likely to remain the keystone, absorbing the bulk of the available resources and increasingly oriented toward strong accountability measures. Those resources must be supplemented and complemented by innovative new initiatives based upon the creative exercise of the spending power. A variety of approaches have been placed upon the federal statute books in recent years, which, if maintained and improved, hold promise of contributing to success, for example: insistence on high content standards and aligned assessments; expanded preschool education; high quality teacher training; smaller learning communities; content oriented after-school programs; and dual language initiatives in addition to the traditional "title" programs. They are reflected, in differing respects, both in the Improving America's Schools Act, enacted during the Clinton administration, and the No Child Left Behind Act, enacted during the administration of George W. Bush.[5]

Beyond these supplementary programs must come a realization that success in education will require increased targeting of resources on the educationally disadvantaged under a wider group of programs than those embraced within the federal educational mission. Improved education can contribute to success in other areas of federal concern such as health, housing, and income maintenance. Progress in these areas may also be essential to improved educational outcomes, particularly for the educationally disadvantaged.

Hunger and substandard housing are barriers to learning. Pervasive poverty impedes educational attainment. Health impairments block educational success. Thus, the effective implementation and delivery of food stamp and school lunch programs, housing programs, income maintenance programs such as TANF, and health insurance programs such as CHIP, are all essential to improvement in education. There is a paramount need for effective integration and collaboration on a holistic basis among a set of mutually supportive and mutually reinforcing programs posited under the General Welfare Clause, as a strategy for meeting its objectives.[6]

That a lead role in program design and implementation was assigned to the states and local school districts under the system of federal grants for educational equity and excellence was essential to its legislative establishment. Federal resources were greatly increased; federal control over curriculum and administration was prohibited. Such a role for state and local authorities is essential if achievement gaps are to be closed and higher levels of educational performance are to be attained through the application of federal resources.

Recent innovative efforts to enhance the program flexibility afforded states and greater encouragement for state initiated program integration, accomplished by legislation enacted in both the Clinton and George W. Bush administrations, reflect this central understanding. In 1994, for example, the Improving America's Schools Act introduced authority for state-level plan consolidation and authority for the administering agency to waive statutory and regulatory provisions that impeded educational progress. These provisions were carried forward (and in some respects expanded) in the No Child Left Behind Act of 2001. Cooperative federalism was the central mechanism of the spending power compromise that emerged in the early part of the nineteenth century; fostering and expanding meaningful federative partnerships, involving local, state, and federal level efforts operating under flexible legislative frameworks, can render that mechanism more effective in the twenty-first.[7]

The public works programs that John Quincy Adams promoted under the rubric of "internal improvement" during his short and troubled tenure reflect an evolution similar to that of education. The modest initiatives begun in the administration of Thomas

Jefferson to help construct a national road and later projects made under presidents who followed, including the C and O Canal, ultimately embraced transcontinental railroads, a massive interstate highway program, and airline transportation subsidies. With progress has come an inevitable set of perplexing challenges in mounting an integrated transportation system, frankly recognized in the Intermodal Surface Transportation Efficiency Act of 1991 and succeeding enactments, of which the current plight of the nation's railroads and airlines is but a part. The early quest for "internal improvement" was the immediate focus of the constitutional dispute over the scope of the spending power. Long after the resolution of that dispute, challenges in the exercise of the spending power persist, requiring the perseverance that Adams acknowledged in his toast of 1828.

President Harry Truman proposed universal health insurance in the 1940s; Medicare and Medicaid were not enacted into law until 1965, representing only a partial implementation of that proposal. The Children's Health Insurance Program (CHIP) went on the books in 1997 after the legislative failure of the far-reaching Clinton health related proposals of 1993 and 1994. Over forty million Americans remain uninsured today; the health care system is afflicted by massive problems of access, particularly for low-income Americans, and of financial viability for hosts of providers. Effectively addressing these issues through consensus-based solutions that are embraced by the vast majority of Americans, patient and provider alike, will call for large doses of patience, perseverance, and a painstaking incremental process.[8]

In confronting these challenges over the long term, we should not forget what has been achieved and conclude that the record of the spending power has been one of unmitigated waste, mismanagement, and dashed expectations. We should avoid the tendency of modern media to feature the shortfalls and bury the accomplishments on the last page. In education, while equity goals remain to be fulfilled, college completion levels have risen substantially for African Americans, Hispanic Americans, and whites, and overall are among the highest of the industrialized nations. The attainment rates of bachelor's degrees by women rose from 18 percent in 1971 to 33 percent in 1999, a profoundly important achievement in gender equity of which we should be justly proud. Federal aid has helped. Federal and state cooperation in transportation has produced an unparalleled network of interstate highways that help unite the country. While facing daunting fiscal problems, Social Security has contributed greatly to erasing the poverty that beset the elderly and today keeps out of poverty a large proportion of that population. While subject to what has been called a crisis, the nation's health-care system, in part aided by federally assisted research, has raised life expectancy in the United States to new and unprecedented levels, and Medicare and Medicaid have improved access for those covered. Maligned as they are, the nation's income-maintenance programs (Food Stamps, Temporary Assistance to Needy Families, Supplemental Security Income, and housing assistance) lift millions of the most vulnerable from poverty and for others make life more bearable. The welfare reform legislation of 1996 holds promise of new transitions for program beneficiaries. Our national charge in the coming decades will be to build upon this foundation in addressing remaining challenges within a constitutional framework that includes a recognized and long-exercised federal spending power.[9]

What is the nature of that framework? John Quincy Adams was convinced that the spending programs he proposed—roads, canals, education, scientific exploration—were within the power of Congress under the General Welfare Clause, without a constitutional amendment. On this score and others, he was much criticized. History has vindicated him.

Over 200 years of broadly encompassing spending power exercise in the Hamiltonian mode, reinforced by Story, and ultimately confirmed by now long-accepted opinions of the Supreme Court, reflect a consensus that the spending power, broadly construed, is part of our set of accepted constitutional canons. That has been accomplished without the amendment Madison and Jefferson vigorously advocated. Proposing and ratifying an explicit amendment to insert that reading into the Constitution now might serve to confuse and unsettle rather than enlighten. We in effect accept that higher lawmaking on the issue took place when the Constitution was ratified, when the practice of appropriating for internal improvement was institutionalized early in our history, or at least, when the Supreme Court affirmed the transformation in the Social Security Act cases as part of the constitutional revolution of 1937. That institutionalization is now deeply ingrained in our society, partly because of wide public support for, and reliance upon, spending power icons such as Social Security, Medicare, postsecondary education assistance, school aid, and transportation subsidies. Joseph Story's conclusion in his 1833 constitutional commentaries that the General Welfare Clause confined Congress to spending but did not confine it to spending only to implement the enumerated powers is a durable proposition of enormous importance to our national growth and progress.[10]

For the reasons stated above, a constitutional amendment to make explicit the Hamiltonian reading on which we have acted, if not since Lincoln, then surely for many generations after him, seems unnecessary, assuming continued adherence to the principles stated in *South Dakota v. Dole*, and potentially restrictive. If there is occasion for a general-welfare amendment, it would be to address the issue first implicitly posed in the Constitutional Convention by Gouverneur Morris: should Congress have the power to legislate in order "to provide for the general Welfare of the United States"? This in effect would disconnect the general-welfare language from the taxing and spending power. Presumably Congress could use it to enact spending power measures directly or to regulate for the general welfare without appropriation and without having to formulate grant conditions attached to the receipt of federal assistance to effect general-welfare policy. Congress, for example, might require equalization of school spending within a state to avoid disparities for those in property-poor areas or adoption of academic content standards in core curricula.

The advantages of such an amendment would seem to be four-fold:

- In order to proceed under the spending power, Congress must assign to a program budgetary resources always in short supply, particularly in times of national security concern. Under the contemplated amendment, Congress would not necessarily have to commit such resources in order to achieve general-welfare objectives that it could not achieve under other enumerated powers, such as the interstate commerce power.
- Under the exercise of the spending power, obtaining adherence of recipients to controversial grant conditions is always problematic and, in the case of state receipients, cannot practically be achieved through strong compliance remedies such as termination of program participation. Under the contemplated amendment, Congress could presumably gain more uniform levels of adherence through judicial action.
- Although the test applied by the Supreme Court decision in *South Dakota v. Dole* gives Congress broad latitude in framing spending power conditions, that result is deeply troubling to many observers.

Under the contemplated amendment, Congress would not have to frame a requirement as a spending-power condition.
- Congress could enact permanent legislation rather than temporary authorizing legislation subject to the vicissitudes of the reauthorization and appropriation processes to achieve general-welfare goals.[11]

Whether these advantages would be real in terms of serious gains in addressing the grave problems the nation faces is a matter beyond the scope of this work. To succeed, such an amendment would require overwhelming public support; a preponderance of the people would have to be clearly persuaded that the problems they want to solve could be successfully addressed only by vesting Congress with such broad, all-encompassing power. Such a course was rejected by the founding framers who feared that it would negate the role of the enumerated powers as a limited grant of legislative authority to Congress and would vitiate a meaningful role for states in a federal system. Constitutional commentators, political and scholarly, saw the General Welfare Clause as a limitation on the power to tax, not an independent license to Congress to regulate for the general welfare. This position was clearly taken by Madison in "Federalist No. 41," as well as by those who favored the Hamiltonian reading of the spending power, including Monroe, Adams, and Story. These statesmen recognized that reading the General Welfare Clause as an authority to regulate, unlimited by the constraints of the spending power, would be a transformation of the basic constitutional understanding. To change that understanding would require a constitutional amendment, truly a second constitution. That federalism remains an abiding value in today's America would present a formidable obstacle to the adoption of such an amendment, as would the requirement in Article V of the Constitution that three-fourths of the state legislatures must approve a constitutional amendment.

Notwithstanding the choice that Article V of the Constitution affords, it is thus unlikely that amending the General Welfare Clause to give greater authority to Congress would be embraced in the near future. Twenty-first century social-welfare legislation will most likely be formulated in the framework of Article I, section 8, clause 1, as it presently stands. Our primary challenge is thus to strengthen the effectiveness of the spending-power exercise under that authority. This can be accomplished through adherence to the principles that have characterized its evolution:

a dedication to fiscal integrity, a commitment to the practice of positive federalism, a willingness to devote adequate resources to essential or priority tasks, and a faith in the power of perseverance that John Quincy Adams invoked when he broke ground for the C and O Canal.

At the same time, we should remember that the Constitution does afford a process of formal change. Madison's veto of the Bonus Bill reminds us of that enduring choice. Even if the people did not embrace that choice in the case of the spending power, the fact that it is available should not be forgotten if, in the future, a need for a greater or different Federal role, in addition to or beyond the spending power, is seen as essential to meeting agreed-upon national goals in one or more areas embraced by that clause. In sum, if there is a lesson to be drawn from the spending power experience, it is this: the Constitution, including its Article V process, provides a wise and well-tested framework for our journey through the centuries. It is not a straitjacket (to use Theodore Roosevelt's term) precluding us from seizing opportunities for growth or progress, or from strongly confronting peril, whenever or wherever it arises. Our basic charter is a flexible instrument for pursuing both our progress and our security authorizing Congress to enlist states in the promotion of national interests within the context of federalism.[12]

Progress under the spending power will also require a holistic approach to the exercise of that power, which must be connected to a vision of "one America" as a transcendent goal. In proposing federal funding for roads and canals in his sixth annual message, Jefferson saw these improvements as opening up "new channels of communication," helping to erase "lines of separation," and serving to "cement" the Union. Despite his Bonus Bill veto, Madison saw internal improvements as "bringing and binding more closely together the various parts of our extended confederacy." Lincoln promoted a transcontinental railroad for the same purpose. Among the framers of Philadelphia, John Dickinson, a member of the Delaware delegation, perhaps put it best. Under the Constitution that embraced that power, Dickinson observed, the nation would be a "United *America*—her sons [and daughters] well prepared to defend their own happiness, and ready to relieve the misery of others...."

In nineteenth-century America, the spending power was seen as a potentially unifying force. In twentieth-century America, it has been so exercised. Social Security, Medicare, Medicaid and Food

Stamps, aid to education and many other programs have been expressions of shared responsibility for the most vulnerable in our society. More recent aspirations for racial reconciliation, the reduction of child and adult poverty, environmental renewal, and the preservation of health and social security guarantees to our senior citizens reflect the unifying "one America" theme. The tragic and horrific events of September 11, 2001, have brought in their wake the need for a heightened level of national unity and common resolve. It is to be hoped that this unity and resolve will extend to the daunting challenges that affect our common defense *and* our general welfare in ways that reinforce both. Our goal should be a United *America* overcoming obstructive division, fully reconciled, and moving from strength to strength facing the future "with candid, fearless eyes."[13]

In pursuing such an inclusive agenda, we must seize the full range of opportunities afforded by a flexibly read General Welfare Clause. We must surmount fragmentation of program and purpose in the exercise of the spending power to address effectively and creatively the issues that confront today's United America. Integrated and coordinated use of resources from a multiplicity of programs and administering agencies at federal, state, and community levels is an imperative. The myriad of related needs of the individual beneficiary must be met in a holistic way, through coordinated, unified, and consolidated application of resources on a cross-program basis.

Rooted in the origins of the nation when "internal improvements" were the major public investment demands of the federal period, the twenty-first century exercise of the spending power must be viewed from a whole-picture perspective that calls upon the collective and indispensable talents of countless separately based and separately funded public servants, both career and noncareer, striving and persevering together. In this way can we realize the full force and the full promise of the authority that the framers wisely bestowed when they granted to Congress the power to tax in order to "provide for the common Defence and general Welfare of the United States."

Appendix

The Constitution, Article I, Section 8

* * *

Section 8. The Congress shall have Power To lay and collect Taxes, Duties, Imposts and Excises, to pay the Debts and Provide for the common Defence and general Welfare of the United States; but all Duties, Imposts and Excises shall be uniform throughout the United States;

To borrow Money on the credit of the United States;

To regulate Commerce with foreign Nations, and among the several States, and with the Indian Tribes;

To establish an uniform Rule of Naturalization, and uniform Laws on the subject of Bankruptcies throughout the United States;

To coin Money, regulate the Value thereof, and of foreign Coin, and fix the Standard of Weights and Measures;

To provide for the Punishment of counterfeiting the Securities and current Coin of the United States;

To establish Post Offices and post Roads;

To promote the Progress of Science and useful Arts, by securing for limited Time to Authors and Inventors the exclusive Right to their respective Writings and Discoveries;

To constitute Tribunals inferior to the supreme Court;

To define and punish Piracies and Felonies committed on the high Seas, and Offences against the Law of Nations;

To declare War, grant Letters of Marque and Reprisal, and make Rules concerning Captures on Land and Water;

To raise and support Armies, but no Appropriation of Money to that Use shall be for a longer Term than two Years;

To provide and maintain a Navy;

To make Rules for the Government and Regulation of the land and naval Forces;

To provide for calling forth the Militia to execute the Laws of the Union, suppress Insurrections and repel Invasions;

To provide for organizing, arming, and disciplining, the Militia, and for governing such Part of them as may be employed in the Service of the United States, reserving to the States respectively, the Appointment of the Officers, and the Authority of training the Militia according to the discipline prescribed by Congress;

To exercise exclusive Legislation in all Cases whatsoever, over such District (not exceeding ten Miles square) as may, by Cession of Particular States, and the Acceptance of Congress, become the Seat of the Government of the United States, and to exercise like Authority over all Places purchased by the Consent of the Legislature of the State in which the Same shall be, for the Erection of Forts, Magazines, Arsenals, dock-Yards, and other needful Buildings;—And

To make all Laws which shall be necessary and proper for carrying into Execution the foregoing Powers, and all other Powers vested by this Constitution in the Government of the United States, or in any Department or Officer thereof.

Notes

Introduction

1. See chapters 2 and 4, below.
2. *United States v. Butler*, 297 U.S. 1 (1936); *Helvering v. Davis*, 301 U.S. 619 (1937).
3. James Madison, *Notes of Debates in the Federal Convention of 1787 Reported by James Madison*, Bicentennial edition (New York: W.W. Norton, 1987), 7–8. (hereinafter cited as "Madison's *Notes*").
4. Madison's *Notes*, 7–10, 8, 13, 17–19. (Madison's Preface; Madison's post-convention recollections as to the origins of the convention); Lance Banning, *The Sacred Fire of Liberty: James Madison and the Founding of the Federal Republic* (Ithaca: Cornell University Press, 1995), 111–91, provides a study of Madison's contribution to the formulation of the Constitution. Madison's reference to the importance of the tax issue in the framing of the Constitution is reinforced in Roger H. Brown, *Redeeming the Republic: Federalists, Taxation and the Origins of the Constitution* (Baltimore: Johns Hopkins University Press, 1993), 11–50.
5. Madison's *Notes*, 29–33 (Randolph's resolutions); *Records of the Federal Convention of 1787*, ed. Max Farrand, 4 vols. (New Haven: Yale University Press, 1966) (hereinafter cited as *Records*) 1:15–28. Randolph's description of the "blessings" is found in *Records*, 1:24, 26 (McHenry's account). Madison's contribution to the preparation of the Virginia resolutions is discussed in Banning, *The Sacred Fire of Liberty*, 111–37. See Madison's *Notes*, 30–31 (resolutions 2–5); 31–32 (resolutions 6 and 9); See Catherine Drinker Bowen, *Miracle in Philadelphia: The Story of the Constitutional Convention, May to September, 1787* (Boston: Little, Brown and Company, 1966), 32–39. Bowen accepts the conclusion that the Virginia plan was the result of a committee composed of various members of the Virginia delegation to which Madison contributed substantially.
6. Madison's *Notes*, 35; *Records*, 34 (Morris, Mason, emphasis in the original); Bowen, *Miracle*, 41–53, (federal-national distinction). For Justice O'Connor's understanding, see *New York v. United States*, 112 Sup. Ct. 2408, 2422 (1992): "In the end, the Convention opted for a Constitution in which Congress would exercise its legislative authority directly over individuals rather than over States; for a variety of reasons, it rejected the New Jersey Plan in favor of the Virginia Plan."
7. Madison's *Notes*, 35–36; 44–45; *Records*, 1:30–31, Journal.
8. Madison's *Notes*, 43–44, May 31; 112–17, June 13. Madison notes a "silent affirmative nem. con.," indicating unanimity and no controversy, on the issue of the transfer of the powers of the Confederation Congress to the new Con-

gress under the Constitution. *Records,* 1:228–29, Journal) (sixth resolution as adopted relating to powers of the national legislature).

9. Madison's Notes, 117–21; *Records,* 1:241–47. Background on the New Jersey plan is found in Bowen, *Miracle,* 104–15; Christopher Collier and James Lincoln Collier, *Decision in Philadelphia: The Constitutional Convention of 1787* (New York: Ballantine Books, 1987), 136–45; Max Farrand, *The Framing of the Constitution of the United States,* (New Haven: Yale University Press, 1913), 84–90.

10. James Wilson sharply criticized the tax provisions in the New Jersey plan because the taxing power would be in an unicameral legislature without proportional representation. Madison's *Notes,* 124–27 (June 16 debate). The "licentiousness" of the people is considered in Bowen, *Miracle,* 47–49 and Gordon Wood's work on the background of the revolutionary and constitutional period, *The Creation of the American Republic, 1776–1787,* (New York: W.W. Norton, 1969). Madison's *Notes,* 121–29 and *Records* 1:248–80 contain a full account of the important June 16 debate on the New Jersey resolutions, including notes by both Hamilton and Wilson. See Brown, *Redeeming the Republic,* 22–31.

11. The Hamilton sketch is recapitulated in Madison's *Notes,* 129–39. An analysis of the speech is found in Bowen, *Miracle,* 108–15; Collier and Collier, *Decision,* 76–86, and Forrest McDonald, *Alexander Hamilton: A Biography,* (New York : W. W. Norton, 1982), 99–105. Hamilton seemed to backpedal from his ultranational position on the day following his June 18 speech: "He had not been understood yesterday. By an abolition of the States, he meant that no boundary could be drawn between the National & State Legislatures; that the former must therefore have *indefinite authority."* Madison's *Notes,* 152 (emphasis added). Hamilton's own outline of the speech is found in *Records,* 1:304–10.

12. Madison's *Notes,* 148–54; *Records,* 1:312–13, Journal (vote on New Jersey resolutions); see also Madison's *Notes,* 140–48 (Madison's speech that preceded the vote).

13. Ibid., 154–302.

14. Madison's *Notes,* 160–61 (June 20 debate; Roger Sherman's speech). For a portrait of Sherman, see Bowen, *Miracle,* 91–103; Dorothy Horton McGee, *Framers of the Constitution* (New York, Dodd, Mead & Company, 1968), 90.

15. Madison's *Notes,* 213–15 (Madison's speech before the vote); 217–18 (June 29 vote); 218–19 (Ellsworth's speech of June 29, proposing equal vote for each state in Senate as a compromise); 220–22 (Wilson's speech of June 30); 222–23 (Ellsworth's response); 223–25 (Madison's response to Ellsworth); 231–37 (July 2 vote). See also *Records,* 1:460–61; 509–10, Journal. A discussion of the background of the July 2 vote and of Sherman's capacity for the art of compromise is provided in Collier and Collier, *Decision,* 119–35; 166–72. Sherman's first proposal of the compromise on June 11 is recorded in Madison's *Notes,* 98.

16. Madison's *Notes,* 226–27, June 30.

17. Madison's *Notes,* 237–45 (report of the Gerry committee); *Records,* 1:522–23 Yates (notes on the proceedings of the committee and the Franklin compromise).

18. Madison's *Notes,* July 6, 249–50 (Wilson's observations); 251 (Franklin's observations); *Records,* 1:589–91 (Vote of July 12); Madison's *Notes,* 282–88 (July 13. Direct taxation to be proportional to representation); *Records,* 2:13–15, Journal, July 16 (vote on Connecticut Compromise); Madison's *Notes,* 297–98.

19. Madison's *Notes,* 298–99 (debate and vote on sixth resolution, powers of legislature). The general welfare provision in the Articles of Confederation is

found in Farrand, *The Framing of the Constitution of the United States*, 216 (Appendix). It provided that all charges for war and other expenses "incurred for the common defence or general welfare" allowed by Congress would be "defrayed" from a common treasury. If this was regarded as a general spending power, it was presumably embraced within the sixth Randolph resolution and implicitly adopted when that resolution was approved by the committee of the whole and the Convention. Roger Sherman's effort was to make it explicit. See chapter 1, below.

20. Madison's Notes, 298–99 (July 16 debate on rest of sixth resolution); 303–5 (Supremacy Clause); 305–6 (Luther Martin's motion, his version of the supremacy clause as a substitute for the authority in Congress to negative state laws originally proposed in the sixth Randolph resolution). See Banning, *Sacred Fire of Liberty*, 147–48.

21. Madison's *Notes*, 302–3 (Sherman's July 17 proposal, emphasis added); 379–85 (finally adopted resolutions of July 26); *Records*, Journal, 2:21 (Sherman's motion); 2:116–18, 128 (reference to Committee of Detail).

Chapter 1. The Framing of the General Welfare Clause

1. Madison's *Notes*, 385–96 (quoted language is at 386, 388, 392); *Records*, 2:176–90 (text of the August 6 draft of the Constitution).
2. Madison's *Notes*, 389–90. The formula was based on the ratio that had obtained under the Confederation government. The Supremacy Clause had made binding on the courts all acts of the Congress, notwithstanding anything in the constitutions or laws of the state, thus curing the defect that had been contained in the original formulation offered by Luther Martin. Madison's *Notes*, 305–6; see Brown, *Redeeming the Republic*, 197–99 (limitation on states designed to protect federal taxing power and prevent state tax-related reliefs).
3. See Banning, *Sacred Fire of Liberty*, 161: "Clearly, Madison, . . . as he insisted later in his life, had no intention of confiding an indefinite extent of legislative power to the reconstructed Congress. After the report of the Committee of Detail, he proved, in fact, to be the meeting's most consistent advocate of strict, though full, enumeration."
4. Madison's *Notes*, 466 (Martin–Wilson colloquy); 466–69 (debate on taxes on exports); *Records*, 2:303 (Journal); 308 (Madison); 311 (McHenry).
5. Madison's *Notes*, 477; *Records* , 2:321–22, Journal (Madison's proposals). Banning characterizes the August proposals as "far from extensive." Madison's "attempt to add them can be seen more reasonably as one of many indications that he wished to leave as little as he could to implication." See *Sacred Fire of Liberty*, 161.
6. Madison's *Notes*, 478; *Records*, 2:321–22, Journal (Madison and Pinckney proposals).
7. See text below at chapters 2, 4, 6, and 8.
8. Madison's *Notes*, 487–88; *Records*, 2: 334–37, Journal (Morris cabinet proposals).
9. Madison's *Notes*, 494–95 (committee report); 498–502 (tax on exports debate).
10. See Madison's *Notes*, 503–8. A general discussion of the slave trade issue, concluding that the Convention's failure to deal more forcefully with this issue

and limit the extension of slavery was its greatest shortcoming is found in Collier and Collier, *Decision,* 183–204.

11. Madison's *Notes,* 509; *Records,* 2:366–67, Journal, Aug. 22 (Rutledge Committee report, spending power provision).

12. Madison's *Notes,* 509; *Records,* 2:367.

13. Madison's *Notes,* 511; *Records,* 2:368 (postponement of decision on Rutledge committee report).

14. Madison's *Notes,* 511–512; *Records,* 2:368 (August 22 debate on debts).

15. Madison's *Notes,* 519; *Records* 2:382 (debts); Madison's *Notes,* 517; *Records,* 2:381–82, Journal (Supremacy Clause, debts).

16. Madison's *Notes,* 519–522; *Records,* 2:399 (Butler complaint).

17. Madison's *Notes,* 528–30; *Records,* 2:408, Journal.

18. Madison's *Notes,* 530; Records, 2:408, Journal (Sherman's August 25 General Welfare Clause proposal).

19. For further background on Roger Sherman, see McGee, *Framers of the Constitution,* 90. See also Bowen, *Miracle,* 93. On the Connecticut-South Carolina coalition, see Collier and Collier, *Decision,* 183–204.

20. Madison's *Notes,* 530; *Records,* 2:408, 412 (disposition of Sherman's motion). See also Madison's *Notes,* 533 (uniform duties); 540 (Sherman's report on uniformity).

21. Madison's *Notes,* 569; *Records,* 2:473 (August 31 reference to Committee on Unfinished Parts). Hamilton's role toward the end of the Convention is described in *Records,* 3:75, his letter of Aug. 28, 1787, to Rufus King. Hamilton was disappointed in the overall result of the Convention's work but was prepared to support it as a preferable alternative to the existing confederation government. He so observed in the debate of September 6, the day of his return to the Convention. *Records,* 2:524–25; M. E. Bradford, *Founding Fathers, Brief Lives of the Framers of the United States Constitution* (Lawrence: University Press of Kansas, 1994), 120 (Carroll). An account of Carroll's role may be found in Sister Mary Geiger, *Daniel Carroll, A Framer of the Constitution* (Washington, D.C.: Catholic University of America Press, 1943), 120–46. Carroll supported the Constitution as "the best form of government which ever has been offered to the world." Ibid., 141.

22. Madison's *Notes,* 569 (September 1 report of Brearley Committee, Committee on Unfinished Parts).

23. Madison's *Notes,* 573–74; *Records,* 2:493, Journal (Report of Brearley Committee on spending power language, September 4). Punctuation in the Journal version is given.

24. For Madison's later perspective on this, as reflected in his correspondence of 1830, see chapter 10, below.

25. Research has not revealed any specific action on the Madison; Pinckney; Morris proposals by the Brearley Committee or the Rutledge Committee. See *Records,* 2:493–96, Journal.

26. Madison's *Notes,* 575; *Records,* 2:495–96 (adoption of General Welfare Clause by convention, September 4, without record vote); 503 (McHenry's account which is consistent); Brown, *Redeeming the Republic,* 184–85.

27. *Records,* 2: 503–4. (McHenry's reflections regarding harbor improvements on September 4; emphasis is McHenry's).

28. *Records,* 2: 529–30 (McHenry's conversation with Morris and others on September 6).

29. Max Farrand, *The Framing of the Constitution,* 178.

30. *Records*, 2:547, 565, 569; Madison's *Notes*, 608 (appointment of Committee of Style; reference of the convention's version of the taxing and spending power to the committee).

31. *Records*, 2:582, 590, 594; Madison's *Notes*, 620 (report of Committee of Style). The first clause in Article VII, sec. 8 called for the appointment of a treasurer. This was later dropped and the power to tax and spend became clause 1.

32. *Records*, 2:651, 655 (the engrossed version of the Constitution without the semicolon); Madison's notes do not contain the engrossed version.

33. Farrand, *Framing of the Constitution*, 182–83; James Madison, *Letters and Other Writings of James Madison, Fourth President of the United States*, 4 vols. (Philadelphia: J.B. Lippincott, 1865) (hereinafter Madison, *Writings*) 4:168–170 (letter of April 18, 1831 to Jared Sparks; Morris role). See also *Records*, 3:379; App. CCLXXXI, excerpt from Annals of Cong., 5th Cong. 2d and 3rd Sess. II, June 19, 1798 (remarks of Albert Gallatin). See also Madison, *Writings*, 3:485–486.

34. *Records*, 3:379.
35. Madison's *Notes*, 616, 620, 637; *Records*, 2:590, 595, 610, n. 2.
36. Madison's *Notes*, 638–39 (September 14 debate on canals).
37. Madison's *Notes*, 639; *Records*, 2:611.
38. Madison's *Notes*, 641 (September 14 debate.)
39. Ibid., 640 (capitation taxes); 644–45 (duties of tonnage).
40. Ibid., 652–54 (Franklin's speech of September 17).
41. Ibid., 652 (Gerry's speech).
42. Ibid., 650–51.
43. Ibid., 659.
44. Ibid.

Chapter 2. Ratification and the General Welfare Clause

1. See generally *The Debate on the Constitution, Federalist and Antifederalist Speeches, Articles, and Letters During the Struggle over Ratification*, 2 vols. (New York: The Library of America, 1993) (hereinafter *Debate*); Herbert J. Storing, *What the Anti-Federalists Were For* (Chicago: University of Chicago Press, 1981). References here to *The Federalist* are to the versions of the essays contained in the volumes of the *Debate on the Constitution*. The emphasis in this chapter is on those aspects of the ratification struggle that focused on the spending power and the General Welfare Clause.

2. *Debate*, 1:613, 618–19 (New York Journal, Dec. 27, 1787).
3. Ibid., 164, 166–67 (New York Journal, Oct. 18, 1787).
4. Ibid., 167. See Storing, *What the Anti-Federalists Were For*, 35: "The decisive issue here was the power of taxation . . . Under the Constitution, the states would have no constitutional way of influencing the raising of the federal revenue and thus would be closed out from substantial influence on federal policy. The states would at the same time have to sustain themselves with whatever crumbs might be left after the general government had taken its fill." See also Jackson Turner Main, *The Anti-Federalists, Critics of the Constitution, 1781–1788* (New York: W. W. Norton, 1974), 123–24.
5. *Debate*, 1:52, 57 (Oct. 5, 1787, emphasis in original).
6. See Storing, *What the Anti-Federalists Were For*, 15–23, 41–43.

7. *Debate*, 2:623, 633 (June 7,1788, Henry speech).
8. Ibid., 636.
9. Robert Allen Rutland, *The Birth of the Bill of Rights, 1776–1791* (London: Collier-MacMillan, Ltd., 1969); Ralph Ketcham, *James Madison: A Biography* (Charlottesville: University Press of Virginia, 1990), 289–92 (Madison's role); Banning, *Sacred Fire of Liberty*, 264–90.
10. *Debate*, 2:47–48 ("*Federalist* No. 41," Independent Journal, New York, Jan. 19, 1788); Madison, *Writings*, 1:407–08 (Letter to Thomas Jefferson, August 10, 1788); Banning, *Sacred Fire of Liberty*, 198–99 (neither author sanctioned all the views of the other).
11. *Debate*, 2:50.
12. Ibid., 51–53.
13. Ibid., 53–54.
14. Ibid., 54–55. See *United States v. Butler*, 297 U.S. 66–67 (1936); Banning, *Sacred Fire of Liberty*, 195–233. See Leonard R. Sorenson, *Madison on the "General Welfare" of America: His Consistent Constitutional Vision* (Lanham, Md.: Rowman & Littlefield Publishers, 1995).
15. *Debate*, 1:832, 839 (Dec. 11, 1787, Wilson's summation and final rebuttal at the Pennsylvania ratifying convention); 1:63, 64, 66; 67–68 (October 6, 1787 speech).
16. *Debate*, 1:838–40; 864–65 (internal improvement). Storing puts Wilson's key argument succinctly and well: "As bounds cannot be set to a nation's wants, so bounds ought not to be set to its resources....

"This is a powerful argument, given the Anti-Federalists' own desire for a Union government powerful enough to secure the common interests, especially defense. It is an argument that is almost sufficient to justify the Constitution...." Storing, *What the Anti-Federalists Were For*, 29.
17. *Debate*, 1:875–76.
18. Ibid., 622 ("*Federalist* No. 30", *New York Packet*, Dec. 28, 1787). For a discussion of Hamilton's role in the preparation of *The Federalist*, see McDonald, *Alexander Hamilton*, 107–15.
19. *Debate*, 1:622, 625 (quoted language); 625–27 (Hamilton's discussion of the defense aspects of the taxing power).
20. *Debate*, 1:720, 721 (*Federalist* No.36, New York Packet, Jan. 8, 1788); see also Ibid., 722–23.
21. Ibid., 2:824, 825–28, 832 (June 28, 1788).
22. See note 10 above. For example, see *The Debates in the Several States on the Adoption of the Federal Constitution*, ed. Jonathan Elliot, 5 vols. (Philadelphia: J. B. Lippincott, 1836), 4:83–94 (North Carolina); 4:274–76 (South Carolina, Rutledge speech).
23. *Records* 3:99, Appendix A, CXXIII, Letter from Sherman and Ellsworth to Governor of Connecticut, Sept. 26, 1787.
24. *Debate*, 1:412–14 (A Countryman II; attributed to Roger Sherman); 1: 877–84 (Ellsworth speech quoted language is at 877–78); 2:1036–37 (Sherman role); *The Documentary History of the Ratification of the Constitution*, 18 vols. (Madison: State Historical Society of Wisconsin, 1978), 3:561 (Connecticut, Sherman's vote); 15:280–81 (Sherman's observations as a citizen of New Haven).
25. *Elliot's Debates*, 3:463, 466 (Randolph's speech); 4:434 (Baldwin, House of Representatives, Feb. 11, 1796); Bradford, *Founding Fathers*, 205.
26. *Debate*, 1:305, 306.
27. Ibid., 2:547, 548–49.

28. Storing, *What the Anti-Federalists Were For*, 64–70 (Bill of Rights).
29. *Debate*, 2:557–574 (ratifying resolutions for Virginia and North Carolina).
30. *Debate*, 1:1094, 1095, 1096, 1097, 1098, 1102, 1104. For documentation on the Delaware ratification, see *Documentary History*, 3:37–115.
31. See Ralph Ketcham, *The Anti-Federalist Papers and the Constitutional Convention Debates* (New York: Penguin Books, 1986), 237, 243 (reprints document entitled, "The Address and Reasons of Dissent of the Minority of the Convention of Pennsylvania to their Constituents" [December 18, 1787].

Chapter 3. The Washington Administration

1. *Compilation of Messages and Papers of the Presidents, 1789–1902*, edited by J. D. Richardson, 10 vols. (Washington, D.C.: GPO, 1903) (hereinafter *Papers of the Presidents*), 1:53.
2. *Papers of the Presidents*, 1:52.
3. Ibid., 65.
4. Ibid., 66. For Washington's final recommendations on this subject, see chapter 4, below, at note 21.
5. *Papers of the Presidents*, 1:66.
6. Ibid. A discussion of Washington's commitment to education as reflected in his farewell address is found in Matthew Spalding and Patrick J. Garrity, *A Sacred Union of Citizens, George Washington's Farewell Address and the American Character* (Lanham, Md.: Rowman and Littlefield, 1996), 80–81.
7. *Papers of the Presidents*, 66.
8. Douglas Southall Freeman, *Washington* (one volume abridgement) (New York: MacMillan, 1968), 579.
9. John Thomas Flexner, *Washington the Indispensable Man* (Boston: Little, Brown and Company, 1974), 221: "Taking literally the separation of powers, Washington did not mobilize congressional support for programs he favored. It was his constitutional duty to make recommendations to Congress in his annual address, and this he did, although charily and always in terms of general principles rather than specifics. But once the legislative debates began, he meticulously kept hands off. He considered that legislative action had ceased to be his concern, until, according to constitutional provision, a bill that had been enacted was placed on his desk for approval or veto."
10. Alexander Hamilton, *The Works of Alexander Hamilton, Comprising His Correspondence and His Political and Official Writings*, edited by J. C. Hamilton, 7 vols. (New York: Charles S. Francis Co., 1851) (hereinafter Hamilton, *Works*), 3:1, 13–18, 43–48, Report on Finance, Jan. 14, 1790 (proposals); ibid., 20–21 (composition of debt), quoted language is at 14. See McDonald, *Alexander Hamilton*, chapters 7–9; ibid., 143–61. The components of the debt the new government inherited are also described by McDonald, 145–49 and recapitulated at 148. The same work provides a concise summary of the major points in Hamilton's 1790 Report on Public Credit with respect to funding and assumption, including the advantages of assumption. Ibid., 167.
11. Hamilton,*Works*, 3:14–15. See chapter 2, above, at note 16 (Wilson's argument); Hamilton's argument may be found in *Debate* 2:825–27 (June 28, 1788).
12. Madison, *Writings*, 1:507, 508–9, Madison to Pendleton, March 4, 1790; 507, Madison to Jefferson, Feb. 14, 1790; McDonald, *Alexander Hamilton*, 177–78; see ibid., 187 (summary of the legislative enactments of the first Con-

gress to implement Hamilton's report); 181–88 (description of the relationship between the assumption and the location of the seat of government issues to which the author attributes enactment of Hamilton's assumption proposal despite Madison's initial opposition).

13. Hamilton, *Works*, 3:95 (public credit); 106 (national bank); 149 (mint); 137–45., plans for bank; McDonald, *Alexander Hamilton*, 193–95 (describes considerations supporting the bank proposal). The paragraph in the text benefits from the lucid explanation in this account.

14. Ibid., 199–201; Flexner, *Washington the Indispensable Man*, 240–41; McDonald, *Alexander Hamilton*, 200–210 discusses the relationship of the location issue to the bank legislation and the maneuvering that accompanied the final determinations.

15. Hamilton,*Works*, 4:104, 107–13 (Hamilton's argument, quoted language is at 107–9); Flexner, *Washington the Indispensable Man*, 241–47 provides background on the role of the bank issue in launching the "great schism" between Hamilton, on the one hand, and Madison and Jefferson, on the other; see *Elliot's Debates*, 4:617, Appendix (extracts from Hamilton's bank argument, Feb. 1791). For a characterization of Hamilton's constitutional argument regarding the bank legislation as the "classic exposition of the doctrine of the broad construction of federal powers under the Constitution," see Alfred H. Kelly, Winifred A. Harbison, and Herman Belz, *The American Constitution: Its Origins and Development*, Seventh Ed., 2 vols. (New York: W. W. Norton and Company, 1985), 125, 127.

16. Flexner provides a valuable assessment: "Hamilton, caught by surprise by Madison's about-face, worked feverishly for days on the rebuttal he subsequently submitted to Washington. Strict interpretation, he pointed out, would, by banning any response to new situations, soon make the federal government obsolete. The state governments, being not similarly tied, would keep up to date and therefore take over, thus defeating the object of the federal union. Since Hamilton's argument was—as almost all modern historians agree—unanswerable, Washington had no choice but to sign the bill. It was this act which brought to the surface the fundamental flaw in the harmony of Washington's administration—and of the nation." *Washington the Indispensable Man*, 240–41.

17. Banning argues that Madison's position on these initiatives was consistent with his constitutional philosophy and was not an about face, as Hamilton urged. *Sacred Fire of Liberty*, 295–98.

18. Alexander Hamilton, *Report on Manufactures: Communication to the House of Representatives, December 5, 1791 from Alexander Hamilton, Secretary of the Treasury, on the Subject of Manufactures*, as reprinted in H. Doc. No. 172, 63rd Cong. 1st Sess. (1913) (hereinafter Hamilton, *Report*), 3–4. (The report covers 62 pages in the House Document version.). The report can also be found in Hamilton, *Works*, 3:192. Punctuation in the House Document varies somewhat from the original. See Jacob Cooke, *Alexander Hamilton* (New York: Charles Scribner and Sons, 1982), 101.

19. Hamilton, *Report*, 4–5. Hamilton's role in the drafting is described in Cooke, *Alexander Hamilton*, 97–99.

20. Hamilton, *Report.*, 9, 10.
21. Ibid., 11–12.
22. Ibid., 14. See also Flexner, *Washington the Indispensable Man*, 247–48.
23. Hamilton, *Report*, 14–16.

24. Ibid., 16; Cooke, *Alexander Hamilton*, 100.
25. Hamilton, *Report*, 17–18
26. Ibid., 18.
27. Ibid., 19–20; 22–27; Richard Brookhiser, *Alexander Hamilton, American* (New York: The Free Press, 1999), 93.
28. Hamilton, *Report*, 37–43 (quoted language is at 38); Cooke, *Alexander Hamilton*, 102; Brookhiser points out that Hamilton advocated that tariffs be used sparingly. *Alexander Hamilton*, 95.
29. Hamilton, *Report*, 38, 39; see Jacob Cooke, "The Reports of Alexander Hamilton" in *Alexander Hamilton A Profile*, ed. Jacob Cooke (New York: Hill and Wang, 1967), 79–81.

Chapter 4. Hamilton's Interpretation—Washington's Legacy

1. See chapter 14 below.
2. Hamilton, *Report*, 40.
3. Ibid.
4. See chapter 2, above, following note 18 (*Federalist*, No. 30).
5. Hamilton, *Report*, 40 (emphasis added); Hamilton, *Works*, 3:249–51. Neither the Cooke nor the Brookhiser biographies dwell on the constitutional significance of the report, although this may be its greatest practical impact.
6. Hamilton, *Report*, 40. Even this limitation has been from time to time ignored in practice in public works appropriations presumably on the thesis, advanced by, among others, Lincoln, that local projects have a general benefit. Hamilton's argument on the bank anticipates some of this general-local distinction. *Elliot's Debates*, 4:617, App.
7. Hamilton, *Report*, 41. See text chapter 2, above, following note 9 (discussion of *"Federalist* No. 41," authored by Madison).
8. Hamilton, *Works*, 4:178–79, letter of Oct. 14, 1791; Samuel Konefsky, "The Powers Ought to be Construed Liberally" in *Alexander Hamilton: A Profile*, ed. Jacob Cooke (New York: Hill and Wang, 1967), 121, 131.
9. Ibid., 126, 127; in the report, Hamilton "fashioned virtually a plenary power out of the taxing, spending . . . [power]." Kelly, Harbison and Belz, *The American Constitution*, 127–28.
10. Hamilton, *Report*, 44, 45.
11. Madison, *Writings*, 1:545, 546–47 (emphasis in the original); Ralph Ketcham, *James Madison: A Biography*, (Charlottesville: University Press of Virginia, 1990), 69 (family connection and friendship with Pendleton). Similar views were expressed in a letter from Madison to Henry Lee, dated January 21, 1792, quoted in Banning, *Sacred Fire of Liberty*, 346.
12. Madison, *Writings*, 3:530; see generally Ketcham, *James Madison*, chapter 13. (Madison as party leader during the Washington administration.) See introduction, above, regarding Hamilton's sketch of the Constitution at the Philadelphia Convention. Banning's analysis is found in *Sacred Fire of Liberty*, 346–47. Madison's February letter to Pendleton is in Madison, *Writings*, 1:548, letter Madison to Pendleton, Feb. 21, 1792.
13. Thomas Jefferson, *The Writings of Thomas Jefferson* (Library Edition), ed. Andrew A. Lipscomb, 20 vols. (Washington, D.C.: Thomas Jefferson Memo-

rial Association, 1903) (hereinafter Jefferson, *Writings*), 8:341, 344–45, Letter to the President of the United States, May 23, 1792. Jefferson charged that the ultimate objective of the Hamiltonians was to substitute a monarchy on the model of the British Constitution for the American republican form of government. Ibid., 344.

14. Ibid., 344, 347; George Washington, *Writings*, ed. John Rhodehamel (New York: Library of America, 1997) 809, 811, Letter to Hamilton, July 29, 1792; Hamilton, *Works*, 4:247, 270, letter of Aug. 18, 1792 and attachment.

15. Jefferson, *Writings*, 8:394, 395. Letter to the President, September 9, 1792. See also ibid., 396–97.

16. Ibid., 397–98 (italics in original)

17. Ibid., 398–406 (quoted language is at 398).

18. Washington, *Writings*, 815, 817–18, Letter to Jefferson, Aug. 23, 1792 (internal dissension); Flexner, *Washington: The Indispensable Man*, 266 (Washington's conversation with Jefferson regarding Jefferson's views on the Report). The growing rift between Hamilton and Jefferson during 1791 and 1792 is described in McDonald, *Alexander Hamilton*, 237–261. The reaction of both Washington and Hamilton to Jefferson's May 23, 1792 letter is described at 252–53.

19. For a general description of the Hamilton-Jefferson rift during Washington's first term, from the perspective of a biographer of Jefferson, see Willard Sterne Randall, *Thomas Jefferson: A Life* (New York: Harper Perennial, 1993), 497–510. Randall attributes much of the infighting to disagreements on foreign policy, as well as domestic policy issues.

20. Douglas Southall Freeman, *Washington* (New York: MacMillan 1968), 588–89, 650–56; *Papers of the Presidents*, 1:162–68 (sixth annual message, Nov. 19, 1794, quoted language is at 166; 125, 127 (fourth annual message, Nov. 6, 1792; 158, Proclamation of Aug. 7, 1794.

21. *Papers of the Presidents*, 1:199, 201 (eighth annual message, Dec. 7, 1796); see Flexner, *Washington: The Indispensable Man*, 355–56 (description of background regarding delivery of message); Freeman, *Washington*, 704–6 (response of Congress to this message).

22. *Papers of the Presidents*, 1:202; see chapter 3 above; Washington, *Writings*, 960, Letter to Hamilton, Sept 1, 1796 (education); Hamilton, *Works*, 6:149, Washington to Hamilton, Sept. 6, 1796 (university); 6:156, 158, Washington to Hamilton, Nov. 2, 1796 (agricultural establishments); 6:167, Hamilton to Washington, Nov. 10, 1796 (outline); 7:611, Hamilton's draft, Dec. 7, 1796).

23. *Papers of the Presidents*, 1:213, 220–21. See Felix Gilbert, "Hamilton and the 'Farewell Address' " in Cooke, *Alexander Hamilton: A Profile*, 106, and Spalding and Garrity, *A Sacred Union of Citizens*, 56, on the role of Hamilton and Madison in the drafting of the Farewell Address. ("From the beginning, Hamilton understood himself as acting on Washington's instructions, following the President's intentions, and serving his purpose.")

24. Joseph Story, *Commentaries on the Constitution of the United States* (Boston: Little, Brown and Company, 1891); *United States v. Butler*, 297 U.S. 1 (1936).

25. *Elliot's Debates*, 4:528, 540 (Virginia and Kentucky resolutions); 546, 550–53 (Madison's report); 532 (Delaware reaction). See David McCullough, *John Adams* (New York: Simon and Schuster, 2001), 52–21 (Kentucky resolutions).

Chapter 5. Jefferson's Dilemma

1. David N. Mayer, *The Constitutional Thought of Thomas Jefferson* (Charlottesville: University Press of Virginia, 1994), 218-21; Alf J. Mapp, Jr., *Thomas Jefferson Passionate Pilgrim: The Presidency, the Founding of the University, and the Private Battle* (Lanham, Md.: Madison Books, 1991), 187 (Constitution and federal role); Kelly, Harbison and Belz, *The American Constitution*, 138-55 (Republican constitutionalism).
2. *Papers of the Presidents*, 1:321; Joseph J. Ellis, *American Sphinx: The Character of Thomas Jefferson* (New York: Random House, 1998), 202 (inaugural march).
3. *Papers of the Presidents*, 1:322.
4. Ibid., 322-24.
5. Jefferson, *Writings*, 10:216-17, Letter to John Dickinson, March 6, 1801.
6. Ibid., 303-4, letter to Benjamin Rush, Dec. 20, 1801.
7. Ibid., 301, 302-3, letter to John Dickinson, December 19, 1801.
8. *Papers of the Presidents*, 1: 378-79.
9. Ibid., 379 (emphasis in original).
10. Jefferson, *Writings*, 15:131, 133-34, Letter to Albert Gallatin, June 16, 1817.
11. Jefferson, *Writings*, 11:69, Letter to Judge John Tyler, March 29, 1805.
12. Mapp, *Thomas Jefferson: Passionate Pilgrim*, 46-62; Jefferson, *Writings*, 10:417, 418-20, Letter to Wilson C. Nicholas, Sept. 7, 1803.
13. Ellis, *American Sphinx*, 251 (quote in text). Ellis attributes Jefferson's flexibility not to pragmatism but to the "special, indeed almost mystical place" the West had in this thinking. Ibid., 252. The background of the negotiation with France is spelled out in Jefferson's vivid private correspondence: Jefferson, *Writings*, 10:311-16, Letter to United States Minister to France, Robert Livingston, April 18, 1802; 316-17, Letter to Monsieur DuPont de Nemours, April 25, 1802; 343-45, Letter to Gov. James Monroe, January 13, 1803; 347-51, Letter to Monsieur DuPont de Nemours; 352, 353-54, letter to Robert Livingston, Feb. 3, 1803; 385-86, Letter to Dr. Hugh Williamson, April 30, 1803; 402-3, Letter to General Horatio Gates, July 11, 1803; 407-11, Letter to John Breckinridge, Aug. 12, 1803. See also Dumas Malone, *Jefferson the President: First Term, 1801-05* (Boston: Little, Brown and Company, 1970), 311-32 (hereinafter Malone, *First Term*). For an account of Jefferson's constitutional doubts regarding the authority to implement the Louisiana purchase, see Mapp, *Thomas Jefferson, Passionate Pilgrim*, 57-62; Jefferson, *Writings*, 10: 412, 414, Letter to Secretary of State James Madison, Aug. 25, 1803; 415, 416-17, Letter to Levi Lincoln, August 30, 1803; 424, 425-27, Letter to Robert Livingston, Nov. 4, 1803; 422, Letter to DuPont de Nemours, Nov. 1, 1803; Malone, *First Term*, 318-19.
14. See chapter 14, below, for a discussion of the *Butler* case.
15. *Papers of the Presidents*, 1:379.
16. Ibid., 405, 408-9.
17. Ibid., 409.
18. Ibid.
19. Ibid., 409-10 (emphasis added).
20. See Jefferson, *Writings*, 11:256, Letter to Governor Cabell, June 29, 1807; see also *Writings*, 11:288, letter to Governor Cabell, July 19, 1807; 313, letter to Henry Dearborn, Aug. 9, 1807; 318; 11:213, 228, 233, 239, 341, communications

regarding Burr trial; 310 (Louisiana). *Papers of the Presidents*, 1:425, 429 (seventh annual message, sharply reduced emphasis in internal improvements).
  21. Jefferson, *Writings*, 11:400, 401, Letter to Joel Barlow, Dec. 10, 1807.
  22. Ibid., 401, 402 , letter to General John Mason (embargo); 439, letter to Robert Smith, Feb. 14, 1808 (Jefferson's duty); 430, letter to Joel Barlow, Jan. 24, 1808.
  23. Ibid., 12:51, 93, 248 (enforcement and repeal of embargo).
  24. Ibid., 12:65–66, Letter to Mr. Leiper, May 25, 1808 (emphasis added).
  25. *Papers of the Presidents*, 1:451, 456 (eighth annual message, emphasis added).
  26. Jefferson, *Writings*, 12:230, 231–32, Letter to Dr. Maese, January 15, 1809.
  27. Dumas Malone, *Jefferson the President, Second Term 1805–1809* (Boston: Little, Brown and Company, 1974), 553–60. (hereinafter, Malone, *Second Term*). For an account of Jefferson's struggle to accommodate his constitutional views with his desire to initiate an exploratory mission to the West through the Lewis and Clark expedition, see Stephen E. Ambrose, *Undaunted Courage: Meriwether Lewis, Thomas Jefferson, and the Opening of the American West* (New York: Simon and Schuster, 1996), 68–79 (origin of the expedition); *Papers of the Presidents*, 1:352–54, communication to Senate and House, Jan. 18, 1803; Jefferson, *Writings*, 10: 337, letter to Albert Gallatin, October 13, 1802. Jefferson essentially relied upon a broad reading of the Commerce Clause to justify the appropriation for the Lewis and Clark expedition.
  28. *Papers of the Presidents*, 1:418, 440 (Cumberland Road reports of 1807, 1808).
  29. Malone, *Second Term*, 556.
  30. Jefferson, *Writings*, 11:194, Letter to Albert Gallatin, April 21, 1807.
  31. Ibid., 12:31–32, Letter to Albert Gallatin, April 22, 1808, emphasis added.
  32. *King v. Smith*, 392 U.S. 333, n. 34 (1968).
  33. Jefferson, *Writings*, 12:117, letter of August 6, 1808 (Cumberland Road); *Papers of the Presidents*, 1:457 (report of the Cumberland Road commissioners).
  34. Malone, *Second Term*, 553, 556–59.
  35. Kelly, Harbison, and Belz, *The American Constitution*, 145.

Chapter 6. Madison's Precept

  1. For general background on Madison and his presidency, see Ralph Ketcham, *James Madison*, chapters 19–21; Robert Allen Rutland, *The Presidency of James Madison* (Lawrence: University Press of Kansas, 1990).
  2. *Papers of the Presidents*, 1:466, 467 (Madison, first inaugural).
  3. Ibid., 468.
  4. Ibid., 473, 474, first annual message, November 29, 1809.
  5. Ibid., 482, 484–85, second annual message, December 5, 1810.
  6. Ibid., 485.
  7. Ibid. (emphasis added); see chapter 2.
  8. *Papers of the Presidents*, 1:485.
  9. Ibid., 491, 494–95 (third annual message, November 5, 1811); 499, 500–505 (message of June 1, 1812 regarding relations with Great Britain); 512 (proclamation of June 19, 1812); Rutland, *The Presidency of James Madison*, 99–132.

10. *Papers of the Presidents*, 1:562, seventh annual message, December 5, 1815.
11. Ketcham, *James Madison*, 599–605; Rutland, *The Presidency of James Madison*, 183–97 (background of the seventh annual message).
12. *Papers of the Presidents*, 1:563–66 (Madison, seventh annual message, defense recommendations); Rutland, *The Presidency of James Madison*, 195.
13. *Papers of the Presidents*, 567.
14. Ibid. (emphasis added).
15. Ibid., 567–68 (emphasis added).
16. Ibid., 568.
17. Ibid.
18. Ibid. See also Rutland, *The Presidency of James Madison*, 196 (political reaction to message) and Ketcham, *James Madison*, 602–4.
19. *Papers of the Presidents*, 1:573, 576 (eighth annual message); ibid., 579.
20. Madison, *Writings*, 3:34, 35 (Letter to Thomas Jefferson, Feb. 15, 1817).
21. Ketcham, *James Madison*, 609.
22. *Papers of the Presidents*, 1:584–85 (veto message of March 3, 1817); Rutland, *The Presidency of James Madison*, 206.
23. *Papers of the Presidents*, 584–85. See Sorenson, *Madison on the "General Welfare" of America*, 81–94.
24. Rutland, *The Presidency of James Madison*, 206; Ketcham, *James Madison*, 609–10; *Elliot's Debates*, 4:46 (Clay's views on the bill).
25. *Annals of Congress*, 14th Congress, second session, 1059–62 (House override vote, March 3, 1817). Available at http://memory.loc.gov. See also Jefferson, *Writings*, 15:131. Not surprisingly, Jefferson agreed with Madison's veto action.

Chapter 7. Monroe's Turn

1. *Papers of the Presidents*, 2:4,8, Monroe Inaugural Address, March 4, 1817; ibid., 11, 18, first annual message.
2. Madison, *Writings*, 3:50–51, letter to President Monroe, November 29, 1817 (emphasis in the original); See ibid., 53–54, Letter to Henry St. George Tucker, Dec. 23, 1817.
3. Ibid., 3: 54, 55, letter to President Monroe, Dec. 27, 1817.
4. Ibid. The reference is to Article IV, section 3, clause 2 of the Constitution: "The Congress shall have Power to dispose of and make all needful Rules and Regulations respecting the Territory or other Property belonging to the United States. . . ."
5. Harry Ammon, *James Monroe: The Quest for National Identity* (Charlottesville: University Press of Virginia, 1990), 386–92 ("The discussions in the House had shown that the majority favoring improvements would never approve an amendment granting a power which they insisted was already within the authority of Congress." Ibid., 390). See also chapter 6, above, at note 25. Article V of the Constitution provides that an amendment to the Constitution may be proposed whenever two-thirds of both houses of Congress "shall deem it necessary." Such an amendment becomes part of the Constitution when ratified by the legislatures of three-fourths of the states.
6. Ammon, *James Monroe*, 390–92. See chapter 8, below.
7. *Papers of the Presidents*, 2:142 (veto message of May 4, 1822).
8. Ibid., 142–43. (emphasis added)

9. Ibid., 143. See *Annals of Congress*, House of Representatives, 17th Cong., 1st Sess., 1809–63 (veto and memo, May 4, 1822); 1872–75 (override vote, May 6, 1822). For discussion of the vote on the Bonus Bill veto, see chapter 6 above, at note 25.

10. The Monroe Memorandum of May 4, 1822 is set forth in full in *Papers of the Presidents*, 2:144–83.

11. *Helvering v. Davis*, 301 U.S. 619, 640 (1937).

12. *Papers of the Presidents*, 2:148; 145–48, Monroe's summary of pre-Constitution history. See Introduction above.

13. *Papers of the Presidents*, 2:150–54; quoted language is at 153.

14. Ibid., 155–56. Compare Madison's discussion in the Bonus Bill veto, chapter 6.

15. *Papers of the Presidents*, 2:157–62, quoted language is at 162.

16. Ibid., 162.

17. Ibid., 163 (emphasis added). See James Monroe, *The Political Writings of James Monroe*, edited by James P. Lucier, (Washington, D.C.: Regnery Publishing, 2001), 549–602 (1817 memo).

18. *Papers of the Presidents*, 2:163.

19. Ibid., 163.

20. Ibid., 164. Here Monroe may have underestimated the impact of grant conditions.

21. 197 U.S. 1, 62–67 (1936).

22. *Papers of the Presidents*, 2:164 (emphasis in the original).

23. Ibid.

24. Ibid., 164–65. See particularly Jefferson's statement, chapter 5, above, at note 10.

25. *Papers of the Presidents*, 2:165.

26. Ibid., (emphasis added); compare Sherman's report to the Governor of Connecticut discussed above chapter 2.

27. *Papers of the Presidents*, 2:165–66.

28. Ibid., 166.

29. Ibid.

30. Ibid.

31. Ibid., 166–67. See *Report on Manufactures*, discussed above in chapter 4.

32. *Papers of the Presidents*, 2:167 (emphasis added); the quoted language is relied upon in the majority opinion in *United States v. Butler*; see chapter 14.

33. *Papers of the Presidents*, 2:167–73. Monroe's summary is at 173; for this purpose Monroe did not distinguish between money raised by land sales and that raised through taxation and then appropriated, 171.

34. Ibid., 177–79. A review of Madison's correspondence with Monroe between May 1822 and the end of 1823 reveals no comment, critical or otherwise, by Madison regarding the Monroe memorandum; the former president engaged in gracious correspondence with his successor on other matters during that period. See Madison, *Writings*, 3:267 et seq.

35. *Papers of the Presidents*, 2:185, 190 (December 3, 1822, sixth annual message); see chapter 8 (John Quincy Adams perspective).

36. *Papers of the Presidents*, 2:191 (emphasis added).

37. Ibid., 207, 216 (seventh annual message, December 2, 1823)

38. Ibid., 248, 255 (eighth annual message, December 7, 1824); for a sample of congressional support for the constitutionality of subscriptions to a canal company during this period, see the observations of Mr. Cambreling, Jan. 18, 1825 to the effect that such legislation could be derived from an implied power re-

lated to the defense and post-roads power in Article I, section 8. *Elliot's Debates*, 4:479. For the survey legislation itself, see Act of April 30, 1824, *U.S. Statutes at Large* 4 (1824–35): 22. The act authorized the president to initiate necessary surveys of road and canal routes that the president deemed of national importance.

39. Noble Cunningham, Jr. *The Presidency of James Monroe*, (American Presidency Series) (Lawrence: University Press of Kansas, 1996), 167.

40. Ammon, *James Monroe*, 388–92, provides background on the formulation of the memorandum. Quote is at 392.

41. See *South Dakota v. Dole*, 483 U.S. 203 (1987).

42. See text below in chapter 8. Kelly, Harbison, and Belz, *The American Constitution*, 153.

43. Joseph Story, *Commentaries on the Constitution of the United States*, 5th ed., 2 vols. (Boston: Little, Brown and Company, 1891); *United States v. Butler*, 297 U.S. 1, 62–67 (1936); Cunningham, *The Presidency of James Monroe*, 165–67.

CHAPTER 8. JOHN QUINCY ADAMS'S "SPIRIT OF IMPROVEMENT"

1. Paul C. Nagel, *John Quincy Adams: A Public Life, A Private Life* (New York: Alfred A. Knopf, 1998), 296.

2. Samuel Flag Bemis, *John Quincy Adams and the Union* (New York: Alfred A. Knopf, 1956), 11.

3. Ibid., 11–54 (detailed description of the 1824 campaign and the ensuing election). Bemis describes the pre-election encounter between Clay and Adams and notes that Adams was out of character in not supplying the details of the conversation in his diary. Ibid., 39–41. Bemis dismisses the "corrupt bargain" charge and provides the following assessment: "The implicit but certainly not corrupt bargain between Adams and Clay was the least questionable of the several deals . . . that Adams made to secure election by the House of Representatives." Ibid., 58. For another sympathetic perspective on the election of 1824, see Lynn Hudson Parsons, *John Quincy Adams* (Madison, Wis.: Madison House, 1998), 169–77. For an account of the reaction of the Jackson camp to the Adams-Clay arrangement, see Robert V. Remini, *Andrew Jackson the Course of American Freedom, 1822–1832* (Baltimore: Johns Hopkins University Press, 1998), 74–99.

4. Nagel, *John Quincy Adams*, 296 (describes the Adams presidency in this fashion); Bemis, *John Quincy Adams and the Union*, 71–91 (problems of a minority president); 126–51; Remini, *The Course of American Freedom*, 100–115 (Jackson camp's opposition to Adams).

5. John Quincy Adams, *Memoirs of John Quincy Adams*, ed. Charles Francis Adams, 12 vols. (Freeport, N.Y.: Books for Libraries Press, 1969). Hereinafter referred to as *JQA Memoirs*. See 4:462–64 (1819 Monroe cabinet sessions); 6:450–52 (1825 conversation with Senator Barbour). See also John Adams and John Quincy Adams, *The Selected Writings of John and John Quincy Adams*, eds. Adrienne Koch and William Peden (New York: Alfred A. Knopf, 1946), 373 (John Quincy Adams's eulogy for Monroe including discussion of Monroe's internal-improvement policies).

6. See text below at note 33; JQA, *Memoirs*, 7:79–80 (conversation with Rep. Bailey).

7. Bemis, *John Quincy Adams and the Union*, 58 (Adams appointed Clay "as an experienced and talented Western man because they agreed on national policies...."); JQA, *Memoirs*, 8:173–74 (Jan. 18, 1830, JQA's post-presidential explanation of his reasons for appointing Clay as secretary of state); Parsons, *John Quincy Adams*, 173–74 ("Thus, both temperamentally and philosophically, Clay was pushed away from Jackson and Crawford, and drawn toward Adams.")

8. See text below this chapter at note 27.

9. See text below at notes 47–51.

10. See text below at note 52. For a positive assessment by Adams, see JQA, *Memoirs*, 8:233–34 (entry of June 25, 1830).

11. JQA, *Memoirs*, 6:518–19 (entry for March 4, 1825, JQA's account of the inauguration); Remini, *The Course of American Freedom*, 102–3 (Jackson's reaction); Parsons, *John Quincy Adams*, 176 (an account of the event from the Adams perspective).

12. *Papers of the Presidents*, 2:294–97 (inaugural address); Bemis, *John Quincy Adams and the Union*, 52.

13. *Papers of the Presidents*, 2:298, reference to Monroe era (emphasis added).

14. Ibid., 298–99.

15. Ibid, 299.

16. JQA, *Memoirs*, 4:462–64 (entry of December 1819, indicates that the memorandum was designed to reconcile Monroe's signing of internal-improvement legislation contrary to his constitutional views; includes "moral certainty" and "nice distinctions" quotes).

17. Bemis, *John Quincy Adams and the Union*, 63–64 (JQA's views).

18. JQA, *Memoirs*, 6:518–19. (JQA's account of the postinaugural address part of the day). The circumstances surrounding the Adams inaugural and his transition into the White House are described in Nagel, *John Quincy Adams*, 298–300.

19. *Papers of the Presidents*, 2:299, 307–8 (first annual message); JQA, *Memoirs*, 7: 66 (anxiety); 8:48–50 (ground breaking at the C and O Canal); Parsons, *John Quincy Adams*, 185 (supplies an account of the groundbreaking where, contrary to his usual form, Adams connected with the people).

20. *Papers of the Presidents*, 2:307–8.

21. Ibid., 311 (emphasis added).

22. Ibid., 311–12. For JQA's affinity for the positions of Washington, see Bemis, *John Quincy Adams and the Union*, 61–63.

23. *Papers of the Presidents*, 2:313 (emphasis added); see also ibid., 312.

24. Ibid., 315–16.

25. Ibid., 316 (emphasis added).

26. Remini, *The Course of American Freedom*, 110; Parsons, *John Quincy Adams*, 181 (suggestion was "especially unfortunate").

27. JQA, *Memoirs*, 7: 59–61; quote is at 61; Bemis, *John Quincy Adams and the Union*, 66–70 (describes these discussions in dialogue style).

28. JQA, *Memoirs*, 7:62–63 (entry of Nov. 26, 1825).

29. Ibid., 63 (entry of Nov. 26); see Parsons, *John Quincy Adams*, 180 (cabinet discussions).

30. JQA, *Memoirs*, 7: 64–65 (entry of Nov. 28, discussion with Wirt); 7:67 (entry of Dec. 2, printing); 7:71–72 (entry of Dec. 6, transmission of message).

31. See Parsons, *John Quincy Adams*, 181. Remini, *The Course of American*

Freedom, 100–142 (describes the anti-Adams coalition and its subsequent victory); JQA, *Memoirs*, 8:327, entry of Feb. 25, 1831 gives Adams's postpresidential perspective on the matter. Parsons describes other factors leading to John Quincy Adams's political demise in 1828 including his support for opening up the treaty with the Creek Indians and his refusal to play appointive politics or participate in electioneering. Ibid., 181–85; 191–92.

32. See JQA, *Memoirs*, 7:77–78 (entry of Dec. 10, discussion with Edward Livingston). For a general discussion of the critical reception of the message, see Nagel, *John Quincy Adams*, 301–3.

33. JQA, *Memoirs*, 7:79–80 (entry of Dec. 14, discussion with Bailey, emphasis added); Bemis, *John Quincy Adams and the Union*, 75.

34. JQA, *Memoirs*, 7:105–6 (entry of Jan. 17, discussion of Jefferson-Madison reaction).

35. Jefferson, *Writings*, 16:140 (letter to James Madison, Dec. 24, 1825).

36. Jefferson, *Writings*, 17:442–48. Apparently none of this dispute crept into Jefferson's correspondence with John Quincy Adams's father, John Adams, during 1825. For background on this correspondence, see McCullough, *John Adams*, 603–8.

37. Madison, *Writings*, 3:511 (letter to Thomas Jefferson, Dec. 28, 1825).

38. Ibid., 506 (letter to Thomas Ritchie, Dec. 18, 1825. Ritchie was a prominent Richmond newspaper publisher).

39. See Jefferson, *Writings*, 16:143 (letter to William B. Giles, December 25, 1825).

40. *Papers of the Presidents*, 2:350, 360 (Second Annual Message, Dec. 2, 1826).

41. John Quincy Adams, *Memoirs*, 7:190, 191 (Nov. 30, 1826); *Papers of the Presidents*, 2:378, 388 (Third Annual Message, Dec. 4, 1827).

42. IV *U.S. Statutes at Large (Stat)* (1846) (19th and 20th Congresses). Act of May 28, 1828, *U.S. Statutes at Large* 4(1824–1835): 293 (C and O Canal); Act of May 19, 1828, *U.S. Statutes at Large* 4:275 (harbor legislation; completion of Cumberland Road to Zanesville); Act of May 23, 1828, *U.S. Statutes at Large* 4:282; Act of May 23, 1828, *U.S. Statutes at Large* 4:290. (Delaware Bay); Act of May 23, 1828, *U.S. Statutes at Large* 4:288 (harbor improvements; lighthouses). For the impact of the opposition of the Jacksonians to Adams's program see Remini, *The Course of American Freedom*, 129. Adams took an active role in the discussions leading up the the appointment of the president and directors of the canal company. See JQA, *Memoirs*, 8:23–24, 26, 35, 37–38. For Adams's description of the ground breaking, see, Ibid., 48–50, July 4, 1828.

43. *Papers of the Presidents*, 2:407, 411–12, 417 (Fourth Annual Message, Dec. 2, 1828). The virulence of the election of 1828 is described in Remini, *The Course of American Freedom*, 133–35.

44. Madison, *Writings*, 3:483, letter to Thomas Jefferson, Feb. 17, 1825. See also 490 (letter to Matthew Carey, May 12, 1825).

45. Ibid., 528 (letter of September 20, 1826 to Martin Van Buren).

46. Ibid., 530 (amendment).

47. John Adams and John Quincy Adams, *Selected Writings*, 384 (John Quincy Adams's Madison eulogy).

48. Ibid., 373, 375–378 (John Quincy Adams's Monroe eulogy). See Parsons, *John Quincy Adams*, 208–9. Adams's target in the eulogy was Andrew Jackson's handling of internal improvements).

49. John and John Quincy Adams, *Selected Writings*, 376–78 (emphasis in original).

50. Ibid., 377–78. Adams's diary entries for 1822 and 1823 do not record extensive participation on his part in the cabinet debates on the issue during the Monroe Administration. See e.g., JQA, *Memoirs*, 5:516–17 (entry of May 4, 1822, transmission of Monroe veto message and memorandum; Monroe apparently informed Adams and Calhoun and read portions of the message to them; Adams records no comment); Ibid., 6:105–10 (debate on 1822 annual message that followed the May veto and contained the compromise portion based on the May legal memorandum referred to here as the "Monroe Memorandum;" Adams records considerable cabinet discussion on the message as a whole but little on the internal improvement portion).

51. *Congressional Record*, 49th Cong., 1st Sess., vol. 17, part 8, appendix 226–29, letter, JQA to Andrew Stevenson, July 11, 1832; *Elliot's Debates*, 4:449, House, Oct. 25, 1803, John Quincy Adams's Senate speech; see also speech of Sen. Rodney, ibid., 448. JQA, *Memoirs*, 6:418 (conversation with Governor Eustis, Oct. 22, 1824, JQA's constitutional view regarding internal improvement); 450–52 (quoted conversation with Senator Barbour of Virginia, Dec. 22, 1824).

52. Adams and Adams, *Selected Writings*, 389. (letter to Reverend Charles Upham, Feb. 2, 1837). Compare John Quincy Adams's 1830 assessment in JQA, *Memoirs*, 8:232 (June 25, 1830 following the Maysville Road veto discussed, below in chapter 9). Earlier in his public career, during his service in the United States Senate, Adams had championed internal improvement initiatives. See JQA, *Memoirs*, 1:460.

53. For Adams on the Smithsonian, see Nagel, *John Quincy Adams*, 374–75; Bemis, *John Quincy Adams and the Union*, 521–23; and Margaret C. S. Christman, *1846 Portrait of the Nation* (Washington, D.C.: Smithsonian Institution Press, 1996), 12–21. For the Cumberland Road and C and O Canal enactments, see references to U.S. *Statutes at Large*, cited above at note 42.

54. See below in chapter 11 (Lincoln's 1848 internal improvement speech before the House).

55. Parsons, *John Quincy Adams*, 200.

56. *Weekly Compilation of Presidential Documents* 34:15–16 (Jan. 12, 1998) (remarks of President Clinton at Democratic National Committee Luncheon in New York, Jan. 8, 1998). JQA, *Memoirs*, 8:243, 246 (JQA's assessment of his reasons for returning to political life. For a less charitable description of JQA's motivation in taking on the gag rule, presented from a Jacksonian perspective, see Robert V. Remini, *Andrew Jackson*, vol. 3, *The Course of American Democracy, 1833–1845* (Baltimore: Johns Hopkins University Press, 1998), 405–7: John Quincy Adams's aim was to even the score with Jackson by disrupting Congress during Jackson's last year in office. An account of Adams's fight against the gag rule is found in William Lee Miller, *Arguing About Slavery: John Quincy Adams and the Great Battle in the United States Congress* (New York: Random House, 1998).

57. J. David Greenstone, *The Lincoln Persusasion: Remaking American Liberalism* (Princeton: Princeton University Press, 1993) 191, 192. See generally ibid., 191–214.

58. Adams and Adams, *Selected Writings*, 389 (John Quincy Adams's letter to Reverend Charles Upham, Feb. 2, 1837). Bemis, *John Quincy Adams and the Union*, 64 (quotes John Randolph of Virginia as fearing that if Congress had power to construct internal improvements, it had the power to "emancipate every slave in the United States.")

59. Adams and Adams, *Selected Writings*, 390, 392 (1842 address to constituents, emphasis added).

60. Greenstone, *Lincoln Persuasion*, 192. Adams did not support outright abolition. With respect to the states, he thought it was beyond the power of Congress under the Constitution; with respect to the District of Columbia it was unlikely to happen given the politics and impractical in any event since slave holders would move their slaves out of the District. See Parsons, *John Quincy Adams*, 232–33, for a discussion of John Quincy Adams's views and his ambivalence on the issue. For a description of Adams's role as defense attorney in the *Amistad* case, see ibid., 236–40.

CHAPTER 9. INTERNAL IMPROVEMENTS IN THE AGE OF JACKSON

1. Remini, *Course of American Freedom*, 156–80.
2. *Papers of the Presidents*, 2:436, 437 (Jackson, inaugural address, March 4, 1829).
3. Ibid., 442, 451 (first annual message, Dec. 8, 1829).
4. Ibid., 451–52.
5. Ibid., 452.
6. Arthur Schlesinger Jr. *The Age of Jackson* (Boston: Little, Brown and Company, 1945), 58. Donald B. Cole, *The Presidency of Andrew Jackson* (Lawrence: University Press of Kansas, 1993) (American Presidency series), 65; see ibid., for an insight on the political context of the veto. See Remini, *Course of American Freedom*, 251–56, for an account of the Maysville Road legislation and Jackson's veto of it.
7. *Papers of the Presidents*, 2:483, 484–85 (veto message of May 27, 1830). Compare Monroe's treatment of the precedents in his 1822 memorandum, described above in chapter 7.
8. *Papers of the Presidents*, 2:485–86. In this passage, Jackson evidently interpreted Madison's Bonus Bill Veto as an affirmation of the distinction between the power to appropriate for, and the power to construct, roads and canals. However, the evidence suggests that Madison did not accept that distinction and maintained that the General Welfare Clause did not even authorize mere appropriations for such purposes. See chapter 4, above, regarding his letter to Pendleton, and chapter 8, above, regarding Madison's proposed constitutional amendment suggested to Senator Van Buren. See also chapter 10, footnote 8.
9. Ibid., 487 (emphasis added). See discussion of Virginia and Kentucky resolutions, chapter 4, at note 25.
10. *Papers of the Presidents*, 2:487. See note 26 below.
11. *Papers of the Presidents*, 2:488.
12. Ibid., 488–89. (The "interpose" quote is at 488 emphasis in the original).
13. Ibid., 489. See chapter 5, Jefferson on taxation.
14. *Papers of the Presidents*, 2:490.
15. Ibid.
16. Ibid. See Remini, *Course of American Freedom*, 116–42 for a discussion of Jackson's ideas on reform, including his concerns about corruption; ibid., 256 for his views on corruption and internal improvements.
17. *Papers of the Presidents*, 2:490–91.
18. Ibid., 491.
19. Ibid., 491–92 (emphasis added). Jackson's distinctions reflected Monroe's compromise. See chapter 7.

20. *Papers of the Presidents*, 2:491.
21. Remini, *The Course of American Freedom*, reproduction of cartoon facing page 257. Ibid., 252–56 for a discussion of Jackson's exercise of this power with respect to internal improvements in the context of the Maysville Road. For John Quincy Adams's observations, see JQA, *Memoirs*, 8:230 (entry of June 6, comment on Jackson's vetoes of internal improvements) and 8:206 (entry of March 23, "Senate now as servile as in my time they were factious. . . .").
22. See chapter 8 above.
23. JQA, *Memoirs*, 8:230, 233–34, entry of June 25, 1830; for Jackson's reaction, see Remini, *Course of American Freedom*, 255.
24. Hofstadter, *Great Issues in American History*, 267–71, Clay speech; emphasis in the original.
25. See current Title 23 of the United States for a modern version of formula grant state administered internal-improvement legislation. The Intermodal Surface Transportation Act of 1991 (ISTEA), discussed in chapter 16, is one example.
26. *Papers of the Presidents*, 2:500, 511–17 (Jackson, second annual message, Dec. 6, 1830). Further background may be found in the following sources: ibid., 544, 545 (third annual message, Dec. 6, 1831); 591, 597–603 (fourth annual message, Dec. 4, 1832). See also JQA, *Memoirs*, 8:503, entry of December 5, 1832 (John Quincy Adams's reaction); Parsons, *John Quincy Adams*, 213 for an account of JQA's reaction to the message as a whole. For further Jacksonian perspectives on the internal improvement General Welfare Clause issue, see *Papers of the Presidents*, 3:97, 120–21 (sixth annual message); 292, 298–301 (farewell address); Remini, *Course of American Democracy*, 414–17.
27. Cole, *The Presidency of Andrew Jackson*, 67. See e.g., Act of March 2, 1831, *U.S. Statutes at Large* 4 (1824–1835): 469; Act of July 3, 1832, *U.S. Statutes at Large* 4: 551,553, 557; Act of March 2, 1833, *U.S. Statutes at Large* 4:648; Act of July 24, 1834, *U.S. Statutes at Large* 4:680 (Ohio, Indiana, Illinois). See also references to ancillary state legislation in these acts. Jackson also signed legislation providing for river and harbor improvements as well as surveys. See e.g., Act of March 2, 1833, *U.S. Statutes at Large* 4:645.

Chapter 10. Madison's Testament, Story's Commentary, and the Postulates of the Antebellum Presidents

1. For the twentieth century judicial adoption of Story's view on the spending power, see *United States v. Butler*, 297 U.S. 1 (1936).
2. Madison, *Writings*, 4:121 (letter of Nov. 27, 1830); Drew McCoy, *The Last of the Fathers: James Madison and the Republican Legacy* (Cambridge: Cambridge University Press, 1989), 77–78. See also 148 (assessment of Stevenson).
3. Madison,*Writings*, 4:122–24 (emphasis omitted).
4. Ibid., 4:124–25 (emphasis in the original).
5. Madison, *Writings*, 4:124–25.
6. Ibid., 125–28 (emphasis added); McCoy, *Last of the Fathers*, 78.
7. Madison, *Writings*, 4:128. See Sorenson, *Madison on the "General Welfare" of America*, 95–105.
8. Ibid., 128–31; 134–39. For Madison's supplemental memorandum, see 134. Here Madison makes clear that he objected to both the interpretation of the

General Welfare Clause as a general power to legislative for the general welfare and the interpretation of the clause as a license to spend for general welfare purposes beyond those reflected in the enumerated powers.

9. Madison, *Writings*, 4:143, 146–50, letter to Reynolds Chapman, Jan. 6, 1831 (emphasis in the original). See McCoy, *The Last of the Fathers*, 79–83, for a discussion of Madison's regard for legislative precedent as a guide to constitutional interpretation.

10. *Encyclopedia Britannica*, 25:970, 3rd ed., 1911; Joseph Story, *Commentaries on the Constitution of the United States* (1833; reprint, with an introduction by Ronald D. Rotunda and John E. Nowak, Durham: Carolina Academic Press, 1987), vi–xiv. This volume—hereafter referred to as Story, Abridgement—reprints the 1833 abridgement. See especially viii–xi for the quoted assessments of Story.

11. Joseph Story, *Commentaries on the Constitution of the United States*, 5th ed., ed., Melville Bigelow, 2 vols. (Boston: Little, Brown and Co., 1891), 1:661–62 (Hereafter Story, *Commentaries*) References here are to the 1891 version unless otherwise indicated in order to provide insight on the source available to late nineteenth century legal scholars. The 1891 edition was subject to editing after Story's death in 1845.

12. Story, *Commentaries*, 1:662.

13. Story, *Commentaries*, 1:662–63 (emphasis in the original).

14. Story, *Commentaries*, 1:664. In the abridged version, Story followed this analysis with a long discussion of the policy reasons for a broad taxing power. Story, Abridgement, 331–35.

15. Story, *Commentaries*, 1:664–66.

16. Story, *Commentaries*, 1:665–66 (emphasis in the original).

17. Story, *Commentaries*, 1:667–69 (citing "Federalist no. 40.")

18. Story, *Commentaries*, 1:669–71.

19. Story, *Commentaries*, 1:670–71. See also Story, Abridgement, 347–50, 453–58 (power to make roads and canals); quoted language is at 347; elsewhere in the abridgement, Story discussed the Louisiana experience as a precedent for broad construction, a point made often by John Quincy Adams. Ibid., 459–65. See ibid., 329–57 (taxation).

20. In the two-volume version, Story supported his conclusions and analysis as to the scope of the General Welfare Clause with an explanation of the proceedings of the 1787 Convention, with a stout defense of the need for a general power of taxation (consistent with that of Hamilton in "Federalist" No. 30), and with lengthy quotations from Hamilton's interpretation in his *Report on Manufactures* (see chapter 4 above) and Monroe's 1822 memorandum (see chapter 7 above). Story also paid tribute to John Quincy Adams's 1832, post-presidential letter to Andrew Stevenson as a "masterly exposition" of the clause. Ibid, 678 n. 3. Finally, Story cited as supportive of his position Jackson's 1830 Maysville Road veto message. Ibid., 727 n. 1. See generally ibid., 672–728. Story insisted that a broadly read spending power was distinct from, and did not duplicate, the enumerated powers. Thus, a broad and distinct spending power could reasonably coexist with the enumerated powers that followed in Article 1, section 8 of the Constitution. In fully quoting Madison's Bonus Bill Veto message and his 1830 letter to Andrew Stevenson and in responding to both, Story engaged Madison on the issue far more directly than had Hamilton, Monroe, and John Quincy Adams. Story summarized the arguments pro and con for a broad reading of the spending power; those in favor he encapsulated as: (1) "the language of the clause [the General Welfare Clause] conferring the power"; (2) "the na-

ture of the power, which renders it in the highest degree expedient, if not indispensable, for the due operations of the national government"; and (3) "the early, constant, and decided maintenance of it [the broad reading] by the government and its functionaries, as well as by many of our ablest statesmen, from the commencement of the Constitution." Ibid., 716–17. In short, (1) plain language; (2) expediency (or indispensability); and (3) government practice were the principal considerations underpinning the broad reading.

21. *South Dakota v. Dole*, 483 U.S. 203 (1987).

22. For Jackson's views regarding Story, see Remini, *Course of American Democracy*, 266–67.

23. For John Quincy Adams's observations regarding Martin Van Buren, see his *Memoirs*, 9:368–69. During his legislative years, Van Buren confessed to his own inconsistency on the constitutional issue. *Elliot's Debates*, 4:477–78.

24. *Papers of the Presidents*, 4:194–202 (second annual message, Dec. 6, 1842); 4:330, 331–32 (Tyler veto message of June 11, 1844).

25. Ibid., 610, 611–12 (Polk veto message of Dec. 15, 1847); See ibid., 373, 378–79 (Polk inaugural address, March 4, 1845); 460–66 (Polk's veto of Aug. 3, 1846).

26. Ibid., 612; see also ibid., 618–24 (veto message of Dec. 15, 1847). Polk appeared to take issue with Monroe's change of heart regarding the power of appropriation. Ibid., 619–20. See chapter 7, above.

27. *Papers of the Presidents*, 4: 625–26.

28. Ibid., 629, 654–62 (Polk, fourth annual message, Dec. 5, 1848).

29. See chapter 11, below (Lincoln, election of 1848, internal improvements); *Papers of the Presidents*, 5:4, 5–6 (Zachary Taylor, inaugural address, March 5, 1849).

30. Ibid., 63–64, Fillmore: (biographical notes by J. D. Richardson); 77, 90 (first annual message, Dec. 2, 1850).

31. Ibid., 90–91.

32. Ibid, 90. See chapter 2, above, debates on ratification.

33. *Papers of the Presidents*, 5:113, 130 (Fillmore, second annual message, Dec. 2, 1851); 163, 181 (Fillmore, third annual message, Dec. 6, 1852: the government "should lend its powerful strength to the improvement of such means of intercommunication as are necessary to promote our internal commerce and strengthen the ties which bind us together as a people.")

34. Ibid., 5:247–56 (Pierce veto message of May 3, 1854); see ibid., 207, 218–19 (first annual message, Dec. 5, 1853).

35. Ibid., 248–49, 250–51.

36. Ibid., 252–53; to the same effect, see ibid., 257–71 (Pierce veto message of Dec. 30, 1854); 273, 290–92 (second annual message); 327, 341–50 (third annual message); 386–88 (internal-improvement vetoes of 1856).

37. *Papers of the Presidents*, 5:543–50 (Buchanan veto message of Feb., 24, 1859); see also ibid., 430, 434–35 (Buchanan, inaugural address, March 4, 1857); 436, 456–57 (first annual message); 599–607 (veto message of Feb. 1, 1860).

38. Ibid., 5:543–50; discussion of spending power is at 547.

39. Ibid., 5:547–49.

40. Ibid., 5:549.

41. Ibid., 5:608–14 (veto message of June 22, 1860, homestead legislation).

CHAPTER 11. LINCOLN'S GENERAL WELFARE CLAUSE

1. See Paul Simon, *Lincoln's Preparation for Greatness: The Illinois Legislative Years* (Norman: University of Oklahoma Press, 1965), 48–53, 76–97;

151–57 (Lincoln's continuing support for state internal improvements during Illinois legislative years despite fiscal problems); 155 ("Lincoln consistently supported bigger and more internal improvements."); 155–56 (federal aid proposal of 1839). See also Abraham Lincoln, *Collected Works of Abraham Lincoln / The Abraham Lincoln Association, Springfield, Illinois*, 9 vols., ed. Roy P. Basler (New Brunswick, N.J.: Rutgers University Press, 1953) 1:132–34; 135–38 (resolution and remarks regarding distribution of proceeds from sale of public lands); 1:196 (support for Illinois and Michigan Canal); Abraham Lincoln, *Abraham Lincoln: His Speeches and His Writings*, ed. Roy P. Basler (Cleveland: World Publishing Co., 1946; New York: Da Capo Press, 1990), 90–113 (Sub-Treasury speech); Lincoln, *Collected Works*, 1:307 (resolutions at a Whig meeting, March 1, 1843); 1:309, 312–14 (campaign circular from Whig committee, March 4, 1843, distribution of public land proceeds); 1:318 (letter to John Bennett, March 7, 1843, authorship of portion of circular); 1:329 (speech at Whig barbecue in Jacksonville, Illinois, journal report; internal-improvement aspect); 1:394–95 (letter to Orville Browning, June 24, 1847, preparation for trip to Chicago River and Harbor Convention).

2. Lincoln, *Abraham Lincoln: His Speeches*, 547 (Lincoln's presidential campaign autobiography).

3. Paul Findley, *A. Lincoln: The Crucible of Congress, The Years Which Formed His Greatness* (New York: Crown Publishers, 1979), 260–61.

4. Ibid., 159–60; Lincoln, *Abraham Lincoln: His Speeches*, 547, 553–54.

5. Lincoln, *Collected Works*, 1:480–90 (speech about internal improvements in U.S. House of Representatives); 483–84 (the general-local distinction). See David Herbert Donald, *Lincoln*, (New York: Simon and Schuster, 1995), 128. Donald finds Lincoln's stance in the speech opposing change in the Constitution a "peculiar position" given Lincoln's later association with the Thirteenth Amendment. However, in the context of the 1848 speech, the position seems reasonable. Lincoln supported congressional aid for internal improvements (without amendment) because, so he argued, the text of the Constitution, as interpreted by respected scholars, warranted it. On the other hand, he consistently maintained that, absent an amendment, there was no authority in the Constitution to interfere with slavery in states where it existed. See text below, following note 9. This was essentially the same position taken by John Quincy Adams. See text below, this chapter, following note 22. For Polk's second veto, see chapter 10 above, text at note 25.

6. Lincoln, *Collected Works*, 1:485 (emphasis in the original); for other policy aspects of the speech, see ibid., 481–85.

7. Ibid., 485–486 (constitutional analysis emphasis in the original). See Story, *Abridgement*, 453–56.

8. Lincoln, *Collected Works*, 1:486 (emphasis in original); 490–92 (letter to William H. Herndon, June 22, 1848, remarks on internal-improvement speech). For other observations on the question of internal improvements during Lincoln's House term, see Lincoln, *Abraham Lincoln: His Speeches*, 233, speech in the U.S. House of Representatives, July 27, 1848 (the Taylor speech).

9. Lincoln, *Collected Works*, 2:158 (speech at Peoria, Illinois, September 17, 1852, opposition to Pierce's internal-improvement record); 220–21 (fragments on government, attributed tentatively to July 1854).

10. See Abraham Lincoln, *Abraham Lincoln: Speeches and Writings, 1859–1865*, (New York: The Library of America, 1989), 59, 86–87 (speech at Cincinnati, Ohio, Sept.17, 1859); *Papers of the Presidents*, 6:5, 10 (inaugural address, no recommendations for amendments).

11. See generally chapter 10, following note 25.
12. See Phillip Shaw Paludan, *The Presidency of Abraham Lincoln*, American Presidency Series (Lawrence: University Press of Kansas, 1994), 319 ("Lincoln's great accomplishment was to energize and mobilize the nation. . . .").
13. *Papers of the Presidents* 6:20 (Lincoln, special session message, July 4, 1861). See Donald, *Lincoln*, 301–4, regarding the special session message.
14. *Papers of the Presidents*, 6:27 (emphasis in the original). Donald, *Lincoln*, 296–97, describes the determination of Arkansas, North Carolina, Tennessee, and Virginia to join the original seven seceding states of the deep South as a result of Lincoln's earler call for militiamen to suppress obstruction of the law. This left in the Union the four border states: Delaware, Kentucky, Maryland, and Missouri, a fragile coalition that Lincoln sought to maintain throughout the war.
15. *Papers of the Presidents*, 6:27 (emphasis in the original). Compare Jackson's antinullification proclamation. Ibid., 2:640. For Lincoln's treatment of the secession as a rebellion or insurrection, see Donald, *Lincoln*, 302–3. A general study of Lincoln and American constitutionalism may be found in Herman Belz, *Abraham Lincoln, Constitutionalism, and Equal Rights in the Civil War Era* (New York: Fordham University Press, 1998).
16. *Papers of the Presidents*, 6:28 (emphasis in the original). Compare Lincoln's internal improvement speech, discussed this chapter following note 4.
17. *Papers of the Presidents*, 6:28.
18. Ibid., 29–30.
19. Ibid., 30. For John Quincy Adams's first annual message and its invocation of a similar role for government, see text above, chapter 8. See Greenstone, *Lincoln Persuasion*, 235 (Lincoln and opportunity).
20. *Papers of the Presidents*, 6:30–31 (emphasis in the original). Donald, *Lincoln*, 304–6, describes the reaction to the special session message; see also Papers of the President, 6:44, 58 (Dec. 3, 1861).
21. *Papers of the Presidents*, 6:44, 46 (first annual message, December 3, 1861). Donald, *Lincoln*, 320, ("perfunctory document").
22. *Papers of the Presidents*, 6:52–53.
23. JQA, *Memoirs* , 5:210; 5:4, 12, 14 (John Quincy Adams's 1820 views on slavery).
24. *Papers of the Presidents*, 6:44, 54 (first annual message, colonization); 68 (message of March 6, 1862, compensated emancipation); 126, 136–42 (second annual message, 1862; constitutional amendment); Donald, *Lincoln*, 343–44 discusses the colonization proposal; See Belz, *Abraham Lincoln, Constitutionalism, and Equal Rights in the Civil War Era*, 101–18 (Republican emancipation legislation).
25. *Papers of the Presidents*, 6:68–69 (message of March 6, 1862); Paludan, *Presidency of Abraham Lincoln*, 126–28 (background of and flaws in compensated emancipation proposal). Lincoln may also have seen this proposal as supported by the Common Defense Clause in Article I, section 8, clause 1.
26. Donald, *Lincoln*, 346–49 (discusses this message, including the positive reaction to it as well as the lack of any practical response by potentially affected border states). For Lincoln's plea to the border states, see Lincoln, *Collected Works*, 5:317 (July 12, 1862); for his draft bill, see ibid., 324.
27. Lincoln, *Collected Works*, 5:336 (July draft of Emancipation Proclamation). See Gideon Welles, *The Diary of Gideon Welles*, 2 vols. (Boston: Houghton Mifflin Company, 1911) 1:70–71 (conversation about military necessity, July 13, 1862); Paludan, *Presidency of Abraham Lincoln*, 147–49, 154–55.

28. *Papers of the Presidents*, 6:136–42 (Lincoln, second annual message; constitutional amendment proposal). The message also repeated Lincoln's earlier proposal for compensated emancipation legislation, suggesting that he did not conceive the idea of a constitutional amendment as a cure for spending power problems in the earlier proposal. Paludan, *Presidency of Abraham Lincoln*, 163–66 (constitutional amendment proposal and its relationship to other initiatives, quoted language is at 164).

Chapter 12. Lincoln's General Welfare Legacy

1. *Papers of the Presidents*, 6:126, 128 (Lincoln, second annual message, Dec. 2, 1862).
2. Ibid., 132–33. G. S. Boritt, *Lincoln and the Economics of the American Dream* (Memphis: Memphis State University Press, 1978), 210–14 (accounts of Lincoln's ample support of government aid to the transcontinental railroad and the Illinois and Michigan Canal); Boritt quoted language is at 214. Heather Cox Richardson,*The Greatest Nation of the Earth: Republican Economic Policies During the Civil War* (Cambridge: Harvard University Press, 1997), 170–208.For the supportive role of Lincoln in railroad legislation, see Paludan, *Presidency of Abraham Lincoln*, 116–17.
3. *Papers of the Presidents*, 6:133. See Richardson, *Greatest Nation of the Earth*, 149–54; Paludan, *Presidency of Abraham Lincoln*, 113–16 (same).
4. *Papers of the Presidents*, 6:133–34.
5. *Papers of the Presidents*, 6:135.
6. Ibid., 179, 186–91.
7. Richardson, *Greatest Nation of the Earth*, 139–49, quoted language is at 149 and 168. Richardson sees the Homestead Act as representing an expansion of the government's role in economic activity and as removing public lands as a tax base, thus ensuring the ultimate need for income taxes to pay for government programs.
8. See Donald, *Lincoln* , 424.
9. *Papers of the Presidents*, 6:186–87. See Lincoln, *Collected Works*, 4:201, speech to the Germans, Feb. 12, 1861; in favor of parceling government lands to give every poor man a home.
10. See text above, chapter 10 regarding Buchanan's veto; Richardson, *Greatest Nation of the Earth*, 141–49 (account of the pre–Civil War homestead legislation and the passage of the act in 1861). Opposition to the Buchanan veto evidently played a role in the campaign of 1860 and was a theme, albeit a minor one, in Republican appeals to the voters. See generally, Emerson D. Fite, *The Presidential Campaign of 1860* (New York: Macmillan, 1911), 125, 198–204, 235, 330–40. This political aspect presumably played a role in Lincoln's support for the legislation from both a constitutional and policy perspective.
11. See Richardson, *Greatest Nation of the Earth*, 148–49 (final passage of Homestead Act). Richardson, to be sure, does not attribute passage of this legislation to the General Welfare Clause but rather to the view that Congress had authority to enact legislation of benefit to the people. The specific authority would be the power to dispose of public lands. See ibid., 143.
12. *Papers of the Presidents*, 6:179, 187.
13. *Papers of the Presidents*, 6:243, 249 (Lincoln, fourth annual message; Dec. 6, 1864, emphasis added).

14. Ibid., 250–51 (railroads; people's department).
15. Ibid., 252. See text above, chapter 11 at note 23.
16. Ibid., 253–54.
17. Ibid., 255
18. Act of July 2, 1862; ch. 130, *U.S. Statutes at Large* 12 (1862): 503.
19. Paludan, *Presidency of Abraham Lincoln*, 115. See Richardson, *Greatest Nation of the Earth*, 155–60, (account of the passage of the first Morrill Act); ibid., 156 (Morrill's objectives: "[Morrill] concentrated on establishing that a college bill would increase agricultural production and thus contribute to national prosperity.... Particularly attractive to Morrill's Republican listeners was his argument that agricultural colleges could slow the growing emigration from rural to urban areas.") See *Congressional Globe*, 37th Cong., 2nd Sess. App. 256–57.
20. Act of July 2, 1862, ch. 130, sections 1–5; section 5 (fourth).
21. See chapter 10 above, text following note 36, for Buchanan veto. For Morrill's 1858 defense of his bill, see Richardson, *Greatest Nation of the Earth*, 155.
22. See *Papers of the Presidents*, 7:112 and 479, for views of Grant and Hayes; Paludan, *Presidency of Abraham Lincoln*, 115, assessment of the relationship between Lincoln's views on labor and the Morrill Act ("free labor" quote). Lincoln's 1859 agriculture speech in Milwaukee, Wisconsin, is found in Lincoln, *Speeches and Writings 1859–1865*, 90, 97–100. For Morrill's 1858 defense of his bill, see Congressional Globe, 35th Cong., 1st Sess. 1692–97, including Morrill's contention that constitutional authority for the measure was to be found in the power over public lands. See also Richardson, *Greatest Nation of the Earth*, 155. The Senate debate is found in *Congressional Globe*, 37th Cong 2nd. Sess, 2160, 2187, 2248–50; 2275–77, 2328–29, 2366, 2394–96, 2440–43, 2625–34. Most of the debate relates to the concerns expressed by Senator Lane of Kansas and others that bill would cause Western lands to be acquired by speculators making it unavailable to help meet state priorities. For references to the *Congressional Globe*, see http://memory.loc.gov. See Lincoln, *Collected Works* 6:123 (letter of March 2, 1863 regarding New Mexico).
23. Paludan, *Presidency of Abraham Lincoln*, 117–18 (flaws in the land grant program). See Alexander Groth, *Lincoln: Authoritarian Savior* (New York: University Press of America, 1996) for a portrait of a strong, nondeferential wartime president.

CHAPTER 13. RECONSTRUCTION, T. R., AND WILSON'S REALIGNMENT

1. *Papers of the Presidents*, 7:55–56 (Grant, Proclamation of March 30, 1870).
2. See also ibid., 96, 112 (Grant, second annual message, 1870). For an overall insight into the Grant Administration that focuses on the disappointments, as well as on Grant's detached approach to public administration, see Morton Keller, *Affairs of State: Public Life in Late Nineteenth-Century America* (Cambridge: Harvard University Press, 1977), 259–62.
3. *Papers of the Presidents*, 7:442, 444 (Hayes, inaugural address March 5, 1877); 458, 479 (Hayes, first annual message); 492, 506 (second annual message); 557, 579 (third annual message Dec. 1, 1879); Hayes's diary entry of Oct. 18,

1877. The correspondence and diary entries of Rutherford B. Hayes may be found at http://www.ohiohistory.org/onlinedoc/hayes, website of the Hayes Presidential Library in Fremont, Ohio.

4. Ari Hoogenboom, *The Presidency of Rutherford B. Hayes* (Lawrence: University Press of Kansas, 1988), 119–20.

5. Ibid., 62; Hayes, letter of March 9, 1886 to Hon. Isaac Taylor, letter of March 27, 1886 to General J. M. Comly, letter of Aug. 24, 1880, to Mr. Frank Hatton.

6. *Papers of the Presidents*, 7:601, 602–3 (Hayes, fourth annual message Dec. 6, 1880, emphasis added); Hayes, diary entry of Aug. 24, 1880, California speech; Keller, *Affairs of State*, 132 (quoted language).

7. Hoogenboom, *Presidency of Rutherford B. Hayes*, 59; Hayes, letter of Sept. 7, 1883 to W. J. Davis ("Universal education is the common interest of the whole people."); diary entry of Oct. 18, 1877, reflects reliance on John Quincy Adams for presidential precedents. Background regarding the Hayes-Tilden election and the causes of Hayes's conflict with Congress and his own party, factors that complicated his ability to implement his policies, is found in Keller, *Affairs of State*, 262–66.

8. *Papers of the Presidents*, 8:6, 8–9 (Garfield, inaugural address, March 4, 1881).

9. Ibid., 8:37, 58 (Chester Arthur, first annual message Dec. 6, 1881); 126, 144; 170, 184 (succeeding annual messages); Hayes, diary entry of Dec. 10, 1881; Keller, *Affairs of State*, 134 (quoted language); see ibid., 132–36 for a general discussion of Reconstruction era federal aid to education.

10. Ibid., 8:95 (Arthur, letter of April 17, 1882, transmitting request for appropriations to repair levees).

11. Ibid., 9:54 (Benjamin Harrison, first annual message) Dec. 3, 1889.

12. Ibid., 55–56 (Harrison). See Second Morrill Act, Act of Aug. 30, 1890, 7 U.S.C. 321., See Keller, *Affairs of State* 132 (use of public domain to aid education).

13. *Papers of the Presidents*, 9:389, 390 (Cleveland, second inaugural address, March 1893); 434, 456–57 (first annual message, second term, Dec. 4, 1893); Keller, *Affairs of State*, 299 (Cleveland vetoes).

14. Ibid., 8:580, 581 (Cleveland, first term, third annual message, Dec. 6, 1887); 773, 778 (fourth annual message, Dec. 3, 1888, constitutional concerns).

15. Ibid., 9:401 (Cleveland, special session message of Aug. 8, 1893).

16. Ibid., 10:26 (McKinley, first annual message, Dec. 6, 1897); 82 (second annual message, Dec. 5, 1898); 191 (message of Dec. 3, 1900).

17. Henry F. Pringle, *Theodore Roosevelt: A Biography* (New York: Harcourt, Brace & World, 1931), 336.

18. *Papers of the President*, 10:417, 424–26 (Theodore Roosevelt, first annual message, Dec. 3, 1901), regulation; labor; quoted language is at 424–25. Ibid., 10:432 (reclamation).

19. George E. Mowry, *The Era of Theodore Roosevelt and the Birth of Modern America, 1900–1912* (New York: Harper & Row, 1958), 121.

20. *Papers of the Presidents*, 10:432

21. Ibid., 10:433.

22. Ibid., 434–36, quoted language is at 436; see Mowry, *Era of Theodore Roosevelt*, 124–25 (background on reclamation legislation).

23. *Presidential Messages and State Papers*, ed. Julius Muller, 10 vols. (New York: Review of Reviews Company, 1917) (hereafter *Presidential Messages*),

9:3090–3091 (T. Roosevelt, fifth annual message). For another insight on Roosevelt's perspective on constitutional interpretation, see Pringle, *Theodore Roosevelt*, 336.

24. Mowry, *Era of Theodore Roosevelt*, 214; see ibid., 197–225, increasing progressivism.

25. *Presidential Messages*, 9:3134, 3143 (T. Roosevelt, Message of Dec. 3, 1907, income tax).

26. Ibid., 3240–41 (Taft, Message of June 16, 1909 income tax).

27. U.S. Constitution, Amendment XVI.

28. Mowry, *The Era of Theodore Roosevelt*, 263–64.

29. Ibid., 263.

30. *Presidential Messages*, 10:1–4 (Woodrow Wilson, inaugural address, 1913).

31. Ibid.,10:4, 37, 41–42 (Wilson, first annual message Dec. 2, 1913).

32. Ibid., 133, 153 (third annual message, December 1915); 162, 164 (speech at Pittsburgh, Pa., January 1916, part of western-preparedness tour); Keller, *Affairs of State*, 298–99 (Grover Cleveland compared to Theodore Roosevelt and Woodrow Wilson).

33. See chapter 14 below; Act of Feb. 23, 1917, *Statutes at Large* 39 (1917): 929.

34. John Milton Cooper, Jr. *The Warrior and the Priest: Woodrow Wilson and Theodore Roosevelt* (Cambridge: Harvard University Press, 1983), 187–221; 225–27; Pringle, *Theodore Roosevelt*, 382–84, 397–400.

35. Cooper, *Warrior and the Priest*, 189–91; Pringle, *Theodore Roosevelt*, 336.

36. Cooper, *Warrior and the Priest*, 229–47.

37. Ibid., 217–18.

38. Ibid., 198.

39. Woodrow Wilson, *The New Freedom: A Call for the Emancipation of the Generous Energies of a People* (New York: Doubleday, Page and Co., 1913), 164.

40. Ibid., chapters 4, 10, 11.

41. Woodrow Wilson, *Constitutional Government in the United States* (1907; reprint, Holmes Beach, Fla.: Gaunt, 1997), 192.

CHAPTER 14. THE NEW DEAL AND JUDICIAL RESOLUTION

1. *Agricultural Adjustment Act of 1933, U.S. Statutes at Large* 48 (1933): 31; *United States v. Butler*, 297 U.S. 1 (1936); *Steward Machine Co. v. Davis*, 301 U.S. 548 (1937); *Helvering v. Davis*, 301 U.S. 619 (1937).

2. Arthur M. Schlesinger, Jr., *The Age of Roosevelt: The Coming of the New Deal* (Boston: Houghton Mifflin Company, 1938), 27–67 (Agricultural Adjustment Act, generally); 29 (Wallace); 36 (domestic allotment plan).

3. Ibid, 37–38.

4. Ibid., 37 (use of spending power).

5. Ibid., 39 (drafting); 40 (Schlesinger's characterization).

6. Ibid., 40–45 (legislative enactment); 45–49 (agricultural adjustment administration; Peek); 59–60 (cotton).

7. *United States v. Butler*, 297 U.S. 1, 53–54 (1936).

8. Ibid., 55–57.

9. Ibid., 57–61. .

10. Ibid., 62; United States v. Butler, Brief for United States in *Landmark Briefs and Arguments of the Supreme Court of the United States: Constitutional Law*, ed., Phillip Kurland and Gerhard Casper (University Publications of America, n.d.), 30: 288–325. In the context of much scholarly criticism of the briefs filed by the Roosevelt Administration in defense of its New Deal program, Felix Frankfurter is quoted as expressing high praise for the government's brief in *Butler*. See William E. Leuchtenburg, *The Supreme Court Reborn: The Constitutional Revolution in the Age of Roosevelt* (New York, Oxford: Oxford University Press, 1995), 232.

11. The brief cited a number of the observations of those who participated in the state ratifying conventions to the effect that General Welfare Clause was intended to confer a broad power of appropriation comparable to that provided in the Articles of Confederation. Brief for United States, *Landmark Briefs and Arguments* 30:294–301. As for pre-1936 statutes based upon a broad reading of the spending power (in the fashion of Hamilton), the brief cited statutes providing for relief of distress, appropriations for the public health, including the Public Health Service; the second Morrill Act of August 30, 1890; appropriations for the Bureau of Education established in 1867; appropriations for vocational education (presumably, the legislation enacted during the Wilson Administration); science-related appropriations for the Bureau of Mines and the National Bureau of Standards; appropriations for vocational rehabilitation; appropriations to compensate farmers for loss suffered due to the suppression of the boll weevil, appropriations to carry out the Federal Farm Loan Act, and other appropriations to carry out the work of the Department of Agriculture. Ibid., 306–22. The brief concluded: "[I]f the Madisonian theory were to be adopted today, it would mean the destruction of many of our most familiar and significant governmental policies and activities. . . . These governmental activities have become so interwoven into our commercial, social, and economic life that to strike them down now would result in catastrophic dislocations. An acceptance at this late date of the Madisonian view . . . would retard the development of public health, education, the sciences, and social welfare, all of which to a large measure are dependent on Federal aid and encouragement." Ibid., 322–23.

12. *United States v. Butler*, 297 U.S. 63–64.
13. Ibid., 64.
14. Ibid., 64–65.
15. Ibid., 65.
16. Ibid., 65 (Madison).
17. Ibid., 65–66 (Hamilton).
18. Ibid., 66 (resolution and conclusion).
19. Ibid., 66–78. For a sharp critique of this part of the Butler Court's decision, see David E. Engdahl, "The Spending Power," *Duke Law Journal* 44:1 (1994). Engdahl argues that, while the Court relied upon Hamilton in reaching its conclusions regarding the scope of the spending power, as described in the text above, it demonstrated a profound misunderstanding of Hamilton's thinking in striking down the Agricultural Adjustment Act on Tenth Amendment grounds. Engdahl observes, "The rule of decision in *Butler* . . . is precisely Madison's view, applied notwithstanding the Court's simultaneous nominal endorsement of Hamilton's view. The majority's seeming obliviousness to this flagrant self-contradiction makes its opinion in Butler one of the truly ridiculous opinions delivered in two centuries of Supreme Court jurisprudence." Ibid., 36–37. Engdahl argues that the Court's mistake was to deny the application of the

"general principle of extraneous ends" to the spending power. Given the grant of the spending power, Congress could employ it to achieve good policy objectives even though not within the scope of an enumerated power, just as Congress could use the enumerated powers to achieve such objectives, e.g., using the interstate commerce clause to promote consumer interests.

20. *United States v. Butler*, 78–81. Quoted language is at 81.
21. Ibid., 81, 82–83.
22. Ibid., 83–85. Quoted language is at 85.
23. Ibid., 86.
24. Ibid., 86–87. Engdahl does not spare Stone's opinion the same criticism that he levels at the majority—gross misunderstanding of Hamilton. See Engdahl, "The Spending Power," 38–43.
25. See David Kyvig, *Explicit and Authentic Acts, Amending the U.S. Constitution* (Lawrence: University of Kansas Press, 1996), 289–314 (failure of Congress to propose constitutional amendment to address the problem). For legislative practice, see preceding chapters in this work.
26. Schlesinger, *Coming of the New Deal*, 297–315, 299–301 (Perkins); see chapter 8, above.
27. Schlesinger, *Coming of the New Deal*, 301–3 (unemployment compensation); 303–4 (aged).
28. Ibid., 303–6 (committee).
29. Ibid., 303–4 (policy on the aged); 306–7 (committee's view on the program for the aged).
30. Ibid., 309–13 (legislative adoption and evaluation).
31. *Steward Machine Co. v. Davis*, 301 U.S. 548 (1937). For the act in question, see *Statutes at Large*, 49 (1935): 620.
32. *Steward Machine Co.*, 574–76 (description of unemployment compensation program).
33. Ibid., 573, 578 (complaint).
34. Ibid., 585–87; quoted language is at 586–87.
35. Ibid., 587–89 (economic pressure vs. cooperative federalism).
36. Ibid., at 589–90 (motive vs. coercion).
37. Ibid., 593–94 (conditions).
38. Ibid., 597.
39. Ibid., 598 (separate dissenting opinion by Justice McReynolds quoting Franklin Pierce veto message); 609 (dissenting opinion by Justice Sutherland, joined in by Justice Van Devanter); 616 (separate dissenting opinion of Justice Butler).
40. *Statutes at Large* 49 (1935): 620 (social security act; retirement benefits); 301 U.S. 634–36.
41. *Helvering v. Davis*, 301 U.S. 619, 640 (Cardozo's spending power resolution, emphasis added). See Engdahl, "The Spending Power," 43–49 for a critique of Cardozo's opinion. Engdahl proposes abandoning the General Welfare Clause as the source of the spending power, despite the historical precedents that based the power on that source beginning with Hamilton's *Report on Manufactures*.
42. *Helvering v. Davis*, 301 U.S. 640, 641
43. Ibid., 642–45. Article VI, para. 2 of the U. S. Constitution is the Supremacy Clause.
44. Ibid., 646 (Analysis of Amendment X). *New York v. United States*, 112 Sup. Ct. 2408, 2417 (1992) (majority opinion of Justice O'Connor). The opinion reflects

the Court's contemporary understanding of the spending power and federalism.

45. 301 U.S. 646; see chapter 1 above.

46. See chapters 15 and 16 below.

47. Leuchtenburg, *Supreme Court Reborn*, 235 (quote); 213–36 ("constitutional revolution" of 1937); 216–18 (role of the Agricultural Adjustment Act and Social Security cases). See Bruce Ackerman, *We the People, Vol. 1, Foundations* (Cambridge: Harvard University Press, 1991), 105–30.

48. Leuchtenburg, *Supreme Court Reborn*, 131–62 (court packing). The court-packing proposal was sent to Congress in February of 1937; the Social Security Cases were handed down in May of 1937; the court-packing plan was sent back to committee in July 1937. See Bruce Ackerman, *We the People, Vol. 2, Transformations* (Cambridge: Harvard University Press, 1998), 312–44, for another account of the court packing episode and its implications.

49. Barry Cushman, *Rethinking the New Deal Court: The Structure of a Constitutional Revolution* (New York: Oxford University Press, 1998), 21–23 (court-packing plan was on the decline when the Social Security Act decisions were handed down); 29–31 (expresses doubt that the election of 1936 was a major factor in influencing the Court in the Social Security Act cases); see also G. Edward White, *The Constitution and the New Deal* (Cambridge: Harvard University Press, 2000), 13–32, 198–239.

50. Leuchtenburg, *Supreme Court Reborn*, 96–100 (impact of *Butler* on administration thinking about the Supreme Court); 218–19 (role of Social Security Act cases in the Court's turn-about and constitutional revolution).

51. See text above following note 15.

52. See text above at notes 10–11.

53. See text above at notes 34 and 41. Note that Cardozo was careful not to "resurrect the contest."

54. Laurence Tribe, *American Constitutional Law* (Mineola, N.Y.: Foundation Press, 1978), 249. See ibid., 247–50 for a general discussion of the spending power.

55. 301 U.S. 598–609 (McReynolds opinion); 301 U.S. 609–16 (Sutherland opinion in which Van Devanter joined). In *Steward Machine Co.*, Justices Van Devanter and Sutherland dissented on other grounds. In his opinion, Justice Sutherland indicated that he had no trouble with the "familiar case of federal aid upon conditions which the state, without surrendering any of its powers, may accept or not as it chooses." 301 U.S. 612. In *Helvering v. Davis*, Justices Van Devanter and Sutherland joined the Court's opinion upholding the Social Security Act's retirement insurance program. For an analysis of this vote, see Cushman, *Rethinking the New Deal Court*, 22.

56. Ackerman, *We the People, Vol. 1, Foundations*, 47.

Chapter 15. Truman to Ford—Toward Consensus

1. See generally David McCullough, *Truman* (New York: Simon and Schuster, 1992), 473–74 ("compulsory health insurance to be funded by payroll deductions"; "all citizens would receive medical and hospital service irrespective of their ability to pay"); 468 (federal aid to housing and urban redevelopment); 485 ("landmark" employment legislation of 1946); 586 (1948 State of the Union message: national health insurance; a "massive housing program"; aid to educa-

tion; farm supports; natural resource conservation); 651 (1948 special session message: eight point program, including housing; aid to education; and farm supports). See also 723–923 (Truman's second term occupied with foreign policy and Korean War); 915 (GI Bill; 8 million veterans attended college); 984 (1965 signature of Medicare bill at Truman Library in Truman's presence).

2. See Geoffrey Perret, *Eisenhower* (Holbrooke, Mass.: Adams Media Corporation, 1999), 421 (social security); 510 (no intent to roll back New Deal; proposal to extend social security to pre-1935 retirees, adding to pool of social security recipients). For observations on the Federal Aid Highway Act, see House Committee on Public Works and Transportation, *Intermodel Surface Transportation Efficiency Act of 1991*, 102d Cong., 1st sess., 1991, H. Rept. 171(l), 1–2; *Federal Aid Highway Act of 1956*, Public Law 627, 84th Cong., 2d sess., *U.S. Statutes at Large*, 70 (1956): 374, 397.

3. *National Defense Education Act of 1958*, Public Law 864, 85th Cong., 2d sess., *U.S. Statutes at Large* 72 (1958): 1580; Perret, *Eisenhower*, 509–10 (HEW); 561 (NDEA); *Public Papers of the Presidents, Dwight D. Eisenhower, 1953* (Washington, D.C.: GPO) (Public Papers), 94–98 (HEW. Quoted language is at 95); *Public Papers, Eisenhower, 1958*, 527, 671 (NDEA).

4. James N. Giglio, *The Presidency of John F. Kennedy* (Lawrence: University Press of Kansas, 1991), 27–30; see ibid., 29 (Kennedy adopted "wisdom that great presidents were powerful instruments who advanced social justice at home"); Arthur Schlesinger Jr., *A Thousand Days* (Boston: Houghton Mifflin Company, 1965), 620–63.

5. *The Mutual Educational and Cultural Exchange Act of 1961*, Public Law 256, 87th Cong., 1st sess., *U.S. Statutes at Large* 75 (1961): 527, Fulbright-Hays Act; *Public Papers, John F. Kennedy, 1961*, 614 (remarks on signing bill).

6. *Higher Education Facilities Act of 1963*, Public Law 204, 88th Cong., 1st sess., *U.S. Statutes at Large* 77 (1963): 363; Giglio, *Presidency of John F. Kennedy*, 106–7.

7. *Manpower Development and Training Act of 1962*, Public Law 415, 87th Cong., 2d sess., *U.S. Statutes at Large* 76 (1962): 23; Giglio, *Presidency of John F. Kennedy*, 106.

8. Ibid., 101–3.

9. Ibid., 113 (Jan. 21, 1961 order on food assistance to the needy; pilot food stamp program); *Public Papers, Kennedy, 1961*, 31 (Feb. 1961 press conference, mention of food stamp project).

10. See generally Giglio, *Presidency of John F. Kennedy*, 154–58.

11. See generally Robert Dallek, *Flawed Giant: Lyndon Johnson and His Times 1961–1973* (New York: Oxford University Press, 1998). Despite the New Deal court decisions, Johnson had some concern as to how the courts might treat his far-reaching reforms. Lyndon Baines Johnson, *The Vantage Point: Perspectives of the Presidency, 1963–1969* (New York: Holt, Rinehart and Winston, 1971), 547.

12. *Elementary and Secondary Education Act of 1965*, (ESEA), Public Law 10, 89th Cong., 1st sess., *U.S. Statutes at Large*, 79 (1965): 27. See Senate Committee on Labor and Public Welfare, Elementary and Secondary Education Act of 1965, 89th Cong., 1st sess., 1965; S. Rept., 146; Dallek, *Flawed Giant*, 195–203; Johnson, *The Vantage Point*, 206–12; quote is at 206. This legislation is constitutionally grounded on the General Welfare Clause. See Michael S. Sorgen, William A. Kaplin, Patrick S. Duffy, and Ephraim Margolin, *State, School and*

Family: Cases and Materials on Law and Education (New York: Matthew Bender, 1979), 14-4-14-17; 14-1-14-92; Judith A Winston, "Excellence and Equal Opportunity in Education: No Conflict of Laws," *Administrative Law Review* 53 (2001): 997, 1003.

13. *ESEA*, sec. 205(a)(2) (1965); Dallek, *Flawed Giant*, 197–98 (services to private school children; role of administration); 199–203 (Johnson's role in gaining enactment of ESEA, quote is at 203); *Public Papers, Lyndon B. Johnson, 1965–I*, 407–8 (signing statement). For a variety of current perspectives on how to make the Title I program work more effectively, see The Civil Rights Project, Harvard University, *Hard Work for Good Schools: Facts Not Fads in Title I Reform*, ed. Gary Orfield and Elizabeth H. DeBray, 1999.

14. *Higher Education Act of 1965*, Public Law 329, 89th Cong., 1st sess., *U.S. Statutes at Large* 79 (1965): 1219. See William A. Kaplin and Barbara A. Lee, *The Law of Higher Education: A Legal Guide for Student Affairs Professionals* (San Francisco: Jossey Bass Publishers, 1997).

15. *Economic Opportunity Act of 1964*, Public Law 452, 88th Cong., 2nd sess., *U.S. Statutes at Large* 78 (1964): 508; Dallek, *Flawed Giant*, 107–11 (Johnson's role; program administration); Johnson, *The Vantage Point*, 69–87, quote is at 70; *The Food Stamp Act of 1964*, Public Law 525, 88th Cong., 2d sess., *U.S. Statutes at Large* 78 (1964): 703. For Johnson's role in establishing the Department of Housing and Urban Development, see Dallek, *Flawed Giant*, 228–29.

16. *Social Security Amendments of 1965*, Public Law 97, 89th Cong., 1st sess., *U.S. Statutes at Large* 79 (1965): 286 (adding Title XVIII (Medicare) and Title XIX (Medicaid) to the Social Security Act); see Dallek, *Flawed Giant*, 203–11; Johnson, *The Vantage Point*, 212–21. (enactment, Johnson's role and perspective).

17. *National Foundation on the Arts and Humanities Act of 1965*, Public Law 209, 89th Cong., 1st sess. *U.S. Statutes at Large* 79 (1965): 845.

18. See Richard Nixon, *RN, The Memoirs of Richard Nixon* (New York: Simon & Schuster, 1990), 670–71 (list of accomplishments at end of first term as Nixon saw them); *Federal Water Pollution Control Act Amendments of 1972*, Public Law 500, 92d Cong. 2d sess., *U.S. Statutes at Large* 86 (1972): 833.

19. Nixon, *RN*, 426–28 (Nixon's account of welfare reform in which Daniel Patrick Moynihan, then serving in the White House, played a substantial role). See *Social Security Amendments of 1972*, Public Law 603, 92d Cong., 2d sess., Title III, *U.S. Statutes at Large* 86 (1972): 1329, 1465 (substantially amended Title XVI of the Social Security Act relating to supplemental security income for the aged, blind, and disabled).

20. *Emergency School Aid Act*, Public Law 318, 92d Cong., 2d sess., *U.S. Statutes at Large* 86 (1972): 235, 354; Nixon, *RN*, 439–43 (emergency school aid, quoted language is at 441); 435–45 (civil rights generally).

21. The National Institute of Education was established by sec. 301 of the Education Amendments of 1972, Public Law 318, 92d Cong., 2d sess., *U.S. Statutes at Large* 86 (1972): 328–332; Nixon, *RN*, 671.

22. Ibid., 671.

23. *Education for All Handicapped Children Act of 1975*, Public Law 142, 94th Cong., 1st sess., *U.S. Statutes at Large* 89 (1975): 773; *Public Papers, Gerald Ford, 1975–II*, 1935 (Washington, D.C.: GPO) (signing statement); John Robert Greene, *The Presidency of Gerald Ford* (Lawrence: University Press of Kansas, 1995), 85, 164.

Chapter 16. Carter to Clinton—Accommodating Budget and National Investment Imperatives

1. *Department of Education Organization Act*, Public Law 88, 96th Cong., 1st sess., *U.S. Statutes at Large* 93 (1979): 668; *Education Amendments of 1978*, Public Law 561, 95th Cong., 2d sess., *U.S. Statutes at Large* 92 (1978): 2143; Jimmy Carter, *Keeping Faith, Memoirs of a President* (New York: Bantam Books, 1982), 75–76, 83–87. Carter's long battle over energy policy and resultant legislation is discussed, 91–124. For a Carter cabinet secretary's account of the Carter presidency's contribution in spending power areas, see Joseph A. Califano, Jr., *Governing America: An Insider's Report from the White House and the Cabinet* (New York: Simon and Schuster, 1981). See particularly chapters 7–9. For two perspectives on the museum services program administered by the then federal Institute of Museum Services and first implemented during the Carter Administration, see Peggy Loar and Theodore Sky, "General Operating Support for Museums: Problems in Paradise," *Journal of College and University Law* 7 (1980–81): 267 and Theodore Sky, "The Institute of Museum Services and the Conservation of America's Heritage," *Dickinson Law Review* 93 (1989): 659.

2. *Comprehensive Environmental Response, Compensation and Liability Act of 1980*, Public Law 510, 96th Cong., 2d sess., *U.S. Statutes at Large* 94 (1980): 2767 (Superfund); Carter, *Keeping Faith*, 581–82.

3. *Family Support Act of 1988*, Public Law 485, 100th Cong., 2d sess. *U.S. Statutes at Large* 102 (1988): 2343; Lou Cannon, *President Reagan: The Role of a Lifetime* (New York: Public Affairs, 1991), 756.

4. *Education Consolidation and Improvement Act of 1981*, Title V–D of the Omnibus Budget Reconciliation Act of 1981, Public Law 35, 97th Cong., 1st sess., *U.S. Statutes at Large* 95 (1981): 357, 463; Public Law 297, 100th Cong., 2nd sess. (1988) later modified some of the consolidating provisions of the ECIA; Cannon, *President Reagan*, 730–31 (Nation at Risk); Terrel H. Bell, *The Thirteenth Man: A Reagan Cabinet Memoir* (New York: The Free Press, 1988), 114–43. For a sense of President Reagan's overall approach to federal programs in the context of his penultimate annual message, see *Public Papers, Ronald Reagan, 1988–I*, 84, "Address before a Joint Session of Congress on the State of the Union" Jan. 25, 1988 (focus on deficit control and welfare reform).

5. *South Dakota v. Dole*, 483 U.S. 203, 207 (1987) (citation omitted); Cannon, *President Reagan*, 207–15 (social security), 720 (judicial appointment philosophy; Reagan "was more successful in judicial selection than in any other area of domestic governance"); see also, 720–29.

6. Cannon, *President Reagan*, 756–57 ("The deficits were rooted in Reagan's incompatible 1980 campaign promises to boost military spending, cut taxes, and balance the federal budget.") See generally *Balanced Budget and Emergency Deficit Control Act of 1985*, Public Law 177, 99th Cong., 1st sess., Title II, *U.S. Statutes at Large* 99 (1985): 1038 (Gramm-Rudman-Hollings legislation to establish deficit control mechanism). The mechanism included successively lower annual deficit targets; if not met, the law called for sequestration of excess budgetary resources.

7. *Budget Enforcement Act of 1990*, Public Law 508, 101st Cong., 2d sess., Title XIII, *U.S. Statutes at Large* 104 (1990): 1388–573.

8. *Intermodal Surface Transportation Efficiency Act of 1991*, Public Law

240, 102d Cong., 1st sess.; *U.S. Statutes at Large* 105 (1991): 1914 (ISTEA) *Public Papers, George H. W. Bush, 1991–I*, 704 (remarks on proposed legislation).

9. The Clean Air Act Amendments are in Public Law 549, 101st Cong., 2d sess., *U.S. Statutes at Large* 104 (1990): 2399. For President Bush's perspective on this legislation, see, *Public Papers, George H. W. Bush, 1990–II:* 1600, 1601, Remarks on Signing the Bill Amending Clean Air Act; George Bush, *All the Best, George Bush: My Life in Letters and Other Writings* (New York: Simon and Schuster, 1999), 487 (entry of Nov. 16, 1990, regarding signing: "I realize more fully now how important this legislation was"). For an overview of Bush's approach to federal programs, see *Public Papers, George H. W. Bush, 1992–93-I:* 156, State of the Union Message, Jan. 28, 1992 (focus on desert storm, economy, education, health care reform, including health insurance tax credit).

10. President's Education Summit, Charlottesville, Virginia, 1989; *Public Papers, George H. W. Bush 1989–II:* 1271 (Remarks at university convocation in Charlottesville, Sept. 28, 1989); 1279 (joint statement on the education summit); *Public Papers, George H. W. Bush, 1990-I*: 274, Feb. 26, 1990 (remarks to governors); *Public Papers, 1991–I*, 395, 399 (address on education strategy and related fact sheet).

11. *Budget Enforcement Act*, Title XIII (1990); George Bush, *All the Best*, 483; see also 475, 480, 481, 582 (other observations on budget issue).

12. President Bill Clinton, *Between Hope and History: Meeting America's Challenges for the 21st Century* (New York: Random House, 1996), 22; ibid, 19–58; E. J. Dionne, Jr., *They Only Look Dead, Why Progressives Will Dominate the Next Political Era* (New York: Simon & Schuster, 1996), 113 (quotation); 109–17 (1993 budget battle).

13. See generally President Clinton's State of the Union messages, 1993–2000 in *Public Papers, William J. Clinton, 1993–2000*. For the 1993 budget legislation that set the stage for the Clinton approach to general-welfare investment in the framework of deficit reduction, see *Omnibus Budget Reconciliation Act of 1993*, Public Law 66, 103d Cong., 1st sess., *U.S. Statutes at Large* 107 (1993): 312.

14. *Goals 2000: Educate America Act*, Public Law 227, 103d Cong., 2d sess., *U.S. Statutes at Large* 108 (1994): 125; *Improving America's Schools Act*, Public Law 382, 103d Cong., 2d sess., *U.S. Statutes at Large* 108 (1994): 3518 (IASA); Clinton, *Between Hope and History*, 43; *Public Papers, William J. Clinton, 1994–II:* 1811 (remarks on signing IASA, Framingham, Mass., Oct. 20, 1994). For a general overview of this legislation and some of its key policy underpinnings, see Richard W. Riley, "The Improving America's Schools Act and Elementary and Secondary Education Reform," *Journal of Law and Education* 24 (1995): 513; Marshall S. Smith and Jennifer O'Day, "Systematic School Reform" in *The Politics of Curriculum and Testing, The Politics of Education Association Yearbook*, edited by Susan Fuhrman and Betty Malen (1990), 233. For a later State of the Union perspective, see *Public Papers, 1998–I*, 112, Address before a Joint Session of the Congress on the State of the Union, Jan. 27, 1998 (focus on deficit reduction, social security preservation, education, including Pell Grants, class size reduction, school construction, welfare reform, health security); U.S. Department of Education, National Center for Education Statistics, *The Condition of Education, 2000*, NCES 2000–062, (Washington, D.C.: GPO, 2000) Indicator 13, 15, 16, 17, 18, 37, 38 (indicators of progress or need for improvement respecting various measures); *Elementary and Secondary Education Act*, Title XIV in Public Law 382, 103d Cong., 2d sess., *U.S. Statutes at Large* 108 (1994): 3887–3912 (flexibility provisions). For a post-administration reflection on

the education goals and accomplishments of the Clinton Administration, see Richard W. Riley, "Education Reform through Standards and Partnerships, 1993–2000," *Phi Delta Kappan* 83 (2002): 700.

15. *Personal Responsibility and Work Opportunity Reconciliation Act* of 1996, Public Law 193, 104th Cong., 2d sess., *U.S. Statutes at Large* 110 (1996): 2105 (PRWORA). The Temporary Assistance to Needy Families Program is established under Title IV of the Social Security Act, as amended by PRWORA; *Public Papers, William J. Clinton, 1996–II*, 1325, 1328 (remarks and signing statement); Dionne, *They Only Look Dead*, 130–35 (Clinton 1994 unenacted welfare reform effort).

16. Social Security Act, as amended by PRWORA, secs. 401–8, *U.S. Statutes at Large* 110 (1996): 2113–42.

17. PRWORA, Title IV; *U.S. Statutes at Large* 110 (1996): 2260–2277; see Clinton, *Between Hope and History*, 133–35 (immigration), *Public Papers, 1996–II*, 1328–29; *Budget of the United States Government, Fiscal Year 1999*, 61 (FY 1999 Budget).

18. See *FY 1999 Budget*, 224–25; Robert A. Moffitt, "From Welfare to Work: What the Evidence Shows," in *Welfare Reform and Beyond, The Future of the Safety Net*, Edited by Isabel V. Sawhill, R. Kent Weaver, Ron Haskins and Andrea Kane (Washington, D.C.: Brookings Institution, 2002), 79; see this work generally for comprehensive background material on welfare reform and reauthorization.

19. See *FY 1999 Budget*, 51–60; 223–27 (education, training and income security); 225–26 (30 million were poor in 1996 after accounting for government programs).

20. See Bipartisan Commission on Entitlement Reform, *Staff Report on Entitlement Options* (December, 1994). This is the so-callled Kerry-Danforth Commission staff report. See *FY 1999 Budget*, 219–22; 229–232 (Medicare, social security).

21. See *Health Care Security for All Americans, Message from the President of the United States*, 103d Cong., 1st sess., 1993, H. Doc. 137; White House Domestic Policy Council, *Health Security: The President's Report to the American People* (Washington, D.C.: GPO), 1993; Dionne, *They Only Look Dead*, 129; see ibid., 118–30. See *Balanced Budget Act of 1997*, Public Law 33, 105th Cong., 1st sess., *U.S. Statutes at Large* 111 (1997): 251, 552–70 (CHIP). Hillary Rodham Clinton, *Living History* (New York: Simon & Schuster, 2003), 143–55, 182–92, 245–49.

CHAPTER 17. THE SPENDING POWER, THE CONSTITUTIONAL AMENDMENT, AND THE EVOLVING AMERICAN PRESIDENCY

1. Ackerman, *v. 1 Foundations* (chapters 1, 3–5); David Kyvig, *Explicit and Authentic Acts: Amending the U.S. Constitution, 1776–1995* (Lawrence: University Press of Kansas, 1996).

2. This is the thrust of chapters 1–14 above.

3. See chapters 1 and 14 above.

4. Ackerman, *v. 1 Foundations*, 6–7 (brief summary of basic idea); 58–67 (three regime perspective).

5. See generally chapter 8, above, regarding Adams (Adams-Bailey conversation).

6. See text above, chapter 9 (Jackson and the Maysville veto). For a concrete and sympathetic description of the evolution of Jefferson's constitutional thinking, see Kyvig, *Explicit and Authentic Acts*, 128–33; Ackerman, v. 1, *Foundations*, 268 (transformative statutes).

7. *United States v. Butler*, 297 U.S. 1 (1936); Story, *Commentaries*, discussed above in chapters 10 and 14.

8. See chapters 1, 2, 4, and 9 above.

9. Kyvig, *Explicit and Authentic Acts*, 480–84; see also, 128–33 (evolution of thinking regarding the place of the constitutional amendment in internal improvement era); 289–314 (describes Franklin Roosevelt's consideration and rejection of a constitutional amendment as a means of confronting obstacles to the New Deal posed by the Court). See Ackerman, *v. 2, Transformations*, chapters 11 and 12 (full account of the Roosevelt court-packing episode. Chapter 12 also describes role of Social Security Act cases in dampening momentum for Roosevelt's initiative); Ackerman, *v. 1 Foundations*, 268 (higher lawmaking through transformative statutes).

10. Ackerman, v. 2, *Transformations*, 315, emphasis in the original. See Kyvig, *Explicit and Authentic Acts*, 480: "[T]he failure to amend the Constitution in this instance [respecting internal improvement], though a restraining influence on federally financed national economic development, had far less consequence than the abandonment of amendment during the New Deal over a century later."

11. See text above, chapters 5, 6 and 7.

12. See text above, chapter 10 at notes 7 and 9 (Madison's observations on the second constitution and his 1831 letter). I do not suggest that this hypothesis (or the related concern) accords in any way with Ackerman's own thought-provoking concept. It merely represents my own effort to relate the spending power conundrum in the framework that Ackerman's historical analysis of the three regimes suggests. See Ackerman, v. 1, *Foundations*, 268–69 (compares classic and modern higher lawmaking); see Ackerman, v. 2, *Transformations*, 334–35 (switch of which Social Security Act decisions were a part "took the sails out of the movement for Article Five amendments"); see also ibid., 345–46.

13. See chapter 18 below where this is taken up at greater length.

14. See chapter 1 for a discussion of Randolph's resolutions.

15. Ackerman, v. 1, *Foundations*, 67.

16. See chapters 5–10, above.

17. See text above, chapter 8 at note 52 and chapter 13 at notes 3–7.

18. See chapter 13 above.

19. See chapter 14; see Ackerman,v. 2, *Transformations*, 350.

20. See chapters 15 and 16 above. Ackerman suggests that it was only with the election of 1940 that the New Deal constitutional changes were institutionalized: "Only after Roosevelt defeated Willkie did it become obvious that further serious appeals to the People to reverse the judicial revolution were utterly fruitless." Ackerman, v. 2 *Transformations*, 361. See *South Dakota v. Dole*, 483 U.S. 203 (1987).

21. See chapter 16 above.

Chapter 18. "Perseverance"

1. See JQA, *Memoirs* 8:48–50, July 4, 1828. Quoted language is at 50.
2. See chapter 15 above.

3. For a comprehensive account of the evolution of the federal role in education by the longest serving United States Secretary of Education, see Richard W. Riley, "Redefining the Federal Role in Education: Toward a Framework for Higher Standards, Improved Schools, Broader Opportunities and New Responsibilities for All," *Journal of Law and Education* 23 (1994): 295.

4. United States Department of Education, *The Condition of Education 2000*, Indicator 13, p. 23 (reading scores increased for 8th grade students and remained same for 4th and 12th graders, 1992 and 1998); 15, p. 25 (mathematics, scores up for all groups, 1990–96); Riley, "Education Reform through Standards and Partnerships, 1993–2000," *Phi Delta Kappan* 83 (2002): 700, 703; Rod Paige, "An Overview of America's Education Agenda," *Phi Delta Kappan* 83 (2002): 708, 710.

5. The latest reauthorization of federal aid to elementary and secondary programs was enacted in 2001 with the strong backing of the Bush Administration. See *No Child Left Behind Act of 2001*, Public Law 110, 107th Cong., 2d sess., *U.S. Statutes at Large* 115 (2001): 1425. The following titles of the ESEA as amended by this legislation relate to the programs mentioned in the text: Title II (teacher training); Title III (language instruction for limited English-speaking children); Title IV (21st century schools); Title V-D-1 (smaller learning communities). See also the following provisions of the ESEA as amended by the *Improving America's Schools Act, U.S. Statutes at Large* 108 (1994): 3518: Titles I, II, VII, X–I and Section 10105.

6. One example is the effort to achieve greater client participation in the Children's Health Insurance Program (CHIP), during the Clinton administration; it reflected a coordinated, interagency effort, involving a number of departments and agencies. For an early plea for integrated, allied services in federal program administration, see Elliot Richardson, *The Creative Balance: Government, Politics, and the Individual in America's Third Century* (New York: Holt, Rinehart and Winston, 1976), 152–93 (calls for simplification and synthesis to respond to the complexity explosion).

7. Department of Education Organization Act, section 103, *U.S. Statutes at Large* 93 (1979): 668, 670.

8. The Intermodal Surface Transportation Efficiency Act, enacted during the George H. W. Bush administration was an effort to address some of the transportation problems through an integrated, intermodal approach. See chapter 16 above. On Truman's role in health care, see chapter 15.

9. On success in education, see United States Department of Education, *The Condition of Education, 2000*, Indicator 38, p. 56 (attainment: completion rates for 25- to 29-year-olds increased across all educational levels, for all racial-ethnic groups); supplemental table 38–3, page 156 (attainment of bachelor's degree for females: 18.1 percent in 1971, 33.0 percent in 1999 more than that of men.); see Social Security Administration, *Fast Facts and Figures about Social Security* (Washington, D.C.: GPO, 2001), 8 (overall 8 percent of aged Social Security beneficiaries were poor; without Social Security, the total poverty rate would have been 48 percent assuming no other changes); Wendell E. Primus, Kathryn Porter, Margery Ditto, and Mitchell Kent, *The Safety Net Delivers: The Effects of Government Benefit Programs in Reducing Poverty* (Washington, D.C.: Center on Budget and Policy Priorities, 1996), 1 (safety net programs lifted 27 million people out of poverty in 1995); U.S. Census Bureau, *Statistical Abstract of the United States: 2001* (Washington, D.C.: GPO, 2001), Table 96, p. 173 (life expectancy for persons born in the United States in 1999 is 77).

10. See chapter 10 above regarding Story's role.

11. Ackerman, v. 2, *Transformations*, 338, note 67, cites the following proposals to authorize Congress to provide for the general welfare as having been introduced into the New Deal Congress: H. R. J. Res. 316, 74th Cong., 1st sess. (1935) (Rep. Keller); S.J. Res. 8, 75th Cong., 1st sess. (1937) (Sen. Logan) as responses to the court-packing scheme. See Kyvig, *Explicit and Authentic Acts*, 297 regarding Roosevelt administration's consideration of idea of reviving language considered by the 1787 Constitutional Convention giving Congress power to "legislate in all cases for the general interests of the Union." Senator Costigan is cited in this work as urging consideration of an amendment that would empower Congress to "legislate for the general welfare where states could not effectively do so." Ibid., 296–97. In *South Dakota v. Dole*, 483 U.S. 203, 207–8 (1987), the Supreme Court held that conditions of federal grants, to be authorized, must be related "'to the federal interest in particular national projects or programs.'"

12. See the opinion of Justice O'Connor writing for the majority in *New York v United States*, 505 U.S. 144, 166 (1992): "Our cases have identified a variety of methods, short of outright coercion, by which Congress may urge a State to adopt a legislative program consistent with federal interests." The opinion cites the spending power as the first such method, through the authority of Congress to attach conditions on the receipt of federal funds. (Compare Laurence H. Tribe and Michael C. Dorf, *On Reading the Constitution* [Cambridge: Harvard University Press, 1991], 6. "In the Constitution of the United States, men like Madison bequeathed to subsequent generations a framework for balancing liberty against power."

13. For John Dickinson's Fabius VIII letter, see *The Debate on the Constitution, Federalist and Antifederalist Speeches, Articles, and Letters During the Struggle over Ratification*, 2 vols. (New York: Library of America, 1993), 2:424, 428. The "fearless eyes" quotation is from Wilson's first inaugural address, *Presidential Messages*, 10:2 (March 4, 1913).

Bibliography

Abbot, W. W., ed. *The Papers of George Washington, The Journal of the Proceedings of the President 1793–1797*. Edited by Dorothy Twohig. Charlottesville: University Press of Virginia, 1981.

Ackerman, Bruce. *We the People*. Vol. 1 *Foundations*. Cambridge: Harvard University Press, 1991.

———. *We the People*. Vol. 2 *Transformations*. Cambridge: Harvard University Press, 1998.

Adams, John Quincy. *Memoirs of John Quincy Adams*. Edited by Charles Francis Adams. 12 vols. Freeport, N.Y.: Books for Libraries Press, 1969.

———. *The Great Design, Two Lectures on the Smithson Bequest by John Quincy Adams*. Edited by Wilcomb E. Washburn. Washington, D.C.: The Smithsonian Institution, 1965.

Adams, John, and John Quincy Adams. *The Selected Writings of John and John Quincy Adams*. Edited by Adrienne Koch and William Peden. New York: Alfred A. Knopf, 1946.

Ambrose, Stephen E. *Undaunted Courage, Meriwether Lewis, Thomas Jefferson, and the Opening of the American West*. New York: Simon and Schuster, 1996.

Ammon, Harry. *James Monroe: The Quest for National Identity*. Charlottesville: University Press of Virginia, 1990.

Banning, Lance. *The Sacred Fire of Liberty: James Madison and the Founding of the American Republic*. Ithaca: Cornell University Press, 1995.

Bell, Terrel H. *The Thirteenth Man: A Reagan Cabinet Memoir*. New York: The Free Press, 1988.

Belz, Herman. *Abraham Lincoln, Constitutionalism and Equal Rights in the Civil War Era*. New York: Fordham University Press, 1998.

Bemis, Samuel Flagg. *John Quincy Adams and the Union*. New York: Alfred A. Knopf, 1956.

Beschloss, Michael, general editor. *The Presidents*. New York: American Heritage, 1999.

Bipartisan Commission on Entitlement Reform, *Staff Report on Entitlement Options*. Washington, D.C., 1994.

Boritt, G. S. *Lincoln and the Economics of the American Dream*. Memphis: Memphis State University Press, 1978.

Bowen, Catherine Drinker. *Miracle in Philadelphia, The Story of the Constitutional Convention, May to September, 1787*. Boston: Little, Brown and Company, 1966.

Bradford, M. E. *Founding Fathers, Brief Lives of the Framers of the United States Constitution*. Lawrence: University Press of Kansas, 1981.

Brookhiser, Richard. *Alexander Hamilton, American.* New York: The Free Press, 1999.
Brown, Roger H. *Redeeming the Republic, Federalists, Taxation and the Origins of the Constitution.* Baltimore: Johns Hopkins University Press, 1993.
Budget of the United States Government, Fiscal Year 1999. Washington, D.C.: GPO.
Burns, James MacGregor. *Roosevelt: The Lion and the Fox.* New York: Harcourt Brace & Company, 1984.
Bush, George H. W. *All The Best, George Bush: My Life in Letters and Other Writings.* New York: Simon and Schuster, 1999.
Califano, Joseph, A. Jr. *Governing America: An Insider's Report from the White House and the Cabinet.* New York: Simon and Schuster, 1987.
Cannon, Lou. *President Reagan, The Role of a Lifetime.* New York: Public Affairs, 1991.
Carter, Jimmy. *Keeping Faith, Memoirs of a President.* New York: Bantam Books, 1982.
Christman, Margaret C. S. *1846 Portrait of the Nation.* Washington, D.C.: Smithsonian Institution, 1996.
The Civil Rights Project. *Hard Work for Good Schools: Facts Not Fads in Title I Reform.* Edited by Gary Orfield and Elizabeth H. DeBray. Cambridge: Harvard University Press, 1999.
Clinton, Hillary Rodham. *Living History.* New York: Simon & Schuster, 2003.
Clinton, President Bill. *Beyond Hope and History: Meeting America's Challenge for the 21st Century.* New York: Random House, 1996.
Cole, Donald B. *The Presidency of Andrew Jackson.* Lawrence: University Press of Kansas, 1993.
Collier, Christopher, and James Lincoln Collier. *Decision in Philadelphia: The Constitutional Convention of 1787.* New York: Ballantine Books, 1987.
Compilation of the Messages and Papers of the Presidents, 1789–1902. Edited by J. D. Richardson. 10 vols. Washington, D.C.: GPO, 1903.
Cooke, Jacob E. "The Reports of Alexander Hamilton," in *Alexander Hamilton: A Profile.* Edited by Jacob Cooke. New York: Hill and Wang, 1967.
———. *Alexander Hamilton.* New York: Charles Scribner's Sons, 1982.
Cooper, John Milton, Jr. *The Warrior and the Priest: Woodrow Wilson and Theodore Roosevelt.* Cambridge: Harvard University Press, 1983.
Cunningham, Noble E., Jr. *The Presidency of James Monroe.* Lawrence: University Press of Kansas, 1996.
Cushman, Barry. *Rethinking the New Deal Court: The Structure of a Constitutional Revolution.* New York: Oxford University Press, 1998.
Dallek, Robert. *Flawed Giant: Lyndon Johnson and His Times 1961–1973.* New York: Oxford University Press, 1998.
Davis, David Brion, and Steven Mintz. *The Boisterous Sea of Liberty, A Documentary History of America from Discovery through the Civil War.* New York: Oxford University Press, 1998.
Davis, Kenneth S. *FDR: The New Deal Years 1933–37.* New York: Random House, 1986.
The Debate on the Constitution, Federalist and Anti-Federalist Speeches, Articles and Letters During the Struggle Over Ratification. Edited by Bernard Bailyn. 2 vols. New York: Library of America, 1993.

Debates in the Several States Conventions on the Adoption of the Federal Constitution. Edited by Jonathan Elliot. 5 vols. Philadelphia: J.B. Lippincott, 1836.

Dionne, E.J. Jr. *They Only Look Dead: Why Progressives Will Dominate the Next Political Era.* New York, Simon and Schuster, 1996.

Documentary History of the Ratification of the Constitution. 18 vols. Madison: State Historical Society of Wisconsin, 1976–95.

Donald, David Herbert. *Lincoln.* New York: Simon and Schuster, 1995.

Edelman, Peter. *Searching for America's Heart: RFK and the Renewal of Hope.* Washington, D.C.: Georgetown University Press, 2003.

Ellis, Joseph J. *American Sphinx, The Character of Thomas Jefferson.* New York: Vintage Books, Random House, 1998.

Engdahl, David E. "The Spending Power," *Duke Law Journal* 44 (1994):1.

Farrand, Max. *The Framing of the Constitution of the United States.* New Haven: Yale University Press, 1913.

Findley, Paul. A. *Lincoln: The Crucible of Congress.* New York: Crown Publishers, Inc., 1979.

Fisher, Louis. *American Constitutional Law,* 4th ed. Durham, N.C.: Carolina Academic Press, 1990.

Flexner, John Thomas. *Washington the Indispensable Man.* Boston: Little, Brown and Company, 1974.

Flower, Milton E. *John Dickinson, Conservative Revolutionary.* Charlottesville: University Press of Virginia, 1983. (Published for the Friends of the John Dickinson Mansion).

Freeman, Douglas Southall. *Washington,* an abridgement in one volume by Richard Harwell of the seven-volume *George Washington* by Douglass Southall Freeman. New York: MacMillan Publishing Company, 1968.

Geiger, Sister Mary. *Daniel Carroll: A Framer of the Constitution.* Washington, D.C.: The Catholic University of America Press, 1943.

Giglio, James N. *The Presidency of John F. Kennedy.* Lawrence: University Press of Kansas, 1991.

Gilbert, Felix. "Hamilton and the 'Farewell Address,'" in *Alexander Hamilton: A Profile.* Edited by Jacob Cooke. New York: Hill and Wang, 1967.

Greene, John Robert. *The Presidency of Gerald Ford.* Lawrence: University Press of Kansas, 1995.

Greenstone, J. David. *The Lincoln Persuasion: Remaking American Liberalism.* Princeton: Princeton University Press, 1993.

Groth, Alexander J. *Lincoln: Authoritarian Savior.* Lanham, Md.: University Press of America, 1996.

Hamilton, Alexander. *The Works of Alexander Hamilton, Comprising His Correspondence and His Political and Official Writings.* Edited by J. C. Hamilton. 7 vols. New York: Charles S. Francis, Co., 1851.

Hamilton, Alexander. *Report on Manufactures, Communication to the House of Representatives, December 5, 1791 from Alexander Hamilton, Secretary of the Treasury, on the Subject of Manufactures,* as reprinted in H. Doc. No. 72, 63rd Cong. 1st Sess. (1913).

Hayes, Rutherford B. *Correspondence and Diaries.* Hayes Presidential Library. www.ohiohistory.org.

Hofstadter, Richard, ed. *Great Issues in American History From the Revolution to the Civil War, 1765–1865.* New York: Vintage Books, 1958.

Hoogenboom, Ari. *The Presidency of Rutherford B. Hayes.* Lawrence: University Press of Kansas, 1988.

Jefferson, Thomas. *The Writings of Thomas Jefferson.* Library Edition. Edited by Andrew A. Lipscomb, 20 vols. Washington, D.C.: Thomas Jefferson Memorial Association, 1903.

Johnson, Haynes and David S. Broder. *The System: The American Way of Politics at the Breaking Point.* Boston: Little, Brown and Company, 1997.

Johnson, Lyndon Baines. *The Vantage Point, Perspectives of the Presidency 1963–1969.* New York: Holt, Rinehart and Winston, 1971.

Kaplin, William A., and Barbara A. Lee. *The Law of Higher Education: A Legal Guide for Student Affairs Professionals.* San Francisco: Jossey Bass Publishers, 1997.

Keller, Morton. *Affairs of State, Public Life in Late Nineteenth-Century America.* Cambridge: Harvard University Press, 1997.

Kelly, Alfred H., Winifred A. Harbison, and Herman Belz. *The American Constitution: Its Origins and Development.* Vol. I. 7th edition. New York: W.W. Norton & Company, 1991.

Ketcham, Ralph. *The Anti-Federalist Papers and the Constitutional Convention Debates.* New York: Mentor, 1986.

———. *James Madison: A Biography.* Charlottesville: University Press of Virginia, 1990.

Klein, Joe. *The Natural: The Misunderstood Presidency of Bill Clinton.* New York: Doubleday, 2002.

Kmiec, Douglas W., and Stephen B. Presser. *The American Constitutional Order: History, Cases, and Philosophy.* Cincinnati: Anderson Publishing Co., 1998.

Konfesky, Samuel J. "The Powers Ought To Be Construed Liberally" in *Alexander Hamilton: A Profile.* Edited by Jacob Cooke. New York: Hill and Wang, 1967.

Kyvig, David. *Explicit and Authentic Acts: Amending the U.S. Constitution, 1776–1995.* Lawrence: University Press of Kansas, 1996.

Larson, John Lauritz. "Jefferson's Union and the Problem of Internal Improvement," in *Jeffersonian Legacies.* Edited by Peter S. Onuf. Charlottesville: University Press of Virginia, 1993.

Leuchtenberg, William E. *The Supreme Court Reborn: The Constitutional Revolution in the Age of Roosevelt.* New York: Oxford University Press, 1995.

Lincoln, Abraham. *The Collected Works of Abraham Lincoln.* Edited by Roy P. Basler. 9 vols. New Brunswick, N.J.: Rutgers University Press, 1953.

———. *Abraham Lincoln: His Speeches and Writings.* Edited by Roy P. Basler. New York: Da Capo Press, 1990. (Unabridged republication of the edition published in Cleveland, Ohio, 1946).

———. *Abraham Lincoln: Speeches and Writings 1859–1865.* Edited by Don E. Fehrenbacher. New York: Library of America, 1989.

Link, Arthur S. *Wilson: The New Freedom.* Princeton: Princeton University Press, 1956.

Loar, Peggy, and Theodore Sky. "General Operating Support for Museums:

Problems in Paradise." *Journal of College and University Law* 7 (1980–81): 267.

Ludwikowski, Rett R., and William F. Fox, Jr. *The Beginnings of the Constitutional Era: A Bicentennial Comparative Analysis of the First Modern Constitutions.* Washington, D.C.: The Catholic University of America Press, 1993.

McCoy, Drew R. *The Last of the Fathers: James Madison and the Republican Legacy.* Cambridge: Cambridge University Press, 1989.

McCullough, David. *Truman.* New York: Simon and Schuster, 1992.

———. *John Adams.* New York: Simon and Schuster, 2001.

McGee, Dorothy Horton. *Framers of the Constitution.* New York: Dodd, Mead & Company, 1968.

McDonald, Forrest. *Alexander Hamilton: A Biography.* New York: W. W. Norton, 1982.

McPherson, James M. *Abraham Lincoln and the Second American Revolution.* New York: Oxford University Press, 1990.

Madison, James. *Notes of Debates in the Federal Convention of 1787 Reported by James Madison.* Bicentennial edition. New York: W. W. Norton, 1987; Athens, Ohio: Ohio University Press, 1987.

———. *Letters and Other Writings of James Madison: Fourth President of the United States.* 4 vols. Philadelphia: J.B. Lippincott, 1865.

Madison, James, Alexander Hamilton, and John Jay. *The Federalist Papers.* Edited by Isaac Kramnick. London: Penguin Books, 1987.

Malone, Dumas. *Jefferson The President, First Term, 1801–1805.* Boston: Little, Brown and Company, 1970.

———. *Jefferson the President, Second Term, 1805–1809.* Boston: Little, Brown and Company, 1974.

Mayer, David N. *The Constitutional Thought of Thomas Jefferson.* Charlottesville: University Press of Virginia, 1994.

Mapp, Alf J., Jr. *Thomas Jefferson: Passionate Pilgrim: The Presidency, the Founding of the University, and the Private Battle.* Lanham, Md.: Madison Books, 1991.

Miller, William Lee. *Arguing About Slavery, John Quincy Adams and the Great Battle in the United States Congress.* New York: Vintage Books, 1998.

Moffitt, Robert A. "From Welfare to Work: What the Evidence Shows," in *Welfare Reform and Beyond: The Future of the Safety Net.* Edited by Isabel A. Sawhill, R. Kent Weaver, Ron Haskins and Andrea Kane. Washington, D.C.: The Brookings Institution, 2002.

Monroe, James. *The Political Writings of James Monroe.* Edited by James P. Lucier. Washington, D.C.: Regnery Publishing, 2001.

Mowry, George E., *The Era of Theodore Roosevelt and the Birth of Modern America, 1900–1912.* New York: Harper & Row, 1958.

Nagel, Paul C. *John Quincy Adams: A Public Life, a Private Life.* New York: Alfred A. Knopf, 1998.

Nixon, Richard N. *RN: The Memoirs of Richard Nixon.* New York: Simon and Schuster, 1990.

Paige, Rod. "An Overview of America's Education Agenda." *Phi Delta Kappan* 83 (2002): 708.

Paludan, Phillip Shaw. *The Presidency of Abraham Lincoln.* Lawrence: University Press of Kansas, 1994.

Parsons, Lynn Hudson. *John Quincy Adams.* Madison, Wis.: Madison House, 1998.

Perret, Geoffrey. *Eisenhower.* Holbrook, Mass.: Adams Media Corporation, 1999.

Presidential Messages and State Papers. Edited by Julius W. Muller. 10 vols. New York: Review of Reviews Company, 1917.

Primus, Wendell E., Kathryn Porter, Margery Ditto and Mitchell Kent. *The Safety Net Delivers: The Effects of Government Programs in Reducing Poverty.* Washington, D.C.: Center on Budget and Policy Priorities, 1996.

Pringle, Henry F. *Theodore Roosevelt: A Biography.* New York: Harcourt, Brace & World, 1931.

Public Papers of the Presidents of the United States: Dwight Eisenhower, 1953. Washington, D.C.: GPO, 1960.

Public Papers of the Presidents of the United States: John F. Kennedy, 1961. Washington, D.C.: GPO, 1962.

Public Papers of the Presidents of the United States: Lyndon B. Johnson, 1965-1. Washington, D.C: GPO, 1966.

Public Papers of the Presidents of the United States: Gerald Ford, 1975-2. Washington, D.C.: GPO, 1977.

Public Papers of the Presidents of the United States: Ronald Reagan, 1981-89. Washington, D.C.: GPO, 1982-1991.

Public Papers of the Presidents of the United States: George H. W. Bush, 1989-93. Washington, D.C.: GPO, 1990-1993.

Public Papers of the Presidents of the United States: Bill Clinton, 1993-2001. Washington, D.C: GPO, 1994-2002.

Randall, J. G., and Richard N. Current. *Lincoln the President.* Vol. 2, *Midstream to the Last Full Measure.* New York: Da Capo Press, 1997.

Randall, Willard Stone. *Thomas Jefferson: A Life.* New York: Harper Perennial, 1994.

The Records of the Federal Convention of 1787. Edited by Max Farrand. 4 vols. New Haven: Yale University Press, 1966.

Remini, Robert V. *Andrew Jackson,* Vol. 2 *The Course of American Freedom, 1822-1832.* Baltimore: Johns Hopkins University Press, 1998.

———. *Andrew Jackson.* Vol. 3. *The Course of American Democracy, 1833-1845.* Baltimore: Johns Hopkins University Press, 1998.

Richardson, Elliot. *The Creative Balance: Government, Politics, and the Individual in America's Third Century.* New York: Holt, Rinehart and Winston, 1976.

Richardson, Heather Cox. *The Greatest Nation of the Earth: Republican Economic Policies during the Civil War.* Cambridge: Harvard University Press, 1997.

Riley, Richard W. "The Improving America's Schools Act and Elementary and Secondary Education Reform." *Journal of Law and Education,* 24 (1995): 513.

———. "Redefining the Federal Role in Education: Toward A Framework for

Higher Standards, Improved Schools, Broader Opportunities and New Responsibilities for All." *Journal of Law and Education*, 23 (1994): 295.

———. "Education Reform through Standards and Partnerships, 1993–2000." *Phi Delta Kappan* 83 (2002): 700.

Rutland, Robert Allen. *The Birth of the Bill of Rights, 1776–1791*. London: Collier-MacMillan, Ltd., 1962.

———. *The Presidency of James Madison*. Lawrence: University Press of Kansas Press, 1990.

Schlesinger, Arthur M., Jr. *The Age of Jackson*. Boston: Little, Brown and Company, 1945.

———. *The Age of Roosevelt: The Coming of the New Deal*. Boston: Houghton Mifflin Company, 1988.

———. *A Thousand Days: John F. Kennedy in the White House*. Boston: Houghton Mifflin Company; Cambridge: The Riverside Press, 1965.

Schneider, Norris F. *The National Road: Main Street of America*. Columbus: Ohio Historical Society, 1975.

Simon, Paul. *Lincoln's Preparation for Greatness: The Illinois Legislative Years*. Norman: University of Oklahoma Press, 1965.

Sky, Theodore. "The Institute of Museum Services and the Conservation of America's Heritage." *Dickinson Law Review* 93 (1989): 659.

Smith, Marshall S., and Jennifer O'Day. "Systemic School Reform," in *The Politics of Curriculum and Testing, The Politics of Education Association Yearbook*, 233. Edited by Susan Fuhrman and Betty Malen, 1990.

Social Security Administration. *Fast Facts and Figures About Social Security*. Washington, D.C.: GPO, 2001.

Sorenson, Leonard R. *Madison on the "General Welfare" of America: His Consistent Constitutional Vision*. Lanham, Md.: Rowman & Littlefield Publisher, 1995.

Sorgen, Michael S., William A. Kaplin, Patrick S. Duffy, and Ephraim Margolin. *State, School and Family: Cases and Materials on Law and Education*. New York: Matthew Bender, 1979.

Spalding, Matthew, and Patrick J. Garrity. *A Sacred Union of Citizens, George Washington's Farewell Address and the American Character*. Lanham, Md.: Rowman and Littlefield Publishers, Inc., 1996.

Stone, Goeffrey R., Louis M. Seidman, Cass R. Sunstein, and Mark V. Tushnet. *Constitutional Law*, 3d edition. New York: Aspen Law and Business, 1996.

Storing, Herbert J. *What the Anti-Federalists Were For*. Chicago: University of Chicago Press, 1981.

Story, Joseph. *Commentaries on the Constitution of the United States*, 5th ed., 2 vols. Boston: Little, Brown and Company, 1891.

———. *Commentaries on the Constitution of the United States*. Abridgement, 1833. Reprint with an Introduction by Ronald D. Rotunda and John E. Nowak, Durham: Carolina Academic Press, 1987.

Tribe, Laurence H. *American Constitutional Law*. Mineola, N.Y.: Foundation Press, 1978.

Tribe, Laurence H., and Michael C. Dorf. *On Reading the Constitution*. Cambridge: Harvard University Press, 1991.

United States v. Butler, Brief for the United States in *Landmark Briefs and Arguments of the Supreme Court of the United States: Constitutional Law.* Edited by Phillip Kurland and Gerhard Casper. Vol. 30. Arlington, Va.: University Publications of America, 1975.

United States Census Bureau. *Statistical Abstract of the United States, 2001,* 121st edition. Washington, D.C.: GPO, 2001.

United States Department of Education, National Center for Education Statistics. *The Condition of Education 2000.* NCES 2000-062. Washington, D.C.: GPO, 2000.

Washington, George. *Writings.* Edited by John Rhodehamel. New York: Library of America, 1997.

Welles, Gideon. *Diary of Gideon Welles.* 3 vols. New York: Houghton Mifflin Company, 1911.

White, G. Edward. *The Constitution and the New Deal.* Cambridge: Harvard University Press, 2000.

White House Domestic Policy Council. *Health Security: The President's Report to the American People.* Washington, D.C.: GPO, 1993.

Wilson, Woodrow. *The New Freedom: A Call for the Emancipation of the Generous Energies of a People.* New York: Doubleday, Page & Company, 1914.

———. *Constitutional Government in the United States.* New York: Columbia University Press, 1908; Holmes Beach, Fla.: Gaunt, Inc., 1997.

———. *Congressional Government: A Study in American Politics.* New York: Meridian Books, 1956.

Winston, Judith A. "Achieving Excellence and Equal Opportunity in Education: No Conflict of Laws." *Administrative Law Review* 53 (2001): 997.

Wood, Gordon S. *The Creation of the American Republic, 1776-1787.* New York: W.W. Norton, 1972.

CASES

Helvering v. Davis, 301 U.S. 619 (1937).
King v. Smith, 392 U.S. 333 (1968).
New York v. United States, 505 U.S. 144 (1992).
South Dakota v. Dole, 483 U.S. 203 (1987).
Steward Machine Co. v. Davis, 301 U.S. 548 (1937).
United States v. Butler, 297 U.S. 1 (1936).

Index

Academic Facilities Act of 1963, 331, 336; providing assistance to colleges and universities for improving or constructing facilities, 332

Ackerman, Bruce, 29, 320, 324, 358, 359, 361, 363, 364, 367, 419n, 421n

Adams, John, 107, 108, 167, 187

Adams, John Quincy, 26, 28, 29, 117, 128, 147, 160, 167–85, 187–99, 202, 204, 207–10, 220–21, 230–32, 234–37, 244, 245, 252, 255, 256, 260, 261, 269, 270, 272, 276–78, 287, 291, 298, 299, 307, 319, 324, 329, 337, 346, 359–62, 364, 367, 368, 371, 374–76, 378, 379, 397–403n; Constitutional thought and convictions, 26–29, 168–71, 179–81, 184, 190–93, 208, 359–64, 376, 403n; election of 1824, 167–68, 397n; election of 1828, 399n; Inaugural address regarding internal improvement, aid, constitutionality, 172–77; Internal Improvements, constitutional amendment on, 184; legacy of, 193–95; Lincoln, Abraham, comparison with, 193–97, 255–61; measures approved during administration, 188–89; program goals, 170–71, 173; post-presidential service in Congress, eulogy of Madison, 190; post-presidential service in Congress, eulogy of Monroe and position on internal improvements, 190–93, 399n; President Clinton on post-presidential service, 195–96; Stevenson, Andrew, 1832 post-presidential letter to, 192–93, 403n

—As president: assumed spending law's validity and would not veto, 180; Chesapeake and Ohio Canal, 188, 371, 399n; coherent program of internal improvement, 195; Cumberland Road (National Road), 188–89; First Annual Message, 177–82; —, constitutional views on authority, 179–81; —, educational proposals, 178–79; —, internal improvement program, 177–78, 368; —, "liberty is power," 181; —, "lighthouses of the skies," 179; —, reception, 183–89

—As Secretary of State under Monroe: constitution, civil rights, and slavery, 255–56, 401n; "Moral certainty" that Congress would not propose constitutional amendment on internal improvements, 175, 398n

—As Senator: position on Louisiana Purchase, 117; sponsorship of internal improvement legislation, 170–71, 400n

Agricultural Adjustment Act, 304–5, 306–8, 312, 320–22, 368, 410–11n, 413n; price subsidy in return for farmer's agreement to limit output, 305; regulation of production as an invasion of Tenth Amendment, 310

Agricultural Adjustment Administration, 27

Aid to Families with Dependent Children (AFDC), 339

America 2000, 348

American System, 170, 200, 205, 232–35, 289

Ammon, Harry, 161, 395n

Anti-Federalists, 55, 56, 58–62, 64–66, 70, 74–76, 360, 387–89n

appropriation of federal funds for internal improvements anticipated broader general welfare projects, 209

Area Redevelopment Bill, 331

Articles of Confederation, 21, 24, 38, 42–43, 46, 66, 72, 100, 156, 214–15, 218, 225–27, 230, 384, 411
Arthur, Chester A., 283, 287–88, 290
assumption of the debt, 38, 82–84, 103, 389n, 390n
assumption of jurisdiction, 159, 161, 169, 184, 190, 250, 299

Baldwin, Abraham, 46, 74
Banning, Lance, 101, 385n, 390n
Barbour, James, 146, 182, 193, 397n, 400n
Barlow, Joel, 121, 122, 125, 394n
Bell, Terrell H., 345, 416n
Belz, Herman, 129, 162
Bemis, Samuel Flag, 167, 397n
bills for appropriating money originate in House, 34
Bipartisan (Kerry-Danforth) Commission on Entitlement Reform, 418n
Boritt, G. S., 263
Bowen, Catherine Drinker, 42
Brandeis, Louis D. (Justice), 310, 313
Brearley, David, 46
Brearley Committee, 48–49, 386n
broad exercise of spending power, as vindicating its promise of opportunity and progress, 252
broad reading of Constitution to achieve economic independence, 98
Brookhiser, Richard, 90
Brown, Roger H., 47, 383–86n
Brown vs. Board of Education, 278, 339
Brutus I and VI, 56–59
Bryan, Samuel, 58
Buchanan, James, 26, 232, 236–39, 249, 253, 259, 266, 267, 272, 273, 275, 277, 283, 289, 290, 367, 407n; Homestead bill veto, 239–40, 266–67; Land Grant College bill veto, 237–39, 272–75; views on General Welfare Clause, 237–39
Budget Enforcement Act of 1990, 347, 348; establishes framework for deficit control in federal spending, 347
Bureau of Mines, 411
Bush, George H. W., 305, 342, 346–48, 368, 417n, 420n; Budget Enforcement Act (BEA), 348; Clean Air Act, 347; education initiatives, 347; Intermodal Surface Transportation Efficiency Act, 347
Bush, George W., 373–74, 420n
Butler, Pierce, 41, 46
Butler, Pierce (Justice), 316

Calhoun, John C., 136, 138, 183, 194, 208, 400n
Cannon, Lou, 344–45, 416n
Cardozo, Benjamin (Justice), 10, 149, 310, 314–18, 321–23, 328, 365–66, 412–13n; *Helvering v. Davis,* opinion in, 27, 317–20; *Steward Machine Co. v. Davis,* opinion in, 27, 314–16
Carroll, Daniel, 46, 53, 386n
Carter, Jimmy, 305, 342–43, 368, 416n; Department of Education Organization Act, 343; education legislation, 342–43; environmental legislation (Superfund), 343
Cass, Lewis, 235
Chapman, Reynolds, 218, 219
Children's Health Insurance Program (CHIP), 353, 374
Civil Rights Act of 1964, 278
Clay, Henry, 138, 141–43, 146, 147, 167, 168, 170, 171, 180, 182, 183, 207, 208, 232, 233, 289, 397n, 398n
Clean Air Act, 347, 417n
Cleveland, Grover, 283, 288–92, 298, 300; championed lower tariffs and diminished revenues, 290; nonpaternalistic government, belief in, 290
Clinton, Bill, 119, 171, 195–96, 305, 342, 348–54, 369, 373–74, 400n, 417–18n, 420n; administration objectives for domestic program, 349; Children's Health Insurance Program (*see* health reform proposals); contribution to exercise of General Welfare Clause, 348–54; Earned Income Tax Credit, 348; education legislation, 350–51; fiscal and budgetary policies, 348–54, 417n, 420n; Goals 2000 (*see* education legislation); health reform proposals and achievements, 352–54; Improving Ameri-

ca's Schools Act (*see* education legislation); as president, 348–54; programmatic presidency, 368–69; service of John Quincy Adams, comments on, 195–96; welfare reform legislation (PRWORA), 351–52
Cole, Donald B., 210
Committee of Style, 283, 288–92, 298, 300
Committee on Unfinished Parts, 25
Committee of the Whole, 22, 23, 244, 385
Community Development Block Grant, 332
Congress: could appropriate money for internal improvements, 158; could provide for the general Welfare of the United States through spending-power, 377–78
Connecticut Compromise, 23, 71
Constitution: Article 1, section 8, clause 1: 9, 10, 19, 25, 48, 50–53, 56, 62, 64, 66, 69, 72, 83–85, 96, 106, 136, 144, 148, 162, 181, 184–85, 217, 222–23, 230, 236, 248, 249, 259, 266, 289, 296, 346, 360, 378, 406n; Bill of Rights, 55, 59–62, 75, 216, 388n, 428n; Common Defense Clause, 329, 346, 406n; Constitutional amendment, need for, 25–29, 376–79, 421n; enumerated powers, 9, 19, 22, 28, 33–37, 39–41, 43–45, 49–51, 55–56, 59, 62, 65–67, 69–70, 75, 79, 84–86, 93, 96, 97, 100, 104, 115, 118, 122, 139, 141, 144, 152–58, 162, 169, 176, 187, 189, 190, 212, 217, 223–27, 229–31, 237, 239, 247, 249, 267, 275, 309, 322, 358, 360, 366, 377, 403n, 412n; Fifteenth Amendment, 283, 284, 286, 288–89; Fourteenth Amendment, 279, 284, 286; Necessary and Proper Clause, 44, 57, 84, 85, 225–27, 238, 309, 360; Ratification, 15, 25, 31, 55–60, 62, 67–69, 72–76, 83, 95, 98, 111, 121, 143, 268, 269, 307, 359, 363, 364, 387–89n, 404n, 421n, 423n, 424n; Sixteenth Amendment, 296, 301, 303; Supremacy Clause, 24, 35, 139, 385n; Territory and Property Clause, 146, 237–39, 275–76; Thirteenth Amendment, 262, 269, 405n

Constitutional Convention, 15, 19, 21–25, 33–43, 45–47, 49–57, 59–62, 64, 66–75, 81, 86, 95, 99–101, 132, 135, 141, 151, 185, 213, 215–17, 220, 229, 230, 247, 248, 255, 256, 308, 319, 360, 371, 377, 383–89n, 391n, 403n, 405n, 421–23n
constitutional revolution of 1937, 27, 303, 320, 324, 334, 364, 365, 376, 413n, 419n; switch in concern from property rights to civil liberties, 320
constrain exercise of spending power, budgetary rather than constitutional concerns have come to, 341
Cooke, Jacob, 87
Cooper, John Milton, 300
Corporation of Boston, 190
court-packing plan, 364, 413n
"costly failures," Nixon viewed a number of the New Deal and Great Society programs as, 339
Crawford, William H., 167
creation of a stable domestic market for agricultural products, 89
Cumberland Road/National Road, 111, 124–26, 128, 144–47, 158, 160, 161, 169, 174, 178, 191, 193, 194, 201, 202, 210, 360, 363, 367, 370, 399n; Congress authorized subject to consent of affected states, 124
Cushman, Barry, 320, 413n

Dallek, Robert, 336
debts as valid against United States as under the Confederation, 42
Delaware, 78, 108, 259, 379, 406n
Democratic-Republican Party (Jefferson's Republican Party), 107, 220; support for internal improvements if carried out by "authorized means," 131
Department of Agriculture, 255, 263, 277, 290, 411n
Department of Education Organization Act of 1979, 343, 420n
Department of Health, Education, and Welfare, 330, 340, 343
Desert Storm, 347, 417n
Dickinson, John, 46, 113, 114, 379
Dionne, E. J., 349, 353
direct grants of legislative power, au-

thority of Congress to spend "for public purposes... is not limited" in constitution, 27
Donald, David Herbert, 252, 254, 265, 405n
"Dualist democracy" and spending power, 358–66
DuPont, Pierre, 117, 393n

Earned Income Tax Credit, 348
Eaton, John, 286
Economic Opportunity Act of 1964, 334, 337, 415n
Education of All Handicapped Children Act (EHA), 341
Education Consolidation and Improvement Act (ECIA), 344, 416n
Eisenhower, Dwight David, 303, 328–30, 341, 368, 372, 414n; exercise of General Welfare Clause, 328–30; National Defense Education Act, 329; organization of Department of Health, Education, and Welfare, 329; position on not wanting to roll back the New Deal, 328; social security legislation, 328
Elementary and Secondary Education Act of 1965 (ESEA), 330, 332, 334, 336, 340, 344, 372, 373, 414n, 415n, 417n, 420n
Ellis, Joseph, 111
Ellsworth, Oliver, 71–73, 75, 384n
Emancipation Proclamation, 260, 269
Emergency School Aid Act, 340, 415
Employment Act of 1946, 328
enhance division of labor between manufacturing and agricultural pursuits, aid to manufactures would, 88
Environmental Protection Agency (EPA), 339
exercise of federal spending power, budget controls replaced Madisonian constitutional theory as limit on, 346

Family Assistance Program (FAP), 339
Family Support Act of 1988, 344
Farrand, Max, 50

federal aid for manufactures, strategies, 90
Federal-Aid Highway Act of 1956, 328, 329
federal aid to education, corollary to Fourteenth and Fifteenth Amendments, 284
Federal Farm Loan Act, 411n
"Federalist No. 41," 25, 55, 62–68, 71, 75, 76, 93, 96, 97, 100, 141, 202, 224, 225, 227, 361, 362, 378, 388n
Federalist Papers, 62, 67, 72, 156
federal programs, impact of, 420n
Federal Reserve Board, 349
federal route must prevail over state, 127
Fillmore, Millard, 232, 234–36, 404n; General Welfare Clause and, 235–36
Finch, Robert, 339
Findley, Paul, 243–44
fiscal weakness of Congress under the Articles, James Madison described, 20
Flexner, John Thomas, 104, 105, 389n, 390n
Food and Nutrition Service, 333
Food Stamp Act of 1964, 333, 337
Food Stamps, 351, 374, 414n
Ford, Gerald, 305, 327, 340, 341, 368
Fourteenth Amendment, 197, 278, 279, 358
Frank, Jerome, 305
Franklin, Benjamin, 23, 24, 52, 54, 81, 384n; canal proposals, 52–53; contribution to Connecticut Compromise, 23; position on appropriation measures, 23–24; remarks on signing of Constitution, 54
free trade proponents, Hamilton case for federal aid for manufactures, 90, 91, 331
Freeman, Douglas Southall, 81
Fulbright-Hayes Act, 331
Fulton, Robert, 121, 122

Gallatin, Albert, 51, 115, 125–27, 153, 387n, 394n
Garfield, James A., 257
General Welfare Clause (Spending Power, Spending Clause), 10, 19–21, 24–29, 33, 35, 38, 39, 41, 43–49, 51–57,

59–63, 65–69, 71–76, 79, 84, 86, 87, 91–95, 97–109, 115, 118, 128, 130, 133, 139–41, 144, 146, 148, 151–53, 155–59, 161–63, 168, 169, 176, 177, 181, 184–87, 190–93, 195, 197–99, 202, 203, 207, 209–18, 221–28, 230–33, 235–39, 243, 244, 247–49, 251, 254, 258, 259, 266, 267, 269, 270, 272, 273, 275, 278, 288, 292–96, 298, 300–304, 307–9, 315–17, 319, 321–23, 327–30, 333, 334, 337, 341, 346, 349, 352, 354, 355, 357–60, 362–66, 368, 374, 376, 378, 385–87n, 401–4n, 407n, 411n, 412n, 414n; Adams (J. Q.) convinced that spending programs within power of Congress under, 376; Court upheld the Social Security Act's programs, 304; description of, 19; did not confer a separate power independent of the spending power, 51, 95, 157, 308; Hamilton reading of, 97, 307; history of, 10; Jackson argues could be exercised only through appropriation for general welfare purposes of national dimension, 210; Lincoln supported federal assistance for internal improvements under, 244; McKinley proposed no major government programs posited on, 291; not a grant of broad authority to regulate separate from power to appropriate, 153, 308; people's blessing be asked through a formal amendment to the Constitution, 101; powerful and broadly phrased charter for vigorous national government, Hamilton saw, 79; providing the authority to carry out investment activities, 48; Republican presidents who succeeded Lincoln took broad view of, 288; spending authority not confined to purposes encompassed within enumerated powers (Hamilton), 19; spending power confined to federal spending implementing enumerated powers (Madison), 19; Supreme Court permitted changes without constitutional amendment, 364; used to encourage state legislative programs, 421n; within framework of role of the constitutional amendment, 367. *See also* Adams, J. Q.; Hamilton, Alexander; Madison, James; Monroe, James; Story, Joseph

Gerry committee, 23, 384; Senate involve an equal voice for each state, bills for appropriation originate in House, 23–24

Gettysburg Address, 264

Gilman, Nicholas, 46

Goals 2000: Educate America Act, 350, 417n

Goldwater, Barry, 333

Gramm, Rudman, Hollings legislation, 346

Grant, Ulysses S., 27, 283–85, 319, 367, 408n

Great Society, 20, 27, 115, 195, 299, 302, 304, 310, 333, 334, 336, 338–40, 343, 344, 353, 360

Greenspan Commission of 1983, 344

Greenstone, J. David, 196–97

Hamilton, Alexander, 10, 19, 20, 22, 23, 25, 27–29, 46, 49, 52, 55, 62, 63, 67–73, 75, 79, 81–108, 18, 120, 136, 141, 155, 156, 173, 208, 217, 218, 221, 229–31, 278, 294, 298–304, 307, 309, 310, 312, 316, 317, 321, 323, 324, 334, 341, 345, 346, 359–65, 368, 384n, 386n, 388–92n, 403n, 411n, 412n; contribution to Farewell Address and Eighth Annual Message, 392n; contribution to Interpretation of General Welfare Clause, 19, 25–26, 93–99, 315–17, 358–66; Monroe and, 156; program of public investment to enhance national growth, 70; Report on Manufactures, 86–99; —, interpretation of General Welfare Clause, 93–99, 391n; —, proposal for bounties, 90–92; —, response of Jefferson to, 102–5; —, response of Madison to, 99–101; Story and, 229; Supreme Court opinions and, 27, 304–24
—In Constitutional convention: Constitution, assessment of, 386n; service on Committee on Style, 49; speech on framework of Constitu-

tion, 22–23, 384 n; views on need for "indefinite" authority, 23, 384 n
—In ratification period, contribution to Federalist Papers, 55, 69–71
—In Washington administration, as secretary of treasury: creation of national mint, 83–84; economic plans, 82–86; national bank, 83–86, 390 n; new excise taxes, 83–84
Hamiltonian reading of the spending power, Lincoln's administration marks effective end of Executive Branch opposition to, 26
Harbison, Winifred A., 129
Harrison, Benjamin, 27, 283, 287–90, 319, 367; constitutionality of federal aid to education, views on, 288; signing and significance of Second Morrill Act, 288
Harrison, William Henry, 233, 273
Hayes, Rutherford B., 27, 276, 285–88, 299, 319, 367, 368, 372, 408 n; administration of Bureau of Education, 286; aid to education, support for federal, 285–88, 368, 372; constitutionality of federal aid for education, 285–88; General Welfare Clause legacy, 367–68; identification with John Quincy Adams, 287
health care reform, 353–54
Helvering v. Davis, 149, 313, 316, 319, 322, 328, 329, 369, 383 n, 396 n, 410 n, 412 n, 413 n
Henry, Patrick, 59, 60, 73, 388 n
Higher Education Act of 1965, 276, 334, 336, 344, 415 n
"Higher Lawmaking," 29, 357–66; when popular movement results in formal amendment to Constitution pursuant to Article V procedures, 358
Highway Trust Fund, 324
Hobby, Oveta Culp, 330
Homestead Act of 1862, 262, 264–65, 267, 274, 337, 407 n
homestead legislation, 239–40, 264–66, 274, 407 n
Hoogenboom, Ari, 287
Housing Act of 1949, 328, 332
Hufstedler, Shirley, 343

Illinois and Michigan Canal, 263
Improving America's Schools Act, 350, 374, 417 n, 420 n
income tax as basis for social legislation since 1912, 296
Individuals with Disabilities Education Act (IDEA), 341
Interior Department, 276
Intermodal Surface Transportation Efficiency Act of 1991 (ISTEA), 347, 375, 402 n, 420 n
internal-improvement: bill, 144; issue, 218; legislation, 146, 171, 189, 230, 232, 244, 247, 273, 362, 367, 370, 398 n, 402 n; policies, 146, 171, 195, 397 n
Interstate Commerce Act of 1887, 292
Interstate Commerce Clause, 139, 294, 308, 412 n. *See also* Constitution

Jackson, Andrew, 26, 167, 168, 170–72, 181, 188, 191, 194, 195, 198–210, 212, 220, 221, 225, 230, 233–35, 244, 253, 277, 298, 362–64, 367, 397 n, 398 n, 400–404 n; General Welfare Clause legacy, 368; Inaugural address and annual messages, 200–207; Maysville Road Veto, 198, 200, 203, 211, 233, 362, 400 n, 403 n; —, and constitutionality of internal improvement legislation, 200–203; opposition to John Quincy Adams's administration, 26, 199–200; post-Maysville policy, 207–10; presidential campaign of 1824, 167–68; presidential campaign of 1828, 189, 195–96; signing of internal improvement legislation, 210–11, 402 n
Jefferson, Thomas, 10, 19, 26, 27, 63, 79, 84–86, 88, 93, 102–5, 107, 108, 111–31, 133–35, 137–39, 141, 142, 144, 146, 148, 153, 154, 156, 157, 169, 171, 172, 174, 176, 183, 185–87, 189, 190, 193, 198, 201, 220–23, 228, 232, 237, 244, 245, 247, 254, 270, 276, 283, 300–302, 329, 347, 358, 359, 362, 364, 367, 371, 375, 379, 393–94 n, 399 n, 401 n, 419 n; Kentucky Resolutions, role in, 107–8; and Madison vision of federal government held in check by limited body of enumerated powers, 79, 82; "sound principle" of federalism,

frugality, fiscal restraint, limited taxation, 113; value of sciences in higher education, 120; views on General Welfare Clause, 26, 79, 115–16, 120–21, 124, 185–87, 358–67, 395n, 399n
—As president: constitutional amendment for improvements, 115–16, 120–22, 128–29; correspondance with Joel Barlow, 121; Cumberland (National) Road, 124–29; education and support for seminaries of learning, 120; Gallatin report, 125; inaugural addresses and annual messages, 111–16, 118–21, 123–24; internal improvement, 119–20, 123–24; Lewis and Clark expedition, 394n; Louisiana Purchase and General Welfare Clause, 116–18, 393n; war and embargo effects on internal improvements, 121–24
—In Washington administration as secretary of state: on national bank, 84–86; opposition to views in Report on Manufactures, 102–5
Johnson, Andrew, 284
Johnson, Lyndon Baines, 20, 171, 299, 331–38, 341, 367, 368, 372, 414n, 415n; constitutional concerns, 414n; contribution to exercise of General Welfare Clause, 337–39; education initiatives, 334–36, 371; federal support for the arts and humanities, 338; Food Stamp Act, 337; Great Society, 334–36; health initiatives, medicare and medicaid, 337–38; poverty program, 336–37
Johnson, Richard M., 200
Johnson, Samuel, 49

Keller, Morton, 286, 288
Kelly, Alfred H., 129
Kennedy, John Fitzgerald, 171, 330–33, 335–37, 341, 368, 414n; Academic Facilities Act of 1963, 331; elementary and secondary education proposals, 332; food stamp program, 332–33; Fullbright-Hayes legislation, 331; General Welfare Clause, 330–33; housing, manpower legislation, and medicare, 332

Kent, James, 245, 246
Kentucky Resolutions of 1798 and 1799, 107
Kerry-Danforth Commission, 418n
Ketcham, Ralph, 136, 142
King, Rufus, 46, 49, 386n
Konefsky, Samuel, 98, 99, 391n
Kyvig, David, 357, 363, 412, 419n, 421n

Land Reclamation Act of 1902, 294
Lane, 408
Leiper, 123, 125
Leuchtenberg, Charles, 320, 413n
Lincoln, Abraham, 10, 11, 15, 26, 171, 195–97, 235, 240, 241, 243–75, 276–79, 285, 287, 288, 289, 319, 346, 359, 360, 364, 367, 371, 377, 379, 391n, 404–8n; administration marks effective end of Executive Branch opposition to Hamiltonian reading of spending power, 26; congressional aid for internal improvements, as the text of Constitution warranted, 405; emancipation policies, 248, 255–61, 268–70; General Welfare Clause, and early emancipation proposals, 255–61; General Welfare Clause, providing for general welfare, 243–49, 271–79, 367–68, 405n; General Welfare Clause, views and legacy, 26–27, 259–64, 266–67, 271–79, 407n; greatest contributions of emancipation, enfranchisement, reconstruction, equal opportunity, preserve the Union, 277; Homestead Act, 264–67; Internal Improvement proposals and legislation, 253–55; Internal Improvement speech of 1848, 243–47, 367, 405n; land grant college legislation (Morrill Act), 270–77, 408n; messages, 249–51, 253–55, 261–62; no authority in Constitution to interfere with slavery in states where it existed, 405n; service in Illinois, in legislature, and internal improvements, 243–47
Lincoln, Levi, 393
Livingston, Robert, 116, 393
Love Canal, 343
"Liberation of the People's Vital Energies, The," 300

INDEX

Louisiana Purchase, 111, 116, 117, 134, 175, 193, 360, 362, 393 n, 403 n

Madison, James, 10, 15, 19–29, 35–41, 43–50, 52–56, 60, 62–72, 74–76 , 79, 83–86, 93, 95–97, 99–101, 104, 107, 108, 111, 115, 116, 130–48, 153, 154, 156–58, 162, 169, 171, 173, 174, 176, 184–187, 189–90, 193, 194, 198, 201, 202, 207, 209, 212–21, 224–232, 237, 244, 249, 266, 270, 276, 278, 290, 294, 298, 299, 304, 307, 309, 317, 321, 323, 358–65, 367, 369, 371, 376, 378, 379, 383 n, 385 n, 390 n, 391 n, 395–96 n, 399 n, 401–3 n, 421 n; Bonus Bill Veto, 130, 138–43, 147, 148, 218, 225, 359, 379, 396 n, 401 n, 403 n; constitutional convention and advocacy of enumerated powers, 20, 21, 23, 24, 52–53, 385 n; constitutional convention authorship of notes, 21; constitutional convention public investment proposals, 35–40, 52–53, 385 n; constitutional convention service on Committee on Style, 49; educational proposals, 131–32, 135–36; General Welfare Clause confered no power to spend on purposes outside the enumerated powers, 49, 67, 217; in House during Washington administration, opposition to assumption, 83; in House opposition to national bank legislation, 84–86; in House response to Report on Manufactures, 99–101; in House views on General Welfare Clause, 99–101, 107–8; inaugural addresses and annual messages, 130–38, 369–70; internal improvements, "intermediate course" prescribed by constitutional amendment for, 219; internal improvements, need for as policy matter, 134–35, 138–43; internal improvements, proposal for constitutional amendment on, 135, 140–41; interpretation of General Welfare Clause, 138–43; Jackson, Andrew on, 401 n; precepts of Constitution as "cement" of Union, 130; ratification debates, co-authorship of Federalist Papers, 55; ratification debates, General Welfare Clause, reference to enumerated powers, 25, 62–68; retirement letter to Reynolds Chapman (1831), 218–19; retirement letter to Andrew Stevenson (1830), 212–19, 402–3 n; retirement opposition to broad interpretation of General Welfare Clause, 185–87, 212–19; retirement and proposed amendment to Constitution sent to Martin Van Buren, 189–90; Story, Joseph on, 225–32, 403 n; testament paramount starting point for Democratic antebellum presidents who vetoed internal-improvement legislation, 232; Virginia resolutions, 107–8

Maese, Dr., 124
Malone, Dumas, 126
manufactures (Hamilton) essential for nation's security, defense, growth and prosperity, 87
manufacturing subsidy, most "positive and direct" form, 91
Marshall, John (Chief Justice), 220
Martin, Luther, 35, 385 n
Mason, George, 22, 42, 312
Maysville Road veto, 198, 200–203, 207–9, 211, 233, 234, 362, 401–3 n; rejected appropriation for internal improvement within single state, 198, 202–5
McCoy, Drew, 213, 215
McDonald, Forrest, 104
McHenry, James, 25, 48, 51, 53, 217, 386 n
McKinley, William, 283, 291, 292
McReynolds, James C. (Justice), 316
Medicaid, 9, 338, 344, 353, 375, 376, 379
Medicare, 9, 332, 334, 337, 338, 344, 352–54, 375, 376, 379, 414 n
Missouri Compromise, 269
Monroe, James, 10, 26, 28, 44, 111, 117, 130, 137, 143–63, 167, 169, 170, 173–78, 80, 181, 184–87, 190–94, 201–3, 206, 208–10, 218, 221, 224–26, 229, 230, 232, 244, 246, 248, 255, 270, 278, 291, 298, 307, 319, 324, 329, 346, 359–61, 370, 378, 393 n, 395–401 n, 403 n, 404 n; Clay, Henry, opposition regarding internal imporovement

veto, 146–47; constitutional amendment and congressional opposition to, 395 n; Cumberland road repair legislation, approval of, 160–61; General Welfare Clause, views on, 26, 151–60, 169–70; inaugural address and annual messages, 145, 160–61, 369–70; Madison, James, correspondence with, 145–46; Memorandum, 144, 150, 160, 169, 181, 184, 186, 187, 190, 202, 210, 218, 224, 226, 307, 397 n, 401–2 n; —, Adams (J. Q.) and preparation of, 147–48, 175–76, 191–92, 398 n, 400 n; —, General Welfare Clause as authorizing appropriations for purposes beyond the enumerated powers, 153–56; —, General Welfare Clause as authorizing internal improvement spending, 158–59; —, General Welfare Clause as not authorizing Congress to construct roads and canals and assume jurisdiction, 157–59, 359; —, General Welfare Clause as spending not regulatory power, 151–53; —, historical significance, 26, 161–63, 370; —, Madison, James, no reaction to, 396 n; Marshall, Chief Justice John, views on, 163; —, Story, Joseph, views on, 163, 225, 229–30, 403 n; survey legislation of 1824, approval by, 161, 397 n; veto of 1822 internal improvement legislation, 147–59, 369–70

Montpelier, 123, 143, 212, 213, 218

Morrill, Justin Smith, 274, 275, 408 n

Morrill Land Grant College Act, 238, 262, 265, 270–77, 285, 288, 298, 311, 331, 371, 408 n

Morris, Gouverneur, 21, 28, 36–38, 40–42, 46, 48–53, 61, 95, 132, 153, 217, 248, 255, 308, 363, 377; cabinet proposals, 37–38; General Welfare Clause and alleged manipulation of punctuation, 49–52; General Welfare Clause harbor improvements, 25, 48–49; national government, nature of, 22

Mowry, George, 293, 295, 296

Moynihan, Daniel Patrick, 339, 415 n

Museum Services Program, 344, 416 n

Mutual Educational, Cultural, and Exchange Act of 1961, 331

Nagel, Paul C., 167, 194

National Bank, 81, 82, 84, 234; proper exercise of government and Necessary and Proper Clause, 85

National Banking Act, 265

National Bureau of Standards, 411 n

National Commission on Excellence in Education, 345

National Defense Education Act of 1958 (NDEA), 372, 414 n

National Endowment for the Humanities, 338, 344

National Endowment for the Arts, 338, 344

National Foundation on the Arts and Humanities Act of 1965, 338 n

National Institute of Education (NIE), 340, 415 n

national legislature: lay and collect taxes/duties/imposts/excises, pay debts, provide for common defense and general welfare, 92

national university, Madison recommended federal spending for, 136

National v. Local Distinction, 210, 405 n

Nation at Risk, A, 345; identified shortcomings in the quality of elementary and secondary education, 344

New Deal, 10, 20, 27, 195, 299, 302, 304, 310, 312, 319–22, 324, 327, 328, 330, 331, 334, 338–41, 343, 345, 353, 358–61, 363, 364, 366, 368–70, 410–14 n, 419 n, 421 n. *See also* Franklin Roosevelt

New Freedom, 27, 300–302, 410 n

New Frontier, 331, 332

New Jersey resolutions, 22–23

New Nationalism, 300

Nicholas, Wilson, 117

Nixon, Richard Milhous, 303, 305, 346, 368, 415 n; Emergency School Aid Act, 331–40; General Welfare Clause, contribution to exercise of, 338–40; Supplemental Security Income, 339; welfare reform, 339

No Child Left Behind Act, 373, 374, 420 n

Nowak, John E., 220

obstructions to foreign trade "accelerate" its "internal improvements," 89
O'Connor, Sandra Day, 345, 383n, 421n
Office of Economic Opportunity, 337
Office of Education, 340
Old Age Survivors and Disability Insurance (OASDI), 317

Pacific Railroad, 263, 268
Paige, Rod, 372–73
Paludan, Phillip Shaw, 260, 271, 274, 408n
Parsons, Lynn Hudson, 183–84, 195
Paterson, William, 22
peacetime defense establishment necessary, 63–64
Pendleton, Edmund, 100, 389, 391n
perils of American System, 234
Perkins, Frances, 312, 313
Perret, Geoffrey, 328, 330
perseverance, adoption of spending power initiative requires, 371
Personal Responsibility and Work Opportunity Reconciliation Act of 1996 (PRWORA), 351, 418n
Philadelphia ratifying convention, 69
Pierce, Franklin, 26, 232, 236, 237, 239, 247, 249, 253, 259, 266, 272, 277, 298, 316, 323, 367, 405n, 412n; General Welfare Clause, views on, 236–37; land grants for care of indigent insane, veto of, 236–37
Pierce, William, 47
Pinckney, Charles, 35–40, 45, 47–49, 52, 81, 371, 385n, 386n
political independence, economic independence was to follow, 90
Polk, James Knox, 26, 201, 232–34, 237, 239, 244–46, 249, 253, 259, 273, 277, 298, 367, 404n, 405; General Welfare Clause, views on, 233–34; Internal improvement appropriations vetoes, 233–34; Maysville road veto, role in, 201; opposition to American System, 234
power in Congress: to authorize expenditure of public moneys for public purposes not limited by Constitution, 310; to perform acts which did not disturb the great body of state power, 150
power in each branch [of the taxing/spending power] is broad and unqualified, and drawn with peculiar fitness to other, 155
power of direct taxation, serves domestic as well as national defense needs, 69
power to appropriate money not a power to do any other thing not authorized in the Constitution, 96
presidential veto, evolved from reinforcing constitutional limitation to reinforcing desired programmatic goals, 369
principal purposes of new form of government: general welfare along with national defense and security of liberty, 21
programs for emancipation as "compensated emancipation," 257
progressive legislation of Lincoln: railroad assistance, land-grant colleges aid, homestead legislation, Department of Agriculture, 277

Randolph, Edmund, 21, 41, 42, 54, 59, 60, 73, 74, 86, 217, 366, 383n
Randolph resolution, 24, 34, 35, 43, 366, 385n
Reagan, Ronald, 305, 342–46, 369, 416n; budget deficits, 416n; education initiatives, 343–46; General Welfare Clause, exercise of, 343–46; New Deal, efforts to constrain, 343–44; Social Security, position on, 346; Supreme Court appointments, 345, 416n; Supreme Court decision in *South Dakota v. Dole*, 345–46; Supreme Court sustaining grant conditions established under federal interstate highway program, 345
Reconstruction, 283–89
Reed, Stanley, 305, 321
Rehnquist, William H. (Chief Justice), 345
Remini, Robert V., 182
Report on Manufactures proposed encouraging manufacturing and ex-

panding the means of transportation, 99
response to dissolution of the Union: nature of federalism, role of central government, implications of a free labor society, 249
Richardson, Heather Cox, 265, 407n
Riley, Richard W., 350–51, 372, 420n
Roberts, Owen (Justice), 44, 306–8, 310, 321, 322, 360
Roosevelt, Franklin, 10, 27, 171, 299, 303–8, 312, 318, 320–23, 327, 337, 363, 365, 368, 410n, 419n, 421n, 425n, 428n; administration's brief in Butler case, 307, 321–22, 411n; agricultural adjustment legislation, 305–6; Constitutional Revolution of 1937, 320–24; Court-packing plan, 320–24, 363, 368; General Welfare Clause legacy, 27, 368; New Deal programs, 27, 304–34; position on constitutional amendment to support New Deal program, 363, 419n; Social Security legislation, 312–14
Roosevelt, Theodore, 97, 283, 284, 291–96, 298–300, 302, 303, 313, 319, 359, 368, 379, 409n, 411–12n, 413n; adoption of Sixteenth Amendment, 295
—As president: Annual messages and role of government, 291–96; conservation and reclamation measures, 293–95; Constitution, legacy and views on, 27, 292–93, 299–300, 368; interstate commerce power, 292; Sixteenth Amendment, 295–96; Campaign for presidency in 1912, 300; Progressive Party, 299, 313; Woodrow Wilson and, 299–303
Rotunda, Ronald D., 230
Rutland, Robert Allen, 136, 137, 142
Rutledge, John, 45
Rutledge Committee, 36, 39, 40, 43, 45, 50, 386n

Schlesinger, Arthur M., 200, 305, 312
Schurz, Carl, 286
Scott, General Winfield, 236
Second Morrill Act, 276, 289, 307, 409n, 411n
Sherman, Roger, 24, 25, 33, 41–47, 49–51, 54, 67, 71–73, 153, 214, 215, 217, 218, 226, 363, 384–86n, 396n; national debt and want of power to draw forth national resources, great matters that press, 23; role in Constitutional Convention, 23, 25, 41–47; —, and Connecticut Compromise, 43; —, and General Welfare Clause, initial proposal of, 41–46; —, and Morris attempt to expand General Welfare Clause, opposition to, 49–52; —, and tax power, recognition of need for adequate, 23; role in ratification debate, 71–73
Shultz, George, 339
significance of Louisiana controversy, distinctively American form of constitutional politics, 129
slavery, 255–61, 268–70, 385n, 400n, 401n; barrier to full expression of a pro internal-improvement policy, 196
Smith-Hughes Vocational Educational Act of 1917, 298
Social Security, 9, 19, 20, 171, 304, 317, 319, 322, 324, 327, 330, 332, 337, 341, 344, 346, 352, 354, 368, 376, 379, 380, 414n, 417n, 419n
Social Security Act of 1933, 27, 28, 304, 312, 314, 315, 317–19, 321–23, 334, 339, 344, 359, 361–66, 369, 376, 413n, 415n, 418n, 419n
South Dakota v. Dole, 345, 377, 397n, 404n, 421n
Soviet Union, 329, 347
spending power. *See* General Welfare Clause
Sputnik, 329
Stevenson, Andrew, 192, 193, 212–16, 218, 226, 227, 230, 359, 362, 400n, 402n, 403n
Steward Machine Co. v. Davis, 313–19, 322, 364, 365, 410n, 412n, 413n
Stone, Harlan Fiske (Chief Justice), 276, 310–12, 316, 322, 366, 412n
Story, Joseph, 26, 44, 66, 67, 107, 118, 153, 163, 195, 197, 212, 213, 215, 218–32, 237, 245, 246, 248, 259, 278, 298, 302, 307–310, 317, 322–24, 346, 360, 361, 363, 366, 367, 376, 378, 392n, 396n, 397n, 401–5n
—General Welfare Clause: Commen-

taries on the Constitution, 26, 219–32; justification for conclusions about, 403–4 n; not confined to enumerated powers, 225–32; qualification of taxing and spending power, 221–25; Madison, James, refutation of, 225–32, 403 n; service on Court, 219; Supreme Court and *United States v. Butler,* 300–10

Superfund legislation, 343

Supplemental Security Income Program (SSI), 9, 339, 376, 415 n; various measures to aid with income-maintenance payments, 339

Sutherland, George (Justice), 316, 323, 412 n, 413 n

Taft, William Howard, 27, 284, 295, 296, 303

Taney, Roger Brooke (Chief Justice), 221

taxing power supports establishment of public credit, 106

Taylor, Zachary, 232, 234, 235, 243, 273; and Millard Fillmore proponents of Clay's American System, 232–33

Temporary Assistance to Needy Families (TANF), 351, 376, 418 n

Title IV (Higher Education Act of 1965), 276, 336, 344, 420 n

Title VI (Civil Rights Act of 1964), 278

Townsend, Francis E., 313

transcontinental railroad, 266, 379, 407 n

Tribe, Laurence, 323

Truman, Harry S., 171, 304, 327, 328, 332, 336, 341, 375, 413 n, 414 n; General Welfare Clause and, 327–28

Tugwell, Rexford, 305

Tyler, John, 116, 232, 233, 253, 393 n

United States Department of Education, 342–43

United States v. Butler, 20, 27, 44, 99, 163, 276, 278, 304–7, 309, 310, 312, 315–17, 319–23, 328, 359–61, 363, 366, 383 n, 388 n, 392 n, 393 n, 396 n, 402 n, 410–13 n, 419 n; confronted issue posed by dispute between Hamilton and Madison and adopted Hamilton's view, 20

vagueness of the General Welfare Clause as a means of dramatizing their opposition to direct taxation, 57

Van Buren, Martin, 183, 188–90, 194, 200–202, 207, 213, 233, 235, 399 n, 401 n, 404 n

Van Devanter, Willis (Justice), 316, 323, 412 n, 413 n

veteran's preference amendment, 266

Virginia plan, 22, 23

Virginia Resolutions of 1798, 21–23, 73, 107, 108, 202, 225, 228, 230, 346, 362, 383 n

vision of government spending by "just repartition" of surplus and constitutional amendment needed to justify initiatives, 115

Wagner-Lewis Bill, 313

Wallace, Henry, 305

War of 1812, 130, 132, 133

Washington, Bushrod, 74

Washington, George, 23, 46, 73, 74, 79–82, 84–85, 88, 93, 95, 98, 102–7, 115, 120, 131, 135, 178, 179, 182, 194, 247, 270, 276, 284, 287, 334, 363, 369, 371, 389–92 n, 398 n; in Constitutional Convention, 23

—As president: annual messages and legislative role, 80–82, 105–7, 389 n; contribution to evolution of General Welfare Clause, 105–8; Farewell Address, 105–7, 389 n, 392 n; General Welfare Clause as basis for recommendations, 107; Hamilton, collaboration with, 108; inaugural address, 79–80; Jefferson, communication and correspondence with, 102–5; internal improvement recommendations, 79–80, 105–6; national university, 80–81, 105–6, 178–79, 276; Report on Manufactures, reaction to, 104–5, 392 n; rift between Hamilton & Jefferson, 102–5; Whiskey Rebellion, 105

Whig, 10, 232–36, 243, 244, 247, 252, 253, 263, 268, 273, 277, 405 n; tradition of Executive Branch deference on legislative matters, 253

Whiskey Rebellion, 105

White, G. Edward, 320, 413n, 429n
White House, 26, 122, 133, 189, 197–99, 243, 244, 247–49, 258, 273, 283, 284, 289–91, 296, 298, 303, 307, 313, 328, 330, 343, 346, 371, 398n, 415n, 416n, 418n
Williamson, Hugh, 46, 393n
Wilson, James, 23–25, 28, 52, 53, 55, 67–72, 75, 217, 384n, 385n, 388n
Wilson, Woodrow, 27, 171, 284, 290, 296–303, 307, 319, 359, 363, 368, 408n, 410n, 411n, 421n; calling for new and active role for government, 298; campaign of 1912, 300–301; constitutional authority, views on, 284, 298–99, 302; *Constitutional Government*, 302–3; Hamiltonian concept of constitutional flexibility, 301; *New Freedom*, 27, 300–302, 410n; presidency and exercise of spending power, 296–99; realignment of Democratic Party in favor of vigorous government, 296–99; reducing tariffs, reforming banking and currency laws, better rural credit facilities, water conservation, and land reclamation, 297; Roosevelt, Theodore, response to, 299–303
Wirt, William, 183, 398n

Yates, Robert, 59, 63, 384n